THE GAP BETWEEN
RICH AND POOR

THE GAP BETWEEN RICH AND POOR

Contending Perspectives on the Political Economy of Development

edited by Mitchell A. Seligson

Westview Press / *Boulder and London*

Copyright © 1984 by Westview Press, Inc.

Published in 1984 in the United States of America by Westview Press, Inc., 5500 Central Avenue, Boulder, Colorado 80301; Frederick A. Praeger, Publisher

Library of Congress Cataloging in Publication Data
Main entry under title:
The Gap Between rich and poor.
    Includes index.
    1. Income distribution—Developing countries—
Addresses, essays, lectures. 2. Economic development—
Addresses, essays, lectures. 3. International economic
relations—Addresses, essays, lectures. I. Seligson,
Mitchell A.
HC59.72.I5G36 1984   338.9   84-5113
ISBN 0-86531-691-0
ISBN 0-86531-692-9 (pbk.)

Printed and bound in the United States of America

10   9   8   7   6   5   4   3   2   1

For Amber Lara Seligson,
who, far more than most North American children,
has had the opportunity to observe at first hand
the gap between the rich and poor

Contents

Preface

Few residents of industrialized nations are not forcibly struck by the vast gap in wealth separating them from those who reside in the poor countries of the world. Whether they travel to those countries or visit them vicariously through television and film, the gap is probably the single most vivid impression that remains in their minds. There is a second gap, one that exists within the poor countries themselves, between the tiny affluent minority and the vast majority of the poor. This dichotomy can be observed in urban areas as well as in rural villages.

For the social scientist who has observed these gaps, two questions immediately arise. First, what causes the gaps? Second, are the gaps narrowing or widening? These two questions have concerned me since my earliest visits to Latin America, where I experienced these two gaps firsthand. This book is an attempt to provide the clearest answers that social science has been able to offer to date.

The book grew out of a graduate seminar I taught at the University of Arizona on the political economy of development. In preparing for the seminar while on sabbatical at the University of Essex in England, it became clear to me that there was a great deal of research addressing the two questions posed above, and I attempted to organize that material for my students. Although there were a number of collections that treated questions of political and economic development, none directly addressed the questions I sought to answer. In addition, the most recent theoretical and empirical research on dependency and world systems was generally absent from these volumes.

In the seminar, my students challenged me to refine my own thinking on the two questions and to probe more deeply the strengths and weaknesses of the existing research. They stimulated me to prepare this volume, which I hope will be of use in undergraduate and graduate courses alike in the fields of economics, political science, sociology, and history. I owe a deep debt of gratitude to those students: James Hansen, James Hawkins, Brian McConnell, Patricia Manning, Sylvia Adriana Pinal C., Francis W. Pumphrey, Marcy I. Rosin, Raúl P. Saba, A. Houman Sadri, Mohammed Sahrifi, and John T. Smith. I also wish to acknowledge the contribution that my colleague Edward N. Muller has made to my thinking on this subject. We have spent many hours discussing the questions addressed in this book. Finally, I would like to thank the many authors and publishers who so kindly granted permission for their works to appear here.

Mitchell A. Seligson
Tegucigalpa, Honduras

PART 1
DEFINING THE GAP
BETWEEN RICH AND POOR

1. The Dual Gaps: An Overview of Theory and Research

Mitchell A. Seligson

The income gap between rich and poor countries has grown dramatically over the past 30 years. In 1950, the average per capita income (in 1980 U.S. dollars) of low-income countries was $164, while the per capita income of the industrialized countries averaged $3,841, yielding an absolute income gap of $3,677. Thirty years later, in 1980, incomes in the poor countries had risen to an average of only $245, while those in the industrialized countries soared to $9,648; the absolute gap in 1980 stood at $9,403. For this period, then, there is clear evidence to support the old adage that "the rich get richer." It is not true that the poor get poorer, but that would be a perverse way of looking at these data. A more realistic view of the increases in "wealth" in the poor countries would show that in this thirty-year period the poor countries increased their incomes by an average of only $2.70 a year, less than what an American might spend for lunch at a neighborhood fast-food stand. And in terms of relative wealth, the poor countries certainly did get poorer; the total income (gross national product or GNP) of the low-income countries declined from 4.3 percent of the income earned by the industrialized countries in 1950 to a mere 2.5 percent by 1980.[1]

One might suspect that these data do not reflect the general pattern of growth found throughout the world, but are influenced by the disappointing performance of a few "basket case" nations. That suspicion is unfounded. The low-income countries comprise nearly half the world's population; more than two billion people live in countries with incomes of less than $400 a year. It is also incorrect to speculate that because some poor countries have recently outperformed the growth rates of the industrialized countries that the gap will soon be narrowed. In Chapter 2, David Morawetz tells us that it could take China, which alone contains some one billion people, 2,900 years to close the gap. Even in the cases of the "miracle countries," like South Korea and

This is an original contribution to this volume.

Taiwan, where growth rates have been twice as high as in the industrialized countries, the gap has doubled.

There is another gap separating rich from poor: within many developing
nations there is a growing internal gap between their own rich and
poor citizens. Poor people who live in poor countries, therefore, are
not only falling further behind the world's rich, but are also falling
further behind their relatively more affluent countrymen. Moreover,
precisely the opposite phenomenon seems to be taking place within the
richer countries, where the gap between rich and poor has been narrowing. The world's poor, therefore, find themselves in a position of
double jeopardy.

The consequences of these widening gaps can be witnessed every
day. In the international arena tensions between the "haves" and "have-
nots" dominate debate in United Nations and other international forums.
The poor countries demand a "New International Economic Order"
(NIEO), which they hope will result in the transfer of wealth away
from the rich countries. The industrialized countries, in turn, have
responded with foreign aid programs that, by all accounts, can only
hope to make a small dent in the problem. Indeed, some argue that
foreign aid actually exacerbates the gap (see Chapter 17). Within the
developing countries, domestic stability is frequently tenuous at best as
victims of the yawning gap between rich and poor (along with their
sympathizers) seek redress through violent means. The guerrilla wars
that spot the globe may be directed by those with linkages to international
movements, but their root causes invariably can be traced to inequality
and deprivation, whether relative or absolute.

Thinking and research on the international and domestic gaps between
rich and poor has been going through a protracted period of debate
that can be traced back to the end of World War II. The war elevated
the United States to the position of world leader, and in that position
the United States found itself confronted with a Western Europe in
ruins. The motivations behind the Marshall Plan for rebuilding Europe
are debated to this day, but one thing remains evident and that is that
unprecedented amounts of aid were given and the expected results were
rapidly forthcoming. War-torn industries were rebuilt, new ones were
begun, and economic growth resumed.

The success of rebuilding Europe encouraged many to believe that
similar success would meet efforts to stimulate growth in the developing
world. More often than not, however, such efforts have failed or fallen
far below expectations. Even when programs have been successful and
nations seemed well on the way toward rapid growth, they nonetheless
continued to fall further and further behind the already wealthy countries.
Moreover, growth seemed to be accompanied by a widening income
gap within the developing countries.

The authors of this collection present a comprehensive treatment of
the thinking that is evolving on the subject of the international and

domestic gaps between rich and poor. Their studies are not confined to a single academic discipline or geographic area. Rather, their work reflects a variety of disciplines, including economics, political science, sociology, history, psychology, and geography, to mention the principal ones, and they have examined the problems from the viewpoint of a single country or region as well as with a macroanalytic approach. This diversity produced three major perspectives on the gap.

In the first, the widening gap between rich and poor nations is viewed as being principally a cultural problem. Specifically, the cultural values associated with industrialization are seen as foreign to many developing nations, which are deeply attached to more traditional cultural values. Yet the values of punctuality, hard work, achievement, and other "industrial" values are keys to unlocking the economic potential of poor countries, according to these scholars. Most adherents of this perspective believe that such values can be inculcated in a population through deliberate effort. Others argue that the values will emerge naturally as the result of a worldwide process of diffusion of values functional for development. This perspective has been incorporated into a more general school of thought focusing on the process called "modernization." Development occurs and the international gap is narrowed when a broad set of modern values *and* institutions are present.

A number of economists, most notably Simon Kuznets, have been associated with the second school of thought, which sees domestic income inequality occurring as an almost inevitable by-product of development. Kuznets traces a path that seems to have been followed quite closely by nations that have become industrialized. The process begins with these nations enjoying relative domestic equality in the distribution of income. The onset of industrialization produces a significant shift in the direction of inequality and creates a widening gap. Once the industrialization process matures, however, the gap is again reduced.

In marked contrast to these two perspectives, which suggest that the phenomena of rich and poor disparity are transitory, there is a third, more recent school of thought that comes to rather different conclusions. The scholars supporting this approach—known as *dependentistas*—observe that the economies of the developing nations have been shaped in response to forces and conditions established by the industrialized nations, and, as a result, their development has been both delayed and dependent. The dependentistas conclude that the failure of poor countries to catch up with the rich ones and the widening internal income gap are both products of the distorted development brought on by dependency relations. A further elaboration on this thinking has emerged in recent years in the form of the "world-system" perspective developed by Immanuel Wallerstein and his followers. According to this group, since the sixteenth century a world capitalist economy has existed, divided geographically (rather than occupationally, as in the earlier system of empires) into three primary zones: core, semiperiphery, and periphery. The core dominates the system and drains the semiperiphery and periphery of their economic surplus. Both of these perspectives contend that the gaps will be perpetuated by the nature of the international system and cannot be narrowed unless a major restructuring of that system is undertaken.

In the remaining chapters of the first part of this book, the principal evidence of the existence of both international and internal gaps is presented. Part Two offers various explanations for both gaps, leading off with Kuznets's discussion of the widening internal gaps. It then surveys some of the best-known cultural explanations and follows with a critique of that perspective. A brief look is taken at an explanation emphasizing domestic determinants of inequality as argued by Michael Lipton in his "urban bias" thesis. Then the dependency perspective is introduced by Theotonio Dos Santos. His discussion is followed by a comparison of modernization and dependency theory. Lastly, world-systems theory and its relationship to the gap between rich and poor is argued by Immanuel Wallerstein and refuted by Tony Smith.

The theories argued in Part Two are confronted by empirical evidence of their validity in Part Three. The authors attempt to find an explanation for the gaps that is actually supported by the data. Adherents to the view that development produces inequality have their say first. Their arguments are followed by a rigorous critique and presentation of counter-evidence. Then a series of authors challenge the entire basis of the argument by showing that the data itself is misleading and that the indicators used are the wrong ones.

The concluding section of the volume, Part Four, offers three case studies. The first of these, by John A. Booth, argues that income inequality is clearly traceable to domestic public policies. In the next chapter, John T. Smith compares capitalist dependency with socialist dependency. The last case study, by Shirley W. Y. Kuo, Gustav Ranis, and John C. H. Fei, examines Taiwan and its success at achieving growth with increased equality. A long-term look into the future is presented by Herman Kahn, who argues that the existence of the gap between rich and poor nations will serve as a catalyst for development that will eventually reduce that gap. The final chapter represents my own effort to synthesize the conflicting perspectives and to help point the way toward research that might ultimately resolve the debate.

In an effort to guide the reader in making the connection between each contribution and the overall theme of the volume, I have prefaced each selection with a short introduction. A special effort has been made to employ the terminology of the respective authors in these introductions, and as a result the particular terms used to describe the poor countries (e.g., developing countries, the Third World, underdeveloped nations, etc.) vary from chapter to chapter. No deeper meaning should be given to the choice of one term over the other or to the lack of consistency throughout the volume in their use. Similarly, in an effort to remain as faithful as possible to the original intent of each author, the footnoting style found in the original piece has been retained.

Notes

1. These figures are based upon the World Bank's *World Development Report, 1980*. New York: Oxford University Press, 1980, p. 34.

2. The Gap Between Rich and Poor Countries

David Morawetz

The enormity and persistence of the per capita income gap between rich and poor countries is the subject of this selection by David Morawetz. He shows, using data gathered by the World Bank, that there are two gaps, the relative and the absolute. Although some areas of the world (China, East Asia and the Middle East) have narrowed the relative gap in the 1950–75 period, others have seen it widen. For the developing countries as a whole, per capita income was only 7.6 percent of the per capita income of the industrialized nations. Even more distressing is the finding that only one country, Libya, was able to narrow the absolute gap during the twenty-five years of post–World War II development covered in this study, and that it will take anywhere from several hundred to over three thousand years for developing countries to close the gap at present growth rates. Morawetz concludes by arguing that closing the relative and absolute gaps may be a goal that is neither attainable nor desirable.

Although during 1950–75 the per capita incomes (as conventionally measured) of the developing countries were growing faster than ever before, so too were those of the developed countries. As a result, the gap between the rich and the poor nations, which had been increasing for 100 to 150 years [Kuznets 1965], continued to widen.

The Relative Gap

Since the developing and developed countries grew in per capita income at almost identical rates during 1950–75 (Table 2.1), the per capita income of the developing countries as a proportion of that of the developed countries stayed fairly constant, at around 7 to 8 percent. In China, East Asia, and particularly in the Middle East, the relative gap narrowed somewhat, whereas in South Asia, Africa, and Latin America it widened.

Reprinted with permission from *Twenty-five Years of Economic Development, 1950–1975*, by David Morawetz, pp. 26–30. Published for the World Bank by The Johns Hopkins University Press, 1977.

Table 2.1.
The Relative and Absolute Gaps in GNP per capita, by Region, 1950-75

Region	Relative gap[a] (percent)		Absolute gap[b] (1974 U.S. dollars)	
	1950	1975	1950	1975
South Asia	3.6	2.5	2,293	5,106
Africa	7.1	5.9	2,208	4,930
East Asia	5.5	6.5[c]	2,248	4,897
China, People's Republic of	4.8	6.1[c]	2,265	4,918
Latin America	20.8	18.0	1,883	4,294
Middle East	19.3	31.7[c]	1,918	3,578
Developing countries	6.7	7.2[c]	2,218	4,863
Developing countries excluding China	7.9	7.6	2,191	4,837

[a] Relative gap is GNP per capita of region as percent of GNP per capita of the OECD countries.

[b] Absolute gap is GNP per capita of the OECD countries ($2,378 in 1950, $5,338 in 1975) less GNP per capita of the region.

[c] Relative gap decreased, 1950-75.

Source: Computed from data tapes, World Bank Atlas (1977), and World Bank, World Tables 1976.

The Absolute Gap

In 1950 the average GNP per capita of the OECD* countries (in conventional 1974 dollars) was $2,191 greater than that of the developing countries. By 1975 this difference had more than doubled, to $4,839 (Table 2.1). There is no single region in which the absolute gap did not at least double. Furthermore, apart from oil-rich Libya, not a single developing country for which data are available for 1950 managed to narrow the absolute gap even slightly during the full twenty-five–year period.[1] Even in fast-growing Korea and Taiwan the absolute gap doubled.

This remarkable situation is the result of the simple algebra of gaps. In brief, a poor country growing faster than a rich one will not even

*OECD stands for the Organization for Economic Cooperation and Development, whose members include Australia, Austria, Belgium, Canada, Denmark, Finland, France, Federal Republic of Germany, Greece, Iceland, Ireland, Italy, Japan, Luxembourg, Netherlands, New Zealand, Norway, Portugal, Spain, Sweden, Switzerland, Turkey, United Kingdom and the United States.—Ed.

Table 2.2.
The Absolute Gap: When Might It Be Closed?[a]

Country[b]	GNP per capita, 1975 (1974 U.S. dollars)	Annual growth rate, 1960-1975 (percent)	Number of years until gap closed if 1960-1975 growth rates continue
OECD countries	5,238	3.7	--
Libyan Arab Republic	4,675	11.8	2
Saudi Arabia	2,767	8.6	14
Singapore	2,307	7.6	22
Israel	3,287	5.0	37
Iran	1,321	6.9	45
Hong Kong	1,584	6.3	48
Korea	504	7.3	69
China (Taiwan)	817	6.3	75
Iraq	1,180	4.4	223
Brazil	927	4.2	362
Thailand	319	4.5	365
Tunisia	695	4.2	422
Syrian Arab Republic	604	4.2	451
Lesoto	161	4.5	454
Turkey	793	4.0	675
Togo	245	4.1	807
Panama	977	3.8	1,866
Malawi	137	3.9	1,920
Malaysia	665	3.8	2,293
Papua New Guinea	412	3.8	2,826
China, People's Republic of	320	3.8	2,900
Mauritania	288	3.8	3,224

[a] Absolute gap is GNP per capita of the OECD countries ($2,378 in 1950, $5,238 in 1975) less GNP per capita of the individual country.

[b] All developing countries with population of 1 million or more whose growth rate of per capita income exceeded that of the OECD countries during 1960-75.
Source: Computed from data tapes, World Bank Atlas (1977).

begin to reduce the absolute gap between them until the ratio of their per capita incomes is equal to the inverse ratio of their growth rates. For example, even though Korea has been growing twice as fast as the OECD countries for the past fifteen years, the absolute gap between them will continue to widen until the per capita GNP of Korea reaches half that of the OECD countries. The proportion is currently not one-half but one-tenth.

Assuming for a moment that historical growth rates continue into the future and ignoring the fact that cross-country comparisons of conventional GNP per capita statistics are misleading, it is possible to calculate for each developing country the number of years that it would take until the absolute gap between it and the OECD countries would be closed (Table 2.2). For the large majority of developing countries containing most of the developing world's population, the gap would never be closed, for their measured rate of growth of per capita GNP has historically been slower than that of the OECD countries. Even among the fastest-growing developing countries, only eight would close the gap within 100 years, and only sixteen would close it within 1,000 years.[2]

Welfare Implications of the Gaps

It is not clear that "narrowing the relative gap" makes much sense as a development objective. To take a simple example, if the per capita income of Bangladesh as conventionally measured rises by $2 while that of the United States rises by $65, the relative gap would be narrowing—yet this hardly seems like a shining goal worth striving toward.[3] "Narrowing the absolute gap" appears to make more intuitive sense in welfare terms. But since it may take centuries before the absolute gap is narrowed—if it is ever narrowed—in most developing countries, to use this as a central goal of development is to guarantee long-term frustration.[4]

Fortunately, there are compelling reasons to believe that most developing countries will not place the closing of the gap at the center of their aspirations. First, not all of them regard the resource-wasting life style of the developed countries as an end toward which it is worth striving; at least some seem to prefer to create their own development patterns based on their own resources, and needs, and traditions.[5]

Second, when thinking of the per capita income that they would like to attain, most people (and governments) tend to think of the income of a close-by reference group. Thus, for example, despite the fact that within most countries there is a clear positive association between income and self-rated happiness, there is no observable tendency for people in poor countries to rate themselves as less happy on average than people in rich countries rate themselves [Easterlin 1974]. There are several possible explanations of this apparent paradox [Abramovitz 1975]. One of them is simply that most people in poor countries do not regard the rich foreigners as part of their reference group and hence are not overconcerned with the gap. They are more concerned, it seems, with their own internal income distributions and their own place within them.[6]

Notes

1. Intuitively, it seems that some of the other oil-exporting countries must surely have narrowed the absolute gap as well. This highlights a problem

existing throughout this and any other study that is based on *real* growth rates. In measuring a nation's increase in GNP, real growth rates—as they are usually calculated—abstract from price effects. The implicit assumption is that, in the long run, a country's consumption possibilities (and hence its economic welfare) are determined by its physical volume of production. Yet for some countries, and in particular for the oil exporters, the change over time in the relative prices of their principal products may be at least as important in determining national consumption possibilities as the change in physical output, if not more so. In such cases, the use of real growth rates to indicate growth in consumption possibilities may involve a serious bias. It certainly does involve such a bias for the oil-exporting countries during 1950–75, and the bias is clearly in a downward direction.

2. These time intervals may be quite different if purchasing-power parity GNP estimates are used, though the direction and magnitude of this difference will not be clear until it is established how growth rates calculated using purchasing-power parities differ from those rates calculated using conventional GNP statistics: see Bhagwati and Hansen [1972], Kravis, Heston, and Summers [1977 and 1977a], and Strout [1977]. For an alternative formulation in which the gap is measured as the number of decades by which specific developing countries lag behind developed countries, see Chenery [1976].

3. In fact, each year's increase in measured GNP per capita in the United States is currently equal to about a century's increase in Bangladesh or India. This is more than a little misleading, however, since a 1 or 2 percent increase in per capita income probably does more to increase economic welfare in Bangladesh than a similar percentage increase does in the United States.

4. The 1974 U.N. General Assembly resolution on the New International Economic Order and the Leontief model [United Nations 1976] both place primary importance on reduction of the gap. Compare Lewis's concluding remarks to a special conference on the gap: "What will happen to the gap between the rich and the poor countries? . . . I do not know the answer and . . . since I think what matters is the absolute progress of the LDCS and not the size of the gap, I do not care" [1972, p. 420].

5. Compare Haq [1976, p. 2]: "Similarly, the concept of catching up must be rejected. Catching up with what? Surely the Third World does not wish to imitate the life styles of the rich nations? It must meet its own basic human needs within the framework of its own cultural values, building development around people rather than people around development."

6. The multicountry study by Cantril [1965] indicates that the elite in developing countries tend to be more concerned with the international gap than poorer people. For some empirical evidence on the income distribution and self-rated happiness, see Morawetz and others [1977].

References

Abramovitz, Moses. 1975. "Economic Growth and Its Discontents." Stanford, California: Stanford University. Typescript.

Bhagwati, Jagdish and Bent Hansen. 1972. "Should Growth Rates be Evaluated at International Prices." In Jagdish Bhagwati and Richard Eckaus, eds., *Development and Planning: Essays in Honor of Paul Rosenstein-Rodan*. London: George Allen and Unwin.

Cantril, Hadley. 1965. *The Pattern of Human Concerns.* New Brunswick, N.J.: Rutgers University Press.

Chenery, Hollis. 1976. "Transitional Growth and World Industrialization." Paper presented at the Nobel Symposium on the International Allocation of Economic Activity. Stockholm. Typescript.

Easterlin, Richard. 1974. "Does Economic Growth Improve the Human Lot?" In David Paul and Melvin Reder, eds., *Nations and Households in Economic Growth: Essays in Honor of Moses Abramovitz.* New York: Academic Press.

Haq, Mahbub ul. 1976. "Concessions or Structural Change." Paper presented at a Special Meeting of the Club of Rome on the New International Order.

Kravis, Irving B., Allan Heston and Robert Summers. 1977. "Real GDP Per Capita for 116 Countries, 1970 and 1974." Department of Economics Discussion Paper no. 391. Philadelphia: University of Pennsylvania.

————. 1977a. "International Comparisons of Real Product and Purchasing Power." United Nations International Comparison Project, Phase II. Washington D.C.: World Bank. Typescript.

Kuznets, Simon. 1965. *Economic Growth and Structure.* New York: W. W. Norton.

Lewis, W. Arthur. 1972. "Objectives and Prognostications." In Gustav Ranis, ed., *The Gap Between Rich and Poor Nations.* London: Macmillan.

Morawetz, David, et al. 1977. "The Income Distribution and Self-rated Happiness: Some Empirical Evidence." *Economic Journal.* Forthcoming.

United Nations. 1976. "The Future of the World Economy." New York: United Nations Department of Economic and Social Affairs.

World Bank. 1976. *World Tables 1976.* Baltimore: Johns Hopkins University Press.

————. 1977. *World Bank Atlas, 1977.* Washington, D.C.: World Bank.

3. Income Inequality: Some Dimensions of the Problem

Montek S. Ahluwalia

The data that have been used by many analysts to show that the gap between rich and poor is considerably wider in the developing economies than it is in the developed ones is presented by this frequently cited study of Montek S. Ahluwalia. The study notes a number of major limitations of the data upon which this conclusion is based, but goes on to argue that these are "the only data we have," and that the conclusions drawn from such data can do more good than harm. Some critics of this view believe, however, that since large sums of development assistance funds are spent based upon the conclusions of studies such as this, faulty conclusions can do considerable harm because such funds will neither produce the desired result nor be of assistance to projects that might truly benefit from them. Moreover, entire national development plans could result in failure if such conclusions were found to be unsupported by better data or better analysis. As the chapters in Part Three will demonstrate, there is considerable controversy over both the quality of the data and the interpretations Ahluwalia has given them.

Recent discussions of economic development reflect an increasing concern with widespread poverty in underdeveloped countries. The fact of poverty is not new: it was always self-evident to those familiar with economic realities. What *is* new is the suspicion that economic growth by itself may not solve or even alleviate the problem within any "reasonable" time period. Indeed it is often argued that the mechanisms which promote economic growth also promote economic concentration, and a worsening of the relative and perhaps even absolute position of the lower-income groups. This pessimistic view has led to some questioning of growth-oriented development strategies which assume that the poverty problem would be solved without much difficulty if growth could be accelerated.

The empirical evidence underlying the new pessimism is limited but persuasive. Detailed studies of the nature and extent of poverty in particular countries show that the problem is of truly gigantic proportions. A study of poverty in India estimated that, in 1960, about 38 percent of the rural population and 50 percent of the urban population lived below a poverty level defined by consumption yielding 2,250 calories.[1] A recent study of Brazil showed that, also in 1960, about 30 percent of the total population lived below a poverty level defined by the minimum wage in northeast Brazil (the poorest region).[2] More importantly, both studies argued that the situation had worsened over the sixties, at least in terms of relative equality. Similarly pessimistic results on changes in relative equality over time were reported in a study of Argentina, Mexico, and Puerto Rico.[3] In addition to these case studies there is some evidence from cross-country analysis of distribution patterns which can be interpreted as showing that economic growth is associated with a worsening in the distribution of income, at least in the initial stages of development.

These studies raise important questions relevant to policy formulation. What is the extent of relative and absolute poverty in underdeveloped countries and does it vary systematically with the level of development? What evidence is there on the relationship between growth and inequality and how far can this relationship be affected by policy? What are the economic characteristics of the poor and what do they imply for distributional strategies? In this chapter we will attempt to sift the available evidence to provide qualitative answers to some of these questions. But first a general caveat is necessary. Analysis of income distribution problems is severely limited by the quality and reliability of the available data and a brief digression on this subject is desirable.

Limitations of the Data

The primary sources of information on patterns of income distribution are sample surveys which provide data on income (and in some cases only consumption) and other socio-economic characteristics of the units sampled. Until recently, data of this type were available for only a few underdeveloped countries and generalizations about patterns of distribution were therefore based on very limited information. For example, Kuznets's (1963) study of cross-country patterns of income distribution included only eleven underdeveloped countries. The situation has changed considerably since then. A large number of surveys have been carried out in underdeveloped countries and results from these surveys are increasingly being used in analyses of income distribution problems.

Unfortunately, the increase in data availability has not been accompanied by an adequate improvement in statistical quality. In many cases the growing interest in the subject has simply led to the proliferation of crude estimates of income distribution for various countries, based on data sources which may be "the best available" but are simply not good enough. An exhaustive review of these problems is beyond the scope of this chapter, but some indication of their importance can be obtained by considering three major sources of error in this field.

First, the income concept used in many surveys falls far short of the comprehensive definition needed. For purposes of welfare measurement, the income concept should refer to "permanent income" and should include income from all sources whether accruing in the form of money income or income in kind (including production for own consumption and investment).[4] Furthermore, if it is to be a measure of welfare, the income concept should be adjusted for tax incidence and transfer payments. In practice, available surveys measure income over a short period— usually a month or at most a year. Frequently they cover only money income, and sometimes only wage income, giving a distorted picture of the true distribution of income in the economy.

Second, even if the income concept is properly defined, it may be difficult to measure in practice. Very different problems arise at the two ends of the income scale. In the highest income groups there is the ever present likelihood of deliberate understatement of income for fear of incurring a tax liability. At the other end of the income scale there is a genuine difficulty in valuing production for own consumption or investment in the subsistence sectors of the economy.[5] Closely related to the measurement problem is the difficulty in using relative money incomes as a measure of relative real incomes, given the wide variation in prices facing different consumers. Rural prices of some goods are typically much lower than urban prices, so that comparisons of urban-rural money incomes typically understate rural real income levels.

Third, there is the problem of accuracy in estimating the distribution of income in the population from the observed distribution in sample surveys. The accuracy of sample estimates depends upon a number of factors relating to the size of the sample and its representativeness. Many available estimates of income distribution are derived from samples that are statistically inadequate in these respects, with the result that sample estimates are both biased and have a large variance. In several cases the samples from which data are available were never originally intended to be representative of the population as a whole.[6] In other cases, despite an attempt at ensuring representativeness, the difficulties of sample design or implementation may have proved ovewhelming. For example, no adequate sampling frame may exist from which to select a sample ensuring proportional coverage of different income groups. The existence of nomadic populations or inaccessible regions presents the most extreme form of this problem.

Because of these problems, available estimates of income distribution in most underdeveloped countries are, at best, approximations of the underlying distribution we wish to measure. Inaccuracy of measurement is not, of course, unique to income distribution; national accounts data are also subject to such errors. But the data limitations for income distribution are usually regarded as more serious. National accounts data are at least collected on a systematic basis and are therefore much more comparable over time and (although to a lesser extent) between countries. No such comparability can be claimed for data on income distribution. Estimates for different countries, and even for the same country at different points of time, are typically based on noncomparable data sources, making intercountry and intertemporal comparisons very hazardous.

These limitations present a familiar dilemma in empirical analysis. The data are very weak, but they are also the only data we have. An extreme response to the problem is to reject any use of most of the available data for analytical purposes. The approach adopted in this chapter is less puristic. We assume that until better data become available, cautious use of existing data—with all its limitations—provides some perspective on the nature of the problem. In common with Kuznets (1955), our excuse "for building an elaborate structure on such a shaky foundation" is the view that "speculation is an effective way of presenting a broad view of the field and . . . so long as it is recognized as a collection of hunches calling for further investigation, rather than a set of fully tested conclusions, little harm and much good may result."

The Extent of Inequality

The first step in defining the dimensions of the problem with which this volume is concerned is to consider the extent of inequality in developed and underdeveloped countries. Cross-section data are particularly useful for this purpose because they reveal possible "uniform patterns" which characterize the problem in different countries. Identifying such uniformities helps to establish "averages" with which levels of inequality observed in particular countries can be compared. They also serve to determine reasonable "benchmarks" in terms of which targets and prospects for improvement can be defined. . . .

The conventional approach to income inequality is to define the problem in purely relative terms. A familiar technique for this purpose is to measure inequality by the extent to which the income share of groups of individuals or households differs from their population share. In this section, we will examine the problem in terms of income shares of the lowest 40 percent, the middle 40 percent, and the top 20 percent of households ordinally ranked by income.[7] For some countries, distribution estimates are available only for individuals in the workforce. We have included these estimates in our data set as the best available approximation to household income distribution.

The choice of income shares instead of one of the various conventional indexes of inequality calls for some explanation.[8] The conventional indexes are designed to provide summary measures of inequality over the entire range of the population and as such may be insensitive to the degree of inequality in particular ranges. Our treatment in terms of the income shares of ordinally ranked income groups enables us to concentrate on inequality at the lower end of the income range, which may be of special interest for policy.

Table 3.1 presents income share data for sixty-six countries cross-classified according to different levels of overall inequality and per capita income levels.[9] The table distinguishes between three inequality levels defined as high, moderate, and low (according to specified ranges of the share of the lowest 40 percent) and three income groupings defined as high, middle, and low (according to specified ranges of per capita GNP). The extent of inequality varies widely among countries but the following broad patterns can be identified.

The *socialist countries* have the highest degree of overall equality in the distribution of income. This is as we would expect, since income from the ownership of capital does not accrue as income to individuals.[10] The observed inequality in these countries is due mainly to inequality in wages between sectors and skill classes. Since the structural factors operating toward equality are the strongest in these countries, their average income share of the lowest 40 percent—amounting to about 25 percent of total income—may be taken as an upper limit for the target income share to which policymakers in underdeveloped countries can aspire.

The *developed countries* are evenly distributed between the categories of low and moderate inequality. The average income share of the bottom 40 percent amounts to about 16 percent, which is lower than the average for socialist countries but better than most of the underdeveloped countries. A major problem in comparing income distribution data between developed and underdeveloped countries is that pretax data does not reflect the equalizing impact of progressive taxes combined with welfare-oriented public transfer mechanisms. These fiscal corrections are generally more substantial and more egalitarian in developed countries. If this factor is taken into account, developed countries may be somewhat more egalitarian than appears from Table 3.1.

Most of the *underdeveloped countries* show markedly greater relative inequality than the developed countries. About half of the underdeveloped countries fall in the high inequality range with another third displaying moderate inequality. The average income share for the lowest 40 percent in all underdeveloped countries as a group amounts to about 12.5 percent, but there is considerable variation around this average. Those of the underdeveloped countries classified in the low inequality category have income shares for the lowest 40 percent averaging 18 percent, as is the case with the most egalitarian of the developed countries. Against this, however, half the underdeveloped countries show income shares of the lowest 40 percent, averaging only 9 percent.

It is worth noting that overall income inequality in the underdeveloped countries is not particularly associated with relatively low income shares for the middle-income group rather than the poorest group. This view

Table 3.1
Cross-classification of Countries by Income Level and Equality

HIGH INEQUALITY — Share of Lowest 40% less than 12%

Country(year)	Per Capita GNP US$	Lowest 40%	Middle 40%	Top 20%
Income up to U.S. $300				
Kenya(1969)	136	10.0	22.0	68.0
S. Leone (1968)	159	9.6	22.4	68.0
Philipp. (1971)	239	11.6	34.6	53.8
Iraq (1956)	200	6.8	25.2	68.0
Senegal (1960)	245	10.0	26.0	64.0
Ivory Coast (1970)	247	10.8	32.1	57.1
Rhodesia (1968)	252	8.2	22.8	69.0
Tunisia (1970)	255	11.4	33.6	55.0
Honduras (1968)	265	6.5	28.5	65.0
Ecuador (1970)	277	6.5	20.0	73.5
Income U.S.300–$750				
Malaysia (1970)	330	11.6	32.4	56.0
Colombia (1970)	358	9.0	30.0	61.0
Brazil (1970)	390	10.0	28.4	61.5
Peru (1971)	480	6.5	33.5	60.0
Gabon (1968)	497	8.8	23.7	67.5
Jamaica (1958)	510	8.2	30.3	61.5
Costa Rica (1971)	521	11.5	30.0	58.5
Mexico (1969)	645	10.5	25.5	64.0
S. Africa (1965)	669	6.2	35.8	58.0
Panama (1969)	692	9.4	31.2	59.4
Income Above U.S. $750				
Venezuela (1970)	1004	7.9	27.1	65.0
Finland (1962)	1599	11.1	39.6	49.3
France (1962)	1913	9.5	36.8	53.7

MODERATE EQUALITY — Share of Lowest 40% between 12% and 17%

Country(year)	Per Capita GNP US$	Lowest 40%	Middle 40%	Top 20%
Income up to U.S. $ 300				
El Salvador (1969)	295	11.2	36.4	52.4
Turkey (1968)	282	9.3	29.9	60.8
Burma (1958)	82	16.5	38.7	44.8
Dahomey (1959)	87	15.5	34.5	50.0
Tanzania (1967)	89	13.0	26.0	61.0
India (1964)	99	16.0	32.0	52.0
Madagasgar (1960)	120	13.5	25.5	61.0
Zambia (1959)	230	14.5	28.5	57.0
Income U.S.300–$750				
Dominican Rep.(1969)	323	12.2	30.3	57.5
Iran (1968)	332	12.5	33.0	54.5
Guyana (1956)	550	14.0	40.3	45.7
Lebanon (1960)	508	13.0	26.0	61.0
Uruguay (1968)	618	16.5	35.5	48.0
Chile (1968)	744	13.0	30.2	56.8
Income Above U.S. $750				
Argentina (1970)	1079	16.5	36.1	47.4
Puerto Rico (1968)	1100	13.7	35.7	50.6
Netherlands (1967)	1990	13.6	37.9	48.5
Norway (1968)	2010	16.6	42.9	40.5
Germany, F.R.('64)	2144	15.4	31.7	52.9
Denmark (1968)	2563	13.6	38.8	47.6
New Zealand (1969)	2859	15.5	42.5	42.0
Sweden (1963)	2949	14.0	42.0	44.0

LOW INEQUALITY — Share of Lowest 40%, 17% and above

Country(year)	Per Capita GNP US$	Lowest 40%	Middle 40%	Top 20%
Chad (1958)	78	18.0	39.0	43.0
Sri Lanka (1969)	95	17.0	37.0	46.0
Niger (1960)	97	18.0	40.0	42.0
Pakistan (1964)	100	17.5	37.5	45.0
Uganda (1970)	126	17.1	35.8	47.1
Thailand (1970)	180	17.0	37.5	45.5
Korea (1970)	235	18.0	37.0	45.0
Taiwan (1964)	241	20.4	39.5	40.1
Surinam (1962)	394	21.7	35.7	42.6
Greece (1957)	500	21.0	29.5	49.5
Yugoslavia (1968)	529	18.5	40.0	41.5
Bulgaria (1962)	530	26.8	40.0	33.2
Spain (1965)	750	17.6	36.7	45.7
Poland (1964)	850	23.4	40.6	36.0
Japan (1963)	950	20.7	39.3	40.0
United Kingdom (1968)	2015	18.8	42.2	39.0
Hungary (1969)	1140	24.0	42.5	33.5
Czechoslavakia (1964)	1150	27.6	41.4	31.0
Australia (1965)	2509	20.0	41.2	38.8
Canada (1965)	2920	20.0	39.8	40.2
United States (1970)	4850	19.7	41.5	38.8

Note: Sources for these data are listed in the Appendix [of the original article. Ed.]. The income shares of each percentile group were read off a free-hand Lorenz curve fitted to observe points in the cumulative distribution. The distributions are for pretax income. Per capita GNP figures are taken from the World Bank data files and refer to GNP at factor cost for the year indicated in constant 1971 U.S. dollars.

was originally put forward by Kuznets (1963) on the basis of data for eighteen countries in which it was observed that the shares of the lowest-income groups in underdeveloped countries were comparable with those in developed countries but the shares of upper-income groups were markedly larger. Kuznets suggested that higher income inequality in underdeveloped countries may be due to greater inequality between the top and middle group and speculated that the equalizing impact of development was perhaps based on a rising share of the middle. Table 3.1 suggests that this generalization is not valid when the sample is widened to include other countries. There are many underdeveloped countries which show high inequality in terms of low income shares for both the middle and the poorest group.

Notes

1. Dandekar and Rath (1971). See also Bardhan (1970) and (1973).
2. Fishlow (1972).
3. Weisskoff (1970).
4. Permanent income takes account of variations over the lifetime of the individual arising from both the age profile of income and random fluctuations around this profile. Income differences due to age are an important element of observed inequality in most samples of individuals at different stages in their working life.
5. Even if the consumption items can be quantified in physical terms, there is the problem of determining the appropriate prices to use in obtaining a "money value" for this consumption. Producer prices (farm gate prices) differ from retail prices, especially in different seasons. The problem of valuing production for direct investment (i.e., various types of labor using farm improvements) is even more complex since there is typically no market for the capital good produced.
6. This is true, for example, of labor force surveys directed at determining the structure of wages, urban household surveys aimed at constructing cost-of-living indexes for particular socio-economic sections of the population and, of course, tax data which cover only a very small percentage of the population.
7. The choice of households rather than individuals as the basic income unit reflects the assumption that income within a household is equally distributed. Even so there are problems arising from variations in household size and age structure. An alternative is to rank the population according to household per capita income, but data on this basis are available only for a few countries.
8. The best known of the various indexes is the Gini coefficient, which is based on the Lorenz curve. Others include the variance of income, the variance of logarithms of income, the coefficient of variation, and also entropy measures borrowed from information theory such as the index developed by Theil (1967). Atkinson (1970) proposes a new measure of inequality which is explicitly related to an underlying social welfare function and therefore provides a more meaningful basis for comparing or ranking alternative distributions.
9. The data are taken from Jain and Tiemann (1974). The original sources for each country as reported in that document are listed in the Appendix to Chapter 1 [in that work].

10. Income distribution data for these countries may overstate income equality since they frequently refer to "workers," which may exclude workers outside the state system who are usually in the lower income ranges.

References

Atkinson, A. B. 1970. "On the Measurement of Inequality." *Journal of Economic Theory*, 2(September): 244–263.

Bardhan, P. K. 1970. "On the Minimum Level of Living and the Rural Poor." *Indian Economic Review*, 5(April): 129–136.

────── . 1973. "On the Incidence of Poverty in Rural Indian in the Sixties." *Economic and Political Weekly*, 8(February special number): 245–254.

Dandekar, V. M. and N. R. Rath. 1971. "Poverty in India." *Economic and Political Weekly*, 6(January 2): 25–48; (January 9): 106–146.

Fishlow, A. 1972. "Brazilian Size Distribution of Income." *Papers and Proceedings of the American Economic Association*, 62(May): 391–402.

Jain, S. and Tiemann, A. 1974. "Size Distribution of Income: A Compilation of Data. Development Research Center Discussion Paper no. 4, mimeographed. Washington, D.C.: World Bank.

Kuznets, S. 1955. "Economic Growth and Income Inequality." *American Economic Review*, 45(March): 1–28.

────── . 1963. "Quantitative Aspects of Economic Growth of Nations: III, Distribution of Income by Size." *Economic Development and Cultural Change*, 11(January): 1–80.

Thiel, H. 1967. *Economics and Information Theory*. Amsterdam: North-Holland.

Weisskoff, R. 1970. "Income Distribution and Economic Growth in Puerto Rico, Argentina and Mexico." *Review of Income and Wealth*, 16(December): 303–332.

PART 2
CONTENDING EXPLANATIONS
OF THE GAPS

4. Economic Growth and Income Inequality

Simon Kuznets

Most debate on the internal gap between rich and poor people in developing nations begins with this seminal presidential address delivered by Simon Kuznets to the American Economic Association in 1954. The address, portions of which are reprinted here, uses limited data from Germany, the United Kingdom, and the United States to draw the conclusion that since the 1920s, and perhaps even earlier, there has been a trend toward equalization in the distribution of income. Kuznets discusses in some detail the possible causes for this trend, examining those factors in the process of industrialization that tend to counteract the trend toward the increasing concentration of savings in the hands of the wealthy. That particular discussion is not in the portions of the address included here, but the interested reader can consult the original piece (see citation at the bottom of this page). Our interest lies in Kuznets's conclusion that the central factor in equalizing income must have been the rising incomes of the poorer sectors outside of the traditional agricultural economy. The critically important notion of the "inverted U curve," although not labeled as such in the address, is introduced in Kuznets's argument that there seems to be a trend of increasing inequality in the early phases of industrialization, followed by declines in the later phases only. Finally, Kuznets opens the debate over the relevance of these findings for the developing nations by examining data from India, Ceylon (today, Sri Lanka), and Puerto Rico. The findings that income inequality in the developing countries is greater than that in the advanced countries, and that such inequality may be growing even greater, form the basis of virtually all subsequent research and debate on this subject.

The central theme of this chapter is the character and causes of long-term changes in the personal distribution of income. Does inequality in the distribution of income increase or decrease in the course of a country's economic growth? What factors determine the secular level and trends of income inequalities?

Reprinted with permission from the *American Economic Review*, vol. 45 (March 1955): 1, 3–6, 17–26.

These are broad questions in a field of study that has been plagued by looseness in definitions, unusual scarcity of data, and pressures of strongly held opinions. . . .

Trends in Income Inequality

Forewarned of the difficulties, we turn now to the available data. These data, even when relating to complete populations, invariably classify units by income for a given year. From our standpoint, this is their major limitation. Because the data often do not permit many size-groupings, and because the difference between annual income incidence and longer-term income status has less effect if the number of classes is small and the limits of each class are wide, we use a few wide classes. This does not resolve the difficulty; and there are others due to the scantiness of data for long periods, inadequacy of the unit used—which is, at best, a family and very often a reporting unit—errors in the data, and so on through a long list. Consequently, the trends in the income structure can be discerned but dimly, and the results considered as preliminary informed guesses.

The data are for the United States, England, and Germany—a scant sample, but at least a starting point for some inferences concerning long-term changes in the presently developed countries. The general conclusion suggested is that the relative distribution of income, as measured by annual income incidence in rather broad classes, has been moving toward equality—with these trends particularly noticeable since the 1920s but beginning perhaps in the period before the first world war.

Let me cite some figures, all for income before direct taxes, in support of this impression. In the United States, in the distribution of income among families (excluding single individuals), the shares of the two lowest quintiles rise from 13½ percent in 1929 to 18 percent in the years after the second world war (average of 1944, 1946, 1947, and 1950); whereas the share of the top quintile declines from 55 to 44 percent, and that of the top 5 percent from 31 to 20 percent. In the United Kingdom, the share of the top 5 percent of units declines from 46 percent in 1880 to 43 percent in 1910 or 1913, to 33 percent in 1929, to 31 percent in 1938, and to 24 percent in 1947; the share of the lower 85 percent remains fairly constant between 1880 and 1913, between 41 and 43 percent, but then rises to 46 percent in 1929 and 55 percent in 1947. In Prussia, income inequality increases slightly between 1875 and 1913—the shares of the top quintile rising from 48 to 50 percent, of the top 5 percent from 26 to 30 percent; the share of the lower 60 percent, however, remains about the same. In Saxony, the change between 1880 and 1913 is minor: the share of the two lowest quintiles declines from 15 to 14½ percent; that of the third quintile rises from 12 to 13 percent, of the fourth quintile from 16½ to about 18 percent; that of the top quintile declines from 56½ to 54½ percent, and of the top 5 percent from 34 to 33 percent. In Germany as a whole, relative income inequality drops fairly sharply from 1913 to the 1920s, apparently due to decimation of large fortunes and property incomes during the war and inflation, but then begins to return to prewar levels during the depression of the 1930s.[1]

Even for what they are assumed to represent, let alone as approximations to shares in distributions by secular income levels, the data are such that differences of two or three percentage points cannot be assigned significance. One must judge by the general weight and consensus of the evidence—which unfortunately is limited to a few countries. It justifies a tentative impression of constancy in the relative distribution of income before taxes, followed by some narrowing of relative income inequality after the first world war—or earlier.

Three aspects of this finding should be stressed. First, the data are for income before direct taxes and exclude contributions by government (e.g., relief and free assistance). It is fair to argue that both the proportion and progressivity of direct taxes and the proportion of total income of individuals accounted for by government assistance to the less privileged economic groups have grown during recent decades. This is certainly true of the United States and the United Kingdom, but in the case of Germany is subject to further examination. It follows that the distribution of income after direct taxes and including free contributions by government would show an even greater narrowing of inequality in developed countries with size distributions of pretax, ex-government-benefits income similar to those for the United States and the United Kingdom.

Second, such stability or reduction in the inequality of the percentage shares was accompanied by significant rises in real income per capita. The countries now classified as developed have enjoyed rising per capita incomes except during catastrophic periods such as years of active world conflict. Hence, if the shares of groups classified by their annual income position can be viewed as approximations to shares of groups classified by their secular income levels, a constant percentage share of a given group means that its per capita real income is rising at the same rate as the average for all units in the country; and a reduction in inequality of the shares means that the per capita income of the lower-income groups is rising at a more rapid rate than the per capita income of the upper-income groups.

The third point can be put in the form of a question. Do the distributions by annual incomes properly reflect trends in distribution by secular incomes? As technology and economic performance rise to higher levels, incomes are less subject to transient disturbances, not necessarily of the cyclical order that can be recognized and allowed for by reference to business cycle chronology, but of a more irregular type. If in the earlier years the economic fortunes of units were subject to greater vicissitudes— poor crops for some farmers, natural calamity losses for some nonfarm business units—if the over-all proportion of individual entrepreneurs whose incomes were subject to such calamities, more yesterday but some even today, was larger in earlier decades, these earlier distributions of income would be more affected by transient disturbances. In these earlier distributions the temporarily unfortunate might crowd the lower quintiles and depress their shares unduly, and the temporarily fortunate might dominate the top quintile and raise its share unduly—proportionately more than in the distributions for later years. If so, distributions by longer-term average incomes might show less reduction in inequality than do the distributions by annual incomes; they might even show an opposite trend.

One may doubt whether this qualification would upset a narrowing of inequality as marked as that for the United States, and in as short a period as twenty-five years. Nor is it likely to affect the persistent downward drift in the spread of the distributions in the United Kingdom. But I must admit a strong element of judgment in deciding how far this qualification modifies the finding of long-term stability followed by reduction in income inequality in the few developed countries for which it is observed or is likely to be revealed by existing data. The important point is that the qualification is relevant; it suggests need for further study if we are to learn much from the available data concerning the secular income structure; and such study is likely to yield results of interest in themselves in their bearing upon the problem of trends in temporal instability of income flows to individual units or to economically significant groups of units in different sectors of the national economy. . . .

Hence we may conclude that the major offset to the widening of income inequality associated with the shift from agriculture and the countryside to industry and the city must have been a rise in the income share of the lower groups within the nonagricultural sector of the population. This provides a lead for exploration in what seems to me a most promising direction: consideration of the pace and character of the economic growth of the urban population, with particular reference to the relative position of lower-income groups. Much is to be said for the notion that once the early turbulent phases of industrialization and urbanization had passed, a variety of forces converged to bolster the economic position of the lower-income groups within the urban population. The very fact that, after a while, an increasing proportion of the urban population was "native," i.e., born in cities rather than in the rural areas, and hence more able to take advantage of the possibilities of city life in preparation for the economic struggle, meant a better chance for organization and adaptation, a better basis for securing greater income shares than was possible for the newly "immigrant" population coming from the countryside or from abroad. The increasing efficiency of the older, established urban population should also be taken into account. Furthermore, in democratic societies the growing political power of the urban lower-income groups led to a variety of protective and supporting legislation, much of it aimed to counteract the worst effects of rapid industrialization and urbanization and to support the claims of the broad masses for more adequate shares of the growing income of the country. Space does not permit the discussion of demographic, political, and social considerations that could be brought to bear to explain the offsets to any declines in the shares of the lower groups, declines otherwise deducible from the trends suggested in the numerical illustration.

Other Trends Related to Those in Income Inequality

One aspect of the conjectural conclusion just reached deserves emphasis because of its possible interrelation with other important elements in the process and theory of economic growth. The scanty empirical evidence suggests that the narrowing of income inequality in the developed countries is relatively recent and probably did not characterize the earlier stages of their growth. Likewise, the various factors that have been suggested above would explain stability and narrowing in income in-equality in the later rather than in the earlier phases of industrialization and urbanization. Indeed, they would suggest widening inequality in these early phases of economic growth, especially in the older countries where the emergence of the new industrial system had shattering effects on long-established pre-industrial economic and social institutions. This timing characteristic is particularly applicable to factors bearing upon the lower-income groups: the dislocating effects of the agricultural and industrial revolutions, combined with the "swarming" of population incident upon a rapid decline in death rates and the maintenance or even rise of birth rates, would be unfavorable to the relative economic position of lower-income groups. Furthermore, there may also have been a preponderance in the earlier periods of factors favoring maintenance or increase in the shares of top-income groups: in so far as their position was bolstered by gains arising out of new industries, by an unusually rapid rate of creation of new fortunes, we would expect these forces to be relatively stronger in the early phases of industrialization than in the later when the pace of industrial growth slackens.

One might thus assume a long swing in the inequality characterizing the secular income structure: widening in the early phases of economic growth when the transition from the pre-industrial to the industrial civilization was most rapid; becoming stabilized for a while; and then narrowing in the later phases. This long secular swing would be most pronounced for older countries where the dislocation effects of the earlier phases of modern economic growth were most conspicuous; but it might be found also in the "younger" countries like the United States if the period preceding marked industrialization could be compared with the early phases of industrialization, and if the latter could be compared with the subsequent phases of greater maturity.

If there is some evidence for assuming this long swing in relative inequality in the distribution of income before direct taxes and excluding free benefits from government, there is surely a stronger case for assuming a long swing in inequality of income net of direct taxes and including government benefits. Progressivity of income taxes and, indeed, their very importance characterize only the more recent phases of development of the presently developed countries; in narrowing income inequality they must have accentuated the downward phase of the long swing, contributing to the reversal of trend in the secular widening and narrowing of income inequality.

No adequate empirical evidence is available for checking this conjecture of a long secular swing in income inequality;[2] nor can the phases be dated precisely. However, to make it more specific, I would place the early phase in which income inequality might have been widening from about 1780 to 1850 in England; from about 1840 to 1890, and particularly from 1870 on in the United States; and from the 1840s to the 1890s in Germany. I would put the phase of narrowing income inequality somewhat later in the United States and Germany than in England—perhaps beginning with the first world war in the former and the last quarter of the nineteenth century in the latter.

Is there a possible relation between this secular swing in income inequality and the long swing in other important components of the growth process? For the older countries a long swing is observed in the rate of growth of population—the upward phase represented by acceleration in the rate of growth reflecting the early reduction in the death rate which was not offset by a decline in the birth rate (and in some cases was accompanied by a rise in the birth rate); and the downward phase represented by a shrinking in the rate of growth reflecting the more pronounced downward trend in the birth rate. Again, in the older countries, and also perhaps in the younger, there may have been a secular swing in the rate of urbanization, in the sense that the proportional additions to urban population and the measures of internal migration that produced this shift of population probably increased for a while—from the earlier much lower levels; but then tended to diminish as urban population came to dominate the country and as the rural reservoirs of migration became proportionally much smaller. For old, and perhaps for young countries also, there must have been a secular swing in the proportions of savings or capital formation to total economic product. Per capita product in pre-industrial times was not large enough to permit as high a nationwide rate of saving or capital formation as was attained in the course of industrial development: this is suggested by present comparisons between net capital formation rates of 3 to 5 percent of national product in underdeveloped countries and rates of 10 to 15 percent in developed countries. If then, at least in the older countries, and perhaps even in the younger ones—prior to initiation of the process of modern development—we begin with low secular levels in the savings proportions, there would be a rise in the early phases to appreciably higher levels. We also know that during recent periods the net capital formation proportion, and even the gross, failed to rise and perhaps even declined.

Other trends might be suggested that would possibly trace long swings similar to those for inequality in income structure, rate of growth of population, rate of urbanization and internal migration, and the proportion of savings or capital formation to national product. For example, such swings might be found in the ratio of foreign trade to domestic activities; in the aspects, if we could only measure them properly, of government activity that bear upon market forces (there must have been a phase of increasing freedom of market forces, giving way to greater intervention by government). But the suggestions already made suffice to indicate that the long swing in income inequality must be viewed as part of a wider process of economic growth, and interrelated with similar movements in other elements. The long alternation in the rate of growth of population can be seen partly as a cause, partly as an effect of the long swing in income inequality which was associated with a secular rise in real per capita income levels. The long swing in income inequality is also probably closely associated with the swing in capital formation proportions—in so far as wider inequality makes for higher, and narrower inequality for lower, countrywide savings proportions.

Comparison of Developed and Underdeveloped Countries

What is the bearing of the experience of the developed countries upon the economic growth of underdeveloped countries? Let us examine briefly the data on income distribution in the latter, and speculate upon some of the implications.

As might have been expected, such data for underdeveloped countries are scanty. For the present purpose, distributions of family income for India in 1949-50, for Ceylon in 1950, and for Puerto Rico in 1948 were used. While the coverage is narrow and the margin of error wide, the data show that income distribution in these underdeveloped countries is somewhat *more* unequal than in the developed countries during the period after the second world war. Thus the shares of the lower 3 quintiles are 28 percent in India, 30 percent in Ceylon, and 24 percent in Puerto Rico—compared with 34 percent in the United States and 36 percent in the United Kingdom. The shares of the top quintile are 55 percent in India, 50 percent in Ceylon, and 56 percent in Puerto Rico, compared with 44 percent in the United States and 45 percent in the United Kingdom.[3]

This comparison is for income before direct taxes and excluding free benefits from governments. Since the burden and progressivity of direct taxes are much greater in developed countries, and since it is in the latter that substantial volumes of free economic assistance are extended to the lower-income groups, a comparison in terms of income net of direct taxes and including government benefits would only accentuate the wider inequality of income distributions in the underdeveloped countries. Is this difference a reliable reflection of wider inequality also in the distribution of *secular* income levels in underdeveloped countries? Even disregarding the margins of error in the data, the possibility raised earlier in this chapter that transient disturbances in income levels may be more conspicuous under conditions of primitive material and economic technology would affect the comparison just made. Since the distributions cited reflect the annual income levels, a greater allowance should perhaps be made for transient disturbances in the distributions for the under-developed than in those for the developed countries. Whether such a correction would obliterate the difference is a matter on which I have no relevant evidence.

Another consideration might tend to support this qualification. Under-developed countries are characterized by low average levels of income per capita, low enough to raise the question of how the populations manage to survive. Let us assume that these countries represent fairly unified population groups, and exclude, for the moment, areas that combine large native populations with small enclaves of nonnative, privileged minorities, e.g., Kenya and Rhodesia, where income inequality, because of the excessively high income shares of the privileged minority, is appreciably wider than even in the underdeveloped countries cited above.[4] On this assumption, one may infer that in countries with low average income, the secular level of income in the lower brackets could not be below a fairly sizable proportion of average income—otherwise, the groups could not survive. This means, to use a purely hypothetical figure, that the secular level of the share of the lowest decile could not fall far short of 6 or 7 percent, i.e., the lowest decile could not have a per capita income less than six- or seven-tenths of the countrywide average. In more advanced countries, with higher average per capita incomes, even the *secular* share of the lowest bracket could easily be a smaller fraction of the countrywide average, say as small as 2 or 3 percent for the lowest decile, i.e., from a fifth to a third of the countrywide average—without implying a materially impossible economic position for that group. To be sure, there is in all countries continuous pressure to raise the relative position of the bottom-income groups; but the fact remains that the lower limit of the proportional share in the secular income structure is higher when the real countrywide per capita income is low than when it is high.

If the long-term share of the lower-income groups is larger in the underdeveloped than in the average countries, income inequality in the former should be narrower, not wider as we have found. However, if the lower brackets receive larger shares, and at the same time the very top brackets also receive larger shares—which would mean that the intermediate income classes would not show as great a progression from the bottom—the net effect may well be wider inequality. To illustrate, let us compare the distributions for India and the United States. The first quintile in India receives 8 percent of total income, more than the 6 percent share of the first quintile in the United States. But the second quintile in India receives only 9 percent, the third 11, and the fourth 16; whereas in the United States, the shares of these quintiles are 12, 16, and 22 respectively. This is a rough statistical reflection of a fairly common observation relating to income distributions in underdeveloped compared with developed countries. The former have no "middle" classes: there is a sharp contrast between the preponderant proportion of population whose average income is well below the generally low countrywide average, and a small top group with a very large relative income excess. The developed countries, on the other hand, are characterized by a much more gradual rise from low to high shares, with substantial groups receiving more than the high countrywide income average, and the top groups securing smaller shares than the comparable ordinal groups in underdeveloped countries.

It is, therefore, possible that even the distributions of secular income levels would be more unequal in underdeveloped than in developed countries—not in the sense that the shares of the lower brackets would be lower in the former than in the latter, but in the sense that the shares of the very top groups would be higher and that those of the groups below the top would all be significantly lower than a low countrywide income average. This is even more likely to be true of the distribution of income net of direct taxes and inclusive of free government benefits. But whether a high probability weight can be attached to this conjecture is a matter for further study.

In the absence of evidence to the contrary, I assume that it is true: that the secular income structure is somewhat more unequal in underdeveloped countries than in the more advanced—particularly in those of Western and Northern Europe and their economically developed descendants in the New World (the United States, Canada, Australia, and New Zealand). This conclusion has a variety of important implications and leads to some pregnant questions, of which only a few can be stated here.

In the first place, the wider inequality in the secular income structure of underdeveloped countries is associated with a much lower level of average income per capita. Two corollaries follow—and they would follow even if the income inequalities were of the same relative range in the two groups of countries. First, the impact is far sharper in the underdeveloped countries, where the failure to reach an already low countrywide average spells much greater material and psychological misery than similar proportional deviations from the average in the richer, more advanced countries. Second, positive savings are obviously possible only at much higher relative income levels in the underdeveloped countries: if in the more advanced countries some savings are possible in the fourth quintile, in the underdeveloped countries savings could be realized only at the very peak of the income pyramid, say by the top 5 or 3 percent. If so, the concentration of savings and of assets is even more pronounced than in the developed countries; and the effects of such concentration in the past may serve to explain the peculiar characteristics of the secular income structure in underdeveloped countries today.

The second implication is that this unequal income structure presumably coexisted with a low rate of growth of income per capita. The underdeveloped countries today have not always lagged behind the presently developed areas in level of economic performance; indeed, some of the former may have been the economic leaders of the world in the centuries preceding the last two. The countries of Latin America, Africa, and particularly those of Asia, are underdeveloped today because in the last two centuries, and even in recent decades, their rate of economic growth has been far lower than that in the Western World— and low indeed, if any growth there was, on a per capita basis. The underlying shifts in industrial structure, the opportunities for internal mobility and for economic improvement, were far more limited than in the more rapidly growing countries now in the developed category. There was no hope, within the lifetime of a generation, of a significantly perceptible rise in the level of real income, or even that the next generation might fare much better. It was this hope that served as an important and realistic compensation for the wide inequality in income distribution that characterized the presently developed countries during the earlier phases of their growth.

The third implication follows from the preceding two. It is quite possible that income inequality has not narrowed in the underdeveloped countries within recent decades. There is no empirical evidence to check this conjectural implication, but it is suggested by the absence, in these areas, of the dynamic forces associated with rapid growth that in the developed countries checked the upward trend of the upper-income shares that was due to the cumulative effect of continuous concentration of past savings; and it is also indicated by the failure of the political and social systems of underdeveloped countries to initiate the governmental or political practices that effectively bolster the weak positions of the lower-income classes. Indeed, there is a possibility that inequality in the secular income structure of underdeveloped countries may have widened in recent decades—the only qualification being that where there has been a recent shift from colonial to independent status, a privileged, *nonnative* minority may have been eliminated. But the implication, in terms of the income distribution among the *native* population proper, still remains plausible.

The somber picture just presented may be an oversimplified one. But I believe that it is sufficiently realistic to lend weight to the questions it poses—questions as to the bearing of the recent levels and trends in income inequality, and the factors that determine them, upon the future prospect of underdeveloped countries within the orbit of the free world.

The questions are difficult, but they must be faced unless we are willing completely to disregard past experience or to extrapolate mechanically oversimplified impressions of past development. The first question is: Is the pattern of the older developed countries likely to be repeated in the sense that in the early phases of industrialization in the underdeveloped countries income inequalities will tend to widen before the leveling forces become strong enough first to stabilize and then reduce income inequalities? While the future cannot be an exact repetition of the past, there are already certain elements in the present conditions of underdeveloped societies, e.g., "swarming" of population due to sharp cuts in death rates unaccompanied by declines in birth rates, that threaten to widen inequality by depressing the relative position of lower-income groups even further. Furthermore, if and when industrialization begins, the dislocating effects on these societies, in which there is often an old hardened crust of economic and social institutions, are likely to be quite sharp—so sharp as to destroy the positions of some of the lower groups more rapidly than opportunities elsewhere in the economy may be created for them.

The next question follows from an affirmative answer to the first. Can the political framework of the underdeveloped societies withstand the strain which further widening of income inequality is likely to generate? This query is pertinent if it is realized that the real per capita income level of many underdeveloped societies today is lower than the per capita income level of the presently developed societies before *their* initial phases of industrialization. And yet the stresses of the dislocations incident to early phases of industrialization in the developed countries were sufficiently acute to strain the political and social fabric of society, force major political reforms, and sometimes result in civil war.

The answer to the second question may be negative, even granted that industrialization may be accompanied by a rise in real per capita product. If, for many groups in society, the rise is even partly offset by a decline in their proportional share in total product; if, consequently, it is accompanied by widening of income inequality, the resulting pressures and conflicts may necessitate drastic changes in social and political organization. This gives rise to the next and crucial question: How can either the institutional and political framework of the underdeveloped societies or the processes of economic growth and industrialization be modified to favor a sustained rise to higher levels of economic performance and yet avoid the fatally simple remedy of an authoritarian regime that would use the population as cannon-fodder in the fight for economic achievement? How to minimize the cost of transition and avoid paying the heavy price—in internal tensions, in long-run inefficiency in providing means for satisfying wants of human beings as individuals—which the inflation of political power represented by authoritarian regimes requires?

Facing these acute problems, one is cognizant of the dangers of taking an extreme position. One extreme—particularly tempting to us—is to favor repetition of past patterns of the now developed countries, patterns that, under the markedly different conditions of the presently under-developed countries, are almost bound to put a strain on the existing social and economic institutions and eventuate in revolutionary explosions and authoritarian regimes. There is danger in simple analogies; in arguing that because an unequal income distribution in Western Europe in the past led to accumulation of savings and financing of basic capital formation, the preservation or accentuation of present income inequalities in the underdeveloped countries is necessary to secure the same result. Even disregarding the implications for the lower-income groups, we may find that in at least some of these countries today the consumption propensities of upper-income groups are far higher and savings pro-pensities far lower than were those of the more puritanical upper-income groups of the presently developed countries. Because they may have proved favorable in the past, it is dangerous to argue that completely free markets, lack of penalties implicit in progressive taxation, and the like are indispensable for the economic growth of the now underdeveloped countries. Under present conditions the results may be quite the op-posite—withdrawal of accumulated assets to relatively "safe" channels, either by flight abroad or into real estate; and the inability of governments to serve as basic agents in the kind of capital formation that is indis-pensable to economic growth. It is dangerous to argue that, because in the past foreign investment provided capital resources to spark satisfactory economic growth in some of the smaller European countries or in Europe's descendants across the seas, similar effects can be expected today if only the underdeveloped countries can be convinced of the need of a "favorable climate." Yet, it is equally dangerous to take the opposite position and claim that the present problems are entirely new and that we must devise solutions that are the product of imagination unrestrained by knowledge of the past, and therefore full of romantic violence. What we need, and I am afraid it is but a truism, is a clear perception of past trends and of conditions under which they occurred, as well as knowledge of the conditions that characterize the underde-veloped countries today. With this as a beginning, we can then attempt to translate the elements of a properly understood past into the conditions of an adequately understood present.

Notes

1. The following sources were used in calculating the figures cited: *United States.* For recent years we used *Income Distribution by Size, 1944–1950* (Wash-ington, 1953) and Selma Goldsmith and others, "Size Distribution of Income Since the Mid-Thirties," *Rev. Econ. Stat.*, Feb. 1954, XXXVI, 1–32; for 1929, the Brookings Institution data as adjusted in Simon Kuznets, *Shares of Upper Groups in Income and Savings* (New York, 1953), p. 220.

United Kingdom. For 1938 and 1947, Dudley Seers, *The Levelling of Income Since 1938* (Oxford, 1951) p. 39; for 1929, Colin Clark, *National Income and Outlay* (London, 1937) Table 47, p. 109; for 1880, 1910, and 1913, A. Bowley, *The Change in the Distribution of the National Income, 1880–1913* (Oxford, 1920).

Germany. For the constituent areas (Prussia, Saxony and others) for years before the first world war, based on S. Prokopovich, *National Income of Western European Countries* (published in Moscow in the 1920s). Some summary results are given in Prokopovich, "The Distribution of National Income," *Econ. Jour.,* March 1926, XXXVI, 69–82. See also, "Das Deutsche Volkseinkommen vor und nach dem Kriege," *Einzelschrift zur Stat. des Deutschen Reichs,* no. 24 (Berlin, 1932), and W. S. and E. S. Woytinsky, *World Population and Production* (New York, 1953) Table 192, p. 709.

2. Prokopovich's data on Prussia, from the source cited in footnote 1, indicate a substantial widening in income inequality in the early period. The share of the lower 90 percent of the population declines from 73 percent in 1854 to 65 percent in 1875; the share of the top 5 percent rises from 21 to 25 percent. But I do not know enough about the data for the early years to evaluate the reliability of the finding.

3. For sources of these data see "Regional Economic Trends and Levels of Living," submitted at the Norman Waite Harris Foundation Institute of the University of Chicago in November 1954 (in press in the volume of proceedings). This paper, and an earlier one, "Underdeveloped Countries and the Pre-industrial Phases in the Advanced Countries: An Attempt at Comparison," prepared for the World Population Meetings in Rome held in September 1954 (in press) discuss issues raised in this section.

4. In one year since the second world war, the non-African group in Southern Rhodesia, which accounted for only 5 percent of total population, received 57 percent of total income; in Kenya, the minority of only 2.9 percent of total population, received 51 percent of total income; in Northern Rhodesia, the minority of only 1.4 percent of total population, received 45 percent of total income. See United Nations, *National Income and Its Distribution in Underdeveloped Countries*, Statistical Paper, Ser. E, no. 3, 1951, Table 12, p. 19.

5. Cultures and Growth

Henri Aujac

According to Henri Aujac, culture determines a country's ability to industrialize and the type of industrialization that might occur. Development, from his perspective, is entirely contingent upon culture, which in turn is a product of historical experience. If this view is sustained by research, some of which is reported in the two chapters that follow, the explanation of the persistent and widening gap between rich and poor countries is obvious; developed countries have cultures that have permitted them to industrialize, while those countries that have failed to industrialize, and hence have failed to narrow the international gap, do not possess appropriate cultures. There is a certain circularity in reasoning inherent in this argument. Furthermore, it tends to minimize the chances for cultural change in response to new challenges. What would observers have said in 1800, for example, about the suitability of the culture of the United States for industrialization?

Purpose and Organization of the Study

Ignorance of the links between, on the one side, a country's culture and the social order structuring its society and, on the other, the suitability of the country for one or other type of industrialization, is no doubt the chief cause of the checks experienced by some developing countries in their attempts to industrialize. Iran is a good example; but analogous cases, if less spectacular, can be found throughout the world, notably among the Islamic countries, in black Africa and in Latin America.

We propose to display some of these links, in particular:

- A country's culture and its prevailing social order largely determine its suitability for industrialization and, moreover, condition quite strictly the possible modes of industrialization: some cultures and some social orders favor industrialization, others do not.
- Reciprocally, some forms of industrialization destroy the prevailing culture and social order without replacing them with new ones; the society is then threatened by chaos or regression. Industrialization in this case destroys the society.

Reprinted with permission from *The Political Economy of New and Old Industrial Countries*, edited by Christopher Saunders, pp. 50–61. London: Butterworths, 1981.

To deal with these various points, we shall briefly describe the concepts used and expound the methodology which seems appropriate; we shall then illustrate our approach by a number of examples.

It seems quite plausible that, in a given country, the prevailing cultural and social order cannot fail to influence the sub-sector formed by the industrial society: a culture and social order take centuries to establish and even the oldest industrial societies have existed for less than two centuries; even in these societies, it is not so long ago that the industrial population became superior to the agricultural.

Culture—that is the totality of the intellectual character of a population, and the body of social, religious, ethical, scientific and technical features which constitute the culture—was established in the course of a country's history at a time when its people were struggling to escape from ancestral terrors and to overcome the horrors of famine, war, disease, and death. This culture is based on behavior, hopes and beliefs taught by very long experience to individuals and groups; the culture so formed allows the organization of a generally acceptable community life and promotes relationships between individuals and groups and relations with the outside world.

Such a culture both sustains and is sustained by the general social order structuring the society. This order is made manifest in customs and an informal system of law as well as in organizations and institutions and in the differentiation of social groups; almost always it incorporates a constitution explicitly defining each group's rights and duties. This general social order, more or less accepted by all, is the result of the society's history and the outward expression of its culture.

A general social organization always involves a hierarchical ordering of society, on occasion quite strict, into groups or classes. Less than two centuries ago in every country, and in many countries today, there is a "prince," (i.e., a power center) at the peak of the "social pyramid," a prince who is sometimes considered as having divine characteristics.

It is of interest for our purpose to ascertain the values attached to this general social order. Briefly, they are altruism and devotion to the group. Whether in the family, the army or the nation, each individual is obligated to sacrifice his personal interest and, if necessary, his life for the advantage of the group whether small or large, which claims his loyalty; in return, the group, whether it be the nation or the family, owes its members a duty of protection and succor. Religion is often capable of smoothing the interpersonal relationships which every state establishes by the very fact of its existence.

Within the general social order a series of special orders may be distinguished; these are either *de facto* orders, which are not explicitly structured and involve persons with common intellectual or material interests, or special orders engendered by the various institutions.

An "industrial organization," when it exists, is one of these special orders. In general, its beginnings are timid. Once established, it grows and, within the society at large, generates a new society structured by industrial enterprises, banks, trading firms, transport enterprises, etc., each run by specific actors in the industrial world. Depending on the political regime, these firms may be private enterprises run by capitalists, or state-owned firms run by the bureaucracy; in any case, the corresponding industrial organization determines the hierarchical position of the various participants, in particular that of firms' executives and their workers and employees: the managerial class commands the workers and sets working objectives and discipline, and fixes wages, more or less strictly, depending on the times and the system.

We may examine the industrial order of a liberal capitalistic state as an illustration. The motivations and values used as norms in this order are indeed special. The goal of the industrial capitalist is financial profit; the value recognized by society is money; the relationships between firms and men who run them are governed by competition; moreover, competition exists within the firm among executives seeking to rise to the top of the structure. The principle of the relationships between management and labor is simple: capitalists can exist only if they can preserve the greatest difference between the prices at which they sell the production of the firm and the wages they pay to their workers; in the short term at least, the interests of labor and management are contradictory.

The ethic of this industrial world is thus different from that of the general social organization because it stresses such qualities as individualism, the importance of the leader, the pursuit of personal interest, the need to struggle against others, and the reduction of values to an equivalent in monetary terms.

It can readily be seen how different the general social organization, as analyzed above, is from the picture of the liberal, capitalistic, industrial organization we have presented. To a certain extent, they are incompatible.[1]

So history has seen the formation of a number of different cultures and social orders, and, often, industrialization has equally taken different forms. It would be interesting, but it is not our purpose here, to establish a correspondence between each culture and social order on the one side, and, on the other, the associated mode of industrialization. For the present, we shall try to analyze the relationship between these two concepts but restricting the discussion, for convenience, to the liberal capitalist mode of industrialization, which is only a special case—one of the possible modes. These relationships can be various.

One kind of culture and general social organization may favor the creation and development of industrial organization: we will therefore call it an "industrializing culture and social order." Another type of social order may be unfavorable. The conditions to be satisfied if a culture and social order is to be considered as industrializing will be examined below.

By contrast, it should first be stressed, to avoid mentioning it again, that an industrial organization, which has succeeded in emerging through favorable circumstances, may turn out to be completely incompatible with the culture and the general social order into which it was born. It may then either generate a new general social order which is more favorable, or replace it to become itself the new culture and the new general social order. In the Communist Manifesto, Marx and Engels give the example of the substitution of an industrial, bourgeois organization in place of the feudal general social order which it destroys. This illustrates one kind of possible relationship between the industrial and the general social orders. It sets out a view which has not yet been justified by the facts: almost 150 years after Marx and Engels wrote these lines, the industrializing bourgeoisie, as they perceived it, has nowhere yet succeeded in altogether destroying the previous culture and general social organization.[2]

In what conditions will a general social order foster the birth and growth of industrialization of the liberal capitalist type? To answer this question, we must discover the conditions to be fulfilled by a developing country in order to interest rich countries in investing there.[3] This type of industrialization is obviously very special because foreign investment and capital are involved, but it shows what the promoters of the industrial order demand from the general social order—demands which are expressed quite bluntly, and sometimes with a degree of cynicism. Some of them relate to problems arising from the foreign nationality of the investor, which are of little concern to us here: for instance, a favorable climate in which foreign investors are accepted, if need be as participants in joint ventures; or the provision of guarantees for the repatriation of profits. Other demands, however, reveal requirements felt by any industrial organization which the general social order is expected to meet. These include, among other things:

1. The public authorities must be strong and effective enough to maintain order and, if possible, the stability of the currency.
2. The society must be stable enough, politically and socially, human rights sufficiently respected, and political circles sufficiently honest, respected and respectable, to eliminate the possibility that revolutionary parties can establish themselves and foment rebellion.
3. The general attitude toward a Western-type civilization—that is to say, the profit motive and the consumer society—must be favorable.
4. Transport and communication networks must be cheap and effective.
5. Manpower must be abundant, active, capable, submissive and inexpensive.

There is one last necessary condition for the development of the country to be autonomous:

6. The values of the traditional social organization should permit or, even better, stimulate dynamic people to enter business, as a means to financial gains and power.

Conditions (1) and (2) imply that the general social organization of the country considered must be vigorous and comprise a relatively strict and accepted hierarchy in which the prince, the power groups, or the ruling classes uncontestedly dominate "the people" who supply manpower.

Conditions (3) and (6) stress that there must be at least minimal compatibility between the values of the society at large and those of the industrial society. For example, industrialization will be difficult if the society as a whole believes that trading, manufacturing, and banking are disreputable, or if it condemns the lending of money at interest.

Condition (5) is obviously essential and is often satisfied. At the start of the industrialization process, the first workers are peasants; indeed, infant industries often first appear in rural areas—sometimes to escape the rules of corporations which protect workers—and create a labor force working in both field and factory. This rural labor force, trained by centuries of agricultural toil, has almost all the necessary qualities from the outset. The permanent threat of starvation has taught it that permanent activity and infinite patience are the source of its daily bread. Farmers know that the fruit of their immense toil is at the mercy of random destruction by an act of God—blight, storm, hail, banditry, etc.—that it is absolutely necessary to be content with little, and that when a catastrophe occurs, the only recourse is to heaven and its representatives on earth—or to rich landlords, men of a superior breed whose way of life and reactions are so strange that they seem to live on another planet. Whether toward heaven, the clergy, or the landlord, obedience is the only effective behavior, and the only possible one.

Energetic, obedient and undemanding, the labor force originating in the rural environment has thus many of the basic qualities required. It nevertheless suffers difficulties in adapting to the yoke of working hours and working discipline and especially to the pace of activity necessitated by industrial production. Above all, technological progress today increasingly requires workers to have professional qualifications beyond those of someone migrating from a rural environment. Nowadays, it is the professional qualifications of the labor force which determine what technologies can be introduced in a given country. Adaptation and qualification take time: several years in some cases, a whole generation in others.

The case discussed here occurs frequently in countries which have been industrialized for quite a while; the farmer has moved from field to factory with practically no transition. But peasants sometimes leave the countryside to seek employment in towns and find none, pile up in the suburbs, rapidly lose their earlier qualities of skill and conscientiousness and become unsuitable for industrial tasks. This phenomenon is frequent today in the developing countries.

So we can understand that the characteristics of the culture and of the general social order directly influence the birth and development of industrial organization; and there is reason to believe that only some of these orders are "industrializing." This working hypothesis will now be illustrated using concrete cases.

France and Japan: Two Comparable Cultures with Different Modes of Industrialization

France

Until the French Revolution, society was subject to the authority of a monarchy which had ruled by divine right for 10 centuries. French society was composed of three sharply demarcated hierarchical orders: the clergy, followed by a nobility established by birth and land ownership, and, at the bottom of the pyramid, the "Third Estate," that is to say the "people," comprising the mass of the peasantry and the bourgeois classes—handicraft workers, traders, businessmen, lawyers, notaries, doctors, bankers, ship-owners, etc. God's will, birth, and land ownership were the legitimating basis of this order which determined social prestige and power. The values cherished by this society were military and feudal: submission to the will of God and the King, respect of and for religion, honor, one's word, the hierarchy, fidelity to one's superior, the protection of the weak, and a degree of distrust for newly acquired social position or wealth. Relationships between men in this type of society were the opposite of those prevailing in a developed commercial and industrial society.

The financing of the whole system was based on the exploitation of the peasantry who could be "taxed and put to forced labor at will," paying farm rents and sharecropping dues to the nobility and a series of direct and indirect taxes to the royal tax inspectors. The peasants were extremely poor, living on the border of famine, and incapable of constituting a market of any kind.

This social organization was unfavorable to industrialization for both economic and cultural reasons, namely:

- Markets were local and not very dynamic; transport was dangerous and expensive, and business hampered by excise taxes.
- In the towns, the strict rules of the guilds limited the volume of production and the number of apprentices. This effectively stopped any growth or development of the economy.

- The nobles, although enjoying the highest incomes, were debarred from business or industrial activities. At best, without derogation to their rank, they could indulge in foreign trade or in branches of business such as mining and metallurgy which were considered direct extensions of agricultural activity.
- The most prized investment, yielding prestige and wealth, was land purchase, and the purchase or construction of castles, following the royal example. Savings were thus channelled chiefly to property and only limited resources were devoted to handicraft and manufacturing trades.

In spite of these handicaps, manufacturing and handicrafts developed. Some rich members of the bourgeoisie became interested in new industries, in particular textiles, and they evaded the corporative rules by employing the rural peasants in their homes. The bourgeoisie would supply the raw materials and market the finished products.

The royal power also generated a limited degree of industrialization in response to two areas of concern. The desire for power led the King, often at war to extend or defend his kingdom and in need of arms and warships, to establish arsenals and foster the development of privately owned arms factories, while the desire for wealth implied the circulation of a substantial quantity of gold, to be seized in case of need; thus the foreign balance had to be positive. However, the King, the court, the nobility, and the rich bourgeoisie were accustomed to importing luxury goods from abroad. These goods had to be produced in France, and as private firms were incapable of doing so, the royal manufactories had to be created for the purpose.

In short, industrialization was begun under the monarchy. However, to accelerate this process, it would have been necessary, among other things, to abolish corporative regulations, to permit handicraft workers and industrialists to produce and to use the labor force as they saw fit, to channel available capital to their activities, to do away with the internal customs, and to improve transport. We shall see how far the Revolution of 1789 contributed to meeting these conditions.

The bourgeois revolution of 1789, at least in appearance, destroyed the general social organization of the monarchy and replaced it with a new one: the orders were abolished, the King was executed, and many of the nobility fled the country. All citizens were proclaimed equal before the law. The change, nevertheless, was not as deep as it seemed. The new order was, indeed, not based on birth, but the concept of power and privilege through land ownership remained intact. The bourgeoisie became landed proprietors, bought castles and tried to reinstate the old system, but this time to their own benefit. In addition, the aristocracy, which had returned to France after 1815, was reasonably successful in reconstituting its former landed property rights. Instead of a substitution of the nobility by the bourgeoisie, the two classes merged, the bourgeoisie taking the nobility as its model and adopting land ownership as the outward sign and justification of its membership of the highest class.

Thus, the change in the general social order was restricted to the higher classes. By contrast, things hardly changed for the laboring classes. Indeed, for some, conditions worsened, as they were no longer protected by corporate regulations. However, living conditions did improve for the peasants, who were freed of all tax to the local seigneur; many purchased small holdings—becoming "lords of their own domains"—to which they held a fierce attachment.

From an economic viewpoint, the bourgeoisie had achieved the abolition of the guild rules, which had hamstrung freedom to establish enterprises and to exploit the labor force. Does this mean that the conditions for true industrialization had now been satisfied?

In reality, some characteristics and values of monarchical times remained deeply engraved in the collective memory, subsisting for 150 years, or from four to five generations, up to World War II; even today, there are still traces of them:

- As regards the exercise of royal authority, the collective subconscious remembers that the subject owes obedience to the state, and in particular to the head of state, and that in return the state has a duty of protection and assistance.
- The ownership of land rather than other property remained preeminent in conferring social prestige long after the revolution, and still survives today. For more than half a century after the revolution, only those who were able to prove high enough landed incomes were entitled to vote and thus able to exercise political power. Because of this, for a good part of the nineteenth century, industrial activity was seen basically as a means of becoming rich faster, in order to purchase domains and castles and thus gain access to privileged status.[4]

A few teachings still remain as vestiges of the guild regulations and their spirit: the golden rule of a society *"à la française"* is to live, however modestly, and to let live. Too overt a search for financial profit, in particular through competition—branded in short order as "unbridled"— is viewed as almost tantamount to usury and as almost contemptible. Such attitudes, which are quite common, are obviously not likely to generate much industrial dynamism.

It is not surprising that in these circumstances French industrialization, except for some rare periods of its history, has recorded only a moderate rate of growth.

There have, however, been periods of strength, of which we may distinguish five:

1. In the period of the First Empire, as under any authoritarian system, the regime wished to mask the absence of freedoms by an increase in general welfare; this, coupled with the absence of British competition during the continental blockade, led it to promote industry.
2. The restoration of absolute monarchy in 1815 and—even more— the regime of Louis-Philippe (July 1830) helped the business world to seize political power, while the development of the railways stimulated that of industry.
3. Under the Second Empire, France reached the stage of an urbanized society, with further substantial industrial development.
4. In the 1890s the second "Industrial Revolution," under the Third Republic, was based on the development of electricity, chemicals, the automobile and aviation—developments intensified during World War I and immediately after.
5. We must wait until 1947 for the next surge in industrial progress— a surge of unprecedented magnitude and duration. It can be attributed to a variety of causes and conditions:
   a. people who had suffered severely from wartime privations and still held modest expectations, while scarcities brought high prices—conditions favoring capital accumulation;
   b. a well-qualified labor force but a stock of capital equipment badly in need of modernization;
   c. American aid under the Marshall Plan, which very soon after the war put abundant capital at the disposal of the government for promoting industrial reconstruction;
   d. the planning system of Jean Monnet which provided capital to industry, but only for projects introducing modern techniques and international competitiveness—conditions favorable to the creation of a modern and efficient production capacity; and
   e. finally, a country which had lost the battle of 1940, which had known privation, and which had seen its factories, its railways, its industry and agriculture in ruins, was able—despite profound political divergences—to find itself united in attacking the priority task of reconstructing the national economy.

During the process of industrial development, the proletariat expanded, as did the trade unions and political parties favorable to labor. First came the Republican party during the July Monarchy, then the Socialist party, followed by the Communist party under the Third Republic. From the 1848 Revolution down to our time, the general social organization of French society was—or more accurately, appeared to be—threatened by working-class claims only on very rare occasions: during the 1848 Revolution, the Paris Commune in 1870, the take-over of power by the Popular Front in 1936, when France was liberated in 1945, and in May 1968. Whenever conflicts of interest between the commanding capitalistic minority and the submissive majority have appeared insoluble within the industrial order, the reaction of the ruling classes has been sharp and often bloody, and—what concerns us here—has quickly produced a reinforcement of the general social order by a return to the former monarchic-style order. In other words, when capitalists and business leaders are incapable of maintaining their domination over the working class and thus no longer control the industrial order, the mobilization of the old organization, which is still the structuring element of society as a whole even if masked, secures their victory.

Several conclusions seem to flow from this rapid overview of the history of French industrialization:

- The often lengthy religious, political, and social history which preceded industrialization progressively forged a national culture, to wit, a set of morals, behavior patterns, relationships between men, and values. Experience proves that this culture changes its basic features only slowly, over several generations. It thus closely conditions the pace and mode of industrialization, as well as the type of industrial society which can develop in the country. From this standpoint, French culture still transmits values which do not correspond to those of a dynamic industrial society.
- To endure, that is to maintain capitalistic domination over labor, to be able to accumulate capital fast enough, and to counterbalance the discipline forced upon workers by an adequate distribution of wealth, the industrial order needs the support of a solidly grounded general social order. The older the order, the more solid it appears. It is the ultimate but up to now unshakable support for the defense of the industrial order.

Japan

The situation in Japan toward the middle of the nineteenth century was similar in many ways to that prevailing in France a hundred years earlier. The general social order was still strong, but it was beginning to deteriorate through the influence of the monetary economy. It consisted of:

1. an emperor, of divine descent, respected by all, but enjoying no real power;
2. a shogun, always a member of the same family, holding authority and with an efficient government organization at his disposal which allowed him to dominate the nobility of "Daimyo";
3. the lords and vassals constituting the samurai, a military class which learned the techniques of management in the shogunate administration and formed a set of competent, patriotic, and reforming men who were to play a decisive role in Japan's industrialization; and

4. the people, the majority being peasants working on the lands of the samurai, together with handicraft workers, traders, etc.; their level of education was higher than in Europe at the same period; almost half the population was literate.

Religion and education taught that society is necessarily a patriarchal and hierarchical organization, in which an individual has value only inasmuch as he contributes to the welfare of the community as a whole. The social system was financed by farmers who paid extremely heavy taxes, sometimes amounting to over 50 percent of their harvest, to the emperor, the shogun, and the samurai. Such a social structure is not particularly conducive to industrialization. Corporative regulations limited the development of handicrafts and small industry. The samurai, an active and dynamic class, could not conduct business: their code of honor forbade profit-seeking and taught them to hold money in contempt. Nevertheless, the development of the monetary system eroded this general social order somewhat, for instance, by enriching traders and by fostering a certain development of handicraft and even of industrial activities, ruining a number of the samurai in the process.

The main participants in the beginnings of industrialization toward the middle of the nineteenth century were rich peasants and certain samurai. They might be taken as the advance signs of the rise of a bourgeois society, but they were weak, and the shogunate order still remained intact as an extremely centralized feudal organization. So one might have forecast that, as in France, Japan's industrial development would remain restricted; but one would have been wrong, and we now turn to the reasons.

The arrival of American (1854) and British (1866) fleets at the Japanese ports to open up the country to foreign trade had two consequences: it was to generate an upheaval in the general social order, and it led to Japan's rapid industrialization.

It was the samurai military class which wrought both changes. The shogun, who had accepted the foreigners' demands, lost status. The emperor retrieved power, assisted by young samurai, who were versed in business matters, competent, and ardently patriotic. This involved a return to the old feudal system which had been adulterated by the shoguns' ambitions: the restoration of the Meiji. Several revolutionary measures were taken: farmers became owners of the lands they tilled, all men were declared to be equal, and education became available to all. In practice, the change does not really seem to have affected the traditional order. The samurai remained in control of the levers of power. The peasant's lot did not improve materially for an income tax replaced the old taxes—an exchange of one burden for another.

The samurai drew two lessons from the entry by force of foreign warships into their ports: freedom of trade meant that industrial countries with a fleet of warships could force less-developed countries to open their borders to them; and to remain independent, the country must acquire military strength. This implied a powerful arms industry. At this point, the conditions for rapid industrialization had been satisfied:

- The ruling class had set itself an aim: the country's independence. This could not be achieved without a powerful industry.
- This class held large financial resources, much greater than the rich traders or wealthy handicraft workers could mobilize to equip heavy industries.
- The workers accepted the aims set by the ruling class and were ready to pay the price in terms of effort.

Industrialization gathered pace thereafter with great efficiency: arms industries, shipyards, steel plants, and the many activities generated by the navy and the army were rapidly established. In parallel, a major effort was undertaken to improve the country's infrastructures with the building of rail and road networks, ports, etc.

Thus, within a few decades Japan became a great industrial power, with features that may still be observed today in the Japanese economy. These include a traditional industry, especially in textiles and food, with small- and average-size firms, and a modern industrial sector comprising heavy industries, transport industries, mechanical industries, etc., using modern techniques and structures which were set up by the state in the form of powerful public corporations and then resold cheaply to a capitalistic family.

As industrialization proceeded, both the male and female labor force increased greatly but its composition has unusual characteristics. The Meiji Restoration did not bring about a rural exodus and the dawn of industrialization took place in traditional industries in rural areas using the especially submissive female labor force. Only toward the end of World War I did the number of male workers equal that of women, mainly through the development of heavy and arms industries.

Only a small percentage of the labor force was unionized, and the unions were ineffective. From the outset, the development of unions was opposed by the government in the name of military imperatives: in 1900, unions were even abolished, together with the then nascent Democratic Socialist party. The union movement recovered strength after World War I, but was torn by internal disputes and ideological discussions. It was repressed in 1931, when the military order took over, and finally abolished in 1937 when it was replaced by an official union which supported austerity and work in the name of solidarity with the fighting forces.

Thus, during the whole Meiji period, and until 1945, the general social order remained unchallenged. The industrial order developed within it, with no urgent social problems raised by the struggle between capitalists and workers. The still neo-feudal state generated first state, then private, capitalism—dynamic and with modern structures—by providing funds, markets, and a cheap and docile labor force. The authorities used the centralized administration, inherited from the shogunate period, with considerable efficiency and drew full benefit from the lessons taught by the foreigners: navies and armies open external markets; power derives from the use of the most modern techniques and is based on the country's industrialization.

A half-century earlier, France had experienced the bourgeois revolution; because the social fabric was impregnated by the monarchical order, it could build up only a not very dynamic industry based on private ownership of the means of production, consisting mainly of small- and medium-size firms. By contrast, Japan, attacked by Western imperialists, recovered its strength by returning to its previous mode of social organization, the imperial feudal order. The state devoted its efforts and abundant financial means to the creation of a powerful, dynamic industry with the most modern structures and techniques, in order to procure the arms needed to make other nations respect its boundaries and to secure *lebensraum*. Thus two societies, quite similar at the outset, yielded two very different patterns of industrialization: in France, where the bourgeois seized power, industry grew at a moderate pace; in Japan, the warrior class took over authority and modern-style industrialization was introduced directly.

It may be interesting to analyze the links between culture, the general social order, and the industrialization policy since the end of World War II. In 1945, several Japanese towns were destroyed, some by atomic, others by phosphorus, bombs. The war was over. American forces occupied the country, with General MacArthur acting as proconsul. For the second time, foreigners were to produce a radical change in Japan's general social order. MacArthur took the following measures in particular: the empire was abolished and replaced by American-type democratic institutions; freedom was granted to found unions and political parties; the large family businesses of the heavy and modern industrial sector were broken up; and Japan was obliged to do away with its armed forces and arms industry. The general social order seemed to be deeply shaken. It had lost its traditional legitimacy: the emperor was no longer divine but the U.S. occupation authorities carefully preserved the monarchy while abolishing its powers.

In fact, here again, we have a great upheaval which had no very visible effects on social organization. The habits and beliefs forged by centuries of an earlier social order cannot be changed instantly. The emperor had indeed lost his antique prestige and there had been some renewal of the ruling classes, but a capable administration, a direct inheritance from the Meiji epoch, still controlled the country's destiny, collaborating closely with the business world—the heads of the large banking, commercial, and industrial firms. The population, trained by long practice in a quasi-military discipline and supervised by political parties of which the largest were financed by business interests, integrated willingly into the industrial order.

Today, the position is what one would expect if there had been no significant changes since the Meiji Restoration and the military period, but nevertheless, with one basic difference: the military-style leadership of the state and the Zaibatsu have been put to the service of other aims, not military but civilian; the twin objectives being to raise Japanese living standards and to conquer foreign markets in order to pay for essential imports. The second of these objectives is pursued according to the rules of military strategy: technical superiority will bring victory; production as a whole must be maintained at a reasonable level as regards both the techniques used and the labor force applying them; the resistance of foreign competitors must be studied in all fields, in order rapidly to concentrate resources in quantity where a breakthrough appears possible. Western observers agree that the large Japanese firms do not apply the criteria used in Western countries in deciding on their investments. Japanese investments are, to quote François Perroux, "wagers on new structures," whereas French investments are calculated on the basis of discounted present values and marginal criteria. Indeed, in a society in which large business concerns and the planning authorities collaborate closely, two or three large firms may decide simultaneously to make identical investments, and then compete fiercely with each other. A firm which has beaten its Japanese competitors need have no complexes about its ability to sell on world markets.

Thus the situation is what one would expect if the executives of the large Japanese firms, like the top civil servants, thought of the struggle for world markets as if it were a military struggle: a war must be won and to do so the necessary means must be provided without regard to expense. Victory will recompense the initial sacrifices—and with great profit; by contrast, defeat means ruin.

Such a strategy can be executed only for so long as capital accumulation remains substantial, and while the labor force accepts lower living standards compared with immediate opportunities, knowing that to sacrifice the present to the future is the only way to obtain a greater rise in living standards in the long run; or more simply, the sacrifice is an unavoidable necessity in a country that is deprived of basic raw materials.

Does this mean that there are no imminent dangers? The old general social order is still preserved in the collective memory and still protects the industrial order efficiently. Its legitimacy has nevertheless been seriously eroded. A generation has gone by since the end of World War II, and another will pass before the capitalistic industrial order can take control of the labor force without the help of the traditional social order. It is then that the difficulties will no doubt occur.

Be this as it may, Japanese history from the Meiji Restoration up to the end of World War II shows clearly that the general social order, the expression of a very ancient culture, having forgotten none of the lessons of history, closely conditions the form of industrial development.

Notes

1. The difference would, at least in theory, be smaller if the industrial order had sprung from the desire of the Prince to have, say, a powerful arms industry. Industrial organization would then be directly at the service of the general social order. This would also be true if firms were nationalized bodies—provided that individuals and groups are, rightly or wrongly, certain that the nationalized industrial order thus created is in harmony with the standards they recognize: to wit, the values of the general society to which they belong, and that it operates to their advantage, and not only to that of their governing bureaucracy.

2. We believe that, on the contrary, the industrial order is expanding not in opposition to, but sheltered by, the general social order, by using certain of its structures, in particular the hierarchical institutions, which are favorable to it. When these institutions prove too weak, the industrial order is often unable to force its own hierarchy onto society other than by terror, and it is then threatened with chaos.

3. "A peaceful Asia beckons investors," *Fortune*, October 1977.

4. Admittedly some entrepreneurs actively sought the status of industrialist—many were Protestants—but they magnified it by giving it a social meaning. The industrialist's function is to provide working-class families with their daily bread and, only incidentally, to make a profit. By acting thus, these industrialists have, doubtless unconsciously, tried to reconstitute, but this time at the factory level, the relationships that bound men during the monarchy.

6. The Achievement Motive in Economic Growth

David C. McClelland[1]

In Chapter 5, Aujac argued that certain cultures favor economic growth. David C. McClelland, a psychologist, expands upon ideas developed by Max Weber, who examined the relationship between the Protestant ethic and the rise of capitalism. McClelland posits a more generalized psychological attribute he calls the "need for Achievement" or n Achievement. In this discussion, which is a summary of a book on the subject, McClelland presents some very interesting historical data he believes help explain the rise and decline of Athenian civilization. Turning to the present century, he produces data that show a close association between national levels of n Achievement and rates of economic growth. In seeking to determine what produces this psychological characteristic, McClelland finds that it is not hereditary but is rather instilled in people. It is therefore possible, he claims, to teach people how to increase their need to achieve and by so doing stimulate economic growth in developing countries. McClelland has been responsible for establishing training and management programs in developing countries in hopes that a change in the psychological orientation of public officials will help speed economic growth.

From the beginning of recorded history, men have been fascinated by the fact that civilizations rise and fall. Culture growth, as A. L. Kroeber has demonstrated, is episodic, and sometimes occurs in quite different fields.[2] For example, the people living in the Italian peninsula at the time of ancient Rome produced a great civilization of law, politics, and military conquest; and at another time, during the Renaissance, the inhabitants of Italy produced a great civilization of art, music, letters, and science. What can account for such cultural flowerings? In our time we have theorists like Ellsworth Huntington, who stresses the importance of climate, or Arnold J. Toynbee, who also feels the right amount of challenge from the environment is crucial though he conceives of the environment as including its psychic effects. Others, like Kroeber, have difficulty imagining any general explanation; they perforce must accept

Reprinted with permission of UNESCO from *Industrialization and Society*, edited by Bert F. Hoselitz and Wilbert E. Moore, pp. 74–95. Paris: UNESCO, 1963.

the notion that a particular culture happens to hit on a particularly happy mode of self-expression, which it then pursues until it becomes overspecialized and sterile.

My concern is not with all culture growth, but with economic growth. Some wealth or leisure may be essential to development in other fields—the arts, politics, science, or war—but we need not insist on it. However, the question of why some countries develop rapidly in the economic sphere at certain times and not at others is in itself of great interest, whatever its relation to other types of culture growth. Usually, rapid economic growth has been explained in terms of "external" factors—favorable opportunities for trade, unusual natural resources, or conquests that have opened up new markets or produced internal political stability. But I am interested in the *internal* factors—in the values and motives men have that lead them to exploit opportunities, to take advantage of favorable trade conditions; in short, to shape their own destiny. . . .

Whatever else one thinks of Freud and the other psychoanalysts, they performed one extremely important service for psychology: once and for all, they persuaded us, rightly or wrongly, that what people said about their motives was not a reliable basis for determining what those motives really were. In his analyses of the psychopathology of everyday life and of dreams and neurotic symptoms, Freud demonstrated repeatedly that the "obvious" motives—the motives that the people themselves thought they had or that a reasonable observer would attribute to them—were not, in fact, the real motives for their often strange behavior. By the same token, Freud also showed the way to a better method of learning what people's motives were. He analyzed dreams and free associations: in short, fantasy or imaginative behavior. Stripped of its air of mystery and the occult, psychoanalysis has taught us that one can learn a great deal about people's motives through observing the things about which they are spontaneously concerned in their dreams and waking fantasies. About ten or twelve years ago, the research group in America with which I was connected decided to take this insight quite seriously and to see what we could learn about human motivation by coding objectively what people spontaneously thought about in their waking fantasies.[3] Our method was to collect such free fantasy, in the form of brief stories written about pictures, and to count the frequency with which certain themes appeared—rather as a medical technician counts the frequency with which red or white corpuscles appear in a blood sample. We were able to demonstrate that the frequency with which certain "inner concerns" appeared in these fantasies varied systematically as a function of specific experimental conditions by which we aroused or induced motivational states in the subjects. Eventually we were able to isolate several of these inner concerns, or motives, which, if present in great frequency in the fantasies of a particular person, enabled us to know something about how he would behave in many other areas of life.

Chief among these motives was what we termed "the need for Achievement" (*n* Achievement)—a desire to do well, not so much for the sake of social recognition or prestige, but to attain an inner feeling of personal accomplishment. This motive is my particular concern in this paper. Our early laboratory studies showed that people "high" in *n* Achievement tend to work harder at certain tasks; to learn faster; to do their best work when it counts for the record, and not when special incentives, like money prizes, are introduced; to choose experts over friends as working partners; etc. Obviously, we cannot here review the many, many studies in this area. About five years ago, we became especially interested in the problem of what would happen in a society if a large number of people with a high need for achievement should happen to be present in it at a particular time. In other words, we became interested in a social-psychological question: What effect would a concentration of people with high *n* Achievement have on a society?

It might be relevant to describe how we began wondering about this. I had always been greatly impressed by the very perceptive analysis of the connection between Protestantism and the spirit of capitalism made by the great German sociologist, Max Weber.[4] He argues that the distinguishing characteristic of Protestant business entrepreneurs and of workers, particularly from the pietistic sects, was not that they had in any sense invented the institutions of capitalism or good craftsmanship, but that they went about their jobs with a new perfectionist spirit. The Calvinistic doctrine of predestination had forced them to rationalize every aspect of their lives and to strive hard for perfection in the positions in this world to which they had been assigned by God. As I read Weber's description of the behavior of these people, I concluded that they must certainly have had a high level of *n* Achievement. Perhaps the new spirit of capitalism Weber describes was none other than a high need for achievement—if so, then *n* Achievement has been responsible, in part, for the extraordinary economic development of the West. Another factor served to confirm this hypothesis. A careful study by M. R. Winterbottom had shown that boys with high *n* Achievement usually came from families in which the mothers stressed early self-reliance and mastery.[5] The boys whose mothers did *not* encourage their early self-reliance, or did not set such high standards of excellence, tended to develop lower need for achievement. Obviously, one of the key characteristics of the Protestant Reformation was its emphasis on self-reliance. Luther stressed the "priesthood of all believers" and translated the Bible so that every man could have direct access to God and religious thought. Calvin accentuated a rationalized perfection in this life for everyone. Certainly, the character of the Reformation seems to have set the stage, historically, for parents to encourage their children to attain earlier self-reliance and achievement. If the parents did in fact do so, they very possibly unintentionally produced the higher level of *n* Achievement in their children that was, in turn, responsible for the new spirit of capitalism.

This was the hypothesis that initiated our research. It was, of course, only a promising idea; much work was necessary to determine its validity. Very early in our studies, we decided that the events Weber discusses were probably only a special case of a much more general phenomenon—that it was *n* Achievement as such that was connected with economic development, and that the Protestant Reformation was connected only indirectly in the extent to which it had influenced the average *n* Achievement level of its adherents. If this assumption is correct, then a high average level of *n* Achievement should be equally associated with economic development in ancient Greece, in modern Japan, or in a preliterate tribe being studied by anthropologists in the South Pacific. In other words, in its most general form, the hypothesis attempts to isolate one of the key factors in the economic development, at least, of all civilizations. What evidence do we have that this extremely broad generalization will obtain? By now, a great deal has been collected—far more than I can summarize here; but I shall try to give a few key examples of the different types of evidence.

First, we have made historical studies. To do so, we had to find a way to obtain a measure of *n* Achievement level during time periods other than our own, whose individuals can no longer be tested. We have done this—instead of coding the brief stories written by an individual for a test, we code imaginative literary documents: poetry, drama, funeral orations, letters written by sea captains, epics, etc. Ancient Greece, which we studied first, supplies a good illustration. We are able to find literary documents written during three different historical periods and dealing with similar themes: the period of economic growth, 900 B.C.– 475 B.C. (largely Homer and Hesiod); the period of climax, 475 B.C.– 362 B.C.; and the period of decline, 362 B.C.–100 B.C. Thus, Hesiod wrote on farm and estate management in the early period; Xenophon, in the middle period; and Aristotle, in the late period. We have defined the period of "climax" in economic, rather than in cultural, terms, because it would be presumptuous to claim, for example, that Aristotle in any sense represented a "decline" from Plato or Thales. The measure of economic growth was computed from information supplied by F. Heichelheim in his *Wirtschaftsgeschichte des Altertums*.[6] Heichelheim records in detail the locations throughout Europe where the remains of Greek vases from different centuries have been found. Of course, these vases were the principal instrument of Greek foreign trade, since they were the containers for olive oil and wine, which were the most important Greek exports. Knowing where the vase fragments have been found, we could compute the trade area of Athenian Greece for different time periods. We purposely omitted any consideration of the later expansion of Hellenistic Greece, because this represents another civilization; our concern was Athenian Greece.

When all the documents had been coded, they demonstrated—as predicted—that the level of *n* Achievement was highest during the period of growth prior to the climax of economic development in Athenian

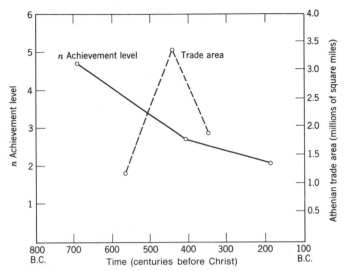

Figure 6.1 Average *n* Achievement level plotted at midpoints of periods of growth, climax, and decline of Athenian civilization as reflected in the extent of her trade area (measured for the sixth, fifth, and fourth centuries B.C. only).

Greece. (See Figure 6.1.) In other words, the maximum *n* Achievement level preceded the maximum economic level by at least a century. Furthermore, that high level had fallen off by the time of maximum prosperity, thus foreshadowing subsequent economic decline. A similar methodology was applied, with the same results, to the economic development of Spain in the sixteenth century[7] and to two waves of economic development in the history of England (one in the late sixteenth century and the other at the beginning of the industrial revolution, around 1800).[8] The *n* Achievement level in English history (as determined on the basis of dramas, sea captains' letters, and street ballads) rose, between 1400–1800, *twice*, a generation or two before waves of accelerated economic growth (incidentally, at times of Protestant revival). This point is significant because it shows that there is no "necessary" steady decline in a civilization's entrepreneurial energy from its earlier to its later periods. In the Spanish and English cases, as in the Greek, high levels of *n* Achievement preceded economic decline. Unfortunately, space limitations preclude more detailed discussion of these studies here.

We also tested the hypothesis by applying it to preliterate cultures of the sort that anthropologists investigate. At Yale University, an organized effort has been made to collect everything that is known about all the primitive tribes that have been studied and to classify the information systematically for comparative purposes. We utilized this cross-cultural file to obtain the two measures that we needed to test our general hypothesis. For over fifty of these cultures, collections of folk tales existed that I. L. Child and others had coded,[9] just as we coded literary documents and individual imaginative stories, for *n* Achievement and other motives. These folk tales have the character of fantasy that we believe to be so essential for getting at "inner concerns." In the meantime, we were searching for a method of classifying the economic development of these cultures, so that we could determine whether those evincing high *n* Achievement in their folk tales had developed further than those showing lower *n* Achievement. The respective modes of gaining a livelihood were naturally very different in these cultures, since they came from every continent in the world and every type of physical habitat; yet we had to find a measure for comparing them. We finally thought of trying to estimate the number of full-time "business entrepreneurs" there were among the adults in each culture. We defined "entrepreneur" as "anyone who exercises control over the means of production and produces more than he can consume in order to sell it for individual or household income." Thus an entrepreneur was anyone who derived at least 75 percent of his income from such exchange or market practices. The entrepreneurs were mostly traders, independent artisans, or operators of small firms like stores, inns, etc. Nineteen cultures were classified as high in *n* Achievement on the basis of their folk tales; 74 percent of them contained some entrepreneurs. On the other hand, only 35 percent of the twenty cultures that were classified as low in *n* Achievement contained any entrepreneurs (as we defined it) at all. The difference is highly significant statistically (Chi-square = 5.97, p <.02). Hence data about primitive tribes seem to confirm the hypothesis that high *n* Achievement leads to a more advanced type of economic activity.

But what about modern nations? Can we estimate their level of *n* Achievement and relate it to their economic development? The question is obviously one of the greatest importance, but the technical problems of getting measures of our two variables proved to be really formidable. What type of literary document could we use that would be equally representative of the motivational levels of people in India, Japan, Portugal, Germany, the United States, and Italy? We had discovered in our historical studies that certain types of literature usually contain much more achievement imagery than others. This is not too serious as long as we are dealing with time changes within a given culture; but it is very serious if we want to compare two cultures, each of which may express its achievement motivation in a different literary form. At last, we decided to use children's stories, for several reasons. They exist in standard form in every modern nation, since all modern nations are involved in teaching their children to read and use brief stories for this purpose. Furthermore, the stories are imaginative; and, if selected from those used in the earliest grades, they are not often influenced by temporary political events. (We were most impressed by this when reading the stories that every Russian child reads. In general, they cannot be distinguished, in style and content, from the stories read in all the countries of the West.)

We collected children's readers for the second, third, and fourth grades from every country where they could be found for two time periods, which were roughly centered around 1925 and around 1950. We got some thirteen hundred stories, which were all translated into English. In all, we had twenty-one stories from each of twenty-three countries about 1925, and the same number from each of thirty-nine countries about 1950. Code was used on proper names, so that our scorers would not know the national origins of the stories. The tales were then mixed together, and coded for n Achievement (and certain other motives and values that I shall mention only briefly).

The next task was to find a measure of economic development. Again, the problem was to insure comparability. Some countries have much greater natural resources; some have developed industrially sooner than others; some concentrate in one area of production and some in another. Economists consider national income figures in per capita terms to be the best measure available; but they are difficult to obtain for all countries, and it is hard to translate them into equal purchasing power. Ultimately, we came to rely chiefly on the measure of electricity produced: the units of measurement are the same all over the world; the figures are available from the 1920s on; and electricity is the *form* of energy (regardless of how it is produced) that is essential to modern economic development. In fact, electricity produced per capita correlates with estimates of income per capita in the 1950s around .90 anyway. To equate for differences in natural resources, such as the amount of water power available, etc., we studied *gains* in kilowatt hours produced per capita between 1925 and 1950. The level of electrical production in 1925 is, as one would expect, highly correlated with the size of the gain between then and 1950. So it was necessary to resort to a regression analysis; that is, to calculate, from the average regression of gain on level for all countries, how much gain a particular country should have shown between 1925 and 1950. The actual gain could then be compared with the expected gain, and the country could be classified as gaining more or less rapidly than would have been expected on the basis of its 1925 performance. The procedure is directly comparable to what we do when we predict, on the basis of some measure of I.Q., what grades a child can be expected to get in school, and then classify him as an "under-" or "over-achiever."

The correlation between the n Achievement level in the children's readers in 1925 and the growth in electrical output between 1925 and 1950, as compared with expectation, is a quite substantial .53, which is highly significant statistically. It could hardly have arisen by chance. Furthermore, the correlation is also substantial with a measure of gain over the expected in per capita income, equated for purchasing power by Colin Clark. To check this result more definitively with the sample of forty countries for which we had reader estimates of n Achievement levels in 1950, we computed the equation for gains in electrical output in 1952–58 as a function of level in 1952. It turned out to be remarkably linear when translated into logarithmic units, as is so often the case with simple growth functions. Table 6.1 presents the performance of each of the countries, as compared with predictions from initial level in 1952, in standard score units and classified by high and low n Achievement in 1950. Once again we found that n Achievement levels predicted significantly ($r = .43$) the countries which would perform more or less rapidly than expected in terms of the average for all countries. The finding is more striking than the earlier one, because many Communist and underdeveloped countries are included in the sample. Apparently, n Achievement is a precursor of economic growth—and not only in the Western style of capitalism based on the small entrepreneur, but also in economies controlled and fostered largely by the state.

For those who believe in economic determinism, it is especially interesting that n Achievement level in 1950 is *not* correlated either with *previous* economic growth between 1925 and 1950, or with the level of prosperity in 1950. This strongly suggests that n Achievement is a *causative* factor—a change in the minds of men which produces economic growth rather than being produced by it. In a century dominated by economic determinism, in both Communist and Western thought, it is startling to find concrete evidence for psychological determinism, for psychological developments as preceding and presumably causing economic changes.

The many interesting results which our study of children's stories yielded have succeeded in convincing me that we chose the right material to analyze. Apparently, adults unconsciously flavor their stories for young children with the attitudes, the aspirations, the values, and the motives that they hold to be most important.

I want to mention briefly two other findings, one concerned with economic development, the other with totalitarianism. When the more and less rapidly developing economies are compared on all the other variables for which we scored the children's stories, one fact stands out. In stories from those countries which had developed more rapidly in both the earlier and later periods, there was a discernible tendency to emphasize, in 1925 and in 1950, what David Riesman has called "other-directedness"—namely, reliance on the opinion of particular others, rather than on tradition, for guidance in social behavior.[10] *Public opinion* had, in these countries, become a major source of guidance for the individual. Those countries which had developed the mass media further and faster—the press, the radio, the public-address system—were also the ones who were developing more rapidly economically. I think that "other-directedness" helped these countries to develop more rapidly because public opinion is basically more flexible than institutionalized moral or social traditions. Authorities can utilize it to inform people widely about the need for new ways of doing things. However, traditional

Table 6.1
Rate of Growth in Electrical Output (1952-1958) and National n Achievement Levels in 1950

Above expectation growth rate			Below expectation growth rate		
National n Achievement levels (1950)[1]	Country	Deviations from expected growth rate[2]	National n Achievement levels (1950)[1]	Country	Deviations from expected growth rate[2]
High n Achievement countries					
3.62	Turkey	+1.38			
2.71	India[3]	+1.12			
2.38	Australia	+ .42			
2.32	Israel	+1.18			
2.33	Spain	+ .01			
2.29	Pakistan[4]	+2.75			
2.29	Greece	+1.18	3.38	Argentina	- .56
2.29	Canada	+ .08	2.71	Lebanon	- .67
2.24	Bulgaria	+1.37	2.38	France	- .24
2.24	U.S.A.	+ .47	2.33	U. So. Africa	- .06
2.14	West Germany	+ .53	2.29	Ireland	- .41
2.10	U.S.S.R.	+1.61	2.14	Tunisia	-1.87
2.10	Portugal	+ .76	2.10	Syria	- .25
Low n Achievement countries					
1.95	Iraq	+ .29	2.05	New Zealand	- .29
1.86	Austria	+ .38	1.86	Uruguay	- .75
1.67	U.K.	+ .17	1.81	Hungary	- .62
1.57	Mexico	+ .12	1.71	Norway	- .77
.86	Poland	+1.26	1.62	Sweeden	- .64
			1.52	Finland	- .08
			1.48	Netherlands	- .15
			1.33	Italy	- .57
			1.29	Japan	- .04
			1.20	Switzerland[5]	-1.92
			1.19	Chile	-1.81
			1.05	Denmark	- .89
			.57	Algeria	- .83
			.43	Belgium	-1.65

Note: Correlation of n Achievement level (1950) x deviations from expected growth rate = .43, $p <$ .01.

[1] Deviations in standard score units. The estimates are computed from the monthly average electrical production figures, in millions of Kwh, for 1952 and 1958, from United Nations, Monthly Bulletin of Statistics (January, 1960), and World Energy Supplies, 1951-1954 and 1955-1958, (Statistical Papers, Series J). The correlation between log level 1952 and log gain 1952-58 is .976. The regression equation based on these thirty-nine countries, plus four others from the same climatic zone on which data are available (China-Taiwan, Czechoslavkia, Rumania, Yugoslavia), is: log gain (1952-58) = .9229 log level (1952) + .0480. Standard scores are deviations from mean gain predicted by the regression formula (M= -.01831) divided by the standard deviation of the deviations from the mean predicted gain (SD = .159).

[2] Based on twenty-one children's stories from second-,third-, and fourth-grade readers in each country.

[3] Based on six Hindi, seven Telegu, and eight Tamil stories.

[4] Based on twelve Urdu and eleven Bengali stories.

[5] Based on twenty-one German Swiss stories, mean = .91; twenty-one French Swiss stories, mean = 1.71; over-all mean obtained by weighting German mean double to give approximately proportionate representation of the two main ethnic populations.

institutionalized values may insist that people go on behaving in ways that are no longer adaptive to a changed social and economic order.

The other finding is not directly relevant to economic development, but it perhaps involves the means of achieving it. Quite unexpectedly, we discovered that every major dictatorial regime which came to power between the 1920s and 1950s (with the possible exception of Portugal's) was foreshadowed by a particular motive pattern in its stories for children: namely, a low need for affiliation (little interest in friendly relationships with people) and a high need for power (a great concern over controlling and influencing other people).

The German readers showed this pattern before Hitler; the Japanese readers, before Tojo; the Argentine readers, before Peron; the Spanish readers, before Franco; the South African readers, before the present authoritarian government in South Africa; etc. On the other hand, very few countries which did not have dictatorships manifested this particular motive combination. The difference was highly significant statistically, since there was only one exception in the first instance and very few in the second. Apparently, we stumbled on a psychological index of ruthlessness—i.e., the need to influence other people (n Power), unchecked by sufficient concern for their welfare (n Affiliation). It is interesting, and a little disturbing, to discover that the German readers of today still evince this particular combination of motives, just as they did in 1925. Let us hope that this is one case where a social science generalization will not be confirmed by the appearance of a totalitarian regime in Germany in the next ten years.

To return to our main theme—let us discuss the precise ways that higher n Achievement leads to more rapid economic development, and why it should lead to economic development rather than, for example, to military or artistic development. We must consider in more detail the mechanism by which the concentration of a particular type of human motive in a population leads to a complex social phenomenon like economic growth. The link between the two social phenomena is, obviously, the business entrepreneur. I am not using the term "entrepreneur" in the sense of "capitalist": in fact, I should like to divorce "entrepreneur" entirely from any connotations of ownership. An entrepreneur is someone who exercises control over production that is not just for his personal consumption. According to my definition, for example, an executive in a steel production unit in Russia is an entrepreneur.

It was Joseph Schumpeter who drew the attention of economists to the importance that the activity of these entrepreneurs had in creating industrialization in the West. Their vigorous endeavors put together firms and created productive units where there had been none before. In the beginning, at least, the entrepreneurs often collected material resources, organized a production unit to combine the resources into a new product, and sold the product. Until recently, nearly all economists—including not only Marx, but also Western classical economists—assumed that these men were moved primarily by the "profit motive." We are all familiar with the Marxian argument that they were so driven by their desire for profits that they exploited the workingman and ultimately forced him to revolt. Recently, economic historians have been studying the actual lives of such entrepreneurs and finding—certainly to the surprise of some of the investigators—that many of them seemingly were not interested in making money as such. In psychological terms, at least, Marx's picture is slightly out of focus. Had these entrepreneurs been above all interested in money, many more of them would have quit working as soon as they had made all the money that they could possibly use. They would not have continued to risk their money in further entrepreneurial ventures. Many of them, in fact, came from pietistic sects, like the Quakers in England, that prohibited the enjoyment of wealth in any of the ways cultivated so successfully by some members of the European nobility. However, the entrepreneurs often seemed consciously to be greatly concerned with expanding their businesses, with getting a greater share of the market, with "conquering brute nature," or even with altruistic schemes for bettering the lot of mankind or bringing about the kingdom of God on earth more rapidly. Such desires have frequently enough been labeled as hypocritical. However, if we assume that these men were really motivated by a desire for achievement rather than by a desire for money as such, the label no longer fits. This assumption also simplifies further matters considerably. It provides an explanation for the fact that these entrepreneurs were interested in money without wanting it for its own sake, namely, that money served as a ready quantitative index of how well they were doing—e.g., of how much they had achieved by their efforts over the past year. The need to achieve can never be satisfied by money; but estimates of profitability in money terms can supply direct knowledge of how well one is doing one's job.

The brief consideration of the lives of business entrepreneurs of the past suggested that their chief motive may well have been a high n Achievement. What evidence have we found in support of this? We made two approaches to the problem. First, we attempted to determine whether individuals with high n Achievement behave like entrepreneurs; and second, we investigated to learn whether actual entrepreneurs, particularly the more successful ones, in a number of countries, have higher n Achievement than do other people of roughly the same status. Of course, we had to establish what we meant by "behave like entrepreneurs"—what precisely distinguishes the way an entrepreneur behaves from the way other people behave?

The adequate answers to these questions would entail a long discussion of the sociology of occupations, involving the distinction originally made by Max Weber between capitalists and bureaucrats. Since this cannot be done here, a very brief report on our extensive investigations in this area will have to suffice. First, one of the defining characteristics of an entrepreneur is *taking risks* and/or innovating. A person who adds up a column of figures is not an entrepreneur—however carefully, efficiently, or correctly he adds them. He is simply following established rules. However, a man who decides to add a new line to his business *is* an entrepreneur, in that he cannot know in advance whether this decision will be correct. Nevertheless, he does not feel that he is in the position of a gambler who places some money on the turn of a card. Knowledge, judgment, and skill enter into his decision making; and, if his choice is justified by future developments, he can certainly feel a sense of personal achievement from having made a successful move.

Therefore, if people with high *n* Achievement are to behave in an entrepreneurial way, they must seek out and perform in situations in which there is some moderate risk of failure—a risk which can, presumably, be reduced by increased effort or skill. They should not work harder than other people at routine tasks, or perform functions which they are certain to do well simply by doing what everyone accepts as the correct traditional thing to do. On the other hand, they should avoid gambling situations, because, even if they win, they can receive no sense of personal achievement, since it was not skill but luck that produced the results. (And, of course, most of the time they would lose, which would be highly unpleasant to them.) The data on this point are very clear-cut. We have repeatedly found, for example, that boys with high *n* Achievement choose to play games of skill that incorporate a moderate risk of failure. . . .

Another quality that the entrepreneur seeks in his work is that his job be a kind that ordinarily provides him with accurate knowledge of the results of his decisions. As a rule, growth in sales, in output, or in profit margins tells him very precisely whether he has made the correct choice under uncertainty or not. Thus, the concern for profit enters in— profit is a measure of success. We have repeatedly found that boys with a high *n* Achievement work more efficiently when they know how well they are doing. Also, they will not work harder for money rewards; but if they are asked, they state that greater money rewards should be awarded for accomplishing more difficult things in games of skill. In the ring-toss game, subjects were asked how much money they thought should be awarded for successful throws from different distances. Subjects with high *n* Achievement and those with low *n* Achievement agreed substantially about the amounts for throws made close to the peg. However, as the distance from the peg increased, the amounts awarded for successful throws by the subjects with high *n* Achievement rose more rapidly than did the rewards by those with low *n* Achievement. Here, as elsewhere, individuals with high *n* Achievement behaved as they must if they are to be the successful entrepreneurs of society. They believed that greater achievement should be recognized by quantitatively larger reward.

What produces high n Achievement? Why do some societies produce a large number of people with this motive, while other societies produce so many fewer? We conducted long series of researches into this question. I can present only a few here.

One very important finding is essentially a negative one: n Achievement cannot be hereditary. Popular psychology has long maintained that some races are more energetic than others. Our data clearly contradict this in connection with n Achievement. The changes in n Achievement level within a given population are too rapid to be attributed to heredity. For example, the correlation between respective n Achievement levels in the 1925 and 1950 samples of readers is substantially zero. Many of the countries that were high in n Achievement at one or both times may be low or moderate in n Achievement now, and vice versa. Germany was low in 1925 and is high now; and certainly the hereditary makeup of the German nation has not changed in a generation.

However, there is substantiating evidence that n Achievement is a motive which a child can acquire quite early in life, say, by the age of eight or ten, as a result of the way his parents have brought him up. . . . The principal results . . . indicate the differences between the parents of the "high n Achievement boys" and the parents of boys with low n Achievement. In general, the mothers and the fathers of the first group set higher levels of aspiration in a number of tasks for their sons. They were also much warmer, showing positive emotion in reacting to their sons' performances. In the area of authority or dominance, the data are quite interesting. The mothers of the "highs" were more domineering than the mothers of the "lows," but the *fathers* of the "highs" were significantly *less* domineering than the fathers of the "lows." In other words, the fathers of the "highs" set high standards and are warmly interested in their sons' performances, but they do not directly interfere. This gives the boys the chance to develop initiative and self-reliance.

What factors cause parents to behave in this way? Their behavior certainly is involved with their values and, possibly, ultimately with their religion or their general world view. At present, we cannot be sure that Protestant parents are more likely to behave this way than Catholic parents—there are too many subgroup variations within each religious portion of the community: the Lutheran father is probably as likely to be authoritarian as the Catholic father. However, there does seem to be one crucial variable discernible: the extent to which the religion of the family emphasizes individual, as contrasted with ritual, contact with God. The preliterate tribes that we studied in which the religion was the kind that stressed the individual contact had higher n Achievement; and in general, mystical sects in which this kind of religious self-reliance dominates have had higher n Achievement.

The extent to which the authoritarian father is away from the home while the boy is growing up may prove to be another crucial variable. If so, then one incidental consequence of prolonged wars may be an increase in n Achievement, because the fathers are away too much to interfere with their sons' development of it. And in Turkey, N. M. Bradburn found that those boys tended to have higher n Achievement who had left home early or whose fathers had died before they were eighteen.[11] Slavery was another factor which played an important role in the past. It probably lowered n Achievement—in the slaves, for whom obedience and responsibility, but not achievement, were obvious virtues; and in the slave-owners, because household slaves were often disposed to spoil the owner's children as a means for improving their own positions. This is both a plausible and a probable reason for the drop in n Achievement level in ancient Greece that occurred at about the time the middle-class entrepreneur was first able to afford, and obtain by conquest, as many as two slaves for each child. The idea also clarifies the slow economic development of the South in the United States by attributing its dilatoriness to a lack of n Achievement in its elite; and it also indicates why lower-class American Negroes, who are closest to the slave tradition, possess very low n Achievement.[12]

I have outlined our research findings. Do they indicate ways of accelerating economic development? Increasing the level of n Achievement in a country suggests itself as an obvious first possibility. If n Achievement is so important, so specifically adapted to the business role, then it certainly should be raised in level, so that more young men have an "entrepreneurial drive." The difficulty in this excellent plan is that our studies of how n Achievement originates indicate that the family is the key formative influence; and it is very hard to change on a really large scale. To be sure, major historical events like wars have taken authoritarian fathers out of the home; and religious reform movements have sometimes converted the parents to a new achievement-oriented ideology. However, such matters are not ordinarily within the policymaking province of the agencies charged with speeding economic development.

Such agencies can, perhaps, effect the general acceptance of an achievement-oriented ideology as an absolute *sine qua non* of economic development. Furthermore, this ideology should be diffused not only in business and governmental circles, but throughout the nation, and in ways that will influence the thinking of all parents as they bring up their children. As B. C. Rosen and R. G. D'Andrade found, parents must, above all, set high standards for their children. The campaign to spread achievement-oriented ideology, if possible, could also incorporate an attack on the extreme authoritarianism in fathers that impedes or prevents the development of self-reliance in their sons. This is, however, a more delicate point, and attacking this, in many countries, would be to threaten values at the very center of social life. I believe that a more indirect approach would be more successful. One approach would be to take the boys out of the home and to camps. A more significant method would be to promote the rights of women, both legally and socially—one of the ways to undermine the absolute dominance of the male is to strengthen the rights of the female! Another reason for concentrating particularly on women is that they play the leading role in rearing the next generation. Yet, while men in underdeveloped countries come in contact with new achievement-oriented values and standards through their work, women may be left almost untouched by such influences. But if the sons are to have high n Achievement, the mothers must first be reached.

It may seem strange that a paper on economic development should discuss the importance of feminism and the way children are reared; but this is precisely where a psychological analysis leads. If the motives of men are the agents that influence the speed with which the economic machine operates, then the speed can be increased only through affecting the factors that create the motives. Furthermore—to state this point less theoretically—I cannot think of evinced substantial, rapid long-term economic development where women have not been somewhat freed from their traditional setting of "Kinder, Küche und Kirche" and allowed to play a more powerful role in society, specifically as part of the working force. This generalization applies not only to the Western democracies like the United States, Sweden, or England, but also to the USSR, Japan, and now China.

In the present state of our knowledge, we can conceive of trying to raise n Achievement levels only in the next generation—although new research findings may soon indicate n Achievement in adults can be increased. Most economic planners, while accepting the long-range desirability of raising n Achievement in future generations, want to know what can be done during the next five to ten years. This immediacy inevitably focuses attention on the process or processes by which executives or entrepreneurs are selected. Foreigners with proved entrepreneurial drive can be hired, but at best this is a temporary and unsatisfactory solution. In most underdeveloped countries where government is playing a leading role in promoting economic development, it is clearly necessary for the government to adopt rigid achievement-oriented standards of performance like those in the USSR.[13] A government manager or, for that matter, a private entrepreneur, should have to produce "or else." Production targets must be set, as they are in most economic plans; and individuals must be held responsible for achieving them, even at the plant level. The philosophy should be one of "no excuses accepted." It is common for government officials or economic theorists in underdeveloped countries to be weighed down by all the difficulties which face the economy and render its rapid development difficult or impossible. They note that there is too rapid population growth, too little capital, too few technically competent people, etc. Such obstacles to growth are prevalent, and in many cases they are immensely hard to overcome; but talking about them can provide merely a comfortable rationalization for mediocre performance. It is difficult to fire an administrator, no matter how poor his performance, if so many objective reasons exist for his doing badly. Even worse, such rationalization permits, in the private sector, the continued employment of incompetent family members as executives. If these private firms were afraid of being penalized for poor performance, they might be impelled to find more able professional mangers a little more quickly. I am not an expert in the field, and the mechanisms I am suggesting may be far from appropriate. Still, they may serve to illustrate my main point: if a country short in entrepreneurial talent wants to advance rapidly, it must find ways and means of insuring that only the most competent retain positions of responsibility. One of the obvious methods of doing so is to judge people in terms of their *performance*—and not according to their family or political connections, their skill in explaining why their unit failed to produce as expected, or their conscientiousness in following the rules. I would suggest the use of psychological tests as a means of selecting people with high n Achievement; but, to be perfectly frank, I think this approach is at present somewhat impractical on a large enough scale in most underdeveloped countries.

Finally, there is another approach which I think is promising for recruiting and developing more competent business leadership. It is the one called, in some circles, the "professionalization of management." Frederick Harbison and Charles A. Myers have recently completed a worldwide survey of the efforts made to develop professional schools of high-level management. They have concluded that, in most countries, progress in this direction is slow.[14] Professional management is important for three reasons: (1) It may endow a business career with higher prestige (as a kind of profession), so that business will attract more of the young men with high n Achievement from the elite groups in backward countries; (2) It stresses *performance* criteria of excellence in the management area— i.e., what a man can do and not what he is; (3) Advanced management schools can themselves be so achievement-oriented in their instruction that they are able to raise the n Achievement of those who attend them.

Applied toward explaining historical events, the results of our researches clearly shift attention away from external factors and to man— in particular, to his motives and values. That about which he thinks and dreams determines what will happen. The emphasis is quite different from the Darwinian or Marxist view of man as a creature who *adapts* to his environment. It is even different from the Freudian view of civilization as the sublimation of man's primitive urges. Civilization, at least in its economic aspects, is neither adaptation nor sublimation; it is a positive creation by a people made dynamic by a high level of n Achievement. Nor can we agree with Toynbee, who recognizes the importance of psychological factors as "the very forces which actually decide the issue when an encounter takes place," when he states that these factors "inherently are impossible to weigh and measure, and therefore to estimate scientifically in advance."[15] It is a measure of the pace at which the behavioral sciences are developing that even within

Toynbee's lifetime we can demonstrate that he was mistaken. The psychological factor responsible for a civilization's rising to a challenge is so far from being "inherently impossible to weigh and measure" that it has been weighed and measured and scientifically estimated in advance; and, so far as we can now tell, this factor is the achievement motive.

Notes

1. This paper is a summary of the author's book, *The Achieving Society*, published by Van Nostrand Co. in Princeton, N.J., in the fall of 1961.
2. A. L. Kroeber, *Configurations of Culture Growth* (Berkeley, California, 1944).
3. J. W. Atkinson (Ed.), *Motives in Fantasy, Action, and Society* (Princeton, N.J., 1958).
4. Max Weber, *The Protestant Ethic and the Spirit of Capitalism*, trans. Talcott Parsons (New York, 1930).
5. M. R. Winterbottom, "The Relation of Need for Achievement to Learning and Experiences in Independence and Mastery," in Atkinson, *op. cit.*, pp. 453–478.
6. F. Heichelheim, *Wirtschaftsgeschichte des Altertums* (Leiden, 1938).
7. J. B. Cortés, "The Achievement Motive in the Spanish Economy between the Thirteenth and the Eighteenth Centuries," *Economic Development and Cultural Change*, IX (1960), 144–163.
8. N. M. Bradburn and D. E. Berlew, "Need for Achievement and English Economic Growth," *Economic Development and Cultural Change*, 1961.
9. I. L. Child, T. Storm, and J. Veroff, "Achievement Themes in Folk Tales Related to Socialization Practices," in Atkinson, *op. cit.*, pp. 479–492.
10. David Riesman, with the assistance of Nathan Glazer and Reuel Denney, *The Lonely Crowd* (New Haven, Conn., 1950).
11. N. M. Bradburn, "The Managerial Role in Turkey" (unpublished Ph.D. dissertation, Harvard University, 1960).
12. B. C. Rosen, "Race, Ethnicity, and Achievement Syndrome," *American Sociological Review*, XXIV (1959), 47–60.
13. David Granick, *The Red Executive* (New York, 1960).
14. Frederick Harbison and Charles A. Myers, *Management in the Industrial World* (New York, 1959).
15. Arnold J. Toynbee, *A Study of History* (abridgment by D. C. Somervell; Vol. I; New York, 1947).

7. Becoming Modern

Alex Inkeles
David H. Smith

This chapter reports on what is perhaps the most extensive investigation ever undertaken to explore the psycho-cultural factors influencing development. Using interview data from some 6,000 young men in six developing countries (Argentina, Chile, India, Israel, Nigeria, and East Pakistan), the authors and their fellow researchers devised an "overall measure of modernization" they call their "OM scale." The characteristics of the "modern man" are described in the portions of their work that follow; the interested reader may consult the original book for the methodological details of the study. The authors discuss the developmental implications of the presence or absence of such modern men in a given society and argue that modern attitudes produce modern behaviors that are essential to development. Moreover, without modern men, modern institutions are bound to fail. In sum, for these researchers, "underdevelopment is a state of mind." The reader should compare the qualities of n Achievement discussed by McClelland with the qualities of OM discussed in this chapter. In what ways are they similar, and how persuasive is the argument that attitudes are, as Inkeles and Smith state, "the essence of national development itself?"

The main purpose of economic development is to permit the achievement of a decent level of living for all people, everywhere. But almost no one will argue that the progress of a nation and a people should be measured solely in terms of gross national product and per capita income. Development assumes, as well, a high degree of political maturation, as expressed in stable and orderly processes of government resting on the expressed will of the people. And it also includes the attainment of popular education, the burgeoning of the arts, the efflorescence of architecture, the growth of the means of communication, and the enrichment of leisure. Indeed, in the end, development requires a transformation in the very nature of man, a transformation that is both a means to yet greater growth and at the same time one of the great ends of the development process.

Reprinted with permission of the publishers from *Becoming Modern: Individual Change in Six Developing Countries*, by Alex Inkeles and David H. Smith. Cambridge, MA: Harvard University Press, 1974.

We have described this transformation as the shift from traditionalism to individual modernity. The object of our research was to delineate the elements of such personal change, to measure its degree, to explain its causes, and to throw some light on its observed and probable future consequences. It is time for us to sum up the progress we made in that task, taking the opportunity, in so doing, to deal briefly with some of the issues we earlier may have left unresolved.

Defining and Measuring Individual Modernity

One who sets out to define and to measure individual modernity is like the animal trainer whose new act requires he learn to ride on the back of his tiger. He may emerge alive, but the chances are very great he will have been knocked about quite a bit in the process. Nevertheless, we accepted as a critical element in the structure of our whole intellectual and scientific enterprise the construction of a reliable, cross-national measure of individual modernity.

We do not claim to have invented the idea of the modern man. The concept was already there when we began our work, even though its content was vague. Inventing types of men has, after all, always been a fundamental preoccupation of sociologists: Karl Marx described the consciousness of the bourgeoisie and the proletariat; Robert Redfield defined the contrasting attributes of the folk and urban types; Everett V. Stonequist gave us the marginal man; David Riesman the inner-, outer-, and other-directed man. These "ideal types" people the pages of almost every well-known sociologist's work. Yet it has been the rare instance, indeed, in which any systematic attempt has been undertaken to measure whether there are real people in the world who, in their own persons, actually incorporate the qualities identified by these ideal types.[1] We were determined to break with this sociological tradition, and firmly committed ourselves to testing how far the set of qualities by which we defined the modern man actually cohered as a psychosocial syndrome in real men.

Our results provide definitive evidence that living individuals do indeed conform to our model of the modern man, that they do so in substantial numbers, and that essentially the same basic qualities which define a man as modern in one country and culture also delineate the modern man in other places. The modern man is not just a construct in the mind of sociological theorists. He exists and can be identified with fair reliability within any population where our test can be applied.

The modern man's character, as it emerges from our study, may be summed up under four major headings. He is an informed participant citizen; he has a marked sense of personal efficacy; he is highly independent and autonomous in his relations to traditional sources of influence, especially when he is making basic decisions about how to conduct his personal affairs; and he is ready for new experiences and ideas, that is, he is relatively open-minded and cognitively flexible.

As an informed participant citizen, the modern man identifies with the newer, larger entities of region and state, takes an interest in public affairs, national and international as well as local, joins organizations, keeps himself informed about major events in the news, and votes or otherwise takes some part in the political process. The modern man's sense of efficacy is reflected in his belief that, either alone or in concert with others, he may take actions which can affect the course of his life and that of his community; in his active efforts to improve his own condition and that of his family; and in his rejection of passivity, resignation, and fatalism toward the course of life's events. His independence of traditional sources of authority is manifested in public issues by his following the advice of public officials or trade-union leaders rather than priests and village elders, and in personal matters by his choosing the job and the bride he prefers even if his parents prefer some other position or some other person. The modern man's openness to new experience is reflected in his interest in technical innovation, his support of scientific exploration of hitherto sacred or taboo subjects, his readiness to meet strangers, and his willingness to allow women to take advantage of opportunities outside the confines of the household.

These *main* elements of individual modernity seem to have in common a thrust toward more instrumental kinds of attitudes and behavior. The more expressive and interpersonal aspects of overall modernization or OM syndrome tended to be less important, by and large, although still significantly involved in the syndrome. This fits well with the relative emphasis on new and more effective ways of doing things as central to the modernization process, with changes in ways of relating to other people coming largely as side effects. The Japanese case is a good example of how the instrumental aspects of OM can be present with, we would judge, many fewer of the expressive elements.

Although these are the principal components, they by no means exhaust the list of qualities which cohere as part of the modernity syndrome. The modern man is also different in his approach to time, to personal and social planning, to the rights of persons dependent on or subordinate to him, and to the use of formal rules as a basis for running things. In other words, psychological modernity emerges as a quite complex, multifaceted, and multidimensional syndrome. . . .

Considering that the modernization process seems to work so consistently in so many different cultural settings, is there then no choice? Must everyone become modern, and to the same degree?

This issue seems to generate the greatest misunderstanding, and satisfying people with regard to it is most difficult. Dispassionate discussion becomes overshadowed by lurid images of modern science turning out a race of automatons, machine-produced golems who are as uniform and unfeeling as are the products of Detroit's massive assembly lines.

Our image of man's nature is not that of a sponge which must soak up everything with which it comes in contact. In our view individual change toward modernization is a process of interaction between the individual and his social setting. Quite contrary to the conception of men as putty passively taking on whatever shape their environment imposes on them, we see the process of individual modernization as one requiring a basic personal engagement between the individual and his milieu. In this engagement the individual must first selectively perceive the lessons the environment has to teach, and then must willingly undertake to learn them, before any personal change can come about.

If the qualities of industrial organization are truly alien to a man, he will not incorporate them. Moreover, even if he finds an organization to be unthreatening or, better, congenial, a man will not necessarily learn new ways unless he personally has the readiness and the capacity to learn. And even if the environment is benign and the individuals are ready to learn, the process will not work if the environment itself is confusing and the messages it conveys are unclear or even contradictory.

In brief, if the process of modernization were at all like the situation described in Aldous Huxley's *Brave New World*, the outcome of our study should have yielded a perfect correlation rather than the much more modest figure it attained. Moreover, *all* the men in our samples should have changed, and all should have become completely modern in short order. Instead, as we know, many did not change at all and most changed only to some degree, so that after years of exposure to the modernizing influences only a modest proportion qualified as truly modern. And these, like all others, became modern with some degree of selectivity, changing fully in some respects but holding to divergent and even traditional views in others. . . .

The Social Significance of Individual Modernization

To a social psychologist, it is gratifying, indeed it is an activity sufficient unto itself, to be able to measure individual modernity, and to show how far and in what ways schooling and jobs bring about increased modernity scores. But the more pragmatic among our readers, and not only those from the developing countries, are likely to ask: "Is this purely an academic exercise? In particular, does it have any practical contribution to make to national development? Are not attitude and value changes rather ephemeral and peripheral? Can you give us any evidence that all this has much to do with the real problem of under-development?"

In response, we affirm that our research has produced ample evidence that the attitude and value changes defining individual modernity are accompanied by changes in behavior precisely of the sort which we believe give meaning to, and support, those changes in political and economic institutions which lead to the modernization of nations.

We were able to document most extensively those behavioral changes accompanying attitudinal modernization in the realm of political and civic action. The modern man more often took an interest in political affairs, he kept informed and could identify important political events and personalities, he often contacted governmental and political agencies, more often joined organizations, more often voted—and all these by large margins. He was in every way a more active participant citizen of his society.[2]

It seems obvious to us that these are precisely the qualities one needs in the citizen of a modern polity. The introduction of modern political institutions imported from outside, or imposed from above by elites, tends to be an empty gesture unless there are active, interested, informed citizens who can make the institutions really work. And, as we have seen, such citizens are the more modern men shaped by the modernizing institutions we have identified, namely, the school, the newspaper, and the factory.

Beyond politics, the modern man showed himself to perform differently from the more traditional man in many realms of action having practical bearing on the process of societal modernization. The more modern man is quicker to adopt technical innovation, and more ready to implement birth-control measures; he urges his son to go as far as he can in school, and, if it pays better, encourages him to accept industrial work rather than to follow the more traditional penchant for office jobs; he informs himself about the goods produced in the more modern sector of the economy, and makes an effort to acquire them; and he permits his wife and daughter to leave the home for more active participation in economic life. In these and a host of other ways, only some of which we have documented, the man who is more modern in attitude and value acts to support modern institutions and to facilitate the general modernization of society.

While it was important to show that men who were more modern in attitude and value also acted in more modern ways, we feel it even more important to challenge the assumption that a "mere" change in attitudes and values cannot in itself be a truly important factor in the process of national development.

In saying this we are not espousing some form of naïve psychological determinism. We are not unaware that a modern psychology cannot alone make a nation modern. We fully understand that to be modern a nation must have modern institutions, effective government, efficient production, and adequate social services. And we recognize full well that there may be structural obstacles to such development stemming not only from nature, but from social, political, and economic causes as well. Narrow class interests, colonial oppression, rapacious great powers, international cartels, domestic monopolies, archaic and corrupted governments, tribal antagonisms, and religious and ethnic prejudices, to name but a few, are among the many objective forces which we know may act to impede modernization.

Nevertheless, we believe a change in attitudes and values to be one of the most essential preconditions for substantial and effective functioning of those modern institutions which most of the more "practical" programs of development hope to establish. Our experience leads us to agree with many of the intellectual leaders of the Third World who argue that, in good part, underdevelopment is a state of mind.[3] It is admittedly difficult with presently available techniques and information to establish the case scientifically, but we are convinced that mental barriers and psychic factors are key obstacles to more effective economic and social development in many countries.

The technology which is, perhaps, the most distinctive ingredient of modernity can be borrowed by and established in developing countries with relative ease. Machinery is influenced by temperature and humidity, but it is otherwise immune to culture shock. Although they travel less well, political, economic, and cultural institutions can also be relatively easily imitated in their totality. Systems of taxation and of voter registration, and even political party systems, are regularly copied from the more advanced countries by those in the earlier stages of development. Patterns of factory management, forms of administration for business and government, new faculties, research institutions, indeed whole universities are being created every day in the developing countries as copies of institutions and procedures originating in the more developed countries.

How many of these transplanted institutions actually take root and bear fruit in their new setting is not precisely known. But the experience of almost everyone who has worked extensively on problems of development is replete with examples of the failure of such transplantation. The disappointment of high hopes and aspirations is endemic among those who have attempted such transplanting, and the hollow shells of the institutions, sometimes transformed into grotesque caricatures of their original design, sometimes barely functioning, often standing altogether abandoned, can be found strewn about in almost any developing country in which one chooses to travel.

In the explanations which are offered for this situation, one hears again and again the echo of one basic refrain: "The people were not ready for it yet." When one probes this generalization, it quickly becomes apparent that the material resources, the manuals for repair and maintenance, the charts and tables for organization, and the guidelines for administration which accompanied the transplanted institutions were meaningless without the support of an underlying and widespread pattern of culture and personality which could breathe life into the otherwise sterile forms and give human meaning and continuity to their activity.

In the last analysis, the successful functioning of these institutions was critically dependent on the availability of individuals who could bring to the job certain special personal qualities. These new institutions required people who could accept and discharge responsibility without constant close supervision, could manifest mutual trust and confidence in co-workers which extended beyond the situations in which one could keep them under direct surveillance, could subordinate the special interests of one's clique or parochial group to the goals of the larger organization, could be flexible and imaginative in the interpretation of rules, could show sympathetic consideration for the feelings of subordinates and openness to their ideas and other potential contributions. These, and a host of other personal qualities requisite to running a complex modern institution effectively, are not in excess supply in any society. In many of the developing countries, moreover, people possessed of the requisite qualities are actually scarce. And in some cases, the small set of individuals who possess the qualities necessary for effectively running the new institutions are either not called upon, or may even be socially ineligible, for service in those roles in which they could be most useful.

Such conditions in the institutions of national standing have their precise analogue in the more commonplace situation of individuals engaged in very modest pursuits, within purely local and parochial settings. In such settings we find most widely diffused the qualities our research has identified as characteristic of the traditional man: passive acceptance of fate and a general lack of efficacy; fear of innovation and distrust of the new; isolation from the outside world and lack of interest in what goes on in it; dependence on traditional authority and the received wisdom of elders and religious and customary leaders; preoccupation with personal and especially family affairs to the exclusion of community concerns; exclusive identification with purely local and parochial primary groups, coupled to feelings of isolation from and fear of larger regional and national entities; the shaping and damping of ambition to fit narrow goals, and the cultivation of humble sentiments of gratitude for what little one has; rigid, hierarchical relations with subordinates and others of low social status; and undervaluing of education, learning, research, and other concerns not obviously related to the practical business of earning one's daily bread.

Of course, not all these qualities are prevalent in all traditional settings, and they are unequally distributed among the men in them. Yet they are extremely common in individuals, and exceptionally pervasive across cultures and settings, in the countries of the less-developed world.

We must acknowledge that some of these qualities of the traditional man facilitate his adaptation to life. Such qualities help men to make a successful adjustment to the real conditions which exist in, and indeed pervade, their life space. But those qualities also tend to freeze people into the situations and positions in which they find themselves, and this, in turn, serves to preserve the outmoded, indeed archaic, and often oppressive institutions which hold the people in their grip. To break out of that iron grip requires, among other things, that people become modern in spirit, that they adopt and incorporate into their personalities the attitudes, values, and modes of acting which we have identified with the modern man. Without this ingredient neither foreign aid nor domestic revolution can hope successfully to bring an underdeveloped nation into the ranks of those capable of self-sustained growth.

Economists define modernity in terms of gross national product per capita, and political scientists in terms of effective institutions for governance. We are of the opinion that neither rapid economic growth nor effective government can develop, or, if introduced, will be long sustained, without the widespread diffusion in the rank and file of the population of those qualities we have identified as those of the modern man. In the conditions of the contemporary world, the qualities of individual modernity are not a luxury, they are a necessity. They are not a marginal gain, derived from the process of institutional modernization, but are rather a precondition for the long-term success of those institutions. Diffusion through the population of the qualities of the modern man is not incidental to the process of social development; it is the essence of national development itself.

Notes

1. There are, of course, some notable exceptions. The most important early example was the effort by Gordon Allport to test Spranger's belief that men could be classified according to the predominance in their personality of "theoretical," "religious," "social," or "economic-and-political" values. See Gordon Allport, Philip Vernon, and Gardner Lindzey, *Study of Values; A Scale for Measuring the Dominant Interests in Personality*, 3rd ed. (Boston: Houghton-Mifflin, 1959). Probably the best-known and most widely studied syndrome is that first proposed by Erich Fromm under the rubric "the authoritarian personality" in *Escape From Freedom* (New York: Farrar and Rinehart, 1941) and later built into the famous "F scale." See Theodor W. Adorno et al., *The Authoritarian Personality* (New York: Harper, 1950).

2. The evidence concerning these differences in political behavior is built into the OM scale, and may be observed by checking the list of questions in Appendix A. [Not reproduced here—Ed.] A full account of the 39 items dealing with political orientations and behavior covered by our questionnaire, the scales those items yielded, and their relation to the independent variables is given in Alex Inkeles, "Participant Citizenship in Six Developing Countries," *American Political Science Review*, 63 (December 1969):1120–1141.

3. In his unpublished contribution to the conference on Alternatives in Development sponsored by the Vienna Institute for Development in June 1971, Dr. Salazar Bondy, a leading intellectual of Peru, wrote as follows: "Underdevelopment is not just a collection of statistical indices which enable a socioeconomic picture to be drawn. It is also a state of mind, a way of expression, a form of outlook and a collective personality marked by chronic infirmities and forms of maladjustment."

8. The Confucian Ethic and Economic Growth

Herman Kahn

The most recent variation on the cultural origins of economic growth derives from the observation that a group of countries that have made spectacular strides since World War II (e.g., Japan, South Korea, Taiwan) are Confucian societies. Until his recent death, Herman Kahn was director of the Hudson Institute "think tank" and was well-known as a futurist. In this contribution, Kahn says that much of the success of these nations can be attributed directly to their cultures. It is interesting to compare the attributes of Confucianism that Kahn suggests are important for development with the attributes of n Achievement and OM discussed in the previous two chapters. It is also worth considering the implication of Kahn's argument for those nations in Latin America, Africa, and elsewhere that have dramatically different traditions. Has the absence of a "Confucian ethic" held back the development of these nations and, if so, is it likely to make closing the gap between them and the developed nations an impossible dream?

Most readers of this book are familiar with the argument of Max Weber that the Protestant ethic was extremely useful in promoting the rise and spread of modernization.[1] Most readers, however, will be much less familiar with the notion that has gradually emerged in the last two decades that societies based upon the Confucian ethic may in many ways be superior to the West in the pursuit of industrialization, affluence, and modernization. Let us see what some of the strengths of the Confucian ethic are in the modern world.

The Confucian Ethic

The Confucian ethic includes two quite different but connected sets of issues. First and perhaps foremost, Confucian societies uniformly promote in the individual and the family sobriety, a high value on education, a desire for accomplishment in various skills (particularly academic and cultural), and seriousness about tasks, job, family, and

Reprinted with permission from *World Economic Development: 1979 and Beyond*, by Herman Kahn. Boulder, CO: Westview Press, 1979.

obligations. A properly trained member of a Confucian culture will be hardworking, responsible, skillful, and (within the assigned or understood limits) ambitious and creative in helping the group (extended family, community, or company). There is much less emphasis on advancing individual (selfish) interests.

In some ways, the capacity for purposive and efficient communal and organizational activities and efforts is even more important in the modern world than the personal qualities, although both are important. Smoothly fitting, harmonious human relations in an organization are greatly encouraged in most neo-Confucian societies. This is partly because of a sense of hierarchy but even more because of a sense of complementarity of relations that is much stronger in Confucian than in Western societies.

The anthropologist Chie Nakane has pointed out that in Western societies there is a great tendency for "like to join like" in unions, student federations, women's groups, men's clubs, youth movements, economic classes, and so on.[2] This tends to set one group in society against another: students against teachers, employees against employers, youths against parents, and so on. In the Confucian hierarchic society, the emphasis is on cooperation among complementary elements, much as in the family (which is in fact the usual paradigm or model in a Confucian culture). The husband and wife work together and cooperate in raising the children; each has different assigned duties and respon-sibilities, as do the older and younger siblings and the grandparents. There is emphasis on fairness and equity, but it is fairness and equity in the institutional context, not for the individual as an individual. Synergism—complementarity and cooperation among parts of a whole—are emphasized, not equality and interchangeability. The major iden-tification is with one's role in the organization or other institutional structure, whether it be the family, the business firm, or a bureau in the government.

Since the crucial issues in a modern society increasingly revolve around these equity issues and on making organizations work well, the neo-Confucian cultures have great advantages. As opposed to the earlier Protestant ethic, the modern Confucian ethic is superbly designed to create and foster loyalty, dedication, responsibility, and commitment and to intensify identification with the organization and one's role in the organization. All this makes the economy and society operate much more smoothly than one whose principles of identification and association tend to lead to egalitarianism, to disunity, to confrontation, and to excessive compensation or repression.

A society that emphasizes a like-to-like type of identification works out reasonably well as long as there is enough hierarchy, discipline, control, or motivation within the society to restrain excessive tendencies to egalitarianism, anarchy, self-indulgence, and so on. But as the society becomes more affluent and secular, there is less motivation, reduced commitment, more privatization, and increasingly impersonal and automatic welfare. Interest in group politics, group and individual selfishness, egoism, intergroup antagonisms, and perhaps even intergroup warfare all tend to increase. It becomes the old versus the young, insiders versus outsiders, men versus women, students versus teachers, and—most important of all—employees against employers. The tendencies toward anarchy, rivalry, and payoffs to the politically powerful or the organized militants become excessive and out of control.

For all these reasons we believe that both aspects of the Confucian ethic—the creation of dedicated, motivated, responsible, and educated individuals and the enhanced sense of commitment, organizational identity, and loyalty to various institutions—will result in all the neo-Confucian societies having at least potentially higher growth rates than other cultures. . . .

Whether or not one accepts our analysis of *why* neo-Confucian cultures are so competent in industrialization, the impressive data that support the final thesis are overwhelming. The performance of the People's Republic of China; of both North and South Korea; of Japan, Taiwan, Hong Kong, and Singapore; and of the various Chinese ethnic groups in Malaysia, Thailand, Indonesia, and the Philippines, discloses extraordinary talent (at least in the last twenty-five years) for economic development and for learning about and using modern technology. For example, the North Vietnamese operated one of the most complicated air defense networks in history more or less by themselves (once instructed by the Soviets), and the American army found that the South Vietnamese, if properly motivated, often went through training school in about half the time required by Americans. We do not gloss over the enormous differences among these neo-Confucian cultures. They vary almost as much as do European cultures. But all of them seem amenable to modernization under current conditions.

Notes

1. Max Weber, *The Protestant Ethic and the Spirit of Capitalism*, translated by Talcott Parsons (New York: Charles Scribner's Sons, 1930).

2. Chie Nakane, *Japanese Society* (Berkeley, Calif.: University of California Press, 1970).

9. On the Sociology of National Development: Theories and Issues

Alejandro Portes

In this chapter, sociologist Alejandro Portes calls into question the value of the cultural explanations of development and underdevelopment that were the subject of Chapters 5 through 8. He begins by criticizing the proponents of this view for having misunderstood Max Weber's explanation of the importance of the Protestant ethic for the rise of capitalism. Portes then enumerates three major flaws in the logic of the culturalists: (1) the failure to consider the importance of structural constraints on development, (2) the anti-developmental role that so-called modern values can have, and (3) the flaw of the "historical fiction" of development. Structural constraints will be elaborated on in greater detail in later chapters of this book dealing with dependency and the world system.

Myron Weiner (1966) notes that, for many scholars, the starting point of any definition of development is not the character of the society but the character of individuals. The same author observes that "although there are differences among social scientists as to how values and attitudes can be changed, it is possible to speak of one school of thought that believes that attitudinal and value changes are prerequisites to creating a modern society, economy, and political system" (Weiner 1966, p. 9).

For Szymon Chodak (1973, p. 11), writers of this school do not ask. "What is development?" or "What happens in its course?" but rather why it happened and what specifically caused the breakthrough from traditional into modern societies. Where such factors were present, development happens; where they are absent, stagnation prevails. The distinctive factor is then sought in the sphere of value orientation. . . .

The search in this case is for those "mental viruses" (McClelland 1967) changing the "spirit" (Inkeles 1969) of men so that they come

Reprinted with permission from the *American Journal of Sociology*, vol. 82 (July 1976), pp. 68–74.

to adapt and promote a modern society. This perspective derives its impetus from the general emphasis in United States sociology on value-normative complexes (Parsons 1964a) as opposed to the structure of material interests in society (Mills 1956). More specifically, the value approach to the problem of development lays claim to, and often labels itself as a direct continuation of, the thesis Max Weber developed in *The Protestant Ethic and the Spirit of Capitalism* (1958).

Weber's argument was, however, securely embedded in a body of research which clearly brought forth the importance of structural forms and the politico-economic interests of groups and classes. Emergence of an urban burgher class out of the feudal "oikos" and the relative vulnerability of feudalism, as opposed for example to the "prebendary" system of China, are subjects examined at length in his work (Weber 1951). The combined effects of the political assault by the central state and the economic assault by rising urban classes on the weakened feudal order meant an increasingly "open" structure for capitalist expansion (Weber 1958; Bendix 1962). Only because of the growing predicament of a lordly class incapable of defending its position by enforcing old prerogatives could the Protestant "spirit" of capitalism, or any other spirit for that matter, transform the economic order to its own advantage (Wallerstein 1974).

Psychological theories of development, such as those proposed by David G. McClelland (1967) and Everett E. Hagen (1962), have chosen to ignore the Weberian treatment of historico-structural issues and concentrate on the primacy of ideas in society: "This is just one more piece of evidence to support the growing conviction among social scientists that it is values, motives, or psychological forces that determine ultimately the rate of economic and social development. . . . *The Achieving Society* suggests that ideas are in fact more important in shaping history than purely materialistic arrangements" (McClelland 1963, p. 17).

Since ideas inhere in individuals, these theories result in an "additive" image of societal development in which the larger the number of people "infected" by the strategic psychological ingredient, the greater the economic growth of the country. This arithmetic approach is concerned neither with differences in positions in the stratification system nor with existing arrangements of economic and political power. Theorists of this persuasion subscribe to the proverb "Where there is a will, there is a way"; their voluntarism is, in turn, predicated on the creation of sufficiently high levels of motivation. In the best known of these theories, the factor responsible for this result is labeled "*n* Achievement": "The mental virus received the odd name of *n*-Ach (short for 'need for Achievement') because it was identified in a sample of a person's thoughts by whether the thoughts had to do with 'doing something well' or 'doing something better' than it had been done before: more efficiently, more quickly, with less labor, with a better result and so on" (McClelland 1966, p. 29). Extrapolating the result to national development, McClelland

(1966, p. 30) reports: ". . . a country that was high in n-Ach level in its children's texts around 1925 was more likely to develop rapidly from 1929 to 1950 than one that was low in n-Ach in 1925. The same result was obtained when 1950 n-Ach levels were related to rates of economic development in the late nineteen-fifties." Apart from "n-Ach," McClelland prescribes a series of additional psychological ingredients making for societal development. Sense of collective responsibility and feelings of superiority over others are the most important ones.

Hagen's (1962) theory of "withdrawal of status respect" is more complex, in a psychoanalytic sense, than McClelland's. It comes, however, to the same formal conclusion. Again, a psychological motor, present in sufficiently large numbers of people, provides the strategic impulse for economic development. In this case, however, the "virus" is not transmitted by children's texts but instead has a gestation period of several generations. Humiliations resulting from status withdrawal among parents have certain psychic consequences for their sons who, in turn, transmit them to their own children. After a complicated evolution of complexes and stages, the "virus" finally matures and is ready to do its work in society. Whether the society is ready for the actions of the new entrepreneurial group is not of major importance to the theory.

More recent, and perhaps more accepted among sociologists, is the theory of "modernity" as a psychosocial complex of values. "Modern man" is characterized, internally, by a certain mental flexibility in dealing with new situations and, externally, by similarity to the value orientations dominant in industrial Western societies (see Lerner 1965). The spirit of modernity is regarded by these writers both as a precondition for societal modernization and as a major consequence of it: "Indeed, in the end, the ideal of development requires the transformation of the nature of man—a transformation that is both a *means* to the end of yet greater growth and at the same time one of the great *ends* itself of the development process (Inkeles 1966, p. 138).

Alex Inkeles identifies nine major attitudes and values distinguishing modern man: (1) readiness for new experience and openness to innovation, (2) disposition to form and hold opinions, (3) democratic orientation, (4) planning habits, (5) belief in human and personal efficacy, (6) belief that the world is calculable, (7) stress on personal and human dignity, (8) faith in science and technology, and (9) belief in distributive justice.

This list is not complemented by a similar description of "traditional man." The latter tends to be defined by default: whatever is not properly modern must be traditional. It is difficult to understand, however, why "traditional man" does not stress "personal and human dignity" or believe in distributive justice.

The list of what goes on to make "modern man" tends to vary from author to author. This is not surprising, since much of what enters into the definition appears to come from introspection. Theorists of this persuasion vie with each other in developing ever more elaborate descriptions of what modern man is like. In doing so, they tend to contradict one another. While, for some, individualism and self-reliance are clearly modern traits, for others the ability to subordinate personal goals to the welfare of the collectivity and the ability to work with others toward its common pursuits constitute the mark of modernity (see Kahl 1968). As seen above, dichotomies between "traditional" and "modern" man are then built by extrapolation, through attributing to the former the reverse of characteristics assigned to the latter (Gusfield 1967).

In addition to the dimensions quoted above, the following are frequently encountered in characterizations of modern man: (1) participation: motivation and ability to take part in organizations and electoral processes; (2) ambition: high mobility aspirations for self and children and willingness to take risks; (3) secularism: limited religious attachments and low receptivity to religious and ideological appeals; (4) information: frequent contact with news media and knowledge of national and international affairs; (5) consumption orientation: desire to own new goods and technologically advanced recreation and labor-saving appliances; (6) urban preference: desire to move to or remain in urban areas; (7) geographic mobility: experience of moving and or willingness to move from original residence in search of better opportunities (Lerner 1965; Kahl 1968; Schnaiberg 1970; Horowitz 1970; Portes 1974). . . .

Discussion

Discussion of this . . . sociology of development must consider, however, several important aspects. A systematic presentation of these will cover three major points: structural constraints, consumption-oriented values, and historical fiction.

Structural Constraints

No matter how compelling the image of highly motivated entrepreneurs racing to break the barriers of stagnation, the fact remains that individual action is highly conditioned by external social arrangements. Despite the frequent application of "tribal" imagery to underdeveloped nations, the reality of such societies is not one of an open frontier awaiting conquest by an entrepreneurial elite. Indeed, a complex structure of economic and political interests penetrates every aspect of them. To think that more modernity, achievement motivation, or status withdrawal will automatically transform these structures is, at best, naive. Regardless of what psychologists may think, societies are not the simple "additive" sum of individual members.

An active set of individuals, motivated by whatever psychological mechanism one may wish to posit, must still cope with existing economic and political arrangements. One way of doing so is to attempt to transform them, in which case "entrepreneurs" must organize themselves and enter the political arena in conflict with entrenched interest groups. The transformation of "modernity" or "*n* Achievement" into potential rebellion and ideologically committed elites is a possibility seldom contemplated in these theories.

A second alternative is that "entrepreneurs" may attempt to work through established channels. This alternative, the most likely one in view of the costs involved, may explain the embracement by established power groups of this perspective as their sociology of development. Highly motivated modern individuals may be extremely functional for maintenance of existing power structures. They may be hired, for example, as highly paid managers of foreign corporations, as has been increasingly the practice of multinational companies (see Blair 1974). They may also be brought into preexisting civilian and military bureaucracies. There are indeed many opportunities for entrepreneurial fulfillment within the existing social order. Altruistic motivations of "moderns" may even be employed in melioristic welfare activities, irrelevant for the structural task of development but functional for legitimizing the existing politico-economic system.

Individual motivations for achievement can be absorbed, fulfilled, and utilized without changing a basic situation of economic subordination and social maldistribution. The issue is not how much individual motivation there is, or what its sources are, but rather to what goals it is directed. The fundamental individualism apparent in theories of achievement and entrepreneurial motivation may be either irrelevant or inimical to struggles for national transformation. Elites committed to the task of development are not formed by "moderns" but by "modernizers"—individuals committed to achievement of collective economic and social change (Kerr et al. 1960).

Consumption-Oriented Values

A second, related aspect has to do with some of the values defined as "modern." That most modern of traits, "empathy," is usually described as ability to comprehend and place oneself symbolically in the midst of urban-industrial life (see Lerner 1965). This, in turn, is directly linked with a "demonstration effect" which raises demands for consumption beyond what a poor country can realistically afford. Excessive, media-promoted demand is a problem faced by both status quo and development-oriented governments in the Third World. For the latter, however, it presents a major difficulty, for it exercises pressure on scarce resources required for long-term investment. The dilemma of choosing between "political" and "economic" strategies (immediate consumption and re-sulting mass political loyalty versus consumption restrictions and long-term planning) emerges here as a major developmental issue (Malloy 1971).

Communications experts agree that modern values are diffused through the mass media. Some argue that advertisements in the commercial media are effective carriers of the "modern" message: "Advertising itself may also be a powerful instrument of development. It is a way of facilitating the distribution of commodities, broadening the market, and making people aware of possibilities with which they would not otherwise be familiar" (Pool 1966, p. 108).

The market is certainly broadened, often for the benefit of multinational enterprises, strains are placed on the country's capacity to import, and new "possibilities" are taught which often bear no relationship to local conditions. Such modern values—premature wants, imported needs and tastes, excessive consumption—are not the values of development. Historical experiences of national development in this century show consistently the necessity for restriction of consumption and for an orientation which places as much emphasis on achievement of national goals as on personal gratification. "Mobilization systems" in the Third World have evolved precisely as attempts to diffuse these "nonmodern" values (Apter 1967).

Finally, much-derided "traditional" cultures have often furnished value legitimations necessary in periods of rapid national change. Secular modernity lacks sufficient cultural depth to match the force of great national traditions. Japanese ideology during the Meiji period furnishes perhaps the best known, but not the only, example of the uses of tradition for development (Bellah 1965; Gusfield 1967; Walton 1976).

Historical Fiction

Theories of modernity share with those of evolutionary differentiation the belief that development proceeds from an early traditional stage toward a terminal "advanced" one. It is proper at this time to complete analysis of the character of this analogy.

As seen above, tradition is described in terms which are only logical counterparts to those embodied in modernity. There is no existing nation in the Third World which can be labeled "traditional" in this sense. The fictional character of the initial stage of the process is due to the fact that it is not based on observation of actual societies but on reflection on the features of the "terminal" stage. Modernity creates tradition very much as in Owen Lattimore's (1962) words, "Civilization gave birth to barbarism."

At the other extreme, as seen above, the current stage of development in industrial societies is unlikely to be replicated in underdeveloped countries. While providing points of reference for developmental efforts, features of currently industrialized nations are products of unique historical processes which already belong to mankind's past. The concrete features of advanced societies of today cannot be reproduced exactly in the future, nor is this the goal of most Third World nations (Illich 1969).

Sociologies of development dominant in the West thus come to posit a transition from a fictional stage to an impossible one. By concentrating on current characteristics of industrial societies, they neglect the fact that these traits, as well as those of underdeveloped societies, are themselves evolving and that social change in each type of society occurs in interaction with the other type. As a contemporary Latin American sociologist states: "A science of development is only science when it abandons the assumption of a formal goal to be reached and attempts instead to comprehend development as a historical process. . . . The object of [such] a theory cannot be to describe the passage from a society that is not really known to one that is not going to exist" (Dos Santos 1970a, p. 174).

References

Apter, David. 1967. *The Politics of Modernization*. Chicago: University of Chicago Press.

Bellah, Robert N. 1965. *Religion and Progress in Modern Asia*. New York: Free Press.

Bendix, Reinhard. 1962. *Max Weber: An Intellectual Portrait*. Garden City, N.Y.: Doubleday.

———. 1967. "Tradition and Modernity Reconsidered." *Comparative Studies in Society and History* 9 (April): 292–346.

Blair, Calvin P. 1974. "Las Empresas multinacionales en el comercio Latinoamericano: Una Mirada hacia el futuro." Mimeographed. Austin: University of Texas.

Chodak, Szymon. 1973. *Societal Development*. New York: Oxford University Press.

Dos Santos, Theotonio. 1970a. "La Crisis de la teoria del desarrollo y las relaciones de dependencia en America Latina." Pp. 147–87 in *La Dependencia politico-economica de America Latina*. Mexico, D.F.: Siglo Veintiuno.

———. 1970b. "The Structure of Dependence." *American Economic Review* 60 (May): 231–36.

Gusfield, Joseph R. 1967. "Tradition and Modernity: Misplaced Polarities in the Study of Social Change." *American Journal of Sociology* 72 (January): 351–62.

Hagen, Everett E. 1962. *On the Theory of Social Change*. Homewood, Ill.: Dorsey.

Horowitz, Irving L. 1966. *Three Worlds of Development*. New York: Oxford University Press.

———. 1970. "Personality and Structural Dimensions in Comparative International Development." *Social Science Quarterly* 51 (December): 494–513.

Illich, Ivan. 1969. *Celebration of Awareness*. New York: Doubleday.

Inkeles, Alex. 1966. "The Modernization of Man." Pp. 138–50 in *Modernization: The Dynamics of Growth*, edited by Myron Weiner. New York: Basic.

———. 1969. "Making Men Modern: On the Causes and Consequences of Individual Change in Six Countries." *American Journal of Sociology* 75 (September): 208–25.

Kahl, Joseph A. 1968. *The Measurement of Modernism*. Austin: University of Texas Press.

Kerr, Clark, John T. Dunlop, Frederick Harbison, and Charles A. Myers. 1960. *Industrialism and Industrial Man: The Problems of Labor and Management in Economic Growth*. New York: Oxford University Press.

Lattimore, Owen. 1962. "La Civilisation, mère de barbarie." *Annales E.S.C.* 17 (January-February): 99.

Lerner, Daniel. 1965. *The Passing of Traditional Society: Modernizing the Middle East.* New York: Free Press.

McClelland, David G. 1963. "Motivational Patterns in Southeast Asia with Special Reference to the Chinese Case." *Journal of Social Issues* 29 (January): 17.

———. 1966. "The Impulse of Modernization." Pp. 28–39 in *Modernization: The Dynamics of Growth,* edited by Myron Weiner. New York: Basic.

———. 1967. *The Achieving Society.* New York: Free Press.

Malloy, James M. 1971. "Generation of Political Support and Allocation of Costs." Pp. 23–42 in *Revolutionary Change in Cuba,* edited by C. Mesa-Lago. Pittsburgh: University of Pittsburgh Press.

Mills, C. Wright. 1956. *The Power Elite.* New York: Oxford University Press.

Parsons, Talcott. 1964a. *The Social System.* New York: Free Press.

———. 1964b. "Evolutionary Universals in Society." *American Sociological Review* 29 (June): 339–57.

Pool, Ithiel de Sola. 1966. "Communications and Development." Pp. 98–109 in *Modernization: The Dynamics of Growth,* edited by Myron Weiner. New York: Basic.

Portes, Alejandro. 1974. "Modernity and Development: A Critique." *Studies in Comparative International Development* 9 (Spring): 247–79.

Schnaiberg, Allan. 1970. "Measuring Modernism: Theoretical and Empirical Explorations." *American Journal of Sociology* 76 (December): 399–425.

Wallerstein, Immanuel. 1974. *The Modern World-System—Capitalist Agriculture and the Origins of the European World-Economy in the Sixteenth Century.* New York: Academic Press.

Walton, John. 1974. "Urban Hierarchies and Patterns of Dependence in Latin America." Paper presented at the May 1974 Seminar on New Directions of Urban Research in Latin America, Institute of Latin American Studies, University of Texas at Austin.

———. 1976. "Elites and the Politics of Urban Development." In *Urban Latin America: The Political Condition from Above and Below,* by A. Portes and J. Walton. Austin: University of Texas Press.

Weber, Max. 1951. *The Religion of China.* New York: Free Press.

———. 1958. *The City.* New York: Free Press.

Weiner, Myron. 1966. "Introduction." Pp. 1–14 in *Modernization: The Dynamics of Growth,* edited by M. Weiner. New York: Basic.

10. Urban Bias and Inequality

Michael Lipton

Michael Lipton is the principal advocate of the thesis that the primary explanation for the internal gap between rich and poor is something he calls "urban bias." He argues that even though developing countries sympathize with the plight of the rural poor, they consistently concentrate scarce development resources in the urban sector. The result is that the urban sectors, which are already well-off in a comparative sense, get an increasing share of national income, which exacerbates the inequalities. In the book from which this chapter is drawn, Lipton tries to show that it is in the interests of the elites of developing countries to maintain this urban bias since they benefit directly from it. Critics of Lipton's thesis claim that historically there has been a rural bias in development and that much political power continues to reside in the hands of the rural elite. One might also ask if there is anything about the cultures found in developing nations that encourages policies favoring one sector over another; rural or urban biases (if they truly exist) might be a function of conditions established by the international environment.

The most important class conflict in the poor countries of the world today is not between labor and capital. Nor is it between foreign and national interests. It is between the rural classes and the urban classes. The rural sector contains most of the poverty, and most of the low-cost sources of potential advance; but the urban sector contains most of the articulateness, organization and power. So the urban classes have been able to "win" most of the rounds of the struggle with the countryside; but in so doing they have made the development process needlessly slow and unfair. Scarce land, which might grow millets and beansprouts for hungry villagers, instead produces a trickle of costly calories from meat and milk, which few except the urban rich (who have ample protein anyway) can afford. Scarce investment, instead of going into water-pumps to grow rice, is wasted on urban motorways. Scarce human

Reprinted with permission from *Why Poor People Stay Poor: A Study of Urban Bias in World Development*, by Michael Lipton, pp. 13–18. First published in Great Britain by Maurice Temple Smith, London, 1977. Permission for U.S. rights granted by Harvard University Press. (References made by the author to other sections of the book from which this selection was drawn have been deleted. Ed.)

skills design and administer, not village wells and agricultural extension services, but world boxing championships in showpiece stadia. Resource allocations, within the city and the village as well as between them, reflect urban priorities rather than equity or efficiency. The damage has been increased by misguided ideological imports, liberal and Marxian, and by the town's success in buying off part of the rural elite, thus transferring most of the costs of the process to the rural poor.

But is this urban bias really damaging? After all, since 1945 output per person in the poor countries had doubled; and this unprecedented growth has brought genuine development. Production has been made more scientific: in agriculture, by the irrigation of large areas, and more recently by the increasing adoption of fertilizers and of high-yielding varieties of wheat and rice; in industry, by the replacement of fatiguing and repetitive effort by rising levels of technology, specialization and skills. Consumption has also developed, in ways that at once use and underpin the development of production; poor countries now consume enormously expanded provisions of health and education, roads and electricity, radios and bicycles. Why, then, are so many of those involved in the development of the Third World—politicians and administrators, planners and scholars—miserable about the past and gloomy about the future? Why is the United Nations' "Development Decade" of the 1960s, in which poor countries as a whole exceeded the growth target,[1] generally written off as a failure? Why is aid, which demonstrably contributes to a development effort apparently so promising in global terms, in accelerating decline and threatened by a "crisis of will" in donor countries?[2]

The reason is that since 1945 growth and development, in most poor countries, have done so little to raise the living standards of the poorest people. It is scant comfort that today's mass-consumption economies, in Europe and North America, also featured near-stagnant mass welfare in the early phases of their economic modernization. Unlike today's poor countries, they carried in their early development the seeds of mass consumption later on. They were massively installing extra capacity to supply their people with simple goods: bread, cloth and coal, not just luxury housing, poultry and airports. Also the nineteenth-century "developing countries," including Russia, were developing not just market requirements but class structures that practically guaranteed subsequent "trickling down" of benefits. The workers even proved able to raise their *share* of political power and economic welfare. The very preconditions of such trends are absent in most of today's developing countries. The sincere egalitarian rhetoric of, say, Mrs. Indira Gandhi or Julius Nyerere was—allowing for differences of style and ideology—closely paralleled in Europe during early industrial development: in Britain, for example, by Henry Brougham and Lord Durham in the 1830s.[3] But the rural masses of India and Tanzania, unlike the urban masses of Melbourne's Britain, lack the power to organize the pressure that alone turns such rhetoric into distributive action against the pressure of the elite.

Some rather surprising people have taken alarm at the persistently unequal nature of recent development. Aid donors are substantially motivated by foreign-policy concerns for the stability of recipient governments; development banks, by the need to repay depositors and hence to ensure a good return on the projects they support. Both concerns coalesce in the World Bank, which raises and distributes some £3,000 million of aid each year. As a bank it has advocated—and financed— mostly "bankable" (that is, commercially profitable) projects. As a channel for aid donors, it has concentrated on poor countries that are relatively "open" to investment, trade and economic advice from those donors. Yet the effect of stagnant mass welfare in poor countries, on the well-intentioned and perceptive people who administer World Bank aid, has gradually overborne these traditional biases. Since 1971 the president of the World Bank, Robert McNamara, has in a series of speeches focused attention on the stagnant or worsening lives of the bottom 40 percent of people in poor countries.[4] Recently this has begun to affect the World Bank's projects, though its incomplete engagement with the problem of urban bias restricts the impact. For instance, an urban-biased government will prepare rural projects less well than urban projects, will manipulate prices to render rural projects less apparently profitable (and hence less "bankable") and will tend to cut down its own effort if donors step up theirs. Nevertheless, the World Bank's new concern with the "bottom 40 percent" is significant.

These people—between one-quarter and one-fifth of the people of the world—are overwhelmingly rural: landless laborers, or farmers with no more than an acre or two, who must supplement their income by wage labor. Most of these countryfolk rely, as hitherto, on agriculture lacking irrigation or fertilizers or even iron tools. Hence they are so badly fed that they cannot work efficiently, and in many cases are unable to feed their infants well enough to prevent physical stunting and perhaps even brain damage. Apart from the rote-learning of religious texts, few of them receive any schooling. One in four dies before the age of ten. The rest live the same overworked, underfed, ignorant and disease-ridden lives as thirty, or three hundred, or three thousand years ago. Often they borrow (at 40 percent or more yearly interest) from the same moneylender families as their ancestors, and surrender half their crops to the same families of landlords. Yet the last thirty years have been the age of unprecedented, accelerating growth and development! Naturally men of goodwill are puzzled and alarmed.

How can accelerated growth and development, in an era of rapidly improving communications and of "mass politics," produce so little for poor people? It is too simple to blame the familiar scapegoats—foreign exploiters and domestic capitalists. Poor countries where they are relatively unimportant have experienced the paradox just as much as others.

Nor, apparently, do the poorest families cause their own difficulties, whether by rapid population growth or by lack of drive. Poor families do tend to have more children than rich families, but principally because their higher death rates require it, if the aging parents are to be reasonably sure that a son will grow up, to support them if need be. And it is the structure of rewards and opportunities within poor countries that extracts, as if by force, the young man of ability and energy from his chronically stagnant rural background and lures him to serve, or even to join, the booming urban elite.

The disparity between urban and rural welfare is much greater in poor countries now than it was in rich countries during their early development. This huge welfare gap is demonstrably inefficient, as well as inequitable. It persists mainly because less than 20 percent of investment for development has gone to the agricultural sector (the situation has not changed much since 1965), although over 65 percent of the people of less-developed countries (LDCs), and over 80 percent of the really poor who live on $1 a week each or less, depend for a living on agriculture. The proportion of skilled people who support development—doctors, bankers, engineers—going to rural areas has been lower still; and the rural-urban imbalances have in general been even greater than those between agriculture and industry. Moreover, in most LCDs, governments have taken numerous measures with the unhappy side-effect of accentuating rural-urban disparities: their own allocation of public expenditure and taxation; measures raising the price of industrial production relative to farm production, thus encouraging private rural saving to flow into industrial investment because the value of industrial output has been artificially boosted; and educational facilities encouraging bright villagers to train in cities for urban jobs.

Such processes have been extremely inefficient. For instance, the impact on output of $1 of carefully selected investment is in most countries two to three times as high in agriculture as elsewhere, yet public policy and private market power have combined to push domestic savings and foreign aid into nonagricultural uses. The process has also been inequitable. Agriculture starts with about one-third the income per head of the rest of the economy, so that the people who depend on it should in equity receive special attention not special mulcting. Finally, the misallocation between sectors has created a needless and acute conflict between efficiency and equity. In agriculture the poor farmer with little land is usually efficient in his use of both land and capital, whereas power, construction and industry often do best in big, capital-intensive units; and rural income and power, while far from equal, are less unequal than in the cities. So concentration on urban development and neglect of agriculture have pushed resources away from activities where they can help growth *and* benefit the poor, and toward activities where they do either of these, if at all, at the expense of the other.

Urban bias also increases inefficiency and inequity *within* the sectors. Poor farmers have little land and much underused family labor. Hence they tend to complement any extra developmental resources received—pumpsets, fertilizers, virgin land—with much more extra labor than do large farmers. Poor farmers thus tend to get most output from such extra resources (as well as needing the extra income most). But rich farmers (because they sell their extra output to the cities instead of eating it themselves, and because they are likely to use much of their extra income to support urban investment) are naturally favored by urban-biased policies; it is they, not the efficient small farmers, who get the cheap loans and the fertilizer subsidies. The patterns of allocation and distribution within the cities are damaged too. Farm inputs are produced inefficiently, instead of imported, and the farmer has to pay, even if the price is nominally "subsidised." The processing of farm outputs, notably grain milling, is shifted into big urban units and the profits are no longer reinvested in agriculture. And equalization between classes inside the cities becomes more risky, because the investment-starved farm sector might prove unable to deliver the food that a better-off urban mass would seek to buy.

Moreover, income in poor countries is usually more equally distributed within the rural sector than within the urban sector.[5] Since income creates the power to distribute extra income, therefore, a policy that concentrates on raising income in the urban sector will worsen inequalities in two ways: by transferring not only from poor to rich, but also from more equal to less equal. Concentration on urban enrichment is triply inequitable: because countryfolk start poorer; because such concentration allots rural resources largely to the rural rich (who sell food to the cities); and because the great inequality of power *within* the towns renders urban resources especially likely to go to the resident elites.

But am I not hammering at an open door? Certainly the persiflage of allocation has changed recently, under the impact of patently damaging deficiencies in rural output. Development plans are nowadays full of "top priority for agriculture."[6] This is reminiscent of the pseudo-egalitarian school where, at mealtimes, Class B children get priority, while Class A children get food.[7] We can see that the new agricultural priority is dubious from the abuse of the "green revolution" and of the oil crisis (despite its much greater impact on *industrial* costs) as pretexts for lack of emphasis on agriculture: "We don't need it," and "We can't afford it," respectively. And the 60 to 80 percent of people dependent on agriculture are still allocated barely 20 percent of public resources; even these small shares are seldom achieved; and they have, if anything, tended to diminish. So long as the elite's interests, background and sympathies remain predominantly urban, the countryside may get the "priority" but the city will get the resources. The farm sector will continue to be squeezed, both by transfers of resources from it and by prices that are turned against it. Bogus justifications of urban bias will continue to earn the sincere, prestige-conferring, but misguided support of visiting "experts" from industrialized countries and international agencies. And development will be needlessly painful, inequitable and slow.

Notes

1. The UN target was a 5 percent yearly rate of "real" growth (that is, allowing for inflation) of total output. The actual rate was slightly higher.

2. Net aid from the donor countries comprising the Development Assistance Committee (DAC) of the Organization for Economic Cooperation and Development (OECD) comprises over 95 percent of all net aid to less-developed countries (LDCs). It fell steadily from 0.54 percent of donors' GNP in 1961 to 0.30 percent in 1973. The real value of aid per person in recipient countries fell by over 20 percent over the period. M. Lipton, "Aid Allocation when Aid is Inadequate," in T. Byres, ed., *Foreign Resources and Economic Development*, Cass, 1972, p. 158; OECD (DAC), *Development Cooperation* (1974 Review), p. 116.

3. L. Cooper, *Radical Jack*, Cresset, 1969, esp. pp. 183–97; C. New, *Life of Henry Brougham to 1830*, Clarendon, 1961, Preface.

4. See the mounting emphasis in his *Addresses to the Board of Governors*, all published by the International Bank for Reconstruction and Development, Washington; at Copenhagen in 1970, p. 20; at Washington in 1971, pp. 6–19, and 1972, pp. 8–15; and at Nairobi in 1973, pp. 10–14, 19.

5. M. Ahluwalia, "The Dimensions of the Problem," in H. Chenery et al., *Redistribution with Growth*, Oxford, 1974.

6. See K. Rafferty, *Financial Times*, 10 April 1974, p. 35, col. 5; M. Lipton, "Urban Bias and Rural Planning," in P. Streeten and M. Lipton, eds., *The Crisis of Indian Planning*, Oxford, 1968, p. 85.

7. F. Muir and D. Norden, "Comonon Entrance," in P. Sellers, *Songs for Swinging Sellers*, Parlophone PMC 111, 1958.

11. The Structure of Dependence

Theotonio dos Santos

In the last chapter, Lipton stressed the importance of the internal determinants of inequality. In this chapter, Theotonio dos Santos, a Brazilian economist, points his finger at external conditions. Dos Santos is a member of what has been called the "dependentista school" of development thinkers, the great majority of whom are Latin American intellectuals. Dependency theory comes in many varieties; indeed, some argue that there is no such thing as dependency "theory." Nonetheless, there is a body of thinking that is common to many of those who form part of this school, and in this chapter dos Santos presents a concise statement of some of its fundamental tenets. He begins by defining dependence and showing its linkages to Marxian theory and goes on to elaborate three basic forms of dependence: (1) colonial, (2) financial-industrial, and (3) multinational. This latter form, arising out of the power of the large multinational corporations that maintain operations in developing countries, is of greatest concern to dos Santos because he sees it as limiting the developmental potential of newly industrializing nations. This new form of dependence restricts the size of the local market and thus contributes to income inequality in developing nations. Ultimately, according to dos Santos, dependent development must culminate in revolutionary movements of the left or right.

This chapter attempts to demonstrate that the dependence of Latin American countries on other countries cannot be overcome without a qualitative change in their internal structures and external relations. We shall attempt to show that the relations of dependence to which these countries are subjected conform to a type of international and internal structure which leads them to underdevelopment or more precisely to a dependent structure that deepens and aggravates the fundamental problems of their peoples.

I. What Is Dependence?

By dependence we mean a situation in which the economy of certain countries is conditioned by the development and expansion of another

Reprinted with permission from *The American Economic Review*, vol. 60 (May 1970), pp. 231–236.

economy to which the former is subjected. The relation of interdependence between two or more economies, and between these and world trade, assumes the form of dependence when some countries (the dominant ones) can expand and can be self-sustaining, while other countries (the dependent ones) can do this only as a reflection of that expansion, which can have either a positive or a negative effect on their immediate development [7, p. 6].

The concept of dependence permits us to see the internal situation of these countries as part of world economy. In the Marxian tradition, the theory of imperialism has been developed as a study of the process of expansion of the imperialist centers and of their world domination. In the epoch of the revolutionary movement of the Third World, we have to develop the theory of laws of internal development in those countries that are the object of such expansion and are governed by them. This theoretical step transcends the theory of development which seeks to explain the situation of the underdeveloped countries as a product of their slowness or failure to adopt the patterns of efficiency characteristic of developed countries (or to "modernize" or "develop" themselves). Although capitalist development theory admits the existence of an "external" dependence, it is unable to perceive underdevelopment in the way our present theory perceives it, as a consequence and part of the process of the world expansion of capitalism—a part that is necessary to and integrally linked with it.

In analyzing the process of constituting a world economy that integrates the so-called "national economies" in a world market of commodities, capital, and even of labor power, we see that the relations produced by this market are unequal and combined—unequal because development of parts of the system occurs at the expense of other parts. Trade relations are based on monopolistic control of the market, which leads to the transfer of surplus generated in the dependent countries to the dominant countries; financial relations are, from the viewpoint of the dominant powers, based on loans and the export of capital, which permit them to receive interest and profits, thus increasing their domestic surplus and strengthening their control over the economies of the other countries. For the dependent countries these relations represent an export of profits and interest which carries off part of the surplus generated domestically and leads to a loss of control over their productive resources. In order to permit these disadvantageous relations, the dependent countries must generate large surpluses, not in such a way as to create higher levels of technology but rather creating superexploited manpower. The result is to limit the development of their internal market and their technical and cultural capacity, as well as the moral and physical health of their people. We call this combined development because it is the combination of these inequalities and the transfer of resources from the most backward and dependent sectors to the most advanced and dominant ones which explains the inequality, deepens it, and transforms it into a necessary and structural element of the world economy.

II. Historic Forms of Dependence

Historic forms of dependence are conditioned by: (1) the basic forms of this world economy which has its own laws of development; (2) the type of economic relations dominant in the capitalist centers and the ways in which the latter expand outward; and (3) the types of economic relations existing inside the peripheral countries which are incorporated into the situation of dependence within the network of international economic relations generated by capitalist expansion. It is not within the purview of this chapter to study these forms in detail but only to distinguish broad characteristics of development.

Drawing on an earlier study, we may distinguish: (1) Colonial dependence, trade export in nature, in which commercial and financial capital in alliance with the colonialist state dominated the economic relations of the Europeans and the colonies by means of a trade monopoly, complemented by a colonial monopoly of land, mines, and manpower (serf or slave) in the colonized countries. (2) Financial-industrial dependence, which consolidated itself at the end of the nineteenth century, characterized by the domination of big capital in the hegemonic centers, and its expansion abroad through investment in the production of raw materials and agricultural products for consumption in the hegemonic centers. A productive structure grew up in the dependent countries devoted to the export of these products (which I.V. Levin labeled export economies [11]; other analysis in other regions [12] [13]), producing what the Economic Commission for Latin America (ECLA) has called "foreign-oriented development" (*desarrollo hacia afuera*) [4]. (3) In the postwar period a new type of dependence has been consolidated, based on multinational corporations which began to invest in industries geared to the internal market of underdeveloped countries. This form of dependence is basically technological-industrial dependence [6].

Each of these forms of dependence corresponds to a situation which conditioned not only the international relations of these countries but also their internal structures: the orientation of production, the forms of capital accumulation, the reproduction of the economy, and, simultaneously, their social and political structure.

III. The Export Economies

In forms (1) and (2) of dependence, production is geared to those products destined for export (gold, silver, and tropical products in the colonial epoch; raw materials and agricultural products in the epoch of industrial-financial dependence); i.e., production is determined by demand from the hegemonic centers. The internal productive structure is characterized by rigid specialization and monoculture in entire regions (the Caribbean, the Brazilian Northeast, etc.). Alongside these export sectors there grew up certain complementary economic activities (cattle-raising and some manufacturing, for example) which were dependent, in general, on the export sector to which they sell their products. There was a third, subsistence economy which provided manpower for the export sector under favorable conditions and toward which excess population shifted during periods unfavorable to international trade.

Under these conditions, the existing internal market was restricted by four factors: (1) Most of the national income was derived from export, which was used to purchase the inputs required by export production (slaves, for example) or luxury goods consumed by the hacienda- and mine-owners, and by the more prosperous employees. (2) The available manpower was subject to very arduous forms of superexploitation, which limited its consumption. (3) Part of the consumption of these workers was provided by the subsistence economy, which served as a complement to their income and as a refuge during periods of depression. (4) A fourth factor was to be found in those countries in which land and mines were in the hands of foreigners (cases of an enclave economy): a great part of the accumulated surplus was destined to be sent abroad in the form of profits, limiting not only internal consumption but also possibilities of reinvestment [1]. In the case of enclave economies the relations of the foreign companies with the hegemonic center were even more exploitative and were complemented by the fact that purchases by the enclave were made directly abroad.

IV. The New Dependence

The new form of dependence, (3) above, is in process of developing and is conditioned by the exigencies of the international commodity and capital markets. The possibility of generating new investments depends on the existence of financial resources in foreign currency for the purchase of machinery and processed raw materials not produced domestically. Such purchases are subject to two limitations: the limit of resources generated by the export sector (reflected in the balance of payments, which includes not only trade but also service relations); and the limitations of monopoly on patents which leads monopolistic firms to prefer to transfer their machines in the form of capital rather than as commodities for sale. It is necessary to analyze these relations of dependence if we are to understand the fundamental structural limits they place on the development of these economies.

1. Industrial development is dependent on an export sector for the foreign currency to buy the inputs utilized by the industrial sector. The first consequence of this dependence is the need to preserve the traditional export sector, which limits economically the development of the internal market by the conservation of backward relations of production and signifies, politically, the maintenance of power by traditional decadent oligarchies. In the countries where these sectors are controlled by foreign capital, it signifies the remittance abroad of high profits, and political

dependence on those interests. Only in rare instances does foreign capital not control at least the marketing of these products. In response to these limitations, dependent countries in the 1930s and 1940s developed a policy of exchange restrictions and taxes on the national and foreign export sector; today they tend toward the gradual nationalization of production and toward the imposition of certain timid limitations on foreign control of the marketing of exported products. Furthermore, they seek, still somewhat timidly, to obtain better terms for the sale of their products. In recent decades, they have created mechanisms for international price agreements, and today the United Nations Conference on Trade and Development (UNCTAD) and ECLA press to obtain more favorable tariff conditions for these products on the part of the hegemonic centers. It is important to point out that the industrial development of these countries is dependent on the situation of the export sector, the continued existence of which they are obliged to accept.

2. Industrial development is, then, strongly conditioned by fluctuations in the balance of payments. This leads toward deficit due to the relations of dependence themselves. The causes of the deficit are three:

a. Trade relations take place in a highly monopolized international market, which tends to lower the price of raw materials and to raise the prices of industrial products, particularly inputs. In the second place, there is a tendency in modern technology to replace various primary products with synthetic raw materials. Consequently, the balance of trade in these countries tends to be less favorable (even though they show a general surplus). The overall Latin American balance of trade from 1946 to 1968 shows a surplus for each of those years. The same thing happens in almost every underdeveloped country. However, the losses due to deterioration of the terms of trade (on the basis of data from ECLA and the International Monetary Fund), excluding Cuba, were $26,383 million for the 1951–66 period, taking 1950 prices as a base. If Cuba and Venezuela are excluded, the total is $15,925 million.

b. For the reasons already given, foreign capital retains control over the most dynamic sectors of the economy and repatriates a high volume of profit; consequently, capital accounts are highly unfavorable to dependent countries. The data show that the amount of capital leaving the country is much greater than the amount entering; this produces an enslaving deficit in capital accounts. To this must be added the deficit in certain services which are virtually under total foreign control—such as freight transport, royalty payments, technical aid, etc. Consequently, an important deficit is produced in the total balance of payments; thus limiting the possibility of importation of inputs for industrialization.

c. The result is that "foreign financing" becomes necessary, in two forms: to cover the existing deficit, and to "finance" development by means of loans for the stimulation of investments and to "supply" an internal economic surplus which was decapitalized to a large extent by the remittance of part of the surplus generated domestically and sent abroad as profits.

Foreign capital and foreign "aid" thus fill up the holes that they themselves created. The real value of this aid, however, is doubtful. If overcharges resulting from the restrictive terms of the aid are subtracted from the total amount of the grants, the average net flow, according to calculations of the Inter-American Economic and Social Council, is approximately 54 percent of the gross flow [5].

If we take account of certain further facts—that a high proportion of aid is paid in local currencies, that Latin American countries make contributions to international financial institutions, and that credits are often "tied"—we find a "real component of foreign aid" of 42.2 percent on a very favorable hypothesis and of 38.3 percent on a more realistic one [5, II, p. 33]. The gravity of the situation becomes even clearer if we consider that these credits are used in large part to finance North American investments, to subsidize foreign imports which compete with national products, to introduce technology not adapted to the needs of underdeveloped countries, and to invest in low-priority sectors of the national economies. The hard truth is that the underdeveloped countries have to pay for all of the "aid" they receive. This situation is generating an enormous protest movement by Latin American governments seeking at least partial relief from such negative relations.

3. Finally, industrial development is strongly conditioned by the technological monopoly exercised by imperialist centers. We have seen that the underdeveloped countries depend on the importation of machinery and raw materials for the development of their industries. However, these goods are not freely available in the international market; they are patented and usually belong to the big companies. The big companies do not sell machinery and processed raw materials as simple merchandise: they demand either the payment of royalties, etc., for their utilization or, in most cases, they convert these goods into capital and introduce them in the form of their own investments. This is how machinery which is replaced in the hegemonic centers by more advanced technology is sent to dependent countries as capital for the installation of affiliates. Let us pause and examine these relations in order to understand their oppressive and exploitative character.

The dependent countries do not have sufficient foreign currency, for the reasons given. Local businessmen have financing difficulties, and they must pay for the utilization of certain patented techniques. These factors oblige the national bourgeois governments to facilitate the entry of foreign capital in order to supply the restricted national market, which is strongly protected by high tariffs in order to promote industrialization. Thus, foreign capital enters with all the advantages: in many cases, it is given exemption from exchange controls for the importation of machinery; financing of sites for installation of industries is provided; government financing agencies facilitate industrialization; loans are available from foreign and domestic banks, which prefer such clients; foreign aid often subsidizes such investments and finances complementary public investments; after installation, high profits obtained in such favorable circumstances can be reinvested freely. Thus it is not surprising that the data of the U.S. Department of Commerce reveal that the percentage of capital brought in from abroad by these companies is but a part of the total amount of invested capital. These data show that in the period from 1946 to 1967 the new entries of capital into Latin America for direct investment amounted to $5,415 million, while the sum of reinvested profits was $4,424 million. On the other hand, the transfers of profits from Latin America to the United States amounted to $14,775 million. If we estimate total profits as approximately equal to transfers plus reinvestments we have the sum of $18,983 million. In spite of enormous transfers of profits to the United States, the book value of the United States's direct investment in Latin America went from $3,045 million in 1946 to $10,213 million in 1967. From these data it is clear that: (1) Of the new investments made by U.S. companies in Latin America for the period 1946–67, 55 percent corresponds to new entries of capital and 45 percent to reinvestment of profits; in recent years, the trend is more marked, with reinvestments between 1960 and 1966 representing more than 60 percent of new investments. (2) Remittances remained at about 10 percent of book value throughout the period. (3) The ratio of remitted capital to new flow is around 2.7 for the period 1946–67; that is, for each dollar that enters $2.70 leaves. In the 1960s this ratio roughly doubled, and in some years was considerably higher.

The *Survey of Current Business* data on sources and uses of funds for direct North American investment in Latin America in the period 1957–64 show that, of the total sources of direct investment in Latin America, only 11.8 percent came from the United States. The remainder is, in large part, the result of the activities of North American firms in Latin America (46.4 percent net income, 27.7 percent under the heading of depreciation), and from "sources located abroad" (14.1 percent). It is significant that the funds obtained abroad that are external to the companies are greater than the funds originating in the United States.

V. Effects on the Productive Structure

It is easy to grasp, even if only superficially, the effects that this dependent structure has on the productive system itself in these countries and the role of this structure in determining a specified type of development, characterized by its dependent nature.

The productive system in the underdeveloped countries is essentially determined by these international relations. In the first place, the need to conserve the agrarian or mining export structure generates a combination between more advanced economic centers that extract surplus value from the more backward sectors and internal "metropolitan" centers on the one hand, and internal interdependent "colonial" centers on the other [10]. The unequal and combined character of capitalist development at the international level is reproduced internally in an acute form. In the second place the industrial and technological structure responds more closely to the interests of the multinational corporations than to internal developmental needs (conceived of not only in terms of the overall interests of the population, but also from the point of view of the interests of a national capitalist development). In the third place, the same technological and economic-financial concentration of the hegemonic economies is transferred without substantial alteration to very different economies and societies, giving rise to a highly unequal productive structure, a high concentration of incomes, underutilization of installed capacity, intensive exploitation of existing markets concentrated in large cities, etc.

The accumulation of capital in such circumstances assumes its own characteristics. In the first place, it is characterized by profound differences among domestic wage-levels, in the context of a local cheap labor market, combined with a capital-intensive technology. The result, from the point of view of relative surplus value, is a high rate of exploitation of labor power. (On measurements of forms of exploitation, see [3].)

This exploitation is further aggravated by the high prices of industrial products enforced by protectionism, exemptions and subsidies given by the national governments, and "aid" from hegemonic centers. Furthermore, since dependent accumulation is necessarily tied into the international economy, it is profoundly conditioned by the unequal and combined character of international capitalist economic relations, by the technological and financial control of the imperialist centers by the realities of the balance of payments, by the economic policies of the state, etc. The role of the state in the growth of national and foreign capital merits a much fuller analysis than can be made here.

Using the analysis offered here as a point of departure, it is possible to understand the limits that this productive system imposes on the growth of the internal markets of these countries. The survival of traditional relations in the countryside is a serious limitation on the size of the market, since industrialization does not offer hopeful prospects. The productive structure created by dependent industrialization limits the growth of the internal market.

First, it subjects the labor force to highly exploitative relations which limit its purchasing power. Second, in adopting a technology of intensive capital use, it creates very few jobs in comparison with population growth, and limits the generation of new sources of income. These two limitations affect the growth of the consumer goods market. Third, the remittance abroad of profits carries away part of the economic surplus generated within the country. In all these ways limits are put on the possible creation of basic national industries which could provide a market for the capital goods this surplus would make possible if it were not remitted abroad.

From this cursory analysis we see that the alleged backwardness of these economies is not due to a lack of integration with capitalism but that, to the contrary, the most powerful obstacles to their full development come from the way in which they are joined to this international system and its laws of development.

VI. Some Conclusions: Dependent Reproduction

In order to understand the system of dependent reproduction and the socioeconomic institutions created by it, we must see it as part of a system of world economic relations based on monopolistic control of large-scale capital, on control of certain economic and financial centers over others, on a monopoly of a complex technology that leads to unequal and combined development at a national and international level. Attempts to analyze backwardness as a failure to assimilate more advanced models of production or to modernize are nothing more than ideology disguised as science. The same is true of the attempts to analyze this international economy in terms of relations among elements in free competition, such as the theory of comparative costs which seeks to justify the inequalities of the world economic system and to conceal the relations of exploitation on which it is based [14].

In reality we can understand what is happening in the underdeveloped countries only when we see that they develop within the framework of a process of dependent production and reproduction. This system is a dependent one because it reproduces a productive system whose development is limited by those world relations which necessarily lead to: the development of only certain economic sectors, to trade under unequal conditions [9], to domestic competition with international capital under unequal conditions, to the imposition of relations of superexploitation of the domestic labor force with a view to dividing the economic surplus thus generated between internal and external forces of domination. (On economic surplus and its utilization in the dependent countries, see [1].)

In reproducing such a productive system and such international relations, the development of dependent capitalism reproduces the factors that prevent it from reaching a nationally and internationally advantageous situation; and it thus reproduces backwardness, misery, and social marginalization within its borders. The development that it produces benefits very narrow sectors, encounters unyielding domestic obstacles to its continued economic growth (with respect to both internal and foreign markets), and leads to the progressive accumulation of balance-of-payments deficits, which in turn generate more dependence and more superexploitation.

The political measures proposed by the developmentalists of ECLA, UNCTAD, Inter-American Development Bank (BID), etc., do not appear to permit destruction of these terrible chains imposed by dependent development. We have examined the alternative forms of development presented for Latin America and the dependent countries under such conditions elsewhere [8]. Everything now indicates that what can be expected is a long process of sharp political and military confrontations and of profound social radicalization which will lead these countries to a dilemma: governments of force, which open the way to facism, or popular revolutionary governments, which open the way to socialism. Intermediate solutions have proved to be, in such a contradictory reality, empty and utopian.

References

1. Paul Baran, *Political Economy of Growth* (Monthly Review Press, 1967).
2. Thomas Balogh, *Unequal Partners* (Basil Blackwell, 1963).
3. Pablo Gonzalez Casanova, *Sociología de la explotación*, Siglo XXI (México, 1969).
4. Cepal, *La CEPAL y el Análisis del Desarrollo Latinoamericano* (1968, Santiago, Chile).
5. Consejo Interamericano Economico Social (CIES) O.A.S., Interamerican Economic and Social Council, External Financing for Development in L.A. *El Financiamiento Externo para el Desarrollo de América Latina* (Pan-American Union, Washington, 1969).
6. Theotonio Dos Santos, *El nuevo carácter de la dependencia*, CESO (Santiago de Chile, 1968).
7. _____ , *La crisis de la teoría del desarrollo y las relaciones de dependencia en América Latina*, Boletin del CESO, 3 (Santiago, Chile, 1968).
8. _____ , *La dependencia económica y las alternotivas de cambio en América Latina*, Ponencia al IX Congreso Latinoamericano de Sociología (México, Nov., 1969).
9. A. Emmanuel, *L'Echange Inégal* (Maspero, Paris, 1969).
10. Andre G. Frank, *Development and Underdevelopment in Latin America* (Monthly Review Press, 1968).
11. I. V. Levin, *The Export Economies* (Harvard Univ. Press, 1964).
12. Gunnar Myrdal, *Asian Drama* (Pantheon, 1968).
13. K. Nkrumah, *Neocolonialismo, última etapa del imperialismo*, (Siglo XXI, México, 1966).
14. Cristian Palloix, *Problemes de la Croissance en Economie Ouverte* (Maspero, Paris, 1969).

12. Modernization and Dependency: Alternative Perspectives in the Study of Latin American Underdevelopment

J. Samuel Valenzuela
Arturo Valenzuela

This chapter contrasts the modernization and dependency perspectives. Since the main notions of modernization theory have been covered in some detail in earlier chapters, only those portions of the Valenzuelas' discussion that elaborate on dependency theory are included here. The Valenzuelas enumerate the principal assumptions held by dependency thinkers and present some of the supporting evidence for the theory's validity, drawing upon the Latin American experience. After evaluating the relative merits of the two perspectives, they conclude that dependency is the superior framework primarily because it is firmly grounded in historical reality.

The Dependency Perspective

Like the modernization perspective, the dependency perspective resulted from the work of many different scholars in different branches of the social sciences. Much of the work proceeded in an inductive fashion. This was the case with economists working in the Economic Commission for Latin America (ECLA) who first sought to explain the underdevelopment of Latin America by focusing on the unequal terms of trade between exporters of raw materials and exporters of manufactured goods. ECLA "doctrine" called for a concerted effort to diversify the export base of Latin American countries and accelerate industrialization efforts through import substitution. However, the continued difficulties with that model of development soon led to a focus on the internal contraints to industrialization, with an emphasis on factors such as the distorting effects of unequal land tenure patterns and the corrosive results of an inflation best explained by structural rather than monetary variables. Soon these two trends came together when scholars, such as

Reprinted with permission from *Comparative Politics*, vol. 10 (July 1978), pp. 543–557.

Osvaldo Sunkel, combined the early emphasis on external variables with the internal constraints to development.[1]

But this dependency perspective was anticipated by Latin American historians who had been working for years on various aspects of economic history. Studies such as those of Sergio Bagú stressed the close inter-relation of domestic developments in Latin America and developments in metropolitan countries. And in Brazil, sociologists such as Florestan Fernandes, Octávio Ianni, Fernando Henrique Cardoso, and Theotonio dos Santos also turned to broad structural analyses of the factors of underdevelopment. The fact that many of these scholars found themselves in Santiago in the 1960s only contributed to further development of the perspective.

In its emphasis on the expansive nature of capitalism and in its structural analysis of society, the dependency literature draws on Marxist insights and is related to the Marxist theory of imperialism. However, its examination of processes in Latin America imply important revisions in classical Leninist formulations, both historically and in light of recent trends. The focus is on explaining Latin American underdevelopment, and not on the functioning of capitalism, though some authors argue that their efforts will contribute to an understanding of capitalism and its contradictions.

Assumptions

The dependency perspective rejects the assumption made by modernization writers that the unit of analysis in studying underdevelopment is the national society. The domestic cultural and institutional features of Latin America are in themselves simply not the key variables accounting for the relative backwardness of the area, though, as will be seen below, domestic structures are certainly critical intervening factors. The relative presence of traditional and modern features may, or may not, help to differentiate societies; but it does not in itself explain the origins of modernity in some contexts and the lack of modernity in others. As such, the tradition-modernity polarity is of little value as a fundamental working concept. The dependency perspective assumes that the development of a national or regional unit can only be understood in connection with its historical insertion into the worldwide political-economic system which emerged with the wave of European colonizations of the world. This global system is thought to be characterized by the unequal but combined development of its different components. As Sunkel and Pedro Paz put it:

> Both underdevelopment and development are aspects of the same phenomenon, both are historically simultaneous, both are linked functionally and, therefore, interact and condition each other mutually. This results . . . in the division of the world between industrial, advanced or "central" countries, and underdeveloped, backward or "peripheral" countries. . . .[2]

The center is viewed as capable of dynamic development responsive to internal needs, and as the main beneficiary of the global links. On the other hand, the periphery is seen as having a reflex type of development; one which is both constrained by its incorporation into the global system and which results from its adaptation to the requirements of the expansion of the center. As dos Santos indicates:

> Dependency is a situation in which a certain number of countries have their economy conditioned by the development and expansion of another . . . placing the dependent countries in a backward position exploited by the dominant countries.[3]

It is important to stress that the process can be understood only by reference to its historical dimension and by focusing on the total network of social relations as they evolve in different contexts over time. For this reason dependence is characterized as "structural, historical and totalizing" or an "integral analysis of development."[4] It is meaningless to develop, as some social scientists have, a series of synchronic statistical indicators to establish relative levels of dependence or independence among different national units to test the "validity" of the model.[5] The unequal development of the world goes back to the sixteenth century with the formation of a capitalist world economy in which some countries in the center were able to specialize in industrial production of manufactured goods because the peripheral areas of the world which they colonized provided the necessary primary goods, agricultural and mineral, for consumption in the center. Contrary to some assumptions in economic theory, the international division of labor did not lead to parallel development through comparative advantage. The center states gained at the expense of the periphery. But, just as significantly, the different functions of center and peripheral societies had a profound effect on the evolution of internal social and political structures. Those which evolved in the periphery reinforced economies with a narrow range of primary exports. The interdependent nature of the world capitalist system and the qualitative transformations in that system over time make it inconceivable to think that individual nations on the periphery could somehow replicate the evolutionary experience of the now developed nations.[6]

It follows from an emphasis on global structural processes and variations in internal structural arrangements that contextual variables, at least in the long run, shape and guide the behavior of groups and individuals. It is not inappropriate attitudes which contribute to the absence of entrepreneurial behavior or to institutional arrangements reinforcing underdevelopment. Dependent, peripheral development produces an opportunity structure such that personal gain for dominant groups and entrepreneurial elements is not conducive to the collective gain of balanced development. This is a fundamental difference with much of the modernization literature. It implies that dependence analysts, though they do not articulate the point explicitly, share the classical economic theorists' view of human nature. They assume that individuals in widely different societies are capable of pursuing rational patterns of behavior; able to assess information objectively in the pursuit of utilitarian goals. What varies is not the degree of rationality, but the structural foundations of the incentive systems which, in turn, produce different forms of behavior given the same process of rational calculus. It was not attitudinal transformations which generated the rapid industrialization which developed after the Great Depression, but the need to replace imports with domestic products. Or, as Cardoso points out in his studies of entrepreneurs, it is not values which condition their behavior as much as technological dependence, state intervention in the economy, and their political weakness vis-à-vis domestic and foreign actors.[7] What appear as anomalies in the modernization literature can be accounted for by a focus on contextual processes in the dependence literature.

It is necessary to underscore the fact that dependency writers stress the importance of the "way internal and external structural components are connected" in elaborating the structural context of underdevelopment. As such, underdevelopment is not simply the result of "external constraints" on peripheral societies, nor can dependency be operationalized solely with reference to clusters of external variables.[8] Dependency in any given society is a complex set of associations in which the external dimensions are determinative in varying degrees and, indeed, internal variables may very well reinforce the pattern of external linkages. Historically, it has been rare for local interests to develop on the periphery which are capable of charting a successful policy of self-sustained development. Dominant local interests, given the nature of class arrangements emerging from the characteristics of peripheral economies, have tended to favor the preservation of rearticulation of patterns of dependency in their interests.

It is also important to note that while relations of dependency viewed historically help to explain underdevelopment, it does not follow that dependent relations today necessarily perpetuate across the board underdevelopment. With the evolution of the world system, the impact of dependent relations can change in particular contexts. This is why Cardoso, in studying contemporary Brazil, stresses the possibility of "associated-dependent development," and Sunkel and Edmundo Fuenzalida are able to envision sharp economic growth among countries most tied into the contemporary transnational system.[9] Because external-internal relations are complex, and because changes in the world system over time introduce new realities, it is indispensable to study comparatively concrete national and historical situations. As Aníbal Quijano says, "The relationships of dependency . . . take on many forms. The national societies in Latin America are dependent, as is the case with the majority of the Asian, African and some European countries. However, each case does not present identical dependency relations."[10] The dependency perspective has thus concentrated on a careful historical evaluation of the similarities and differences in the "situations of dependency" of the various Latin American countries over time implying careful attention to "preexisting conditions" in different contexts.[11]

The description of various phases in the world system and differing configurations of external-internal linkages, follow from this insistence on diachronic analysis and its application to concrete cases. The dependency perspective is primarily a historical model with no claim to "universal validity." This is why it has paid less attention to the formulation of precise theoretical constructs, such as those found in the modernization literature, and more attention to the specification of historical phases which are an integral part of the framework.

The dependency literature distinguishes between the "mercantilistic" colonial period (1500–1750), the period of "outward growth" dependent on primary exports (1750–1914), the period of the crisis of the "liberal model" (1914–1950), and the current period of "transnational capitalism."

As already noted, because of the need for raw materials and foodstuffs for the growing industrialization of England, Germany, the United States, and France, Latin American productive structures were aimed from the outset at the export market. During the colonial period, the economic specialization was imposed by the Iberian monarchies. As Bagú notes in his classic study, "Colonial production was not directed by the needs of national consumers, and not even by the interests of local producers. The lines of production were structured and transformed to conform to an order determined by the imperial metropolis. The colonial economy was consequently shaped by its complementary character. The products that did not compete with those of Spain or Portugal in the metropolitan, international or colonial markets, found tolerance or stimulus. . . ."[12] During the nineteenth century, exports were actively pursued by the politically dominant groups. The independence movement did not attempt to transform internal productive structures; it was aimed at eliminating Iberian interference in the commercialization of products to and from England and northern Europe. The logic of the productive system in this period of "outwardly directed development," in ECLA's terms, was not conducive to the creation of a large industrial sector. Economic rationality, not only of individual entrepreneurs but also of the system, dictated payments in kind and/or extremely low wages and/or the use of slavery, thus markedly limiting the internal market. At the same time, the accumulation of foreign exchange made relatively easy the acquisition of imported industrial products. Any expansion of exports was due more to political than economic factors and depended on a saleable export commodity, and plenty of land and labor, for its success.

There were, however, important differences among regions and countries. During the colonial period these are attributable to differences in colonial administrations, natural resources, and types of production.

During the nineteenth century a key difference was the degree of local elite control over productive activities for export. Though in all countries elites controlled export production initially (external commercialization was mainly under foreign control), toward the end of the century in some countries control was largely relinquished to foreign exploitation. Where this occurred, the economic role of local elites was reduced considerably, though the importance of this reduction varied depending both on the degree to which the foreign enclave displaced the local elite from the export sector and the extent to which its economic activities were diversified. Concurrently, the state bureaucracy expanded and acquired increasing importance through regulations and taxation of the enclave sector. The state thus became the principal intermediary between the local economy and the enclave, which generally had litttle *direct* internal secondary impact. Other differences, especially at the turn of the century, are the varying importance of incipient industrialization, the size and importance of middle- and working-class groups, variations in export products, natural resources, and so on.[13]

The world wars and the depression produced a crisis in the export-oriented economies through the collapse of external demand, and therefore of the capacity to import. The adoption of fiscal and monetary policies aimed at supporting the internal market and avoiding the negative effects of the external disequilibrium produced a favorable climate for the growth of an industrial sector under national auspices. The available foreign exchange was employed to acquire capital goods to substitute imports of consumer articles.[14] The early successes of the transition to what ECLA calls "inwardly directed development" depended to a large extent on the different political alliances which emerged in the various national settings, and on the characteristics of the social and political structures inherited from the precrisis period.

Thus, in the enclave situations the earliest developments were attained in Mexico and Chile, where middle- and lower-class groups allied in supporting state development policies, ultimately strengthening the urban bourgeoisie. The alliance was successful in Chile because of the importance of middle-class parties which emerged during the final period of export-oriented development, and the early consolidation of a trade union movement. The antecedents of the Mexican situation are to be found in the destruction of agricultural elites during the revolution. Such structural conditions were absent in other enclave situations (Bolivia, Perú, Venezuela, and Central America) where the internal development phase began later under new conditions of dependence, though in some cases with similar political alliances (Bolivia, Venezuela, Guatemala, Costa Rica). Throughout the crisis period agrarian-based and largely nonexporting groups were able to remain in power, appealing in some cases to military governments, and preserving the political scheme that characterized the export-oriented period.

In the nonenclave situations, considerable industrial growth was attained in Argentina and Brazil. In the former, export-oriented entrepreneurs had invested considerably in production for the internal market and the contraction of the export sector only accentuated this trend. In Brazil the export-oriented agrarian groups collapsed with the crisis and the state, as in Chile and Mexico, assumed a major developmental role with the support of a complex alliance of urban entrepreneurs, nonexport agrarian elites, popular sectors, and middle-class groups. In Colombia the export-oriented agrarian elites remained in power and did not foster significant internal industrialization until the fifties.[15]

The import substituting industrialization attained greatest growth in Argentina, Brazil, and Mexico. It soon, however, reached its limits, given the parameters under which it was realized. Since capital goods for the establishment of industrial parks were acquired in the central nations, the success of the policy ultimately depended on adequate foreign exchange supplies. After reaching maximum growth through the accumulation of foreign exchange during World War II, the industrialization programs could only continue—given the available political options—on the basis of an increased external debt and further reliance on foreign investments. This accumulation of foreign reserves permitted the success of the national-populist alliances in Argentina and Brazil which gave the workers greater welfare while maintaining investments. The downfall of Perón and the suicide of Vargas symbolized the end of this easy period of import substitution.

But the final blow to "import substitution" industrialization came not from difficulties in the periphery but further transformations in the center which have led, in Sunkel's term, to the creation of a new "transnational" system. With rapid economic recovery the growing multinational corporations sought new markets and cheaper production sites for their increasingly technological manufacturing process. Dependency consequently acquired a "new character" as dos Santos noted, which would have a profound effect on Latin America. Several processes were involved resulting in (1) the investment of centrally based corporations in manufactures within the periphery for sales in its internal market or, as Cardoso and Enzo Faletto note, the "intenationalisation of the internal market"; (2) a new international division of labor in which the periphery acquires capital goods, technology, and raw materials from the central nations, and export profits, along with its traditional raw materials and a few manufactured items produced by miltinational subsidiaries; and (3) a denationalization of the older import substituting industries established originally.[16] Although the "new dependence" is in evidence throughout the continent, the process has asserted itself more clearly in the largest internal markets such as Brazil, where the weakness of the trade-union movement (the comparison with Argentina in this respect is instructive) coupled with authoritarian political structures has created a singularly favorable investment climate.

In subsequent and more recent works writers in the dependency framework have pursued different strategies of research. Generally speaking, the early phases of the historical process have received less attention, though the contribution of Immanuel Wallerstein to an understanding of the origins of the world system is a major addition to the literature.[17] Most writers have preferred to focus on the current "new situation" of dependence. Some have devoted more attention to an effort at elaborating the place of dependent capitalism as a contribution to the Marxist analysis of capitalist society. Scholars in this vein tend to argue more forcefully than others that dependent capitalism is impossible and that socialism provides the only historically viable alternative.[18] Others have focused more on the analysis of concrete cases of dependence, elaborating in some detail the various interconnections between domestic and foreign forces, and noting the possibility of different kinds of dependent development.[19] Still others have turned their attention to characterizing the nature of the new capitalist system, with particular emphasis on the emergence of a "transnational system" which is rendering more complex and problematic the old distinctions of center and periphery.[20] Particularly for the last two tendencies, the emphasis is on the design of new empirical studies while attempting to systematize further some of the propositions implicit in the conceptual framework.

Summary and Conclusions

Modernization and dependency are two different perspectives each claiming to provide conceptual and analytical tools capable of explaining the relative underdevelopment of Latin America. The object of inquiry is practically the only thing that these two competing "visions" have in common, as they differ substantially not only on fundamental assumptions, but also on methodological implications and strategies for research.

Though there are variations in the literature, the *level of analysis* of a substantial tradition in the modernization perspective, and the one which informs most reflections on Latin America, is behavioral or microsociological. The primary focus is on individuals or aggregates of individuals, their values, attitudes, and beliefs. The dependency perspective, by contrast, is structural or macrosociological. Its focus is on the mode of production, patterns of international trade, political and economic linkages between elites in peripheral and central countries, group and class alliances and conflicts, and so on. Both perspectives are concerned with the process of development in national societies. However, for the modernization writer the national society is the basic *unit of analysis*, while the writer in a dependence framework considers the global system and its various forms of interaction with national societies as the primary object of inquiry.

For the dependency perspective, the *time dimension* is a crucial aspect of what is fundamentally a historical model. Individual societies cannot be presumed to be able to replicate the evolution of other societies because the very transformation of an interrelated world system may preclude such an option. The modernization potential of individual societies must be seen in light of changes over time in the interactions between external and internal variables. The modernization perspective is obviously concerned about the origins of traditional and modern values; but, the time dimension is not fundamental to the explanatory pretensions of a model which claims "universal validity." Without knowing the source of modernity-inhibiting characteristics, it is still possible to identify them by reference to their counterparts in developing contexts.

At the root of the differences between the two perspectives is a fundamentally different *perception of human nature*. Dependency assumes that human behavior in economic matters is a "constant." Individuals will behave differently in different contexts not because they are different but because the contexts are different. The insistence on structures and, in the final analysis, on the broadest structural category of all, the world system, follows logically from the view that opportunity structures condition human behavior. Modernizationists, on the other hand, attribute the lack of certain behavioral patterns to the "relativity" of human behavior; to the fact that cultural values and beliefs, regardless of opportunity structures, underlie the patterns of economic action. Thus, the *conception of change* in the modernization perspective is a product of innovations which result from the adoption of modern attitudes among elites, and eventually followers. Though some modernization theorists are now more pessimistic about the development potential of such changes, modernizing beliefs are a prerequisite for development. For dependency analysts the conception of change is different. Change results from the realignment of dependency relations over time. Whether or not development occurs and how it occurs is subject to controversy. Given the rapid evolution of the world system, dependent development is possible in certain contexts, not in others. Autonomy, through a break in relations of dependency, may not lead to development of the kind already arrived at in the developed countries because of the inability to recreate the same historical conditions, but it might lead to a different kind of development stressing different values. Thus, the *prescription for change* varies substantially in the dependency perspective depending on the ideological outlook of particular authors. It is not a logical consequence of the historical model. In the modernization perspective the prescription for change follows more automatically from the assumptions of the model, implying greater consensus.

From a methodological point of view the modernization perspective is much more parsimonious than its counterpart. And the focus of much of the literature on the microsociological level makes it amenable to the elaboration of precise explanatory propositions such as those of David McClelland or Everett Hagen. Dependency, by contrast, is more descriptive and its macrosociological formulations are much less subject to translation into a simple set of explanatory propositions. Many aspects of dependency, and particularly the linkages between external phenomena and internal class and power relations are unclear and need to be studied with more precision and care. For this reason the dependency perspective is an "approach" to the study of underdevelopment rather than a "theory." And yet, precisely because modernization theory relies on a simple conceptual framework and a reductionist approach, it is far less useful for the study of a complex phenomenon such as development or underdevelopment.

But the strengths of the dependency perspective lie not only in its consideration of a richer body of evidence and a broader range of phenomena, it is also more promising from a methodological point of view. The modernization perspective has fundamental flaws which make it difficult to provide for a fair test of its own assumptions. It will be recalled that the modernization perspective draws on a model with "universal validity" which assumes that traditional values are not conducive to modern behavioral patterns of action. Given that underdevelopment, on the basis of various economic and social indicators, is an objective datum, the research task becomes one of identifying modernizing values and searching for their opposites in underdeveloped contexts.

In actual research efforts, the modernity-inhibiting characteristics are often "deduced" from impressionistic observation. This is the case with much of the political science literature on Latin America. However, more "rigorous" methods, such as survey research, have also been employed, particularly in studies of entrepreneurial activity. Invariably, whether through deduction or survey research, less appropriate values for modernization such as "arielismo" (a concern for transcendental as opposed to material values) or "low-achievement" (lack of risk-taking attitudes) have been identified thus "confirming" the hypothesis that traditional values contribute to underdevelopment. If by chance the use of control groups should establish little or no difference in attitudes in a developed and underdeveloped context, the research instrument can be considered to be either faulty or the characteristics tapped not the appropriate ones for identifying traditional attitudes. The latter alternative might lead to the "discovery" of a new "modernity of tradition" literature or of greater flexibility than anticipated in traditional norms or of traditional residuals in the developed country.

The problem with the model and its behavioral level of analysis is that the explanation for underdevelopment is part of the preestablished conceptual framework. It is already "known" that in backward areas the modernity-inhibiting characteristics play the dominant role, otherwise the areas would not be backward. As such, the test of the hypothesis involves a priori acceptance of the very hypothesis up for verification, with empirical evidence gathered solely in an illustrative manner. The focus on individuals simply does not permit consideration of a broader range of contextual variables which might lead to invalidating the assumptions. Indeed, the modernity of tradition literature, which has pointed to anomalies in the use of the tradition modernity "polarities," is evidence of how such a perspective can fall victim to the "and so" fallacy. Discrepancies are accounted for not by a reformulation, but by adding a new definition or a new corollary to the preexisting conceptual framework.

Much work needs to be done within a dependency perspective to clarify its concepts and causal interrelationships, as well as to assess its capacity to explain social processes in various parts of peripheral societies. And yet the dependency approach appears to have a fundamental advantage over the modernization perspective: It is open to historically grounded conceptualization in underdeveloped contexts, while modernization is locked into an illustrative methodological style by virtue of its very assumptions.

Notes

1. See Osvaldo Sunkel, "Politica nacional de desarrollo y dependencia externa," *Estudios Internacionales*, I (April 1967). For reviews of the dependency literature see Norman Girvan, "The Development of Dependency Economics in the Caribbean and Latin America: Review and Comparison," *Social and Economic Studies*, XXII (March 1973); Ronald H. Chilcote, "A Critical Synthesis of the Dependency Literature," *Latin American Perspectives*, I (Spring 1974); and Phillip O'Brien, "A Critique of Latin American Theories of Dependence," in I. Oxaal, et al., eds. *Beyond the Sociology of Development* (London, 1975).

2. Osvaldo Sunkel and Pedro Paz, *El subdesarrollo latinoamericano y la teoría del desarrollo* (Mexico, 1970), p. 6.

3. Theotonio dos Santos, "La crisis del desarrollo y las relaciones de dependencia en América Latina," in H. Jaguaribe, et al., eds. *La dependencia político-económica de América Latina* (Mexico, 1970), p. 180. See also his *Dependencia y cambio social* (Santiago, 1970) and *Socialismo o Fascismo: El nuevo carácter de la dependencia y el dilema latinoamericano* (Buenos Aires, 1972).

4. Sunkel and Paz, p. 39; Fernando Henrique Cardoso and Enzo Faletto, *Dependencia y desarrollo en América Latina* (Mexico, 1969).

5. This is the problem with the studies by Robert Kaufman, et al., "A Preliminary Test of the Theory of Dependency," *Comparative Politics*, VII (April 1975), 303–30, and C. Chase-Dunn, "The Effects of International Economic Dependence on Development and Inequality: A Cross National Study," *American Sociological Review*, XL (December 1975). It is interesting to note that Marxist scholars make the same mistake. They point to features in the dependency literature such as unemployment, marginalization etc., noting that they are not peculiar to peripheral countries but characterize capitalist countries in general. Thus "dependence" is said to have no explanatory value beyond a Marxist theory of capitalist society. See Sanyaya Lall, "Is Dependence a Useful Concept in Analyzing Underdevelopment?," *World Development*, III (November 1975) and Theodore Weisscopf, "Dependence as an Explanation of Underdevelopment: A Critique," (paper presented at the Sixth Annual Latin American Studies As-

sociation Meeting, Atlanta, Georgia, 1976). The point of dependency analysis is not the relative mix at one point in time of certain identifiable factors but the evolution over time of structural relations which help to explain the differential development of capitalism in different parts of the world. As a historical model it cannot be tested with cross national data. For an attempt to differentiate conceptually contemporary capitalism of the core and peripheral countries, and thus more amenable to such criticism, see Samir Amin, *Accumulation on a World Scale* (New York, 1974).

6. Some authors have criticized the focus of the literature on the evolution of the world capitalist system. David Ray, for example, has argued that "soviet satellites" are also in a dependent and unequal relationship vis-à-vis the Soviet Union and that the key variable should not be capitalism but "political power." Robert Packenham has also argued that the most important critique of the dependency literature is that it does not consider the implications of "power." See Ray, "The Dependency Model of Latin American Underdevelopment: Three Basic Fallacies," *Journal of Interamerican Studies and World Affairs*, XV (February 1973) and Packenham, "Latin American Dependency Theories: Strengths and Weaknesses," (paper presented to the Harvard-MIT Joint Seminar on Political Development, February 1974), especially pp. 16–17, 54. This criticism misses the point completely. It is not power relations today which cause underdevelopment, but the historical evolution of a world economic system which led to economic specialization more favorable to some than others. It is precisely this concern with the evolution of world capitalism which has led to the preoccupation in the dependency literature with rejecting interpretations stressing the "feudal" rather than "capitalist" nature of colonial and postcolonial Latin American agriculture. On this point see Sergio Bagú, *Economia de la Sociedad Colonial* (Buenos Aires, 1949); Luis Vitale, "América Latina: Feudal o Capitalista?," *Revista Estrategia*, III (1966) and *Interpretación Marxista de la historia de Chile* (Santiago, 1967); and E. Laclau, "Feudalism and Capitalism in Latin America," *New Left Review*, LXVII (May–July 1971). A brilliant recent exposition of the importance of studying the evolution of the capitalist world system in order to understand underdevelopment which focuses more on the center states than on the periphery is Immanuel Wallerstein, *The Modern World System: Capitalist Agriculture and the Origins of the European World Economy in the Sixteenth Century* (New York, 1974).

7. Cardoso, *Empresário industrial e desenvolvimento econômico no Brazil* (São Paulo, 1964) and *Ideologías de la burguesia industrial en sociedades dependientes* (Mexico, 1971).

8. Cardoso and Faletto, *Dependencia y desarrollo*, p. 20. Indeed, Cardoso argues that the distinction between external and internal is "metaphysical." See his "Teoría de la dependencia o análisis de situaciones concretas de dependencia?," *Revista Latinoamericana de Ciencia Política*, I (December 1970), 404. The ontology implicit in such an analysis is the one of "internal relations." See Bertell Ollman, *Alienation: Marx's Conception of Man in Capitalist Society* (London, 1971). This point is important because both André Gunder Frank and the early ECLA literature was criticized for their almost mechanistic relationship between external and internal variables. Frank acknowledges this problem and tries to answer his critics in *Lumpenbourgeoisie and Lumpendevelopment* (New York, 1967). "Tests" of dependency theory also attribute an excessively mechanical dimension to the relationship. See Kaufman, et al., "A Preliminary Test of the Theory of Dependency."

9. Cardoso, "Associated Dependent Development: Theoretical Implications," in Alfred Stepan, ed. *Authoritarian Brazil* (New Haven, 1973), and Sunkel and Edmundo Fuenzalida, "Transnational Capitalism and National Development," in José J. Villamil, ed. *Transnational Capitalism and National Development* (London, forthcoming). It is thus incorrect to argue that dependency analysts ignore the evidence of certain kinds of economic growth. For fallacies in the dependency literature see Cardoso "Las contradicciones del desarrollo asociado," *Desarrollo Económico*, IV (April-June 1974).

10. Aníbal Quijano, "Dependencia, Cambio Social y Urbanización en América Latina," in Cardoso and F. Weffort, eds. *América Latina: Ensayos de interpretación sociológico político* (Santiago, 1970).

11. Cardoso and Faletto, *Dependencia y desarrollo*, pp. 19–20; Sunkel and Paz, *El subdesarrollo latinoamericano*, pp. 5, 9.

12. Bagú, *Economía de la sociedad colonial*, pp. 122–23.

13. On industrialization see A. Dorfman, *La industrialisación en América Latina y las políticas de fomento* (Mexico, 1967).

14. See M. de C. Tavares, "El proceso de sustitución de importaciones como modelo de desarrollo reciente en América Latina," in Andres Bianchi, ed. *América Latina: Ensayos de interpretación económica* (Santiago, 1969).

15. For detailed discussions of nonenclave versus enclave situations see Cardoso and Faletto, and Sunkel and Paz.

16. Sunkel "Capitalismo transnacional y desintegración nacional en América Latina," *Estudios Internacionales*, IV (January–March 1971) and "Big Business and Dependencia: A Latin American View," *Foreign Affairs*, L (April 1972); Cardoso and Faletto; Dos Santos, *El nuevo carácter de la dependencia* (Santiago, 1966).

17. Wallerstein, *The Modern World System*.

18. V. Bambirra. *Capitalismo dependiente latinoamericano* (Santiago, 1973); R. M. Marini, *Subdesarrollo y revolución* (Mexico, 1969); F. Hinkelammert, *El subdesarrollo latinoamericano: un caso de desarrollo capitalista* (Santiago, 1970).

19. Cardoso, "Teoría de la dependencia." A recent trend in dependency writings attempts to explain the current wave of authoritarianism in Latin America as a result of economic difficulties created by the exhaustion of the easy import substituting industrialization. The new situation leads to a process of development led by the state and the multinational corporations which concentrates income toward the top, increases the levels of capital accumulation, and expands heavy industry; the old populist alliances can therefore no longer be maintained. See Dos Santos, *Socialismo o fascismo: el nuevo carácter de la dependencia y el dilema latinoamericano* (Buenos Aires, 1972); Guillermo O'Donnell, *Modernization and Bureaucratic Authoritarianism: Studies in Latin American Politics* (Berkeley, 1973); Atilio Borón, "El fascismo como categoría histórica: en torno al problema de las dictaduras en América Latina," *Revista Mexicana de Sociología*, XXXIV (April–June 1977); the effects of this situation on labor are explored in Kenneth P. Erickson and Patrick Peppe, "Dependent Capitalist Development, U.S. Foreign Policy, and Repression of the Working Class in Chile and Brazil," *Latin American Perspectives*, III (Winter 1976). However, in the postscript to their 1968 book, Cardoso and Faletto caution against adopting an excessively mechanistic view on this point, against letting "economism kill history": Cardoso and Faletto, "Estado y proceso político en América Latina," *Revista Mexicana de Sociología*, XXXIV (April–June 1977), 383. Articles with dependency perspective

appear frequently in the *Revista Mexicana de Sociología* as well as in *Latin American Perspectives*.

20. Sunkel, "Capitalismo transnacional y desintegración nacional en América Latina," and Sunkel and Fuenzalida, "Transnational Capitalism and National Development."

13. The Present State of the Debate on World Inequality

Immanuel Wallerstein

Immanuel Wallerstein is generally considered the driving intellectual force behind the "world-system" school of thought. He has articulated his view of development in a series of books and articles, perhaps the best known of which is The Modern World-System: Capitalist Agriculture and the Origins of the European World-Economy in the Sixteenth Century *(Academic Press, 1974). Wallerstein sees dependency theory as a sub-set of his broader world-system perspective. In this chapter, he attempts to explain the existence of the gap between rich and poor countries by arguing that all states form part of a capitalist world economy in which the existence of differences in wealth is not an anomaly but rather a natural outcome of the fundamental processes driving that economy. According to this perspective, the gap between rich and poor ultimately will disappear, but only when the capitalist world system that has been in place since the sixteenth century itself disappears.*

It has never been a secret from anyone that some have more than others. And in the modern world at least, it is no secret that some countries have more than other countries. In short, world inequality is a phenomenon about which most men and most groups are quite conscious.

I do not believe that there has ever been a time when these inequalities were unquestioned. That is to say, people or groups who have more have always felt the need to justify this fact, if for no other reason than to try to convince those who have less that they should accept this fact with relative docility. These ideologies of the advantaged have had varying degrees of success over time. The history of the world is one of a constant series of revolts against inequality—whether that of one people or nation vis-à-vis another or of one class within a geographical area against another.

This statement is probably true of all of recorded history, indeed of all historical events, at least since the Neolithic Revolution. What has changed with the advent of the modern world in the sixteenth century

Reprinted with permission from *World Inequality: Origins and Perspectives on the World System*, edited by Immanual Wallerstein, pp. 12–28. Montreal: Black Rose Books, 1975.

is neither the existence of inequalities nor of the felt need to justify them by means of ideological constructs. What has changed is that even those who defend the "inevitability" of inequalities in the present feel the need to argue that eventually, over time, these inequalities will disappear, or at the very least diminish considerably in scope. Another way of saying this is that of the three dominant ideological currents of the modern world—conservatism, liberalism, and Marxism—two at least (liberalism and Marxism) are committed in theory and the abstract to egalitarianism as a principle. The third, conservatism, is not, but conservatism is an ideology that has been very much on the defensive ever since the French Revolution. The proof of this is that most conservatives decline to fly the banner openly but hide their conservative ideas under the mantle of liberalism or occasionally even Marxism.

Surely it is true that in the universities of the world in the twentieth century, and in other expressions of intellectuals, the contending ideologies have been one variant or another of liberalism and Marxism. (Remember at this point we are talking of ideologies and not of political movements. Both "liberal" parties and social democratic parties in the twentieth century have drawn on liberal ideologies.)

One of the most powerful thrusts of the eighteenth-century Enlightenment, picked up by most nineteenth- and twentieth-century thought-systems, was the assumption of progress, reformulated later as evolution. In the context of the question of equality, evolution was interpreted as the process of moving from an imperfect, unequal allocation of privileges and resources to some version of equality. There was considerable argument about how to define equality. (Reflect on the different meanings of "equality of opportunity" and "to each according to his needs.") There was considerable disagreement about who or what were the obstacles to this desired state of equality. And there was fundamental discord about how to transform the world from its present imperfection to the desired future, primarily between the advocates of gradualism based on education to advocates of revolution based on the use at some point in time of violence.

I review this well-known history of modern ideas simply to underline where I think our current debates are simply the latest variant of now classic debates and where I think some new issues have been raised which make these older formulations outdated.

If one takes the period 1945–1960, both politically and intellectually, we have in many ways the apogee of the liberal-Marxist debate. The world was politically polarized in the so-called cold war. There were two camps. One called itself the "free world" and argued that it and it alone upheld the first part of the French Revolution's trilogy, that of "liberty." It argued that its economic system offered the hope over time of approximating "equality" through a path which it came to call "economic development" or sometimes just "development." It argued too that it was gradually achieving "fraternity" by means of education and political reform (such as the 1954 Supreme Court decision in the United States, ending the legality of segregation).

The other camp called itself the "socialist world" and argued that it and it alone represented the three objectives of the French Revolution and hence the interests of the people of the world. It argued that when movements inspired by these ideas would come to power in all non-"socialist" countries, (and however they came to power,) each would enact legislation along the same lines and by this process the whole world would become "socialist" and the objective would be achieved.

These somewhat simplistic ideological statements were of course developed in much more elaborate form by the intellectuals. It has become almost traditional (but I think nonetheless just) to cite W. W. Rostow's *The Stages of Economic Growth* as a succinct, sophisticated, and relatively pure expression of the dominant liberal ideology which informed the thinking of the political leadership of the United States and its Western allies. Rostow showed no modesty in his subtitle, which was "a non-Communist Manifesto."

His basic thesis is no doubt familiar to most persons interested in these problems. Rostow saw the process of change as a series of stages through which each national unit had to go. They were the stages through which Rostow felt Great Britain had gone, and Great Britain was the crucial example since it was defined as being the first state to embark on the evolutionary path of the modern industrial world. The inference, quite overtly drawn, was that this path was a model, to be copied by other states. One could then analyze what it took to move from one stage to another, why some nations took longer than others, and could prescribe (like a physician) what a nation must do to hurry along its process of "growth." I will not review what ideological function such a formulation served. This has been done repeatedly and well. Nonetheless, this viewpoint, somewhat retouched, still informs the developmentalist ideas of the major Western governments as well as that of international agencies. I consider Lester Pearson's "Partners in Progress" report in the direct line of this analytic framework.

In the socialist world in this period there was no book quite the match of Rostow's. What there was instead was an encrusted version of evolutionary Marxism which also saw rigid stages through which every state or geographical entity had to go. The differences were that the stages covered longer historical time and the model country was the USSR. These are the stages known as slavery-feudalism-capitalism-socialism. The absurdities of the rigid formulation which dates from the 1930s and the inappropriateness of applying this on a *national* level have been well argued recently by an Indian Marxist intellectual, Irfan Habib, who argues not only the meaningfulness of the concept of the "Asiatic mode of production" but also the illogic of insisting that the various historical modes of extracting a surplus must each, necessarily, occur in all countries and follow in a specific order. Habib argues:

The materialist conception of history need not necessarily prescribe a set universal periodisation, since what it essentially does is to formulate an analytic method for the development of class societies, and any periodi-sation, theoretically, serves as no more than the illustration of the application of such a method. . . . The crucial thing is the definition of principal contradiction (i.e., class-contradictions) in a society, the marking out of factors responsible for intensifying them, and the deliniation of the shaping of the social order, when a particular contradiction is resolved. It is possible that release from the set P-S-F-C- pattern [primitive communism-slavery-feudalism-capitalism] may lead Marxists to apply themselves better to this task, since they would no longer be obliged to look for the same "fun-damental laws of the epoch" (a favourite Soviet term), or "prime mover," as premised for the supposedly corresponding European epoch.[1]

I give this excerpt from Habib because I very much agree with his fundamental point that this version of Marxist thought, so prevalent between 1945 and 1965, is a sort of "mechanical copying" of liberal views. Basically, the analysis is the same as that represented by Rostow except that the names of the stages are changed and the model country has shifted from Great Britain to the USSR. I will call this approach the developmentalist perspective, as espoused either by liberals or Marxists.

There is another perspective that has slowly pushed its way into public view during the 1960s. It has no commonly accepted name, in part because the early formulations of this point of view have often been confused, partial, or unclear. It was first widely noticed in the thinking of the Latin American structuralists (such as Raúl Prebisch and Celso Furtado) and those allied to them elsewhere (such as Dudley Sears). It later took the form of arguments such as the "development of underdevelopment" (A. G. Frank, in the heritage of Paul Baran's *The Political Economy of Growth*), the "structure of dependence" (Theotonio Dos Santos), "unequal exchange" (Arghiri Emmanuel), "accumulation of world capital" (Samir Amin), "sub-imperialism" (Ruy Mauro Marini). It also surfaced in the Chinese Cultural Revolution as Mao's concept of the continuity of the class struggle under socialist regimes in single countries.[2]

What all these concepts have in common is a critique of the devel-opmentalist perspective. Usually they make it from a Marxist tradition but it should be noted that some of the critics, such as Furtado, come from a liberal heritage. It is no accident that this point of view has been expressed largely by persons from Asia, Africa and Latin America or by those others particularly interested in these regions (such as Umberto Melotti of *Terzo Mondo*).[3]

I would like to designate this point of view the "world-system perspective." I mean by that term that it is based on the assumption, explicitly or implicitly, that the modern world comprises a single capitalist world-economy, which has emerged historically since the sixteenth century and which still exists today. It follows from such a premise that national states are *not* societies that have separate, parallel histories, but parts of a whole reflecting that whole. To the extent that stages exist, they exist for the system as a whole. To be sure, since different parts of the world play and have played differing roles in the capitalist world-economy, they have dramatically different internal socio-economic profiles and hence distinctive politics. But to understand the internal class contradictions and political struggles of a particular state, we must first situate it in the world-economy. We can then understand the ways in which various political and cultural thrusts may be efforts to alter or preserve a position within this world-economy which is to the advantage or disadvantage of particular groups located within a particular state.[4]

What thus distinguishes the developmentalist and the world-system perspective is not liberalism versus Marxism nor evolutionism vs. something else (since both are essentially evolutionary). Rather I would locate the distinction in two places. One is in mode of thought. To put it in Hegelian terms, the developmentalist perspective is mechanical, whereas the world-system perspective is dialectical. I mean by the latter term that at every point in the analysis, one asks not what is the formal structure but what is the consequence for both the whole and the parts of maintaining or changing a certain structure at that particular point in time, given the totality of particular positions of that moment in time. Intelligent analysis demands knowledge of the complex texture of social reality (historical concreteness) within a long-range perspective that observes trends and forces of the world-system, which can explain what underlies and informs the diverse historically concrete phenomena. If synchronic comparisons and abstracted generalizations are utilized, it is only as heuristic devices in search of a truth that is ever contemporary and hence ever-changing.

This distinction of scientific methodology is matched by a distinction of praxis, of the politics of the real world. For what comes through as the second great difference between the two perspectives (the developmentalist and the world-system) is the prognosis for action. This is the reason why the latter perspective has emerged primarily from the intellectuals of the Third World. The developmentalist perspective not only insists that the model is to be found in the old developed countries (whether Great Britain, USA, or USSR) but also that the fundamental international political issues revolve around the relations among the hegemonic powers of the world. From a world-system perspective, there are no "models" (a mechanical notion) and the relations of the hegemonic powers are only one of many issues that confront the world-system.

The emergence of the world-system perspective is a consequence of the dramatic challenge to European political domination of the world which has called into question all Europo-centric constructions of social reality. But intellectual evolution itself is seldom dramatic. The restructuring of the allocation of power in the world has made itself felt in the realm of ideas, particularly in the hegemonic areas of the world, via a growing malaise that intellectuals in Europe (including of course North America) have increasingly felt about the validity of their answers to a series of "smaller" questions—smaller, that is, than the nature of the world-system as such.

Let us review successively six knotty questions to which answers from a developmentalist perspective have increasingly seemed inadequate.

Why have certain world-historical events of the last two centuries taken place where and when they have? The most striking "surprise," at the moment it occurred and ever since, is the Russian Revolution. As we all know, neither Marx nor Lenin nor anyone else thought that a "socialist revolution" would occur in Russia earlier than anywhere else. Marx had more or less predicted Great Britain as the likely candidate, and after Marx's death, the consensus of expectation in the international socialist movement was that it would occur in Germany. We know that even after 1917 almost all the leading figures of the Communist Party of the Soviet Union (CPSU) expected that the "revolution" would have to occur quickly in Germany if the Soviet regime was to survive. There was however no socialist revolution in Germany and nonetheless the Soviet regime did survive.

We do not want for explanations of this phenomenon, but we do lack convincing answers. Of course, there exists an explanation that turns Marx on his head and argues that socialist revolutions occur not in the so-called "advanced capitalist" countries but precisely in "backward" countries. But this is in such blatant contradiction with other parts of the developmentalist perspective that its proponents are seldom willing to state it baldly, even less defend it openly.

Nor is the Russian Revolution the only anomaly. There is a long-standing debate about the "exceptionalism" of the United States. How can we explain that the USA replaced Great Britain as the hegemonic industrial power of the world, and in the process managed to avoid giving birth to a serious internal socialist movement? And if the USA could avoid socialism, why could not Brazil or Russia or Canada? Seen from the perspective of 1800, it would have been a bold social scientist who would have predicted the particular success of the USA.

Again there have been many explanations. There is the "frontier" theory. There is the theory that underlines the absence of a previously entrenched "feudal" class. There is the theory of the USA as Britain's "junior partner" who overtook the senior. But all of these theories are precisely "exceptionalist" theories, contradicting the developmentalist paradigm. And furthermore, some of these variables apply to other countries where they did not seem to have the same consequences.

We could go on. I will mention two more briefly. For a long time, Great Britain's primacy (the "first" industrial power) has been unquestioned. But was Britain the "first" and if so why was she? This is a question that only recently has been seriously adumbrated. In April

1974 at an international colloquium held here in Montreal on the theme of "Failed Transitions to Industrialism: The Case of 17th Century Netherlands and Renaissance Italy," one view put forward quite strongly was that neither Italy nor the Netherlands was the locus of the Industrial Revolution precisely because they were too far *advanced* economically. What a striking blow to a developmentalist paradigm.

And lastly one should mention the anomaly of Canada: a country which economically falls into a category below that of the world's leading industrial producers in structural terms, yet nonetheless is near the very top of the list in per capita income. This cannot be plausibly explained from a developmentalist perspective.

If the world has been "developing" or "progressing" over the past few centuries, how do we explain the fact that in many areas things seem to have gotten worse, not better? Worse in many ways, ranging from standard of living, to the physical environment, to the quality of life. And more to the point, worse in some places but better in others. I refer not merely to such contemporary phenomena as the so-called "growing gap" between the industrialized countries and the Third World, but also to such earlier phenomena as the deindustrialization of many areas of the world (starting with the widely known example of the Indian textile industry in the late eighteenth and early nineteenth century).

You may say that this contradicts the liberal version of the developmentalist perspective but not its Marxist version, since "polarization" was seen as part of the process of change. True enough, except that "polarization" was presumably within countries and not between them. Furthermore, it is not clear that it is "polarization" that has occurred. While the rich have gotten richer and the poor have gotten poorer, there is surely a fairly large group of countries now somewhere in between on many economic criteria, to cite such politically diverse examples as Mexico, Italy, Czechoslovakia, Iran, and South Africa.

Furthermore, we witness in the 1970s a dramatic shift in the distribution of the profit and the international terms of trade of oil (and possibly other raw materials). You may say it is because of the increased political sophistication and strength of the Arab world. No doubt this has occurred, but is this an explanation? I remind this group that the last moment of time in which there was a dramatic amelioration of world terms of trade of primary products was in the period 1897–1913, a moment which represented in political terms the apogee of European colonial control of the world.

Once again it is not that there are not a large number of explanations for the rise in oil prices. It is rather that I find these explanations, for what they're worth, in contradiction with a developmentalist perspective.

Why are there "regressions?" In 1964, S. N. Eisenstadt published an article entitled "Breakdowns of Modernization," in which he discussed the fact that there seemed to be cases of "reversal" of regimes to "a lower, less flexible level of political and social differentiation. . . ."[5]

In seeking to explain the origins of such "reversals," Eisenstadt restricted himself to hesitant hypotheses:

> The problem of why in Turkey, Japan, Mexico, and Russia there emerge in the initial stages of modernization elites with orientations to change and ability to implement relatively effective policies, while they did not develop in these initial phases in Indonesia, Pakistan, or Burma, or why elites with similar differences tended to develop also in later stages of modernization, is an extremely difficult one and constitutes one of the most baffling problems in comparative sociological analysis. There are but four available indications to deal with this problem. Very tentatively, it may perhaps be suggested that to some extent it has to do with the placement of these elites in the preceding social structure, with the extent of their internal cohesiveness, and of the internal transformation of their own value orientation.[6]

As is clear, Eisenstadt's tentative explanation is to be found in anterior factors operating internally in the state. This calls into question the concept of stages through which all not only must pass but all *can* pass, but it leaves intact the state framework as the focus of analysis and explanation. This of course leads us logically to ask how these anterior factors developed. Are they pure historical accident?

Similarly, after the political rebellion of Tito's Yugoslavia against the USSR, the latter began to accuse Yugoslavia of "revisionism" and of returning to capitalism. Later, China took up the same theme against the USSR.

But how can we explain how this happens? There are really two varieties of explanation from a developmentalist perspective. One is to say that "regression" seems to have occurred, but that in fact "progress" had never taken place. The leaders of a movement, whether a nationalist movement or a socialist movement, only pretended to favor change. In fact they were really always "neocolonialist" stooges or "revisionists" at heart. Such an explanation has partial truth, but it seems to me to place too much on "false consciousness" and to fail to analyze movements in their immediate and continuing historical contexts.

The second explanation of "regression" is a change of heart—"betrayal." Yes, but once again, how come sometimes, but not always? Are we to explain large-scale social phenomena on the basis of the accident of the biographic histories of the particular leaders involved? I cannot accept this, for leaders remain leaders in the long run only if their personal choices reflect wider social pressures.

If the fundamental paradigm of modern history is a series of parallel national processes, how do we explain the persistence of nationalism, indeed quite often its primacy, as a political force in the modern world? Developmentalists who are liberals deplore nationalism or explain it away as a transitional "integrating" phenomenon. Marxists who are developmentalists are even more embarrassed. If the class struggle is primary—that is, implicitly the intra-national class struggle—how do we explain the fact that the slogan of the Cuban revolution is "Patria o muerte—venceremos?" And how could we explain this even more astonishing quotation from Kim Il Sung, the leader of the Democratic People's Republic of Korea:

> The homeland is a veritable mother for everyone. We cannot live nor be happy outside of our homeland. Only the flourishing and prosperity of our homeland will permit us to go down the path to happiness. The best sons and daughters of our people, all without exception, were first of all ardent patriots. It was to recover their homeland that Korean Communists struggled, before the Liberation, against Japanese imperialism despite every difficulty and obstacle.[7]

And if internal processes are so fundamental, why has not the reality of international workers' solidarity been greater? Remember World War I.

As before, there are many explanations for the persistence of nationalism. I merely observe that all these explanations have to *explain away* the primacy of internal national processes. Or to put it another way, for developmentalists nationalism is sometimes good, sometimes bad. But when it is the one or the other, it is ultimately explained by developmentalists in an ad hoc manner, adverting to its meaning for the world-system.

An even more difficult problem for the developmentalists has been the recrudescence of nationalist movements in areas smaller than that of existing states. And it is not Biafra or Bangladesh that is an intellectual problem, because the usual manner of accounting for secessionist movements in Third World countries has been the failure to attain the stage of "national integration."

No, the surprise has been in the industrialized world: Blacks in the USA, Québec in Canada, Occitania in France, the Celts in Great Britain, and lurking in the background the nationalities question in the USSR. It is not that any of these "nationalisms" is new. They are all long-standing themes of political and cultural conflict in all these countries. The surprise has been that, as of say 1945 or even 1960, most persons in these countries, using a developmentalist paradigm, regarded these movements or claims as remnants of a dying past, destined to diminish still further in vitality. And lo, a phoenix reborn.

The explanations are there. Some cry, anachronism—but if so, then the question remains, how come such a flourishing anachronism? Some say, loud shouting but little substance, a last bubble of national integration. Perhaps, but the intellectual and organizational development of these ethno-national movements seem to have moved rapidly and ever more firmly in a direction quite opposite to national integration. In any case, what in the developmentalist paradigm explains this phenomenon?

One last question, which is perhaps only a reformulation of the previous five. How is it that the "ideal types" of the different versions of the developmentalist perspective all seem so far from empirical reality? Who has not had the experience of not being quite certain which party represents the "industrial proletariat" or the "modernizing elite" in Nigeria, or in France of the Second Empire for that matter? Let us be honest. Each of us, to the extent that he has ever used a developmentalist paradigm, has stretched empirical reality to a very Procrustean bed indeed.

Can the world-system perspective answer these questions better? We cannot yet be sure. This point of view has not yet been fully thought through. But let me indicate some possible lines of argument.

If the world-system is the focus of analysis, and if in particular we are talking of the capitalist world-economy, then divergent historical patterns are precisely to be expected. They are not an anomaly but the essence of the system. If the world-economy is the basic economic entity comprising a single division of labor, then it is natural that different areas perform different economic tasks. Anyway, it is natural under capitalism, and we may talk of the core, the periphery and the semi-periphery of the world-economy. Since, however, political boundaries (states) are smaller than the economic whole, they will each reflect different groupings of economic tasks and strengths in the world-market. Over time, some of these differences may be accentuated rather than diminished—the basic inequalities which are our theme of discussion.

It is also clear that over time the loci of economic activities keep changing. This is due to many factors—ecological exhaustion, the impact of new technology, climate changes, and the socio-economic consequences of these "natural" phenomena. Hence, some areas "progress" and others "regress." But the fact that particular states change their position in the world-economy, from semi-periphery to core say, or vice versa, does not in itself change the nature of the system. These shifts will be registered for individual states as "development" or "regression." The key factor to note is that within a capitalist world-economy, all states cannot "develop" simultaneously *by definition,* since the system functions by virtue of having unequal core and peripheral regions.[8]

Within a world-economy, the state structures function as ways for particular groups to affect and distort the functioning of the market. The stronger the state machinery, the more its ability to distort the world-market in favor of the interests it represents. Core states have stronger state machineries than peripheral states.

This role of the state machineries in a capitalist world-economy explains the presistence of nationalism, since the primary social conflicts are quite often between groups located in different states rather than between groups located within the same state boundaries. Furthermore, this explains the ambiguity of class as a concept, since class refers to the economy which is worldwide, but class consciousness is a political, hence primarily national, phenomenon. Within this context, one can see the recrudescence of ethno-nationalisms in industrialized states as an expression of class consciousness of lower caste-class groups in societies where the class terminology has been preempted by nationwide middle strata organized around the dominant ethnic group.

If then the world-system is the focus of analysis rather than the individual states, it is the natural history of this system at which we must look. Like all systems, the capitalist world-economy has both cyclical and secular trends, and it is important to distinguish them.

On the one hand, the capitalist world-economy seems to go through long cycles of "expansion" and "contraction." I cannot at this point go into the long discussion this would require. I will limit myself to the very brief suggestion that "expansion" occurs when the totality of world production is less than world effective demand, as permitted by the existing social distribution of world purchasing power, and that "contraction" occurs when total world production exceeds world effective demand. These are cycles of 75–100 years in length in my view and the downward cycle is only resolved by a political reallocation of world income that effectively expands world demand. I believe we have just ended an expansionary cycle and we are in the beginning of a contractual one.

These cycles occur within a secular trend that has involved the physical expansion and politico-structural consolidation of the capitalist world-economy as such, but has also given birth to forces and movements which are eating away at these same structural supports of the existing world-system. In particular, these forces which we call revolutionary forces are calling into question the phenomenon of inequality so intrinsic to the existing world-system.

The trend toward structural consolidation of the system over the past four centuries has included three basic developments:

The first has been the capitalization of world agriculture, meaning the ever more efficient use of the world's land and sea resources in large productive units with larger and larger components of fixed capital. Over time, this has encompassed more and more of the earth's surface, and at the present we are probably about to witness the last major physical expansion, the elimination of all remaining plots restricted to small-scale, so-called "subsistence" production. The counterpart of this process has been the steady concentration of the world's population as salaried workers in small, dense pockets—that is, proletarianization and urbanization. The initial impact of this entire process has been to render large populations more exploitable and controllable.

The second major structural change has been the development of technology that maximizes the ability to transform the resources of the earth into usable commodities at "reasonable" cost levels. This is what we call industrialization, and the story is far from over. The next century should see the spread of industrial activity from the temperature core areas in which it has hitherto been largely concentrated to the tropical and semi-tropical peripheral areas. Industrialization too has hitherto tended to consolidate the system in providing a large part of the profit that makes the system worth the while of those who are on top of it, with a large enough surplus to sustain and appease the world's middle strata. Mere extension of industrial activity will not change a peripheral area into a core area, for the core areas will concentrate on ever newer, specialized activities.

The third major development, at once technological and social, has been the strengthening of all organizational structures—the states, the economic corporate structures, and even the cultural institutions—vis-à-vis both individuals and groups. This is the process of bureaucratization, and while it has been uneven (the core states are still stronger than the peripheral states, for example), all structures are stronger today than previously. Prime ministers of contemporary states have the power today that Louis XIV sought in vain to achieve. This too has been stabilizing because the ability of these bureaucracies physically to repress opposition is far greater than in the past.

But there is the other side of each of these coins. The displacement of the world's population into urban areas has made it easier ultimately to organize forces against the power structures. This is all the more so since the ever-expanding market-dependent, property-less groups are simultaneously more educated, more in communication with each other, and hence *potentially* more politically conscious.

The steady industrialization of the world has eaten away at the political and hence economic justifications for differentials in rewards. The technological advances, while still unevenly distributed, have created a new military equality of destructive potential. It is true that one nation may have 1000 times the fire power of another, but if the weaker one has sufficient to incur grievous damage, of how much good is it for the stronger to have 1000 times as much strength? Consider not merely the power of a weaker state with a few nuclear rockets but the military power of urban guerillas. It is the kind of problem Louis XIV precisely did *not* need to worry about.

Finally, the growth of bureaucracies in the long run has created the weakness of top-heaviness. The ability of the presumed decision makers to control not the populace but the bureaucracies has effectively diminished, which again creates a weakness in the ability to enforce politico-economic will.

Where then in this picture do the forces of change, the movements of liberation, come in? They come in precisely as not totally coherent pressures of groups which arise out of the structural contradictions of the capitalist world-economy. These groups seem to take organizational form as movements, as parties, and sometimes as regimes. But when the movements become regimes, they are caught in the dilemma of becoming part of the machinery of the capitalist world-economy they are presuming to change. Hence the so-called "betrayals." It is important neither to adulate blindly these regimes, for inevitably they "betray" in part their stated goals, nor to be cynical and despairing, for the movements which give birth to such regimes represent real forces, and the creation of such regimes is part of a long-run process of social transformation.

What we need to put in the forefront of our consciousness is that both the party of order and the party of movement are currently strong. We have not yet reached the peak of the political consolidation of the capitalist world-economy. We are already in the phase of its political decline. If your outlook is developmentalist and mechanical, this pair of statements is an absurdity. From a world-system perspective, and using a dialectical mode of analysis, it is quite precise and intelligible.

This struggle takes place on all fronts—political, economic, and cultural—and in all arenas of the world, in the core states, in the periphery (largely in the Third World), and in the semi-periphery (many but not all of which states have collective ownership of basic property and are hence often called "socialist" states).

Take a struggle like that of Vietnam, or Algeria, or Angola. They were wars of national liberation. They united peoples in these areas. Ultimately, the forces of national liberation won or are winning political change. How may we evaluate its effect? On the one hand, these colonial wars fundamentally weakened the internal supports of the regimes of the USA, France and Portugal. They sapped the dominant forces of world capitalism. These wars made many changes possible in the countries of struggle, the metropolises, and in third countries. And yet, and yet— one can ask if the net result has not been in part further to integrate these countries, even their regimes, into the capitalist world-economy. It did both of course. We gain nothing by hiding this from ourselves. On the other hand, we gain nothing by showing Olympian neutrality in the form of equal disdain for unequal combatants.

The process of analysis and the process of social transformation are not separate. They are obverse sides of one coin. Our praxis informs, indeed makes possible, our analytic frameworks. But the work of analysis is itself a central part of the praxis of change. The perspectives for the future of inequality in the world-system are fairly clear in the long run. In the long run the inequalities will disappear as the result of a fundamental transformation of the world-system. But we all live in the short run, not in the long run. And in the short run, within the constraints of our respective social locations and our social heritages, we labor in the vineyards as we wish, toward what ends we choose. . . .

Notes

1. Irfan Habib, "Problems of Marxist Historical Analysis in India," *Enquiry*, Monsoon, 1969, reprinted in S. A. Shah, ed., *Towards National Liberation: Essays on the Political Economy of India* (Montreal: n.p., 1973), 8–9.

2. See my "Class Struggle in China?", *Monthly Review*, XXV, 4, Sept. 1973, 55–58.

3. See U. Melotti, "Marx e il Terzo Mondo," *Terzo Mondo,* No. 13–14, sett. dict. 1971. Melotti subtitles the work: "towards a multilinear schema of the Marxist conception of historical development."

4. I have developed this argument at length elsewhere. See *The Modern World-System: Capitalist Agriculture and the Origins of the European World-Economy* (New York and London: Academic Press, 1974) and "The Rise and Future Demise of the World Capitalist System: Concepts for Comparative Analysis," *Comparative Studies in Society and History,* XVI, 4, Oct. 1974, 387–415.

5. S. N. Eisenstadt, "Breakdowns of Modernization," *Economic Development and Cultural Change,* XII, 4, July 1964, 367.

6. *Ibid.,* pp. 365–366.

7. *Activité Révolutionnaire du Camarade Kim Il Sung* (Pyongyang: Ed. en langues étrangères, 1970). Livre illustré, 52nd page (edition unpaginated). Translation mine—I.W.

8. As to how particular states can change their position, I have tried to furnish an explanation in "Dependence in an Interdependent World: The Limited Possibilities of Transformation Within the Capitalist World-Economy," *African Studies Review,* XVII, 1, April 1974, 1–26.

14. Reiterating the Identity of the Peripheral State

Tony Smith

Proponents of dependency and world-system perspectives argue their cases on historical grounds, as has been demonstrated by the previous three chapters. Hence, if one wants to critique these perspectives on their own terms, one must argue with the validity of their reading of history. This is precisely the approach taken by Tony Smith in this discussion drawn from his book on imperialism. His central argument is that because dependency and world-system theorists are ideologically motivated, they tend to overstate their case. Specifically, they exaggerate the power of the world system and underestimate the role of the state. Smith believes that if more attention were paid by these thinkers to political life in the periphery, they would understand that there is in fact a great deal of national autonomy and hence control over decisions affecting economic growth and distribution.

In order to clarify more sharply the argument presented in the foregoing pages [of Smith's book], let us set it against what is today perhaps the dominant mode of analysis for studying the impact of imperialism on the periphery since the early decades of the nineteenth century. The most distinctive feature of this tendency is its insistence that social developments in Africa, Asia, and Latin America be seen within a historical and global context dominated by the force of imperialism. Political collapse or authoritarianism, social conflict or civil war, economic backwardness or mass poverty: All these are assigned to the responsibility of the workings of an international system dominated first by Britain, then by the United States. One might not take such writing too seriously except that it constitutes much more than simply a movement in the intellectual history of our day: It is an ideology as well, joining southern nationalists and Marxists within the confines of a generally agreed-upon form of historical analysis able to motivate significant political activity on the part of two of the most important political forces of our century. My purpose is to investigate what I consider to be a serious historiographic

Reprinted with permission from *The Pattern of Imperialism: The United States, Great Britain and the Late-industrializing World Since 1815*, by Tony Smith, pp. 69–84. Cambridge: Cambridge University Press, 1981.

failure in this writing with the hope of helping to save what is possible of the study of imperialism from what are today the ravages of the ideologues.

Although it is obviously oversimplifying to reduce a complex and variously interpreted approach to a few propositions, a summary presentation of the general tenets of the "dependency" or "neocolonial" form of historical analysis will be attempted here, although the discussion will later show that there are substantial disagreements among its different proponents. According to the best-known advocates of this perspective (many of whose names will appear in the following pages), sovereign states of the south have long been dependent on the international economic system dominated by the northern capitalist powers (including Japan) for an evolving mixture of technology, financing, markets, and basic imports—dependent to such an extent that these less developed lands may be called "hooked": They cannot do with their dependence, but, just as certainly, they cannot do without it.

They cannot do with their dependence, so the thesis runs, because their form of incorporation into the international system has tended to inhibit their industrialization, relegating them instead to the less dynamic forms of growth associated with agriculture or the extractive industries. A surprising number of these writers—until quite recently the great majority of them—maintained that these countries would simply be unable to move beyond industrialization associated with limited import substitution. As we shall see, such a basic error in analysis is typical of this group's way of thinking, of its preference for conclusions dictated by theoretically logical, if empirically unsubstantiated, concepts drawn on the grand scale. No wonder, then, that a number of statistically minded political economists have sought to test these propositions and been unable to confirm them. It appears as a general rule that those countries most integrated into the world economy have tended to grow more quickly over a longer period than those countries that are not so integrated.[1] For those like Fernando Henrique Cardoso, however, who see the clear evidence that the manufacturing sector *is* expanding dramatically in many Third World countries, the process remains nonetheless neocolonial, as the leading sectors are inevitably controlled by multinational corporations with their headquarters in the north.[2] As a result, for whatever benefits they may bring in the form of managerial and technological know-how, these corporations take more than they give and—what is more important—make it virtually impossible for local, self-sustaining industrialization to occur. This form of analysis, it should be noted, has affinities with Marxism, for it is the economic process that is seen as the dynamic of history. Thus the stages of economic development of the international system (from mercantilism to free trade to finance capital to the multinational corporation, to take one possible way of marking its development through time) come to interact with the various preindustrial economies in ways that may vary but that in every case soon establish the dominance of the world order over the form of growth followed locally. Over time, imperialism changes in form but not in fact.[3] Nor is it argued that the process is sowing the seeds of its own destruction in any dialectically recognizable fashion. For the present at least, the system is still expanding and consolidating its gains.[4]

But if the Third World cannot do with its dependent status, neither can it do without it. For what has occurred is that the local political elites in these areas have almost invariably structured their domestic rule on a coalition of internal interests favorable to the international connection. That is, it is not the sheer economic might of the outside that dictates the dependent status of the south, but the sociological consequences of this power. The result, as most writers of this persuasion see it, is that the basic needs of the international order must be respected by the south if this system is to continue to provide the services that the local elites need, in their turn, in order to perpetuate their rule. In other words, a symbiotic relationship has grown up over time—a relationship in which the system has created its servants, whose need is precisely to ensure the system's survival, whatever the short-term conflicts of interest may be. In the case of decolonization, for example, those nationalists leading the drive against colonialism in Africa and Asia potentially faced two foes in addition to their colonial rulers: rivalrous local class or ethnic groups whose loyalty these nationalists had not managed to secure, and neighboring peoples hostilely anxious to ensure the service of their interests in the wake of the departing northerners. In no significant way is the situation altered once independence is obtained: Civil war and jealous neighbors—in each case potentially abetted by the diffusion of the East-West confrontation—continue to jeopardize these independent regimes. Thus the system has at its disposal sanctions for transgressing its basic rules that are all the more powerful because their greatest force comes *not from an active threat of intervention so much as from a threat of withdrawal*, a withdrawal that would leave these dependent regimes to the fate of civil and regional conflict, which a great many of them would be quite unprepared to face. And once again there are affinities with Marxism, as it is understood that economic forces do not act in any sense alone but must be grasped sociologically as modes or relations of production creating specific configurations of political conflict over time.

Certain of these observations are persuasive and serve as a useful antidote to the claims of those who see in decolonization's "transfer of power" more of a watershed in world history than was actually the case. But at the same time, these insights exist alongside a number of arguments of dubious validity which I will try to link to a single yet fundamental theoretical shortcoming common to this style of thinking. In a word, too many of these writers make the mistake of assuming that because the whole (in this case the international system) is greater

than the sum of its parts (the constituent states), the parts lead no
significant existence separate from the whole but operate simply in
functionally specific manners as a result of their place in the greater
system. As a result, these writers suggest, it is sufficient to know the
properties of the system as a whole to grasp the logic of its parts; no
special attention need be paid specific cases insofar as one seeks to
understand the movement of the whole. "Apart from a few 'ethnographic
reserves,' all contemporary societies are integrated into a world system,"
writes Samir Amin, an Egyptian working in Africa and known in Europe
as a leading dependency theorist. "Not a single concrete socio-economic
formation of our time can be understood except as part of this world
system."[5] As a consequence, in the words of André Gunder Frank, one
of the more influential members of this school who is working on Latin
America, "Underdevelopment was and still is generated by the very
same historical process which also generated economic development:
the development of capitalism itself."[6] In myriad forms, the argument
appears again and again. A writer on contemporary African politics
asserts that underdevelopment "expresses a particular relationship of
exploitation: namely, the exploitation of one country by another. All the
countries named as 'underdeveloped' in the world are exploited by
others and the underdevelopment with which the world is now preoc-
cupied is a product of capitalist, imperialist and colonialist exploitation."[7]
A book comparing China's and Japan's economic growth after their
contact with the West goes so far as to maintain that Ch'ing China and
Tokugawa Japan were similar enough up to the early 1800s, and that
any later difference in their economic performances should be explained
chiefly by the character of their contact with the West:

> This study argues that the paramount influence in the rise of industrial
> capitalism in Japan was . . . [that Japan] occupied a position of relative
> autonomy within the nineteenth-century world political economy. For a
> variety of reasons other societies were more strongly incorporated as eco-
> nomic and political satellites of one or more of the Western capitalist powers,
> which thwarted their ability to industrialize. . . . In contrast . . . China's
> location in the world political economy dominated by the Western capitalist
> nations, must be considered of prime importance in China's failure to
> develop industrial capitalism during the nineteenth and twentieth centuries.
> China was more strongly incorporated than Japan and thus lacked the
> autonomy to develop the same way.[8]

Similarly, two writers maintain that they "view Latin America as a
continent of inadequate and disappointing fulfillment and seek to pinpoint
the co-ordinates of sustained backwardness in examining the process of
economic change in a dependent, peripheral, or colonial area."[9] And a
book on the Middle East concludes: "The products of Turkish craftsmen,
well known and in great demand in Europe during the seventeenth and
eighteenth centuries, declined along with the products of the rest of

the Middle East when Turkey failed to keep pace with the industrial development of the West. Machine production swept craftsmanship off the markets not only in Europe, but also in Turkey. The latter fell back on agriculture, but in 1908, under the Young Turk movement, she began to take an interest in industrial development."[10]

In the United States, this general argument has reached its fullest expression in the work of Immanuel Wallerstein, who has published only the first book in a four-volume series under the instructive title *The Modern World-System: Capitalist Agriculture and the Origins of the European World-Economy in the Sixteenth-Century.*[11] In a companion essay written after the book's completion, Wallerstein approvingly cites Georg Lukács and says that a central tenet of Marxist historiography is that the study of society should "totalize," or begin with an understanding of the whole. The passage from Lukács is worth quoting:

> It is not the predominance of economic themes in the explanation of history which distinguishes Marxism from bourgeois science in a decisive fashion, it is the point of view of the totality. The category of the totality, the domination determining in all domains of the whole over the parts, constitutes the essence of the method Marx borrowed from Hegel and that he transformed in an original manner to make it the foundation of an entirely new science. . . . The reign of the category of the totality is the carrier of the revolutionary principle in science.[12]

Working from this perspective, Wallerstein declares: "The only kind of social system is a world-system, which we define quite simply as a unit with a single division of labor and multiple cultural systems." And he explains:

> But if there is no such thing as "national development" . . . the proper entity of comparison is the world system. . . . If we are to talk of stages, then—and we should talk of stages—it must be stages of social systems, that is, of totalities. And the only totalities that exist or have existed historically are mini-systems ["simple agricultural or hunting and gathering societies"] and world systems, and in the nineteenth and twentieth centuries there has been only one world-system in existence, the capitalist world economy.[13]

Although Wallerstein's position (to which we will return later) is the most detailed yet to appear, the American writer still most frequently cited by those who favor this approach is probably Paul Baran. Appropriately enough, Baran chose as the epigraph for his book *Monopoly Capital* (written with Paul Sweezy) Hegel's dictum "The truth is the whole." And fortunately for our purposes, Baran's writing is a particularly egregious example of this form of reductionist historiography.

Taking the case of Indian economic development, Baran portrays the country under the pressure of British imperialism as a tabula rasa, so that all the land's problems, past or present, supposedly spring directly from this foreign presence. In a passage extraordinary in its exaggeration, he writes:

> Thus, the British administration of India systematically destroyed all the fibres and foundations of Indian society. Its land and taxation policy ruined India's village economy and substituted for it the parasitic landowner and moneylender. Its commercial policy destroyed the Indian artisan and created the infamous slums of the Indian cities filled with millions of starved and diseased paupers. Its economic policy broke down whatever beginnings there were of an indigenous industrial development and promoted the proliferations of speculators, petty businessmen, agents, and sharks of all descriptions.[14]

And he speculates on what India's fate might have been without the British: "Indeed, there can be no doubt that had the amount of economic surplus that Britain has torn from India been invested in India, India's economic development to date would have borne little similarity to the actual somber record. . . . India, if left to herself, might have found in the course of time a shorter and surely less tortuous road toward a better and richer society."[15]

But surely this account—which, it should be noted, is based on virtually no hard evidence—imputes far too much power (for evil or otherwise) to the British. Thus, despite his allegation that India without the British might have found its own autonomous way to industrial development complete with less human suffering, Baran makes no effort to assess the probability that Mogul India could have accomplished such a transformation or to evaluate what price the pre-British system exacted from its subjects. Life was surely not easy under the Mogul in Delhi (warfare was constant, particularly in the years preceding the British takeover, and the taxation levels were quite high), and the most serious accounts of which I am aware dismiss out of hand the likelihood that pre-British India had any capacity in its contemporary form for sustained economic change. As M. D. Morris writes:

> The British did not take over a society that was "ripe" for an industrial revolution and then frustrate that development. They imposed themselves on a society for which every index of performance suggests the level of technical, economic and administrative performance of Europe five hundred years earlier.[16]

Nor is it at all accurate to suggest, as Baran so adamantly does, either that pre-British India was without original sin or that the British were the authors of unmitigated evil. "Parasitic landowners and moneylenders" were not unknown before the British set foot on the subcontinent; British "commercial policy" is now thought by some to have "destroyed" far fewer artisans than was previously believed; British economic policy surely did more to create the foundations for industrial society in India than to "break down whatever beginnings there were" (however much the effort fails by comparison with Meiji Japan); British "land and taxation policy," far from "ruining" the village economy, was surely less exploitive than that of the Great Mogul and probably provided for a modest per capita increase during the nineteenth century; and British "administration," far from destroying "all the fibres and foundations of Indian society," actually accommodated itself rather well to indigenous ways in the manner of most conquerors of large populations.[17] Of course there is no particular reason to sing hosannas about the British presence. For example, British rule clearly inhibited industrialization in the late nineteenth century: The efforts of Lancashire especially were successful in keeping Indian custom duties low until World War I and so stunted the growth of Indian manufactures.[18] But as the Great Mutiny of 1857 demonstrated, India herself possessed strong forces resisting change. In what seems to me to be a balanced judgment of the forces guiding India's development, Barrington Moore puts the effects of British policy within the context of the persisting strength of indigenous practices and institutions:

> In addition to law and order, the British introduced into Indian society during the nineteenth century railroads and a substantial amount of irrigation. The most important prerequisites for commercial agricultural and industrial growth would seem to have been present. Yet what growth there was turned out to be abortive and sickly. Why? A decisive part of the answer, I think, is that *Pax Britannica* simply enabled the landlord and now also the moneylender to pocket the surplus generated in the countryside that in Japan paid for the first painful stages of industrialization. As foreign conquerors, the English were not in India to make an industrial revolution. They were not the ones to tax the countryside in either the Japanese or the Soviet fashion. Hence, beneath the protective umbrella of Anglo-Saxon justice-under-law, parasitic landlordism became much worse than in Japan. To lay all the blame on British shoulders is obviously absurd. There is much evidence . . . to demonstrate that this blight was inherent in India's own social structure and traditions. Two centuries of British occupation merely allowed it to spread and root more deeply throughout Indian society.[19]

In a parallel fashion, when he takes up the question of the reasons for the success of Japanese industrialization, Baran advances the same reductionist formula: Once again the part (Japan) disappears into the momentum of the whole (the dynamism of expansionist capitalistic imperialism):

> What was it that enabled Japan to take a course so radically different from that of all the other countries in the now underdeveloped world? . . . Reduced to its core, it comes down to the fact that Japan is the only country in Asia (and in Africa or in Latin America) that escaped being turned into a colony or dependency of Western European or American capitalism, that had a chance of independent national development.[20]

And then, in explaining why Japan was not so incorporated, Baran refers once more to the properties of the international system: its preoccupation with other parts of Asia, its conviction that Japan was poor in markets and resources, its internal rivalries. That Japan may have escaped colonial rule and initiated the single successful attempt to industrialize outside of North America and Europe in the nineteenth century for reasons having to do with forces internal to the country is not an idea to which Baran pays the slightest heed. Indeed he so ignores conditions in late Tokugawa Japan that he actually calls the Meiji Restoration a bourgeois revolution!

The point of this discussion is not to doubt that the international system under the expansionist force of European and American capitalism had an impact on the internal development of technologically backward areas of the world over the last two centuries. These writers have served a purpose in making us aware of how intense and complex these interactions were (and remain), and there is substance to their criticism that development literature as it is currently written in the United States tends to mask these linkages for its own ideological reasons.[21] Nor is the objection to the simple omission of evidence relevant to the construction of a historical argument. Selective judgment in the presentation of material is an inevitable part of the study of history. Rather, the objection is to a certain style of thinking that, to use two of this school's favorite words, is biased and ideological, distorting evidence as much in its fashion as does the "bourgeois science" it claims to debunk.

As I suggested earlier, the chief methodological error of this kind of writing is to deprive local histories of their integrity and specificity, making local actors little more than the pawns of outside forces. Feudalism as a force in Latin America? Nonsense, says Frank (to be applauded by Wallerstein); because capitalism has penetrated every nook and cranny of the world system, the concept of feudal relations of production cannot be validly used.[22] Destroy the particular, exalt the general in order to explain everything. Cite Hegel: "The truth is the whole." Tribalism as a force in Africa? Colin Leys cannot bring himself to use the word without putting it in quotation marks, asserting that "among Africanists [this] point . . . perhaps no longer needs arguing." " 'Tribalism,' " Leys maintains, "is a creation of colonialism. It has little or nothing to do with precolonial relations between tribes. . . . In neo-colonial Africa class formation and the development of tribalism accompany each other."[23] Why? Because the logic of the whole (capitalist colonialism) has found it expedient to work its will in the part (Africa) through creating, virtually ex nihilo, the divisive force of "tribalism." By such reckoning, all the social structures in history after a certain low level of development in the division of labor could be dissolved—feudal and bureaucratic estates, castes and clans as well as tribes—in favor of class analysis, the only "real" social formation.

Because this approach is formulistic and reductionist, it is bad historiography. It is formulistic in the sense that it seeks to specify universal laws or processes in blatant disregard of the singular or the idiosyncratic. And by the same token it is reductionist, because it forces the particular case to express its identity solely in the terms provided by the general category. The error here, it should be repeated, is not that the approach draws attention to the interconnectedness of economic and political processes and events in a global manner, but that it refuses to grant the part *any* autonomy, *any* specificity, *any* particularity independent of its membership in the whole.

The problem of the relationship of the whole to the parts (like that of politics to economics, or of psychology to sociology) is a recurrent one in the social sciences. The only successful resolution of the problem of understanding their interaction, so far as I am aware, is to recognize that although the whole does have a logic indiscernible from analysis of the parts considered separately, the parts too have their identities— identities that no amount of understanding of the whole will adequately reveal. In his monumental *Critique de la raison dialectique*, Jean-Paul Sartre makes a telling criticism of Marxists who make "a fetish of totalizing," and illustrates it with an example of the problem of relating an individual biography to a social milieu:

"Valéry is a petit bourgeois intellectual, no doubt about it. But not every petit bourgeois intellectual is Valéry. The heuristic inadequacy of contemporary Marxism is contained in these two sentences."[24]

Thus part and whole must be comprehended at once as aspects of each other and yet as analytically autonomous—although the degree of relative independence will obviously be more or less complete depending on the historical moment. The theoretical consequences are clear: Systems composed of complex parts may expect change to come not only from the evolution of the whole (considered dialectically or otherwise), or from influences without in the form of the impingement of other systems, but also from developments *within the parts*, whose movements are endogenously determined. Therefore, in studying the patterns of relations between countries on the periphery and the core lands of Western Europe and the United States, we must be aware not only of the way the system as such is changing (for example, in terms of balance-of-power relations among the great powers, or with respect to changes in the international division of labor), but also of the manner in which parts of this whole (such as the form of state organization on the periphery) may transform themselves for local reasons but with important repercussions for the entire system of relations between strong and weak. Historical analyses that hold to these premises may be difficult to write, as lines of movement become more numerous and more difficult to see synthetically. But only this form of writing can hope to portray at all adequately the complexity that history actually is.

In line with the analysis presented in the first part of this chapter [See original book by Smith, Ed.], the political organization of social life on the periphery emerges as the single most important variable to grasp if we would understand the historical identity of these peoples. For political organization represents the ability of these groups seen in class or communal terms to act historically, to lead their collective lives. The state thus focuses the coalitions and conflicts of present social forces within an organizational entity whose administrative and coercive capacities are the legacy of the past as well as the creation of current generations. Its story is that of the individuality of the people it encompasses in relation to global history. And it is the abrupt dismissal of the importance of analyzing political life on the periphery in other than a reductionist manner that is the cardinal error of the approach we have been reviewing.

Thus, although Immanuel Wallerstein promotes the study of the "world-system," as we saw earlier, the reverse side of the coin is his disinterest in political life on the periphery:

> The world-economy develops a pattern where state structures are relatively strong in the core areas and relatively weak in the periphery. . . . What is necessary is that in some areas the state machinery be far stronger than in others. What do we mean by a strong state machinery? We mean strength vis-à-vis other states within the world-economy including other core-states, and strong vis-à-vis local political units within the boundaries of the state.[25]

Bereft of significant political activity, the periphery is then understood to operate in terms of social groups organized around economic interests. It is therefore international ties of cooperation and conflict based on class that permit a unified analysis of world politics:

> We must maintain our eye on the central ball. The capitalist world economy as a totality—its structure, its historic evolution, its contradictions—is the arena of social action. The fundamental political reality of that world-economy is a class struggle which, however, takes constantly changing forms: class-consciousness versus ethno-nationalist consciousness, classes within nations versus classes across nations.[26]

Although there may be instances aplenty when state action is unimportant, Wallerstein's hasty disregard of its potential significance is in error. Even on his home ground of the sixteenth century, Wallerstein overstates his case. As Theda Skocpol has pointed out, the strong states of that era were not at the core in England and Holland, but on the periphery in Spain and Sweden. Holland was ruled by a federation of merchant oligarchs whereas the English crown, deficient in terms of a bureaucracy or a standing army, was beholden to merchants and local notables.[27] Later history substantiates his position no better. As Alexander Gerschenkron has demonstrated, the "late industrializers" in every case were successful because of exceptionally strong state structures that were determined to modernize. One-time peripheral countries like Russia, Prussia, and Japan could not possibly have developed as they did without the vigorous leadership of the state.[28] Nor is the contemporary governmental structure of the United States the Leviathan one might expect of the "core country of the world economy" any more than are many governments on the periphery today the weak structures one might anticipate on the basis of Wallerstein's writing.

Having created a historical arena in which the only actors are social groups responding to economic interests, Wallerstein is free to weave a tight net of interdependence among the actors in question. As he puts it in an anthology on Africa edited with Peter Gutkind:

> All the authors in this volume stress that there was an asymmetrical and unequal economic relationship between Africa and the industrially highly developed world and that the "change process on the periphery of the world capitalist system is not an endogenous path through stages but a process subject to powerful exogenous factors." [The authors therefore propose] the idea of the world-system and Africa's place in and relationship to this system, "whose fundamental dynamic largely controlled the actors located in both sectors of one united arena."[29]

Arguing from this perspective, Wallerstein and Gutkind arrive at the following startling conclusion:

> Underdevelopment, then, is the product of the operations and contradictions *within* the capitalist system . . . and it is just as clearly revealed in the relations between England and Scotland as between Great Britain and Nigeria. . . . Why is Africa (or for that matter Latin America and much of Asia) so poor? . . . the answer is very brief: we have made it poor.[30]

The problem with this approach is that it accounts only with relative difficulty for the wide variety of differences that occur within this allegedly unified world system. Wallerstein can allude to an international division of labor, to be sure, to explain the diversity he encounters. But his failure to acknowledge a political dynamic proper to these lands and peoples results in the exclusion from his analysis of an extremely significant historical force, which thereby impoverishes his discussion and nullifies many of his conclusions. By reducing the political to the economic, and the local to the international, Wallerstein has created a caricature of the historical process whose shortcomings outweigh its insights.

It is not difficult to anticipate the line of argument to be taken by apologists for the dependency literature. They will claim that at its best this approach is more complex than the foregoing analysis recognizes, that it sees a role for the state on the periphery and for the influence of local forces on developments there that I have altogether failed to appreciate.[31] Of course, some of this writing is of high quality and has produced new insights into the character of historical change in the south. (One thinks, for example, of the work of Fernando Henrique Cardoso.) But what these apologists do not see is that dependency theory serves a historically conditioned ideological function of bringing together Marxists and southern nationalists around certain categories of analysis that serve their respective interests. As a consequence, dependency theory is wedded to its bias of seeing local problems of development in terms of international forces in order to satisfy nationalist sentiments, just as it is committed to downplaying the realm of the political by virtue of its allegiance to Marxism. The limitations of this school are therefore not peculiar to its writers of lesser talent, but are rather more of a family disease. It is ironic that these writers who delight (often with good cause) in exposing the ideologically biased assumptions of mainstream North American work on Third World development should fail to see the historical roots of their own efforts in terms of the groups they represent.

To conclude, let us turn to an interesting example of the issues raised here that occurs in a current debate over the coming to power of "bureaucratic-authoritarian" governments headed by the military in a number of Latin American states (the most important being Brazil, Peru, Chile, Uruguay, and Argentina) since 1964. Among Latin Americanists who have tried to understand this phenomenon, there seems to be general agreement that Guillermo O'Donnell has advanced the most challenging and comprehensive of explanations.[32] While O'Donnell is well aware of the wide variety of factors that might have conspired to produce these bureaucratic-authoritarian governments, his central theoretical arguments make him akin to the writers criticized in the preceding pages. Put too briefly, his core thesis is that a regional economic crisis connected to a specific stage in such an area's economic development provoked a political crisis the resolution of which dictated a specific form of political outcome. Thus, in his analysis, economic forces clearly predominate over political developments in the fashion we have seen to be indicative of the approach to the study of the periphery discussed in the preceding pages. But the argument that most closely links O'Donnell to this general perspective is his insistence that both the origin of the crisis (the inability of these countries to generate internally the capital and organization needed at a certain stage to move ahead economically) and the form of its resolution (with the help offered by multinational corporations who were ready and eager to move into the situation) must be understood at their most basic levels in terms of the development of the world capitalist order. Indeed, as a similar train of events may be expected to manifest itself in other parts of the world, O'Donnell declares that the focus of his work is on Latin America "only in a trivial sense; the pertinent historical context is provided by the political economy of nations that were originally exporters of primary materials and were industrialized late, but extensively, in a position of dependency upon the great centers of world capitalism."[33]

As Albert Hirschman notes with respect to O'Donnell's work, "Considerable intellectual excitement is . . . apt to be generated—quite legitimately so—when a *specific* turn of the political tide is shown or alleged to originate in a *precise* feature of the underlying economic terrain."[34] Nevertheless, as Hirschman and a number of other scholars who contributed to a volume that reviews O'Donnell's work conclude, the evidence now available makes it difficult to accept the core thesis summarized in these lines without significant reservations. Thus, if O'Donnell seems convincing in tying the advent of authoritarian governments on the continent to the demand of certain social groups to end the civil discord attendant upon economic upheavals typified by high rates of inflation, balance-of-payments problems, and the like, he has nonetheless not successfully demonstrated (except perhaps in the case of Argentina) the accuracy of his far more crucial proposition that this basic economic disturbance constituted an epochal crisis in the transition from one economic stage of development to another (the "deepening" of industrialization).[35] Furthermore, relatively less important issues are also open to question, especially whether authoritarian governments need be the inevitable response to such problems (however conceptualized), and whether multinational corporations are particularly keen to work with such regimes (given their equal success in democratic environments).

Yet despite the apparent problems with the central thesis of O'Donnell's work, the richness of its presentation—in particular, its sense of regional history and its recognition of the significance of the role of the state—has allowed it to serve as the basis for alternative formulations designed to explain the rise of authoritarian governments on the continent. The resulting dialogue is a salutary development. In these analyses, political events may be shown to engender economic consequences, local events to have international repercussions, and long-term cultural factors to possess amazing powers of regeneration—at the same time that the political weight of imperialism and the economic strength of the international system are recognized as the forces they are. There is, to be sure, the danger of rampant eclecticism in analyses based on such open-ended premises. Some explanations are obviously superior to others and it should be an essential academic concern to lay out the reasons for this. Nevertheless, eclecticism at least permits a climate for serious intellectual pursuit. This is more than can be said for the stifling narrowness of vision of the reductionist universe, where the political is explained in terms of the economic, where local events are interpreted in terms of external occurrences, and where truth becomes the preserve of those who have mastered the mysteries of the "totality."[36]

Notes

1. See Robert R. Kaufman et al., "A Preliminary Test of the Theory of Dependency," *Comparative Politics*, VII, 3, April 1975; David Ray, "The Depen-

dency Model of Latin America: Three Basic Fallacies," *The Journal of Interamerican Affairs and World Studies*, XV, 1, February 1973; Patrick J. McGowan, "Economic Dependency and Economic Performance in Black Africa," *The Journal of Modern African Studies*, XIV, 1, 1976; and Elliot J. Berg, "Structural Transformation versus Gradualism: Recent Economic Development in Ghana and the Ivory Coast," in Philip Foster and Aristide R. Zolberg, eds., *Ghana and the Ivory Coast: Perspectives on Modernization* (University of California Press, 1971).

2. Fernando Henrique Cardoso, "Associated-Dependent Development: Theoretical and Practical Implications," in Alfred Stepan, ed., *Authoritarian Brazil: Origins, Policies, and Future* (Yale University Press, 1973), and Cardoso, "Dependent Capitalist Development in Latin America," *The New Left Review*, 74, July-August 1972. In the jargon used by proponents of this approach, such countries become part of the "semi-periphery." Although the term is Immanuel Wallerstein's, the earliest use of the concept of which I am aware occurs in the idea of "go-between" countries as expressed in Johan Galtung, "A Structural Theory of Imperialism," *Journal of Peace Research*, 8, 2, 1971. Note how many countries obtain their comparative labels by virtue of international, not domestic, characteristics.

3. Although the local economies as well as the international system are seen to change over time, the dominant partner and therefore the shaper of the overall movement is always the world economy in these analyses. See, among others, Susanne Bodenheimer, "Dependency and Imperialism: The Roots of Latin American Development," in K. T. Fann and Donald C. Hodges, eds., *Readings in U.S. Imperialism* (Porter Sargent, Boston, 1971); and Stanley J. Stein and Barbara H. Stein, *The Colonial Heritage of Latin America: Essays on Economic Dependency in Perspective* (Oxford University Press, 1970).

4. Immanuel Wallerstein does not forsee the end of the system for another century or two. See "Dependence in an Interdependent World: The Limited Possibilities of Transformation within the Capitalist World Order," *African Studies Review*, XVII, 1, April 1974, p. 2.

5. Samir Amin, *Accumulation on a World Scale: A Critique of the Theory of Underdevelopment* (Monthly Review Press, 1974), vol. 1, p. 3.

6. André Gunder Frank, "The Development of Underdevelopment," in James D. Cockcroft et al., *Dependence and Underdevelopment: Latin America's Political Economy* (Doubleday, 1972), p. 9.

7. Walter Rodney, *How Europe Underdeveloped Africa* (Bogle-l'Ouverture, London, 1973), pp. 21–2.

8. Frances V. Moulder, *Japan, China, and the Modern World-Economy: Toward a Reinterpretation of East Asian Development* (Cambridge University Press, 1977), pp. vii–viii.

9. Stein and Stein, *The Colonial Heritage*, p. viii (n. 35).

10. Kurt Grunwald and Joachim O. Ronall, *Industrialization in the Middle East* (Council for Middle Eastern Affairs Press, 1960), p. 331.

11. Immanuel Wallerstein, *The Modern World-System: Capitalist Agriculture and the Origins of the European World-Economy in the Sixteenth Century* (Academic Press, 1974).

12. Georg Lukács, "Rosa Luxembourg, Marxiste," in *Histoire et conscience de classe* (Editions de Minuit, Paris, 1960), pp. 47–8.

13. Immanuel Wallerstein, "The Rise and Future Demise of the World Capitalist System," *Comparative Studies in Society and History*, XVI, 4, September 1974,

p. 390. In the fall of 1977, Wallerstein launched the journal *Review* to encourage the dissemination of these ideas.

14. Paul Baran, *The Political Economy of Growth* (Monthly Review Press, 2nd ed., 1962), p. 149.

15. Ibid., p. 150.

16. Morris D. Morris, "Towards a Reinterpretation of Nineteenth-Century Indian Economic History," *The Indian Economic and Social History Review*, V, March 1968, pp. 6–7.

17. Barrington Moore, Jr., *Social Origins of Dictatorship and Democracy: Lord and Peasant in the Making of the Modern World* (Beacon Press, 1966), n. 28, chapter 6; Angus Maddison, *Class Structure and Economic Growth: India and Pakistan since the Moghuls* (Allen & Unwin, 1971); and M. D. Morris, "Trends and Tendencies in Indian Economic History," *The Indian Economic and Social History Review*, V, 4, December 1968, and Morris, "Towards a Reinterpretation" (n. 48).

18. Romesh Dutt, *The Economic History of India: In the Victorian Age, 1837–1900* (Ministry of Information and Broadcasting, Government of India, 2nd ed., 1970), book 2, chapter 12; book 3, chapter 9; Daniel Houston Buchanan, *The Development of Capitalistic Enterprise in India* (Macmillan, 1934), pp. 465–7. Radhe Shyam Rungta, *The Rise of Business Corporations in India, 1851–1900* (Cambridge University Press, 1970); B. R. Tomlinson, *The Political Economy of the Raj, 1914–1917: The Economics of Decolonization in India* (Macmillan, 1979), chapter 1; and Clive Dewey, "The End of the Imperialism of Free Trade: The Eclipse of the Lancashire Lobby and the Concession of Fiscal Autonomy to India," in Dewey and A. G. Hopkins, eds., *The Imperial Impact: Studies in the Economic History of Africa and India* (Athlone Press, 1978).

19. Moore, *Social Origins of Dictatorship and Democracy* (n. 28), pp. 354–5.

20. Baran, *The Political Economy of Growth* (n. 46), p. 158.

21. André Gunder Frank, "Sociology of Underdevelopment and Underdevelopment of Sociology," in Cockcroft, *Dependence and Underdevelopment* (n. 38); and Susanne J. Bodenheimer, *The Ideology of Developmentalism: The American-Paradigm-Surrogate for Latin American Studies* (Sage Professional Papers in Comparative Politics, 1971).

22. André Gunder Frank, "The Development of Underdevelopment," and "Economic Dependence, Class Structure, and Underdevelopment Policy," in Cockcroft, *Dependence and Underdevelopment* (n. 38); Wallerstein, "The Rise and Future Demise" (n. 45).

23. Colin Leys, *Underdevelopment in Kenya: The Political Economy of Neo-Colonialism, 1964–1971* (University of California Press, 1974), pp. 198–9.

24. Jean-Paul Sartre, *Critique de la raison dialectique* (Gallimard, 1960), p. 44. For a criticism of Sartre on precisely the grounds that he also occasionally rides roughshod over the individual case, see Tony Smith, "Idealism and People's War: Sartre on Algeria," *Political Theory*, I, 4, November 1973.

25. Immanuel Wallerstein, *The Modern World-System* (n. 43), p. 355.

26. Immanuel Wallerstein, "Class Formation in the Capitalist World-Economy," *Politics and Society*, 5, 3, 1975, p. 375.

27. Theda Skocpol, "Wallerstein's World Capitalist System: A Theoretical and Historical Critique," *American Journal of Sociology*, 82, 5, March 1977.

28. Alexander Gerschenkron, "Economic Backwardness in Historical Perspective," in his *Economic Backwardness in Historical Perspective* (Harvard University Press, 1973).

29. Peter C. W. Gutkind and Immanuel Wallerstein, eds., *The Political Economy of Contemporary Africa* (Sage, 1976), pp. 11, 14.

30. Ibid., pp. 12, 27.

31. See, for example, James A. Caporaso, "Dependency Theory: Continuities and Discontinuities in Development Studies," *International Organization*, 34, 4, Autumn 1980.

32. Guillermo A. O'Donnell, *Modernization and Bureaucratic-Authoritarianism: Studies in South American Politics* (Institute of International Studies, Berkeley, 1973).

33. Guillermo A. O'Donnell, "Corporatism and the Question of the State," in James M. Malloy, ed., *Authoritarianism and Corporatism in Latin America* (University of Pittsburgh Press, 1977), p. 54; and see O'Donnell, "Reflections on the Patterns of Change in the Bureaucratic-Authoritarian State," *Latin American Research Review*, 13, 1, 1978, pp. 29–30.

34. Albert O. Hirschman, "The Turn to Authoritarianism in Latin America and the Search for its Economic Determinants," in David Collier, ed., *The New Authoritarianism in Latin America* (Princeton University Press, 1980), p. 68.

35. José Serra, "Three Mistaken Theses Regarding the Connection between Industrialization and Authoritarian Regimes," and Robert R. Kaufman, "Industrial Change and Authoritarian Rule in Latin America: A Concrete Review of the Bureaucratic-Authoritarian Model," in Collier, *The New Authoritarianism* (n. 66).

36. For a rebuttal of attempts to refute such criticisms, see Tony Smith, "The Logic of Dependency Theory Revisited," *International Organization*, 35, Autumn 1981, pp. 755–61.

PART 3
EMPIRICAL STUDIES:
EVIDENCE MEETS THEORY

15. Economic Development and the Distribution of Income

Irma Adelman
Cynthia Taft Morris

This study presents one of the first attempts to apply social science statistical methodology to the problem of the internal gap between rich and poor. The portions reproduced here represent an abbreviated summary of an entire book on the subject, and the interested reader should consult the original source for details of the data and methodology. A principal finding of the study is that economic growth does lead to increasing income inequality, as was suggested in Chapters 3 and 4 by Ahluwalia and Kuznets. But Irma Adelman and Cynthia Taft Morris go beyond that finding to conclude that the poor lose in absolute terms as well. Hence, they support the old adage that "the rich get richer and the poor get poorer." This finding is certainly controversial and has been disputed by critics. Finally, the investigation points to a number of policy instruments developing countries can employ to mitigate the impact of growth on income distribution. These conclusions are at variance with the thinking of many proponents of the dependency and world-system schools who generally see little opportunity for countries on the periphery to counteract the predominant role of systemic constraints on their development, unless they embark upon a revolutionary course.

Our discussion below depicts the typical path of an underdeveloped country undergoing change that is suggested by our analyses. It is based on study of the average characteristics of the different country groupings obtained in our results. Individual countries will of course diverge from this typical path. Our discussion involves a dynamic interpretation of cross-sectional results. . . .

[T]here is no *statistical* justification for interpreting a cross-section as representative of changes over time. We therefore apply theory and historical evidence in order to derive the generalizations that follow.

These generalizations should be viewed as a set of hypotheses regarding the dynamics of economic development and income distribution.

When economic growth begins in a subsistence agrarian economy through the expansion of a narrow modern sector, inequality in the distribution of income typically increases greatly, particularly where expatriate exploitation of rich natural resources provides the motivating force for growth. The income share of the poorest 60 percent declines significantly, as does that of the middle 20 percent,[1] and the income share of the top 5 percent increases strikingly.

The gains of the top 5 percent are particularly great in very low income countries where a sharply dualistic structure is associated with political and economic domination by traditional or expatriate elites. Once countries move successfully beyond the stage of sharply dualistic growth, further development as such generates no systematic advantage or disadvantage for the top 5 percent until they reach the very highest level for underdeveloped countries, when broad-based social and economic advances operate to their disadvantage. Instead, their share increases with greater natural resources available for exploitation and decreases with a larger government role in the economic sphere.

As developing nations become less dualistic, the middle-income group is the primary beneficiary under two possible development strategies available to countries that are at least moderately developed. Widely based social and economic advances, combined with consistent efforts to improve human resources and expand political participation and facilitated by a reasonable abundance of natural resources, typically favor the middle sector. Where resources are sparse, the middle sector may nevertheless benefit through the development of a diversified manufacturing export sector supported by an active government economic role and expanding financial institutions. In contrast, when neither of these strategies is followed but rapid and quite widespread economic growth under moderate dualism nevertheless takes place, the relative position of the middle quintile worsens, with the benefits of economic change going rather to the upper 20 percent of the population.[2]

The position of the poorest 60 percent typically worsens, both relatively and absolutely, when an initial spurt of narrowly based dualistic growth is imposed on an agrarian subsistence economy. Our study suggests that, in an average country going through the earliest phases of economic development, it takes at least a generation for the poorest 60 percent to recover the loss in absolute income associated with the typical spurt in growth. . . .

Our analysis provides some grounds for speculating about the mechanisms that operate before the economic takeoff point to depress the standard of living of the poorest 40 percent. In the very earliest stage of dualistic growth, increased wage payments to indigenous workers in modern plantation, extractive, and industrial enterprises tend to be more than offset by concurrent changes in population, relative prices, tastes, and product availability. The lowering of death rates through the introduction of modern health measures such as malaria control accelerates population growth and thus tends to depress the per capita income of the indigenous population. Since increased cash wages are not immediately matched by increased availability of consumers' goods, higher prices erode gains in money income. Subsistence farmers shifting to cash crops are particularly hard hit by rising prices. Typically they suffer both declines in real income and nutritional deficiencies as they become dependent on the market for major necessities previously produced at home.

As the process of economic growth spreads beyond the narrow expatriate enclave, the factors at work to erode the relative and even the absolute positions of the poorest 40 percent appear to be changes in product mix and technology within both agricultural and nonagricultural sectors, rapid expansion of the urban industrial sectors, continued rapid population increases, migration to the cities, lack of social mobility, and inflation.

Regional income inequality typically increases as the concentration of rapidly growing, technologically advanced enterprises in cities widens the gap between rural and urban per capita income. Income inequality also intensifies in the urban sector with the accumulation of assets in the hands of a relatively small number of owners (usually expatriate) of modern enterprises. This concentration is accelerated by the spread of capital-intensive industrial technology through at least three factors— the ease with which owners of modern enterprises obtain capital abroad, the inability of small-scale enterprises to obtain financing, and a growing preference of medium and large entrepreneurs for advanced modern technologies. This labor-saving bias of technological advance, the rapidity of urban population growth, the migration to cities of unemployed rural workers, and the lack of social mobility all tend to swell the numbers of urban impoverished and to decrease the income share of the poorest segments of the urban population.

Several concomitants of the growth process characteristic of the period before economic takeoff also operate to worsen the absolute position of the poor. As agricultural output expands, the inelasticity of international and domestic demand for many agricultural products tends to reduce the real income of agricultural producers. Import substitution policies can raise the prices of consumers' goods above international levels. Simultaneously, mechanization in industry tends to preempt markets formerly supplied by large numbers of artisans and cottage workers. The destruction of handicraft industries acts to reduce incomes and increase unemployment among rural and urban poor. Finally, inflation, the product of investment efforts typically well beyond capacities to save, drives up prices faster than the wages of low-income workers, who have meager bargaining power. At the same time profits tend to rise both absolutely and relatively.

Thus, to summarize, inflation, population growth, technological change, the commercialization of the traditional sector, and urbanization all combine to reduce the real income of the poorest 40 percent of the population in very low-income countries in the before-takeoff stage of development. Those middle- and upper-income groups benefit that are better able to finance the application of more advanced capital-intensive techniques of production.

These hypotheses and speculations are, broadly speaking, consistent with other studies, both cross-sectional and time series. Sketchy evidence cited by Kuznets on the early stages of economic growth in currently advanced nations suggests a relative worsening of the position of the poor. Cross-sectional and time series studies of contemporary under-developed countries also lend support to the hypothesis that the initial phases of economic growth increase the inequality of income distribution.[3] It is only very recently, however, that evidence has been brought forward of absolute declines in the average income of the poorest 40 to 60 percent of the population as a consequence of economic growth in these countries. . . .

Of the variables of greatest significance in this analysis, the most reliable for increasing the quality of income distribution appear to be the rate of improvement in human resources and direct government economic activity. Increased access to the acquisition of middle-level skills and professional training appears, from our results, to be quite predictable in equalizing effects on the income distribution. The distributional effects of increasing the proportion of government investment in total investment also appear to be favorable to lower- and middle-income recipients. As policy instruments, measures to increase political participation through stronger labor unions are probably less reliable because of their unpredictable impact on the stability of social and political institutions.

While the extent of socioeconomic dualism cannot itself be considered a policy instrument, our results suggest strongly that policies tending to reduce dualism by widening the base for economic growth can be very important for increasing income equality, and particularly for improving the position of the middle-income groups. Instruments having this effect might include providing credit to small, indigenous rural and urban entrepreneurs and expanding technical services to promote the spread of new seeds throughout agriculture.

The consequences for income distribution of increasing the rate of economic growth and improving economic institutions (represented by the development potential variable) are not fully predictable, probably because of the unfavorable effects discussed above. Nevertheless, our results suggest that, once some minimum level of development is reached, a wider coverage of improvements in economic institutions accompanied by either social advances or a shift in trade structure toward more diversified manufacturing exports supported by government policy is likely to increase the share in total income of middle-income groups. Increases in per capita GNP are associated with worsening of the income distribution at low levels of development; only at very high levels for low-income nations is higher per capita GNP associated with a more equal income distribution.

It is quite striking that several variables most closely associated with variations in patterns of income distribution proved to have little importance in our earlier studies of influences on short-term growth rates of per capita GNP. These variables include natural resource abundance, structure of foreign trade, direct economic role of the government, political participation, and even rates of improvement in middle- and higher-level human resources.[4] Yet this study underlines their relevance to differences in the extent of income inequality and thus reinforces the view that the policy instruments that are most effective in improving income distributions are different from those that are best for raising economic growth rates.

Notes

1. There is obviously an overlap between the income share of the poorest 60 percent and that of the middle 20 percent. The former measure is of interest when one is concerned with the position of the poorer "majority" of the population. The latter is of most interest to those concerned with the middle groups, which are assumed by political and economic historians to play key roles in national development.

2. Our hypotheses about changes in relative income shares are consistent with cross-section regressions of various income shares on per capita GDP.

3. For time series studies, see Subramanian Swamy, "Structural Changes and the Distribution of Income by Size: The Case of India," *Review of Income and Wealth*, Series 2 (June 1967), pp. 155–74; Richard Weisskoff, "Income Distribution and Economic Growth in Puerto Rico, Argentina, and Mexico," *Review of Income and Wealth*, 16 (1970); and the references cited on p. 305 of the latter article. For examples of cross-sectional studies, see T. Morgan, "Distribution of Income in Ceylon, Puerto Rico, the United States and the United Kingdom," *Economic Journal*, 43 (1953): 821–35, and H. T. Oshima, "The International Comparison of Size Distribution of Family Incomes with Special Reference to Asia," *Review of Economics and Statistics*, 44 (1962): 439–45.

4. See Irma Adelman and Cynthia Taft Morris, *Society, Politics, and Economic Development* (Baltimore, 1971), chaps. 5–7.

16. The World-Economy and the Distribution of Income Within States: A Cross-National Study

Richard Rubinson

This chapter is an explicit attempt to test some of the concepts presented in Wallerstein's world-system theory. Richard Rubinson asserts that it only makes sense to examine the question of income inequality in a global perspective since individual states are tied together in a single system of production, i.e., the capitalist world economy. Within this economy there is a geographic division of labor in which peripheral states specialize in the production of raw materials while the core states turn those materials into manufactured goods. In this system, the economically more powerful states will enjoy a more equal distribution of income than the less powerful states. Rubinson tests this thesis with historical data from the United States and Great Britain. He then conducts a cross-sectional empirical analysis using income inequality data. The results of both the historical and empirical analysis, according to Rubinson, substantiate the world-system perspective.

The explanation of intercountry differences in inequality has been a central concern of comparative stratification research. Traditional approaches to explaining these differences between countries have been based predominately on a developmental, or modernization model, which explains differences in inequality by the level of a country's economic wealth. Thus, such models account for the well-known fact that richer countries have more equal income distributions than poorer countries (Paukert, 1973) through the mechanism of increasing economic growth. Economic growth is seen to lead to decreases in inequality because it leads to economic differentation and diversification which allows wealth to "trickle down" from elites to the mass of the population (Kerr et al., 1964; Kravis, 1973; Ranis and Fei, 1961) and because it creates so much

Reprinted with permission from the *American Sociological Review*, vol. 41 (August, 1976): 638–659.

wealth that elites give up a share of their reward because the absolute level of their reward is so high (Lenski, 1966; Cutright, 1967).

The results of recent research, however, have begun to cast doubt on these developmental models. First, there is now much evidence that income distributions do not necessarily tend toward greater equality even with high rates of economic growth, and some studies show that inequality increases along with growth (Adelman and Morris, 1973; Girling, 1973; Jeck, 1968; Vandendries, 1974). Second, many studies also show that increasing economic growth does not necessarily lead to the expansion of structural differentiation and economic diversification which are assumed to be the mechanisms leading to greater equality (Furtado, 1972; Galtung, 1971; Girvan, 1973). Consequently, there is a need to consider alternative models to explain inter-country differences in inequality. This chapter, then, attempts to develop such an alternative model and subject it to empirical test using a cross-sectional sample of countries.

The World-Economy as the Focus of Study

One reason for the inadequacy of developmental models is that they are based on the implicit assumption that countries represent separate systems of economic production, so that all countries are assumed to be able to go from an initial stage of underdevelopment to a stage of development. The model to be proposed here makes two different assumptions. First, it is assumed that it is not the effects of wealth or economic production per se that affect inequality; but rather, it is the social control and organization of production that determine the distribution of income. Second, this model assumes that countries do not represent separate systems of production; but rather, that all countries are part of a single system of production which contains multiple political units within it. Thus, this model starts with an analysis of the world-economy rather than with an analysis of the national economy.

In accord with Lenski (1966), this model assumes that the distribution of reward in a system is a function of the organization and differential control that groups have over production. Lenski uses this assumption when he identifies the system of production with technology and then states that the degree of inequality in societies increases as technology advances from hunting and gathering to horticultural to agrarian. Throughout his discussion it is clear that these comparisons are across separate *systems of production.*

Lenski then states that with the appearance of industrial societies, this trend toward increasing inequality reverses itself, since his evidence indicates that the level of inequality in mature industrial societies is less than in agrarian ones. He locates the causes of this reversal in changes in authority relations, the scale of production, changes in labor requirements, and the rise of democracy (1966:308–25). In this analysis of industrial societies, though, Lenski is implicitly identifying nations as separate systems of production. But political boundaries are not always coterminous with the boundaries of production systems. Any analysis must be careful to distinguish between regions or areas *within* a system of production (even though these areas are politically bounded) and the boundaries of the system of production itself. If we define the boundary of a production system by the scope of its division of labor, then the industrial system of production encompasses multiple states. Consequently, it is incorrect to infer that the amount of inequality in this system has decreased merely on evidence that the amount of inequality *within* the political areas of that system has declined. In shifting his discussion from agrarian to industrial technologies, Lenski has misspecified his unit of analysis. In discussing hunting and gathering, horticultural, and agrarian societies, Lenski correctly compares the degree of inequality across systems of production. But when he shifts to industrial technology, he compares the amount of inequality within political *areas* of the industrial system to other *entire* systems of production. The correct comparison for his theory should be between the amount of inequality in agrarian systems and the amount of inequality in the entire industrial system.

An example drawn from the relations of a city to its suburban areas can clarify this point. The city of Baltimore and the area ringing the city are two separate political entities, Baltimore City and Baltimore County. Baltimore County is a suburban area with a high average income, and production is specialized in light industry and advanced technologies. Baltimore City has a lower average income and production is concentrated in heavy industry and commerce. The distribution of income in the county is also more equal than the distribution of income in the city. If an analyst were unaware of the economic relations between the populations in these two political jurisdictions, he might infer that the system of production in the county, because of its type of technology and higher level of wealth, produces a more equal distribution of income than the system of production in the city. But, of course, the city and county are not two separate systems of production but two political areas within a single division of labor. Furthermore, political entities are not usually passive boundaries in production systems but are often organized as mechanisms to protect the economic gains of the population within them. For example, Baltimore County was formed and politically incorporated precisely to protect and maintain the income of its inhabitants from the encroachment of Baltimore City. The difference in the degree of inequality within the city and county does not occur because they are different production systems but because of the differential relations of those political units, and the groups within them, to the overall system of production.

This distinction between a system of production and areas within a system is important for any analysis of income distribution within modern states, since these states are part of a *single* system, the capitalist world-economy. That there is a single system of production has been effectively demonstrated by Wallerstein (1974a; 1974b). Two types of evidence support this claim. First, the division of labor of this system encompasses the entire world. The different states within this system specialize in different types of production, in different types of labor skills and organization, and in different political roles; and all of these specializations are necessary for the functioning of the system. Second, this division of labor has developed as a consequence of the operation of this world-economy, which began in the sixteenth century as a European world-economy and has now expanded to include the entire globe.

When we compare the degree of inequality within modern states, then, we are comparing political units within a larger system. And if we assume that stratification is a function of the organization of production, then we should expect that the income distribution within states is a function of the relation of states, and the economic groups within them, to this world-economy.[1]

The World-Economy and Inequality Within States

This section discusses how the structure of the world-economy operates to affect the degree of inequality within states. The basic idea is that the greater the economic dominance and influence that states (and the economic actors within them) have in the world-economy, the more equal the distribution of power within states, and consequently, the more equal the distribution of reward. Economic dominance and influence over production in a market system can be exercised in a variety of ways, such as through ownership, through financial control, through the ability to set prices, and through the ability to decide what is to be produced and where it will be sold. Thus, like Lenski (1966:44–58), this model assumes that inequality of reward is a function of the distribution of power and control over production. But since the system of production is the world-economy, it is dominance and influence in this larger system which determines the distribution of power within states and, consequently, the distribution of reward. The first part of this section discusses the nature of the world-economy. The second part describes three major means by which control in this system is achieved. And the third part discusses how this control affects the degree of inequality within states.

The Structure of the World-Economy

Following Wallerstein (1974b), I conceptualize the system of production as the capitalist world-economy. Three features of this system are central for understanding its functioning. First, the defining characteristic of this system is that production is undertaken "for sale in a market in which the object is to realize the maximum profit" (Wallerstein, 1974b:398). Second, the political units of this system are states. And third, the division of labor within this system is not only functional but also geographic.

What is unique about the market system is that the market is the primary mechanism for organizing the factors of production and the decisions of economic actors. Polanyi (1944) describes two central features of this type of system. First, under a market system, greater profit accrues to those economic actors that possess larger amounts of resources. Consequently, there is a continual pressure in the market system toward monopolization and the creation of privileged access to resources. Second, the market system is dynamic and creates risks and uncertainties for any specific economic actors, since new areas of demand and new profit opportunities continually arise and often undercut and disadvantage previous centers of profit. Consequently, there is a continual pressure for economic actors to attempt to stabilize these uncertainties to both protect and increase their advantages. These two features of markets, then, lead to continuing attempts for "actors in the market to avoid the normal operation of the market whenever it does not maximize their profit. The attempts of these actors to use non-market devices to ensure short-run profits makes them turn to the political entities which have, in fact, power to affect the market—the nation states" (Wallerstein, 1974b:403). Since states, which are the political units of the world-economy, are organizations with considerable power, economic actors orient their actions toward these political structures to secure privileged access to resources and protection from the risks of the market. Under this production system, then, there is a continuing growth of the power and autonomy of states as different economic actors find it necessary to support the state, and increase its authority, in order to more effectively pursue their economic activities. As Wallerstein says, "The functioning of a capitalist world-economy requires that groups pursue their economic interests within a single world-market while seeking to distort this market for their benefit by organizing to exert influence on states, some of which are more powerful than others but none of which controls the market in its entirety" (1974b:406).

This difference in the strength of state structures is partially a result of the fact that the functional division of labor in the world-economy is also geographic. Different areas of the world, and the states within those areas, tend to specialize in different economic roles (suppliers of raw materials versus suppliers of manufactured goods, for example) and, consequently, occupy different positions in the overall system. This geographic division of labor is itself a consequence of the different times in which areas were incorporated into the world-economy, the types of resources in those areas, and the form and strength of the political structures in those areas at the time of their incorporation into this system. This geographic division of labor has two consequences. First, coalitions of economic interest often form among actors located within different states. For example, in many states the producers of raw materials become aligned with those groups in other states that use those materials in manufacturing. Second, economic actors in some states attempt to control directly and to influence the economic and political process in other states. These two tendencies, in turn, result in international differences in the strength of various states (Wallerstein, 1972).

In this system, actors orient their economic activities to the world-market, but constantly attempt to use their local state structures to secure and advance their economic advantages. And control of production within states becomes subject, in varying degrees, to the actions and influence of actors located within different states.

Power and Control in the World-Economy

Dominance and influence over production in this system can be achieved in three major ways: (1) through the political mechanism of state control and regulation, (2) through direct economic penetration and control of economic activity in other states, and (3) through lessening the dependence of the economic activity within a state on the external market.

Political control, or state strength, refers to the degree to which a state dominates the activities within its population. Since force is an unstable means of control, strong states are those which have transformed force into a stable set of authority relations which give rights of the regulation and control of activities of its population to the state. Thus, the mark of a strong state is not the size of its army or the centralization of power in the hands of an oligarchy, but the degree to which the state apparatus has come to expropriate to itself the rights to control action, among the most important of which are the rights to regulate and control economic activity (see, for example, the papers in Tilly, 1975). Political control is a major mechanism for securing control over production in the world-economy for three reasons. First, strong states are effective mechanisms for protecting economic actors from the risks and uncertainties generated by the world-market. They accomplish this task through the regulation of the economic production within their borders. For example, many of the poorest areas in Latin America today were at one time highly active centers of raw material production in the world-economy. But when the demand for these materials declined, the capital and organization which exploited these resources were withdrawn (Frank, 1972). Strong states, however, are effective mechanisms for preventing such occurrences. They can erect barriers to prevent external control of production by forcing ownership into the hands of indigenous groups. They can regulate the flow of capital and profit to ensure that the gains of production are not withdrawn from the country but channeled into other economic activities within the national economy, and through trade and tariff policies, they can stimulate a diversification of production (Furtado, 1972). Thus, strong states typically have elaborate rules and regulations controlling the production within their boundaries, and much political activity is directed toward controlling economic activity. Second, states are effective mechanisms for securing privileged access to resources and markets, including their own national markets. Economic actors engaged in producing consumption goods, for example, often attempt to influence the state to protect the home market from economic penetration of the manufactures of groups in other states. Similarly, groups attempt to influence the state to secure foreign markets as outlets for their goods and to secure a steady supply of the materials needed for production. Most of the trade and commercial policies of states are directed toward these two ends (Hobsbawm, 1968). Third, states are effective mechanisms for organizing economic actors to work in concert in the world-market. States provide a means for pooling the resources of economic actors and achieve the benefits of economies of scale that large resources have under a market system. These benefits can be achieved either through advantage in direct competition or through control over prices as effected recently by the oil exporting states. The ability of states to act in these ways is a function of both the strength of the state in relation to its own population and of the strength of the state in relation to other states. A strong state structure, therefore, is one of the major means by which states, and the economic actors within them, can gain control and power in the world-economy.

Direct economic penetration and control over the production activities in other states is a second mechanism of control. Direct economic control over the production of raw materials by those who use those materials in manufacture is a means to insure a steady supply of those materials and a way to keep prices at an artificially low level (Furtado, 1972). In states in which much of production is directly controlled by foreign economic actors, those states and their national economic groups have much less control and ability to influence economic activity. This is one reason why nationalization of production is a means to increase the control of states, and their national economic groups, over production in the world-economy.

The third means of control is to decrease the dependence of national economic activity on the external market. If a good deal of the resources needed for production must be purchased from outside the national economy and much of the goods produced must be sold outside, then control over production is reduced. One reason is that this situation makes economic actors more vulnerable to political attempts by other states to restrict supplies and protect their own internal markets for indigenous producers. A second reason is that this situation exposes economic actors more to the risks and uncertainties in the world-market. Consequently, there is a distinct advantage to large size in the capitalist world-economy, for greater size increases the probability of both large amounts of domestic resources and a large internal market for consumption.

These three means of control in the world-economy are not necessarily highly correlated, and states may rank differently on all three. But strong states, with little foreign control over their internal production and a large internal market, are states which have the greatest power and control in the world-economy. Weak states, with a large amount of foreign control over production and a high dependence on foreign markets for both materials and outlets, will be the weakest in control. The empirical analysis will attempt to show that these means of achieving power and control in the world-economy affect the internal distribution of income within states. The remaining part of this section discusses how dominance and control in the world-economy affects the internal distribution of power, and inequality, within the state.

Mechanisms Affecting Income Distribution

Inter-country differences in domination and influence over the process of production affect income distribution in three interrelated ways: (1) through effects on the process of class formation, (2) through effects on the production and occupational structure, and (3) through effects on class relations.

(1) Class formation. Inter-country differences in control over production are reflected in variations in class formation among countries. In dependent countries within the world-economy, a class structure has developed which is dominated by a small economic elite whose predominant interests have been tied to foreign economic actors through mutual interests in the control of production for export. Typically, this economic and political alliance has centered around the production and export of food and raw materials required by the dominant countries in the system. These elites, in turn, have suppressed or limited the development of national groups which have attempted to develop indigenous manufacturing and industrial production. This has occurred because the interests of these export elites are directed toward free trade with other countries, while the interests of the indigenous manufacturing classes rest with restriction of trade to protect their manufactures from those of other countries. Historically, for example, this conflict lay behind the Latin American civil wars of the nineteenth century; and in each instance, the forces of free trade and external orientation were victorious. Consequently, what developed was a class structure consisting of a small but dominant elite based on the export-import sector, controlling an immense share of the wealth of the country, and a small, weak manufacturing class (Amin, 1974; Ehrensaft, 1971; Furtado, 1972; Frank, 1972; Girvan, 1973; Wallerstein, 1974b). This class structure ultimately generates a very unequal income distribution when compared to the dominant countries, which have experienced just the opposite process of class formation. In the latter countries, strong state structures and less direct foreign control shifted the balance of political and economic forces away from the dominance of a small export elite and toward the

development of a much larger and diversified manufacturing class with the consequence that income distribution is more equal (Hobsbawm, 1968; Moore, 1966; Wallerstein, 1972).

Historical studies have shown the type of class formation which develops is a function of the three means of dominance and control over production discussed previously. Thus, in countries where capitalist production was initiated in response to a demand for raw materials by foreign actors, an economic and political alliance developed between local elites and foreign economic actors. This alliance produced forms of direct and indirect foreign control over production (e.g., in terms of what and how much to produce, control of prices, and control of patterns of trade) and led to the decline of indigenous manufacturing. Where states were strong, political action was taken through military and commercial policy to protect indigenous manufactures; but where states were weak (and it has often been the case that the leverage provided by foreign control was one of the major sources undercutting the power of the state), the externally oriented elite proved dominant. Thus, initial differences amoung countries in terms of foreign control, reliance on external markets, and state strength led to different paths of class formation and, consequently, to intercountry differences in income inequality. Wallerstein (1972) shows that the combination of external alliances and a weak state accounted for the decline of the indigenous Polish bourgeoisie, leading to the de-industrialization and peripheralization of Poland, and the dominance of an export-oriented landed elite in that country. On the other hand, a strong state structure combined with limited foreign control led to the dominance of the indigenous bourgeoisie in England and the Netherlands. Amin (1974), Frank (1972) and Sunkel (1973) have documented the peripheralization process in Latin America and Africa.

(2) The production and occupational structure. These differences in class formation have important and long-term effects on the production and occupational structures of countries. In peripheral countries, this export-dominated elite structure has produced a type of development termed "dependent development" (Girvan, 1973).

Typically, one or two areas of export production become well-developed, but are controlled by a small elite. A small service and commercial sector develops in relation to the export sector, but there is no large scale diversification of manufacturing production. That is, under this type of growth, the spread and multiplier effects that economic growth is usually assumed to generate do not develop (Baer, 1967; Furtado, 1972; Singer, 1950). What develops instead is a small labor elite, or aristocracy, which works in the export sector for relatively high wages (often four to ten times the wage for similar work in other sectors), and this produces extreme wage inequalities (Arrighi, 1970; Girling, 1973). In the dominant states in the world-economy, the opposite process occurs. The strong state structures and relatively weak foreign controls allow production to have expansive effects on the national economy. The production and occupational structures become expanded and diversified, with a much lower degree of inequality within the wage sector. Thus, inter-country differences in income inequality result not only from differences of class formation but also from resulting differences in the production and occupational structure.

(3) Class relations. Finally, these processes affect the political relations among classes, particularly by affecting the bargaining power of workers in relation to employers, the state, and each other. In dependent countries, the combination of a smaller wage-labor force and the lower level of skills in the work force have made political organization more difficult. The labor force as a whole has less bargaining power in relation to employers since they face a smaller and more homogeneous set of employers. Since the state is relatively weak, workers cannot effectively use access to the state to apply political leverage to meet demands for higher wages, a strategy which has been the successful one in dominant countries (Shorter and Tilly, 1974). In the dominant countries, the work force is much larger and more organized and, consequently, has more bargaining power. In addition, labor has been able to use the state to press for demands, both in terms of wages and in terms of other measures of redistribution such as tax policy. Finally, as Routh (1965) has shown for England, the relative power of different occupational groups within the work force is more homogeneous in dominant countries, so that if one occupational group makes wage gains, other groups mobilize and apply political and economic pressure to effect similar wage gains. In dependent countries, with a small well-paid labor aristocracy and a large low-wage underemployed work force, this same process does not occur. Thus, the nature of class relations in dominant countries is qualitatively different than in dependent countries, which in turn, has lead to differences in income inequality.

Evidence from Historical Trends

Although long-term historical series on income distribution in countries is very scarce, it can be useful to inspect what data is available to see if the broad patterns are consistent with the hypotheses developed in this paper. The inspection of such historical series may also provide some evidence on whether a developmental or world-economy perspective is more useful in explaining changes in income distribution.

However, the historical series that exist must be interpreted very cautiously for three reasons. First, the necessary data often is not directly available and a considerable amount of work is based on indirect measures in constructing historical time series. Second, most of the historical materials vary in their coverage of the population. What we would like is nationally representative data on income distribution of persons or households. However, there is almost none of this sort of historical data until after World War II. Third, analysts investigating the same countries do not always agree on the course of the historical record. Such disagreement, however, is not surprising given that the data is often piecemeal in character and many assumptions must be made to construct a long time trend. (For discussions of these problems, see Kuznets, 1955; Marchal and Ducros, 1968; Soltow, 1968). Therefore, it is doubtful that the present evidence should be taken as conclusive, though it seems clear that the most reliable data are those that pertain to the post-World War II period.

With this in mind, we now proceed to see how the historical evidence fits with two issues that are suggested by the alternative models of income distribution. The first issue concerns the course of changes in income distribution following a change in a country's relative position in the world-economy. The model developed previously predicts that a country that increases its dominance in the world system should come to have a more equal income distribution, and a country that declines in its relative position should show increasing inequality. A suggestive test of this prediction can be made by comparing the trends in income distribution in the United States and Great Britain.

The United States was originally incorporated into the world-economy in a relatively weak position, but over the last hundred years has become the dominant country in the system. The available historical data for the United States do show that the distribution of income has become more equal during this time. Kuznets (1955) presents data which he interprets to show that income distribution was stable between 1913 and 1930, but that inequality began to decline sometime during the 1930s, with this trend continuing at a greater rate after World War II. Miller (1966) confirms this analysis, arguing that there was a decline of inequality from 1929 to after World War II, with a leveling off in the mid-1950s. Kravis (1962) concludes that there was a decrease in inequality in the United States between 1890 and 1920, followed by a slight increase during the depression, and a continuing decline in inequality from the early 1930s to after World War II, with stability in the post-war period. Thus, the historical record for the United States shows that there has been a decline in income inequality during the time when the United States became the dominant country in the world system, and that this decline in inequality has leveled off since the mid-1950s.

The historical data for Great Britain are not as clear-cut over the long historical period. Soltow's (1968) work on Great Britain indicates that there may have been some decline in inequality between 1801 and 1880 (the period of England's dominance in the world-economy), but he is cautious in drawing this conclusion. Between 1880 and 1911, he finds evidence of some reduction of inequality. Between 1913 and 1960, he shows a definite decline in inequality. Routh (1965), however, finds a general long-term stability in income distribution between 1906 and

1955. This is the time period during which England lost her dominant position to the United States but still remained as the second or third strongest power, at least until after World War II. The decline of England's relative position in the world-economy, which has become so evident since World War II, seems to be matched by an increase in income inequality since sometime in the 1950s. Routh finds the distribution to have become more unequal from 1955 to 1960. Seers (1966) finds a slight increase in inequalities since the war and Nicholson (1967) documents an increase in inequality since 1959. Stark (1972) shows an increase in inequality between 1959 and 1963. Though all of these studies differ in the times during which they show increases in inequality, the overall picture presented is that there has been a definite increase in income inequality in England since the 1950s. Thus, the historical data for the United States and Great Britain are consistent with the idea that changes in income distribution are related to changes in a country's relative position in the world-economy.

A second issue relevant to both the developmental and world-economy models is the relation of changes in income distribution to economic growth. The developmental model predicts that income distribution should become more equal with economic growth. The world-economy model emphasizes changes in a country's position in the world-economy. Thus, it is quite possible for all countries to experience economic growth, yet to retain their relative positions in the system. The world-economy model does not imply that there is no mobility within the system, since countries do change their relative positions; but it is a structural characteristic of the system that the relative positions of most countries remain stable for very long periods of time. Thus, the countries which formed the core of the system in the seventeenth and eighteenth centuries—England, France, Holland, Prussia—are still among the dominant countries in the system. Countries which were incorporated as peripheral areas—Latin America and parts of Africa and Asia—are still in relatively weak positions within the system. Thus, we should expect relatively long periods of stability in income distribution in most countries. This is because, even though almost all countries grow economically, their relative position tends to remain stable for long periods of time. Indeed, almost all studies of historical trends in income distribution show relatively long periods in which income distribution is stable. Such a finding emerges in the studies of the United States and Great Britain noted previously. A hundred-year study of several areas of Germany also shows remarkable periods of stability in income distribution among wage-earners (Jeck, 1968). A study of eight Norwegian cities (Soltow, 1965), however, does show more of a continual decline in inequality. There does emerge, then, a somewhat general picture of long periods of stability in the income distribution of countries of Western Europe and the United States at a time when the aggregate economic output of these countries was showing a marked, long-term increase (Kuznets, 1971:1–50). There is also some recent evidence from longitudinal studies in Latin America which show that income inequality has increased, even in the face of rapid economic growth. For example, Vandendries (1974) shows a marked increase in inequality in Peru from 1954 to 1970, at a time when gross domestic product (GDP) in real terms grew at an annual rate of 5.2 percent. Similarly, a study of Brazil from 1960 to 1970 (Fishlow, reviewed in Girling, 1973) shows a marked increase in inequality while economic growth in real terms increased at a rate of 6 percent annually. From the point of view of the world-economy model, it is interesting to note that the external public debt and profits made by foreign firms, two forms of external control, also increased rapidly during this time period (Donnelly, 1973; U.N. Balance of Payments Yearbook, 1969).

Thus, the evidence from historical movements of income distribution seems to be consistent with the idea that income distribution in a country is a function of the relation of that country to the world-economy. These data do not necessarily invalidate the developmental model, since the time lags necessary to produce changes in inequality as a result of growth are not clear. However, the comparative movements of inequality in the United States and England, the long periods of stability of income distribution, and the increases in inequality in the face of economic growth do suggest that the world-economy model may be more appropriate than the developmental model.

Income Distribution Data

We now turn to an empirical, cross-sectional analysis which examines the relationship between indicators of a country's position in the world-economy and the distribution of income within states. Comparative data on income distribution have been difficult to obtain. The few empirical studies of cross-national income inequality have not even used measures of individual or family income but have employed sectoral income as a proxy (Cutright, 1967; Jackman, 1974). However, using sectoral income[2] for this purpose assumes that the income within each production sector is equally distributed among all economic actors within the sector. This assumption is unrealistic (Husbands and Money, 1970). Recently, due to the work of Adelman and Morris (1971) on underdeveloped countries, the amount of data on the distribution of family and household income has been greatly increased. The data used in this analysis are taken from Paukert (1973). He presents data showing the share of personal pre-tax income accruing to the five quintiles of households in 56 countries. In assembling this information, he used much of the data collected by Adelman and Morris; but he omits their data for four countries because of inadequacies, replaces their data for three countries with data from better sources, recalculates the income distribution for nine countries using more realistic assumptions, and adds data for sixteen developed countries. The result is income distribution data for a highly varied set of countries, except no socialist countries are included.[3]

In the empirical analysis, we test the proposition that power and control in the world-economy reduces the degree of income inequality within states. Three specific hypotheses are tested: (1) the greater the strength of the state, the more *equal* the income distribution; (2) the greater the degree of direct foreign control over production, the more *unequal* the distribution of income; (3) the greater the reliance of a state's production on external resources, the more *unequal* the distribution of income. We test these hypotheses by regressing the share of income accruing to each quintile of households on indicators which measure these three means of power and control in the world-economy. In interpreting the regression results as test of this model, we look for two kinds of evidence. First, we expect that measures of greater power in the world-economy will have negative effects on the overall measure of inequality, the Gini coefficient; and that this overall decline is produced by a reduction of the share of the income of the top quintile and an increase in the share of the income of the bottom quintiles. Thus, besides making inferences from the signs and magnitudes of the regression coefficients, we also consider the overall pattern of the results.

In interpreting the regression coefficients, it is important to remember that they represent the effects of the measures of power in the world-economy on the *relative* shares of income. Thus, although the share of income accruing to the bottom 20 percent of households in the United States is almost equal to the share of income accruing to the bottom 20 percent in Chile (5.6 percent versus 5.4 percent), the *absolute* level of income in the United States is much higher than in Chile (Paukert, 1973:114–5). Similarly, the signs and magnitudes of the coefficients should not be interpreted as absolute increases or decreases in the income of the different quintiles but as increases or decreases in the *relative* share of the income accruing to that quintile. For example, the negative coefficient of $-.297$ representing the effect of the log of kilowatt-hours on the income share of the top quintile (see Table 16.1) does not mean that this group loses absolute income, but that its gain is negative relative to other quintiles.[4]

Analysis of Data

The Effects of Economic Development

We begin the analysis by investigating the relation between the level of economic development and income inequality. The indicator of economic development used is the log of kilowatt-hours consumed per capita. The values of kilowatt-hours (KWH) were obtained from the United Nations Statistical Yearbooks (1950–1969). Log values are used both because this transformation was suggested by the scatter plots and because Jackman (1974) has shown that a log transformation is appropriate for the theoretical models relating economic development to inequality.

Table 16.1

Effects of Ln Kilowatt-Hours per Capita on Income Shares Received by Quintiles (N=47)

Independent Variables	Effects on Income Shares Received by Quintile					Gini Index
	Q_1 Bottom 20%	Q_2 21–40%	Q_3 41–60%	Q_4 61–80%	Q_5 81–100%	
Ln KWH per Capita	−.310[a] ** (.151)[b] −.293[c] **	.201 (.192) .154	.748** (.227) .441**	.791** (.248) .429	−1.41** (.671) −.297**	−.009 (.007) −.183

[a] Unstandardized regression coefficient.

[b] Standard error of coefficient.

[c] Standardized regression coefficient.

*Significant at .10.

**Significant at .05.

Because the data on income distribution is from different years, this measure of economic development, and all other measures used in the analysis, have been matched to the exact year for each case. Because the data are from different years, the year relevant for each country's data was included in the regressions to test for a possible secular increase or decrease in inequality. No such effect was found. Also, following Lieberson and Hansen (1974), the date of independence of each country was controlled, but this variable had no effect on the analysis.

The results of the regressions of the five separate income quintiles and the Gini index on the log of KWH per capita are presented in Table 16.1.

The first number under each quintile is the unstandardized regression slope; the number in parentheses is the standard error; and the third number is the standardized slope, or path coefficient. Table 16.1 shows that the effect of economic development is to decrease slightly the overall degree of income inequality.[5] This is shown by the −.183 standardized regression coefficient for the Gini index. This overall decrease in inequality is due to a relative loss of the share of income of the richest quintile, Q_5, and a relative loss of the share of the poorest quintile, Q_1. The standardized regression coefficient representing the effect of log KWH on Q_5 is −.297, and the coefficient representing the effect of log KWH on Q_1 is $-.293$. The middle three quintiles all increase their relative share of income as a result of higher levels of economic development. The standardized regression coefficients associated with these three quintiles are .154, .441 and .429. This analysis shows that the effect of economic development is to decrease income inequality by expanding the share of income accruing to the middle groups and reducing the share of income accruing to the richest and the poorest group.

Some researchers have argued that economic development is likely to have a curvilinear effect on inequality. That is, at early stages of economic development, income inequality is likely to increase but then the effects of development change to reduce inequality (Adelman and Morris, 1973; Kuznets, 1963; Paukert, 1973). Soltow (1968), however, finds no evidence that such an initial increase in inequality occurred in England's early industrialization. This hypothesis of a curvilinear relation between economic development and inequality was tested by fitting a second-order polynomial regression to the data, which allowed the effects of economic development to be positive initially on inequality and then become negative. The results of these regressions did not support the hypothesis of a curvilinear relation. The signs of the terms were not in the hypothesized direction nor were the coefficients significant. Inspection of the scatter plots also did not reveal any evidence of such a curvilinear relation either.[6]

This analysis replicates other results from cross-sectional studies of the relation between economic development and inequality (Cutright, 1967; Jackman, 1974). The world-economy model does not argue that there are no effects of economic development on inequality, but rather that the consequences of economic growth depend on the social organization under which development occurs. In the empirical analysis that follows, we focus on the social relations of production and show that power and influence over production in the world-economy is an important determinant of income distribution, even controlling for the effects of wealth; and that the effects of wealth tend to weaken and change somewhat when measures of power and influence in the world-economy are considered.

The Effects of State Strength

The first hypothesis we test is that the greater the strength of the state, the more equal the distribution of income within states.[7] State strength has two dimensions. First, states vary by the degree to which they have control over the activities of their own population. Second, states vary by the degree to which they have strength in relation to other states. The indicator we use to measure the first dimension of state strength is the value of government revenues as a percentage of gross domestic product. This indicator measures the degree to which the total economic resources in a state's population are available to the state itself. The data on government revenues are taken from the

Table 16.2
Effects of Ln Kilowatt-Hours per Capita and Government Revenue on Income
Shares Received by Quintiles (N=47)

| Independent Variables | Effects on Income Shares Received by Quintile | | | | | Gini |
	Q_1 Bottom 20%	Q_2 21–40%	Q_3 41–60%	Q_4 61–80%	Q_5 81–100%	Index
Ln KWH	-.381**	.058	.505*	.491*	-.653	-.002
per Capita	(.177)	(.224)	(.260)	(.282)	(.771)	(.008)
	-.360**	.044	.298*	.266*	-.138	-.031
Government Revenue	.114	.101	.172*	.212**	-.535**	-.006**
as % of GDP	(.086)	(.083)	(.096)	(.104)	(.286)	(.003)
	.201	.210	.293*	.310**	-.304**	-.289**

Note: see notes to Table 16.1.

International Financial Statistics Supplement 1972 and supplemented
for five cases from Cross-Polity Time-Series Data by Banks et al. (1970).
Data were not available on nine countries, reducing the number of cases
to forty-seven.

Table 16.2 presents the results of the six equations in which the five
income quintiles and the Gini index have been regressed on the log of
KWH per capita and government revenues as a percentage of GDP. The
results of this analysis support the hypothesis that the greater the degree
of state strength, the lower the degree of income inequality. The effect
of government revenue on the Gini index is −.289. And government
revenue has its predicted positive effects on the bottom four quintiles
and negative effects on the relative income of the top quintile. Government
revenue tends to increase the relative income of the first four quintiles
in an increasing fashion. Its effects are weakest on increasing the relative
income of the bottom quintile and strongest on increasing the relative
income of the fourth quintile. The *unstandardized* slopes associated with
government revenue on the share of the income of the first four quintiles
are .114, .101, .172 and .212. Its strongest effect is in decreasing the
relative income of the richest quintile (the slope is −.535). The independent effects of log KWH are somewhat altered. Particularly, the
negative effect of log KWH on the relative income of the top quintile
is reduced from −1.41 to −.653. That is, the reduction in the relative
income of the top quintile is largely a consequence of greater state
strength rather than a direct consequence of greater economic development.[8]

The effects of government revenue, then, are very strong and independent of economic development. These results speak to a question posed by Jackman (1974). After he showed that the degree of societal democratization had no effect on the distribution of income within countries, he posed the question of what political dimensions, if any, did affect the distribution of income (Jackman, 1974:40). One answer to this question is state strength. Jackman himself suggested another dimension of politics, legislative *efforts* toward reducing inequality. He measures this by constructing an indicator of social insurance program experience (SIPE), proposed by Cutright (1956). This index is constructed by combining the number of five possible types of social insurance programs a country has and the number of years that these programs have been in effect. The data come from the yearbook Social Security Programs throughout the World (1973). Jackman's analysis showed that the SIPE index had the effect of decreasing the degree of *sectoral* income inequality in a sample of 60 nations. He did not have household income data. To test this hypothesis with household income data, we constructed the SIPE index for the countries used in this analysis and included SIPE in the equations with log KWH and government revenues (Jackman did not include a measure of state strength).

The results, presented in Table 16.3, show that support for this argument does not appear when household income distribution is the dependent variable and government revenue is included as an explanatory variable. First, the effect of government revenue is not affected by the inclusion of the SIPE index in the equations. Second, the coefficients associated with the SIPE index are very small. None of them are significant and none of the slopes are even greater than their standard errors. The pattern of effects though is as would be expected, with the SIPE index having positive effects on the bottom four quintiles and a negative effect on the income share of the top quintile. However, the effects are very small and do not alter the effects of government revenues.[9]

The world-economy model argues that state strength decreases income inequality because the state is a mechanism of power and control over production in the world-economy. The analysis has also shown that a measure of direct welfare effort or legislative policy effort as *indicated by SIPE* does not mediate the effects of state strength. Another way to test the idea of the state as a mechanism of control is to use measures of the second dimension of state strength, the strength of states in relation to other states in the world-economy. One measure of this aspect of state strength is the degree of external public debt of states. The data on external public debt come from the World Tables of the International Bank for Reconstruction and Development (1973). The rationale for using the amount of external public debt as a measure of the *weakness* of a state in the world-economy is as follows: the more a state is indebted to other states or to economic actors located within other states, the weaker that state is in the world-system. This is because the higher the

Table 16.3

Effects of Ln Kilowatt-Hours per Capita, Government Revenue and SIPE Index on Income Shares Received by Quintiles (N=47)

Independent Variables	Effects on Income Shares Received by Quintile					
	Q_1 Bottom 20%	Q_2 21–40%	Q_3 41–60%	Q_4 61–80%	Q_5 81–100%	Gini Index
Ln KWH	-.521**	-.082	.449	.439	-.333	.002
per Capita	(.247)	(.312)	(.364)	(.394)	(1.07)	(.011)
	-.492**	-.063	.264	.242	-.070	-.036
Government Revenue	.042	.093	.169*	.210**	.516*	-.005*
as % of GDP	(.067)	(.085)	(.098)	(.106)	(.291)	(.003)
	.107	.193	.268*	.307**	-.294*	.278*
SIPE Index	.005	.005	.002	.002	-.011	-.000
	(.006)	(.007)	(.009)	(.010)	(.027)	(.001)
	.186	.151	.047	.032	-.095	-.095

Note: see notes to Table 16.1

level of debt, the more leverage other states have over that state. The greater the degree of debt, the more constrained are the actions of that state in the world-system (Furtado, 1972; Payer, 1974). Consequently, we use the amount of external public debt as a percentage of GDP as a measure of the weakness of states in relation to other states. A similar measure can be constructed using the amount of foreign reserves that a country possesses. The rationale for using this measure is similar. The more foreign reserves a country possesses, the more it is able to obtain needed resources from other states without incurring an external public debt. The amount of foreign reserves in United States dollars has been obtained from the International Monetary Fund (1972). The model predicts that (1) the greater the degree of external public debt, the more unequal the income distribution and (2) the greater the amount of foreign reserves of a state, the more equal the distribution of income.

The results are presented in Tables 16.4 and 16.5 which do lend some support to these hypotheses. The pattern of results and the signs of the coefficients are all as predicted. External public debt has negative effects on the relative share of the income of the bottom four quintiles and a positive effect on the income share of the top quintile. Foreign reserves has the predicted opposite effects, positive effects on the bottom quintiles and a negative effect on the income of the top quintile. The effects of

Table 16.4

Effects of Ln Kilowatt-Hours per Capita, Government Revenue and External
Public Debt on Income Shares Received by Quintiles (N=40)

Independent Variables		Effects on Income Shares Received by Quintile					
		Q_1 Bottom 20%	Q_2 21-40%	Q_3 41-60%	Q_4 61-80%	Q_5 81-100%	Gini Index
Ln KWH		-.333*	-.099	.471	.391	-.622	-.002
per Capita		(.201)	(.248)	(.297)	(.304)	(.877)	(.009)
		-.303*	.074	.262	.199	-.121	-.041
Government Revenue	.030	.098	.152	.183*	-.471	-.005*
as % of GDP	(.070)	(.087)	(.105)	(.107)	(.311)	(.003)
	.079	.211	.244	.269*	-.265	-.249*
External Public	-.002	-.001	-.005	-.011**	.018	.001
Debt as % of GDP	(.003)	(.003)	(.004)	(.004)	(.012)	(.001)
	-.139	-.003	-.189	-.350**	.231	.191

Note: see notes to Table 16.1

Table 16.5

Effects of Ln Kilowatt-Hours per Capita, Government Revenue and Foreign
Reserves on Income Shares Received by Quintiles (N=41)

Independent Variables		Effects on Income Shares Received by Quintile					
		Q_1 Bottom 20%	Q_2 21-40%	Q_3 41-60%	Q_4 61-80%	Q_5 81-100%	Gini Index
Ln KWH		-.619**	-.089	.413	.551*	-.218	.007
per Capita		(.226)	(.297)	(.335)	(.363)	(.945)	(.010)
		-.523**	-.056	.219	.261	-.042	.123
Government Revenue	.057	.091	.168*	.198*	-.514**	-.005**
as % of GDP	(.065)	(.086)	(.096)	(.104)	(.263)	(.002)
	.156	.194	.287*	.302*	-.319**	-.318**
Foreign Reserves	.317	.439*	.330	.330	-1.43*	-.016*
	(.207)	(.272)	(.308)	(.333)	(.868)	(.009)
	.258	.280*	.168	.150	-.266*	.292*

Note: see notes to Table 16.1

external public debt are not very large. Only its effect in the fourth quintile is significant. For foreign reserves, the effects are larger. Its effects are significant on the second and fifth quintiles and the Gini index. In all cases the slopes are greater than their standard errors. The overall conclusion to be drawn from these two tables is that these measures of the strength of states in relation to other states do have independent, though small, effects in reducing the degree of income inequality.

The set of results from Tables 16.2 through 16.5 provide support for the first hypothesis; that the greater the strength of states, both internally and externally, the more equal the distribution of income within states. The effects of strong states on income distribution are seen to occur because state strength is a mechanism for control over production in the world-economy.

The Effects of Direct Economic Penetration

The second hypothesis derived from the model is that the greater the amount of direct economic penetration and control over economic activities in a state by foreign economic actors, the greater the degree of income inequality in that state. As discussed above with foreign control over production, foreign economic actors obtain political leverage within the state and tend to form political coalitions with certain indigenous elites to repress the demands of the less powerful economic actors (Furtado, 1972; Galtung, 1971; Wallerstein, 1972).

To measure this direct economic penetration, we use the value of debits on investment income. This value measures the amount of all profits made by foreign direct investment. These data are taken from the World Tables of the International Bank for Reconstruction and Development. Debits are measured as a percentage of GDP.[10] Since this is a measure of lack of control over production, the hypothesis is that the greater the amount of debits in a state, the higher the degree of income inequality. The effect of having foreign actors control indigenous production should be to lower the relative income shares of the bottom groups and raise the relative income share of the top quintile. The results of this analysis are presented in Table 16.6.

Included in these equations is a measure of domestic capital formation obtained from the United Nations Statistical Yearbooks (1950; 1969). This measure is included following an argument by Chase-Dunn (1974). It may be argued that foreign capital gravitates to those areas where domestic capital is low, because profits would be higher there, and a low level of domestic capital increases income inequality. Consequently, any effect of debits on income distribution may be spurious due to the level of domestic capital formation.

The results in Table 16.7 show that the greater the level of debits, the higher the degree of income inequality. The effect of debits on the Gini index is .346. Further, the level of debits has negative effects on

Table 16.6

Effects of Ln Kilowatt-Hours per Capita, Government Revenue, Debits on Investment Income and Capital Formation on Income Shares Received by Quintiles (N=39)

Independent Variables	Effects on Income Shares Received by Quintile					
	Q_1 Bottom 20%	Q_2 21-40%	Q_3 41-60%	Q_4 61-80%	Q_5 81-100%	Gini Index
Ln KWH	.619**	-.305	.213	.541	.019	.011
per Capita	(.234)	(.311)	(.365)	(.408)	(1.04)	(.011)
	-.558**	-.215	.113	.267	.038	.206
Government Revenue	.084	.125	.200**	.222**	-.631**	-.007**
as % of GDP	(.060)	(.080)	(.094)	(.105)	(.266)	(.003)
	.240	.284	.340**	.348**	-.396**	-.406**
Debits on Invest.	-.307**	-.317**	-.358*	-.174	1.13**	.013**
Income	(.115)	(.153)	(.179)	(.203)	(.509)	(.005)
	-.387**	-.316**	-.267*	-.120	.313**	.346**
Capital Formation	.021	.145*	.144	.044	-.354	-.004
as % GDP	(.066)	(.088)	(.103)	(.115)	(.293)	(.003)
	.060	.321*	.239	.068	-.217	-.217

Note: see notes to Table 16.1

the relative income shares of the bottom four quintiles and positive effects on the relative share of income of the top quintile. These results support the second hypothesis that the greater the degree of direct foreign control over production within a state, the greater the degree of income inequality within the state. The effects of government revenue again remain basically the same, demonstrating that the various mechanisms of power and control in the world-economy have separate independent effects on the degree of material inequality. These results also replicate a finding by Chase-Dunn (1974) who analyzed the effects of debits and domestic capital formation on economic growth, measured by GDP per capita. The effects of domestic capital formation are opposite to the effects of debits, i.e., foreign controlled capital. As he suggests, this points to the fact that capital does not have uniform effects on economic growth or inequality, but its effects vary by the locus of control of capital. This finding also demonstrates the point made previously that the effects of wealth are a function of the social organization of the production of wealth.

Table 16.7

Effects of Ln Kilowatt-Hours per Capita, Government Revenue and Exports on
Income Shares Received by Quintiles (N=47)

Independent Variables	Effects on Income Shares Received by Quintile					
	Q_1 Bottom 20%	Q_2 21–40%	Q_3 41–60%	Q_4 61–80%	Q_5 81–100%	Gini Index
Ln KWH	-.459**	-.012	.430*	.468*	-.406	.001
per Capita	(.169)	(.222)	(.259)	(.289)	(.760)	(.008)
	-.434**	-.009	.253*	.254*	-.086	.029
Government Revenue	.100	.146*	.220**	.227**	-.693**	-.007**
as % of GDP	(.064)	(.084)	(.099)	(.110)	(.290)	(.003)
	.256	.302*	.349**	.332**	-.394**	-.392**
Exports as % GDP	-.708**	-.627*	-.681*	-.208	2.23*	.027**
	(.263)	(.344)	(.403)	(.449)	(1.18)	(.013)
	-.377**	-.272*	-.226*	-.063	.266*	.307**

Note: see notes to Table 16.1

The Effects of Dependence on External Markets

The third hypothesis derived from the model is that the more a state is dependent on the external market for its production activities, the greater the degree of income inequality. Such dependence subjects economic actors to political attempts by other states to restrict supplies and protect their own internal markets and, in general, reduces control over economic fluctuations in external markets.

To measure this economic dependency on the external market, we use the value of exports and the value of imports, both measured as a percentage of GDP. The reason is that the greater a country's proportion of imports and exports, the more its economic activities are dependent on actions in the external market. Here, the concern is not with whether internal production in a country is controlled by foreign actors as was the case above, but rather, just the fact of having to import or export puts the state and its economic actors in a position of less power and control in the world-economy. The data on exports and imports are obtained from the International Financial Statistics Supplement 1972. The results of this analysis are presented in Tables 16.7 and 16.8.

The results show strong support for the hypothesis. In the case of both imports and exports, the effects are to lower the relative shares of the income of the bottom four quintiles and to raise the share of

Table 16.8

Effects of Ln Kilowatt-Hours per Capita, Government Revenue and Imports on
Income Shares Received by Quintiles (N=47)

Independent Variables	Effects on Income Shares Received by Quintile					
	Q_1 Bottom 20%	Q_2 21–40%	Q_3 41–60%	Q_4 61–80%	Q_5 81–100%	Gini Index
Ln KWH	-.421**	.007	.504*	.461*	-.525	.000
per Capita	(.173)	(.217)	(.265)	(.284)	(.764)	(.008)
	-.397**	.005	.295*	.250*	-.111	.001
Government Revenue	.083	.143*	.176*	.237**	-.641**	-.006**
as % of GDP	(.066)	(.072)	(.101)	(.108)	(.290)	(.003)
	.212	.297*	.289*	.347**	-.365**	-.360**
Imports as % GDP	-.525**	-.666**	-.065	-.401	1.69	.021*
	(.252)	(.317)	(.387)	(.415)	(1.11)	(.012)
	-.296**	-.306**	-.123	-.130	.213	.253*

Note: see notes to Table 16.1

income accruing to the top quintile. The standardized coefficients showing
the effects of exports and imports on raising the overall level of income
inequality (the Gini index) are .307 and .253. Also, the effects of
government revenue remain basically the same when imports and exports
are included in the analysis. These same results occur if both imports
and exports are included together in the same equations. We present
them separately here to show that it is dependence on the external
market that causes the negative effects on income distribution, and such
dependence should occur equally whether actors are dependent on
external markets through exporting or importing.

One possible alternative explanation of these findings is the following.
It can be argued that it is not imports or exports per se which affect
inequality but the type of products that are imported and exported.
Particularly, it can be argued that specializing in the production of food
and raw materials for export has little spin-off effects in the national
economy and this in turn prevents a decrease in income inequality
(Galtung, 1971). Since those countries which specialize in these types
of products also have a very high proportion of exports as a percentage
of their total production, then the effects of exports on income distribution
may be spurious, due not to dependence on external markets but to
the type of product exported. This argument suggests that if one controls

Table 16.9

Effects of Ln Kilowatt-Hours per Capita, Government Revenue, Exports and Value
of Foodstuffs Exported on Income Shares Received by Quintiles (N=47)

Independent Variables	Effects on Income Shares Received by Quintile					Gini Index
	Q_1 Bottom 20%	Q_2 21-40%	Q_3 41-60%	Q_4 61-80%	Q_5 81-100%	
Ln KWH	-.421*	-.013	.357	.389	-.281	.003
per Capita	(.185)	(.249)	(.282)	(.295)	(.817)	(.009)
	-.393*	.010	.207	.204	-.058	.058
Government	.094	.137	.210**	.197*	-.637**	-.009**
Revenue as	(.066)	(.088)	(.100)	(.104)	(.291)	(.003)
% of GDP	.250	.289	.349**	.296*	-.380**	-.389**
Exports as % GDP	-.567**	.576	-.606	-.230	2.01**	.234*
	(.277)	(.372)	(.421)	(.441)	(1.22)	(.131)
	-.308**	-.247	-.205	-.070	.243**	.274*
Value of Food	.009	-.005	.016	-.043**	.057	.000
Exported	(.010)	(.010)	(.016)	(.017)	(.047)	(.001)
	-.120	-.055	-.135	.332**	.176	.109

Note: see notes to Table 16.1

for the type of products imported and exported, the effects of exports
and imports on income inequality will disappear.

To test this alternative hypothesis, we have coded from the Yearbook
of International Trade Statistics (U.N., 1950–69) the type of products
imported and exported for each country. We have used the category
system of the Standard International Trade Classification (SITC) to group
exports and imports into three types of products: foodstuffs (SITC
categories 0 and 1), petroleum products and raw materials (SITC categories 3 and 4) and manufactured goods (SITC categories 5, 6 and 7).
We then included the value of the three types of products into the
equations for exports and imports. The results of including a specification
for type of product show that types of products exported and imported
do not affect the relationships between exports and imports and the
distribution of income.

Tables 16.9 and 16.10 present a sample of these results. Table 16.9
shows the effects of including the value of foodstuffs exported, and
Table 16.10 shows the effects of including the value of manufactured
goods exported. These tables apply only to exports, but the same pattern

Table 16.10

Effects of Ln Kilowatt-Hours per Capita, Government Revenue, Exports and Value of Manufactured Goods Exported on Income Shares Received by Quintiles (N=47)

Independent Variables	Effects on Income Shares Received by Quintile					Gini Index
	Q_1 Bottom 20%	Q_2 21-40%	Q_3 41-60%	Q_4 61-80%	Q_5 81-100%	
Ln KWH	-.477**	-.102	.288	.260	.056	.006
per Capita	(.211)	(.279)	(.320)	(.349)	(.925)	(.010)
	-.455**	-.075	.167	.137	.011	.124
Government	.088	.127	.201**	.179*	-.595**	-.006**
Revenue as	(.067)	(.089)	(.102)	(.111)	(.295)	(.003)
% of GDP	.235	.267	.334**	.269*	-.351**	-.366**
Exports as % GDP	-.587**	-.474	-.442	.171	2.34*	.183
	(.285)	(.377)	(.431)	(.471)	(1.24)	(.134)
	-.319**	-.203	-.149	.052	.263*	.215
Value of	.004	.014	.015	.033	-.066	-.001
Manufactured	(.013)	(.018)	(.021)	(.022)	(.059)	(.001)
Goods Exported	.055	.148	.129	.257	-.202	-.170

Note: see notes to Table 16.1

of findings also appears for imports. As these tables demonstrate, the effects of exports on increasing inequality through reducing the income share of the bottom quintiles and raising the income share of the top quintile remain even when the type of product is controlled. The overall conclusion is that dependence of economic production on the external market causes an increase in the degree of income inequality. These results tend to confirm the third hypothesis derived from the theoretical model, that the dependence of economic production on the external market tends to increase the degree of income inequality.

Summary and Implications

In this paper we have posited a model which explains the income distribution within states as a consequence of the relation of states to the world-economy. The empirical results have supported the three hypotheses derived from this model. Two implications for the comparative study of stratification can be drawn from this analysis. First, since the model developed here is based on the assumption that there is a single

system of production in the modern world system, the empirical confirmation of hypotheses from this model supports the validity of this
assumption. Therefore, it seems crucial that comparative studies of
stratification, and studies of economic and political development in
general, start with the recognition that states are separate *political* units
within one production system, the capitalist world-economy. Such a
model implies that many features of states are a consequence of the
functioning of this whole system and the roles that various actors occupy
in this world-economy. Second, this analysis contradicts the widely held
view that increasing economic and political development will necessarily
lead toward an equalization of incomes within all states. This is because
the operation of the capitalist world-economy as a system of production
generates and maintains a system of stratification in which some states
and economic actors necessarily have more power and control over
production than others. If this is the case, and the degree of inequality
within states is a function of power and control in this world-economy,
then under this system it is not possible for all states to have the same
distribution of income.

Notes

1. Other comparisons of inequality are also possible. For example, one can
construct a world distribution of income with states as the income units and
compare how the distribution of income among states changes over time (Meyer
et al., 1975). Such a comparison would speak to the question of whether the
operation of the world-economy is causing changes in the distribution of income
among states. This chapter, however, compares the distribution of income within
states and studies the way in which the position of states in the world-economy
affects this income distribution.

2. Sectoral income inequality is computed by dividing the percentage of total
domestic product produced in eight economic sectors (agriculture, mining,
manufacturing, etc.) by the number of workers in each sector. A Lorenz coefficient
is then computed based on the degree to which this per worker product is
unequal across the eight sectors.

3. The available income distribution data for socialist countries is not comparable to the data used in this analysis because it covers only the active working
population and sometimes only some segments of this population. Therefore,
we can say nothing directly about whether socialist countries would conform
to this analysis. However, while the processes determining income distribution
within socialist states often are seen as different from those in capitalist states,
a world-economy perspective suggests that some of the same processes may
apply, since these states are also part of the capitalist world-economy. The state-
socialist model of development—the creation of a strong state structure, nationalization and careful regulation of economic activity crossing state boundaries—contains the three elements that we have argued are means to increase
control over production in the world-economy and thus this socialist model of
development should decrease inequality.

4. This interpretation is necessitated by the fact that there is somewhat of
a part/whole problem when the five income quintiles are separately regressed

on the independent variables, since an effect on any one quintile will cause an effect on some other quintile. Because of this complication, the analysis was replicated through the use of canonical correlation, which allows all quintiles to enter the analysis simultaneously. (The second quintile was omitted in the canonical analyses to avoid linear dependency among the quintiles.) The results from the canonical analysis support the results of the regression analyses.

5. Although it has been argued sometimes that inequality affects development, a review of this literature by Cline (1975) concludes that income distribution has a largely neutral effect on economic development.

6. All analyses in this chapter have also been done using several other measures of economic development: gross domestic product per capita, the percentage of the male labor force in industry and the percentage of the male labor force in agriculture. The results are substantially the same.

7. The means and standard deviations of the variables used in these analyses appear in Appendix 1. The correlations among these variables appear in Appendix 2. The list of countries used in the analysis appears in Appendix 3. [See original article.—Ed.] Also, the scatter plots of the variables reveal no nonlinear associations that would necessitate a linear transformation.

8. The inclusion of gross domestic product as part of the indicator for several of the variables raises the possibility of measurement bias (cf. Fuguitt and Lieberson, 1974). To check for such an effect we recomputed the regression equations in two ways. First, we regressed the income shares on raw government revenue, exports, etc., and included GDP in the equations as a control. These equations were then estimated by weighted least squares (wls). A wls estimating procedure was required because of the pattern of the disturbance variances in the unweighted equations. This wls procedure produced the same results as the original equations. Second, we included total GDP in the original equations as another way to test for measurement bias, and the results of this procedure also produced the same pattern of findings as the original equations.

9. An analysis was also performed in which the five quintiles and the Gini index were regressed on the dollar value of social security benefits in a country as a percentage of GDP. The social security benefits data were obtained from the Cost of Social Security Programs published by the International Labour Organization (1961–1968). The results of these regressions show that there are no significant effects of social security benefits on the pre-tax distribution of income.

10. Gross domestic product is a measure of the total amount of goods and services produced within the domestic boundaries of a country. It does not include goods and services produced by citizens outside the domestic boundaries.

References

Adelman, Irma and Cynthia Morris. 1971. An Anatomy of Patterns of Income Distribution in Developing Nations, Part III of the Final Report (Grant AID/csd-2236).

——. 1973. Economic Growth and Social Equity in Developing Countries. Stanford: Stanford University Press.

Amin, Samir. 1974. Accumulation on a World Scale, Volume 1. New York: Monthly Review Press.

Arrighi, Giovanni. 1970. "International corporations, labour aristocracies, and economic development in tropical Africa." Pp. 220–67 in Robert Rhodes (ed.), Imperialism and Underdevelopment. New York: Monthly Review Press.

Baer, Werner. 1961. "The economics of Prebisch and ECLA." Economic Development and Cultural Change 10–11:169–82.

Banks, Arthur. 1970. Cross-Polity Time-Series Data. Cambridge, Mass.: Massachusetts Institute of Technology Press.

Chase-Dunn, Chris. 1974. "The effects of international economic dependence on development and inequality: a cross-national study." Paper presented at the Meetings of the American Sociological Association, Montreal.

Cline, William. 1975. "Distribution and development: a survey of literature." Journal of Development Economics 1:1–42.

Cutright, Phillips. 1965. "Political structure, economic development, and national social security programs." American Journal of Sociology 70:537–50.

————. 1967. "Inequality: a cross-national analysis." American Sociological Review 32:562–78.

Donnelly, John. 1973. "External financing and short-term consequences of external debt servicing for Brazilian economic development." Journal of Developing Areas 7:411–29.

Ehrensaft, Philip. 1971. "Semi-industrial capitalism in the Third World." Africa Today 18:40–67.

Frank, Andre G. 1972. "The development of underdevelopment." Pp. 3–17 in J. D. Cockcroft, A. G. Frank and D. Johnson (eds.), Dependence and Underdevelopment. New York: Doubleday.

Fuguitt, Glenn and Stanley Lieberson. 1974. "Correlation of ratios or difference scores having common terms." Pp. 128–44 in Herbert Costner (ed.), Sociological Methodology, 1973–1974. San Francisco: Jossey-Bass.

Furtado, Celso. 1972. Economic Development of Latin America. Cambridge: Cambridge University Press.

Galtung, Johan. 1971. "A structural theory of imperialism." Journal of Peace Research 8:81–117.

Girling, Robert. 1973. "Dependency and persistent income inequality." Pp. 83–101 in Frank Bonilla and Robert Girling (eds.), Structures of Dependency. Stanford: Institute of Political Studies.

Girvan, Norman. 1973. "The development of dependency economics in the Caribbean and Latin America." Social and Economic Studies 22:1–33.

Hobsbawm, Eric. 1968. Industry and Empire. Middlesex, England: Penguin.

Husbands, C. T. and Roy Money. 1970. "The cross-national study of inequality: a research note." American Sociological Review 35:319–25.

International Bank for Reconstruction and Development (IBRD). 1973. World Tables. Washington, D.C.: IBRD.

International Labour Organization (ILO). 1961–68. The Cost of Social Security. Geneva: ILO.

International Monetary Fund (IMF). 1972. International Financial Statistics 1972, Supplement. Washington, D.C.: IMF.

Jackman, Robert. 1974. "Political democracy and social equality." American Sociological Review 39:29–45.

Jeck, Albert. 1968. "The trends of income distribution in West Germany." Pp. 78–106 in Jean Marchal and Bernard Ducros (eds.), The Distribution of National Income. New York: St. Martin's Press.

Kerr, Clark, J. T. Dunlop, Frederik Harbison and Charles Myers. 1964. Industrialism and Industrial Man. New York: Oxford University Press.
Kravis, Irving. 1962. The Structure of Income. Philadelphia: University of Pennsylvania Press.
————. 1973. "A world of unequal incomes." The Annals of the American Academy of Political and Social Science 409:61–80.
Kuznets, Simon. 1955. "Economic growth and income inequality." American Economic Review 45:1–28.
————. 1963. "Quantitative aspects of the economic growth of nations, VIII: the distribution of income by size." Economic Development of Cultural Change 11:1–80.
————. 1971. Economic Growth of Nations. Cambridge: Harvard University Press.
Lenski, Gerhard. 1966. Power and Privilege. New York: McGraw-Hill.
Lieberson, Stanley and Lynn K. Hanson. 1974. "National development, mother tongue diversity, and the comparative study of nations." American Sociological Review 39:523–41.
Marchal, Jean and Bernard Ducros. 1968. The Distribution of National Income. New York: St. Martin's Press.
Meyer, John, John Boli-Bennett and Chris Chase-Dunn. 1975. "Covergence and divergence in development." Pp. 223–46 in Alex Inkeles (ed.), Annual Review of Sociology, Volume 1. Palo Alto: Annual Reviews Inc.
Miller, Herman. 1966. Income Distribution in the United States. Washington, D.C.: U.S. Government Printing Office.
Moore, Barrington. 1966. Social Origins of Dictatorship and Democracy. Boston: Beacon.
Nicholson, R. J. 1967. "The distribution of personal income." Lloyds Bank Review 83–86:11–22.
Paukert, Felix. 1973. "Income distribution of different levels of development: a survey of evidence." International Labour Review 108:97–125.
Payer, Cheryl. 1974. The Debt Trap. Middlesex, England: Penguin.
Polanyi, Karl. 1944. The Great Transformation. Boston: Beacon.
Ranis, G. and J. C. Fei. 1961. "A theory of economic development." American Economic Review 51:533–65.
Routh, Guy. 1965. Occupation and Pay in Great Britain 1906–1960. Cambridge: Cambridge University Press.
Seers, Dudley. 1956. "Has the distribution of income become more unequal?" Bulletin of the Oxford University Institute of Statistics 18:73–86.
Singer, Hans. 1950. "The distribution of gains between investing and borrowing countries." American Economic Review 40:473–85.
Shorter, Edward and Charles Tilly. 1974. Strikes in France, 1830–1968. Cambridge: Cambridge University Press.
Social Security Administration. 1973. Social Security Programs throughout the World, 1973. Washington, D.C.: U.S. Government Printing Office.
Soltow, Lee. 1965. Toward Income Equality in Norway. Madison: University of Wisconsin Press.
————. 1968. "Long run changes in British income inequality." Economic History Review 21:17–29.
Stark, Thomas. 1972. The Distribution of Personal Income in the United Kingdom, 1949–1963. Cambridge: Cambridge University Press.

Sunkel, Osvaldo. 1973. "Transitional capitalism and national disintegration in Latin America." Social and Economic Studies 22:132–76.

Tilly, Charles. 1975. The Formation of National States in Western Europe. Princeton: Princeton University Press.

United Nations. 1950–69. Statistical Yearbook. New York: United Nations.

—————. 1950–69. Yearbook of International Trade Statistics. New York: United Nations

Vandendries, Rene. 1974. "Income distribution in Peru after World War II." Journal of Developing Areas 8:421–36.

Wallerstein, Immanuel. 1972. "Three paths of national development in the sixteenth century." Studies in Comparative International Development 8:95–101.

—————. 1974a. The Modern World-System: Capitalist Agriculture and the Origins of the European World-Economy in the Sixteenth Century. New York: Academic Press.

—————. 1974b. "The rise and future demise of the world capitalist system: concepts for comparative analysis." Comparative Studies in Society and History 16:387–415.

17. Cross-National Evidence of the Effects of Foreign Investment and Aid on Economic Growth and Inequality: A Survey of Findings and a Reanalysis

Volker Bornschier
Christopher Chase-Dunn
Richard Rubinson[1]

In the last chapter, Rubinson presented data supporting the thesis that income inequality within states is a function of the operation of the world system. In the years immediately preceding and following the publication of Rubinson's study a series of studies were published attempting to test dependency and world-system perspectives with respect to their predictions regarding the gap between rich and poor. In this chapter, the authors summarize much of that research and find strong support for the proposition that dependency (in the form of foreign investment and aid) increases income inequality. The evidence with respect to the impact of dependency on economic growth is found to be equivocal, however. The authors therefore proceed to examine the possible causes of the variations in findings and conduct their own analysis, which leads them to the conclusion that dependency slows growth over the long term. In sum, the research reported here makes a strong case that both of the gaps this book is focused on are products of dependency and the operation of the world capitalist system.

As a theoretical perspective on development, dependency theory emphasizes that a country's position in the world division of labor is a major cause of development and underdevelopment. One focus in dependency theory has been the analysis of the consequences of foreign investment and foreign aid for the development of the structure of the national economy and state, the rate of economic growth, and the degree of inequality within countries. This concern has by now generated a

Reprinted with permission from the *American Journal of Sociology*, vol. 84 (November, 1978): 651–671, 676–679, 682–683.

large number of empirical cross-national studies which have investigated these relationships.

This chapter reviews a subset of these studies. We want to find out what can be concluded from them about the effects of foreign investment and aid on national economic growth and inequality. We do not discuss the extensive theoretical literature on dependency theory or recent extensions of that theory into world-system analysis. Nor do we discuss critiques of these theories.[2] Our aim is to review a set of empirical studies, to explain inconsistent and contradictory findings, and to summarize the conclusions.

A review of these studies is important to the study of national development because the question of the effects of dependence on growth and inequality is widely debated and considered crucial for many theories of development (Frank 1972; Papanek 1972; Singer 1950, 1975; Heintz 1969; Heintz and Heintz 1973; Senghaas 1977). These writings are widely scattered in the literature of the social sciences, and most researchers are familiar with only a limited subset of them. Also, they present many seemingly contradictory findings. Consequently, different researchers draw different conclusions about the relationships, depending on which studies they use. A review, then, will increase our empirical knowledge about the process of development and aid the building of a theory of development.

To anticipate our general conclusions, we find that foreign investment and aid have the long-term effect of decreasing the rate of economic growth and of increasing inequality. This finding is consistent with dependency theory, but we make no claim that any one finding can either prove or disprove such a complex theoretical framework. One reason is that there are many varieties of dependency theory (O'Brien 1975). Another is that no theory of national development is formulated rigorously enough to be capable of a simple confirmation or refutation (Portes 1976). We do insist, however, that any theory of national development must be able to explain this empirical finding.

We limit consideration to cross-national, quantitative studies which analyze the effects of either foreign investment, including multinational enterprises, or foreign aid on economic growth or inequality.[3] We do not imply that other research designs are inferior. There have been excellent case studies, comparative historical studies, and studies using multinational corporations as the unit of analysis. Our purpose, though, is to compare studies which are similar enough to make it possible to draw valid conclusions. Even limiting our scope in this way, we initially find a number of contradictory and inconsistent findings which must be explained.

Our strategy is as follows: First, we discuss the conceptualization of the four main variables with which we are concerned. Second, we discuss the differences in the research designs and measurements in the studies. Third, we compare their results and attempt to explain the contradictory and inconsistent findings. Finally, we state our conclusions and suggest areas for future research.

We are aware that some researchers working within the dependency framework have criticized the type of studies reviewed here for implicitly claiming that dependent development can be explained as a response to external forces, to the neglect of internal processes of class formation and political organization. We do not believe that these studies should be interpreted in this manner. Studying the effects of external forces such as foreign investment, aid, or trade does not imply that internal structures and processes are unimportant or even less important. But we would go further and argue that any such "internal-external" distinction obscures the fundamental point that all these structures and processes are internal to the world-economy. Therefore, we are not claiming that studies of the type reviewed here pertain to the primary dynamic in development and underdevelopment, but just that they treat one important set of processes in understanding the core-periphery division of labor in the world-economy.

Conceptualization of the Major Variables

Table 17.1 lists the 16 studies grouped according to which independent and dependent variables they include. We refer to the two variables whose effects we are studying as investment dependence and aid dependence. Investment dependence is most often conceptualized as the extent to which a country's economy is penetrated and controlled by direct private foreign capital investment. The operations of subsidiaries of multinational corporations (direct investment), rather than portfolio investment, are often the focus of interest. Some studies, however, combine portfolio and direct foreign investment in their measurement of investment dependence.[4] By most theorists and researchers sympathetic to dependency theory, investment dependence is understood as a structural feature of a national economy which gives some degree of economic and political power to those groups whose interests are involved with the foreign investment. By theorists and researchers working in the framework of neoclassical economics, investment dependence is seen as a flow of resources into a country (Chase-Dunn 1975a). These different viewpoints come to affect the way this variable is operationalized in the studies.

Aid dependence refers to the amount of foreign aid, both private and public, that a country receives. Aid dependence also is viewed in two distinct ways. By some researchers, it is seen as creating a control structure by which international or bilateral aid agencies influence the governments that depend on them for resources. By others, aid is seen as a bilateral or multilateral resource flow into countries. Some of the studies we review focus on the extent to which foreign aid is extended as credit, which may result in foreign indebtedness. We include such "debt dependence" in our review of the effects of foreign aid.

Table 17.1
Cross-National Studies of the Effects of Foreign Investment and Aid on
Economic Growth and Equality

Independent Variables	Dependent Variables	
	Economic Growth	Economic Inequality
Investment dependence...	Alschuler	Bornschier (1975, 1978)
	Bornschier (1975)	Chase-Dunn (1975a)
	Bornschier and Ballmer-Cao	Kaufman et al.
	Chase-Dunn (1975a)	Rubinson (1976)
	Evans	...
	Kaufman et al.	...
	McGowan and Smith	...
	Papanek (1973)	...
	Ray and Webster	...
	Rubinson (1977)	...
	Stevenson	...
	Stoneman	...
	Szymanski	...
Aid Dependence..........	Chase-Dunn (1975a)	Chase-Dunn (1975a)
	Griffin and Enos	Rubinson (1976)
	McGowan and Smith	...
	Papanek (1973)	...
	Rubinson (1977)	...
	Stevenson	...
	Stoneman	...
	Szymanski	...

Economic development and income inequality are the two major dependent variables with which we are concerned. A national economy is considered developed if it has high levels of internal differentiation, integration, and energy consumption, employs scientific technology in production, and has a high level of labor productivity in all sectors. Most studies use GNP per capita or GDP per capita, or a growth rate of these, as a measure of economic development.[5] Despite the criticisms of such aggregate measures, they still remain the best single indicators of economic development.

Inequality is most often studied by focusing on income inequality, which refers to the distribution of money income across households or individuals in a country. It is understood that this measure is not an estimate of inequality of wealth, property ownership, or power, but a variable which reflects the outcome of a complex interplay of these and other factors. Some researchers use inequality in land holdings or in the product per worker across economic sectors as a proxy for income inequality, though these measures may not always be valid substitutes for income inequality (Rubinson and Quinlan 1977). . . .

Differences Among the Studies

Sample Size and Composition

The number of countries in these studies varies from 7 to 91. Some of the researchers attempt to overcome the statistical problems of studying a limited number of countries by using data at different time points. For example, Stevenson (1972) pools seven yearly cross-sections on seven Latin American nations to give him a sample size of 49 units to analyze; Stoneman (1975) pools four time periods of 47 countries to give him a sample size of 188. Most researchers include only formally independent nations with populations greater than 1 million. Half of the studies focus on a particular geographic area, and seven of those exclusively on Latin America (Alschuler 1976; Evans 1972; Griffin and Enos 1970; Kaufman, Chernotsky, and Geller 1975; Ray and Webster 1978; Stevenson 1972; and Szymanski 1976) and one on Africa (McGowan and Smith 1978).

Nations are sometimes excluded because of extreme scores on one or more variables. Oil producing countries are excluded by Kaufman et al. (1975) and Rubinson (1977) for this reason. Many authors have also excluded socialist countries either for theoretical reasons or because of problems of data availability. Some studies exclude the most developed countries because they want to study only developing countries (Bornschier 1975; Chase-Dunn 1975a; Papanek 1973; and Stoneman 1975).

Many studies create subsamples and analyze them separately. Bornschier (1975) does his analysis with and without the socialist countries, and Bornschier and Ballmer-Cao (1978) present analyses separately for highly developed countries, large developing countries, and small (and poor) developing countries. Stoneman (1975) divides his sample by geographical area, presenting separate analyses for Latin America, Africa, Asia, and Mediterranean countries. Rubinson (1977) presents analyses for developed and underdeveloped countries. Ray and Webster (1978) present results for their Latin American sample with and without Venezuela.

The sample size and composition of these studies, then, vary greatly. For any one study viewed in isolation, this presents problems of scope and generalizability. But for our purposes, this variability provides distinct advantages. One advantage is that we have replications of many similar samples. Another is that some countries excluded by some studies have been included in others, so we can check on possible biases produced by these exclusions. And, as a third advantage, we can make a wide variety of comparisons for the effects we are studying: the effects in developed versus developing countries, the effects within developing countries, the effects within geographical areas, and the effects between such areas. As we report later, such comparisons allow us to say something about the conditions under which dependence effects occur.

Research Designs

All these studies attempt to infer causal relationships from nonexperimental research designs. The primary difference in these designs lies in the way in which the temporal dimension is employed. There are seven different designs: cross-sectional, pooled cross-sectional, cross-sectional with a percentage growth rate as the dependent variable, the same with the addition of a lagged dependent variable, pooled cross-sectional with a percentage growth rate as the dependent variable, panel analysis, and panel residuals.

A simple cross-sectional design compares measures on variables at one point in time without attempting to measure change over time in any of the variables. This design is employed by Rubinson (1976) and by Bornschier (1978).

A pooled cross-sectional design combines cross-sections for different years into a single analysis. This design is used by Stevenson (1972). Like the simple cross-section, no measure of change is included in the analysis.

The most common design has been a cross-section with a percentage change score used as the dependent variable. For instance, the dependent variable used by Szymanski (1976) is the average yearly growth rate of GDP per capita for the period 1960–72, with the independent variables measured in 1960. This design is also used by Griffin and Enos (1970), Kaufman et al. (1975), and McGowan and Smith (1978). Ray and Webster (1978) also employ it as one of their designs and, using the same data, compare it with others. It should be noted that the time at which independent variables are measured is sometimes not the beginning of the period for which the percentage growth rate is calculated. For example, Kaufman et al. estimate the effect of an independent variable measured in 1929 on a growth rate measured between 1961 and 1969. Most independent variables, however, are measured within the time period for which the percentage growth rate is calculated, but not always at the beginning of this period.

The fourth design is a modification of the previous one, in which a lagged dependent variable is included in the regression equation. Thus, Bornschier and Ballmer-Cao (1978) introduce GNP per capita in 1960 as a control variable in an equation in which the dependent variable is the percentage change in GNP per capita between 1960 and 1975. The inclusion of GNP per capita in 1960 in the equation is intended to control for the relationship between the dependent variable and the independent variables at the first point in time.

The fifth design involves the pooling of cross-sections with the dependent variable being a percentage growth rate. For example, Stoneman (1975) pools four cross-sectional series together, with the dependent variable in each series being a percentage growth rate. Papanek (1973) also uses this design.

The sixth design is panel analysis, in which the dependent variable at time t is regressed on its value at time $t - 1$ (the lagged dependent variable) and other independent variables measured at $t - 1$. For example, Evans (1972) regresses GNP per capita in 1966 on GNP per capita in 1950 and on investment intensity in 1950. This design is also used by Chase-Dunn (1975a) and by Rubinson (1977). And Bornschier (1975) used the same design with panel correlations instead of regressions.

The final design is similar to panel analysis except that the dependent variable is the residuals of the regression of an indicator on itself at an earlier point in time. Thus, Alschuler (1976) uses as his measure of economic growth the residuals from the regression of GNP per capita in 1965 on GNP per capita in 1960. Ray and Webster (1978) also use this method.

These studies, then, employ a great variety of research designs in relation to the handling of the temporal dimension in the measurement of economic growth. Several researchers have investigated the potential biases in the use of different types of change scores and panel designs (Bohrnstedt 1969; Heise 1970; Ray and Webster 1978). With a few exceptions to be noted later, however, we do not find that the different designs used in these studies have affected the findings.

Statistical Estimators

Most of the studies employ linear regression to estimate the relationships between variables. Two studies use partial correlation; three studies use rank order or zero order correlations; and one study uses canonical correlations.

Time Period

The time period most frequently analyzed is the 1960s. Some analysts use data as recent as 1975, and Kaufman et al. (1975) use a measure dating from 1929. Several studies use data from the 1950s to 1970 (Bornschier 1975; Chase-Dunn 1975a; Rubinson 1977; Papanek 1973; and Stoneman 1975). Thus, these studies cover the entire post–World War II period. It is important to keep in mind that the results found during this period may be conditional on certain characteristics of the world-economy during this 20-year period.

Measurement

The studies often use different indicators to measure the four major variables, and we discuss each one in turn. All the studies weight the absolute size of foreign investment (whether stock or flow) and aid by some measure of size, either population, gross product, or energy consumption.

1. *Investment dependence.*—To obtain a measure of an economy's structural dependence on foreign investment most researchers try to approximate a ratio of the value of stock of foreign direct investment to the domestically owned capital stock of the country. This ideal indicator would measure the proportion of the capital ownership of a country that is controlled by foreign actors, that is, it would measure the degree of foreign capital penetration. Data to construct such a measure are not available for most countries, so none of the studies actually uses this measure. Only since the Organization for Economic Cooperation and Development (OECD) study of 1972 have there been estimates of the stock of private foreign direct investment for a large number of underdeveloped countries; but this estimate is available only beginning in 1967. The studies by Bornschier (1978) and Bornschier and Ballmer-Cao (1978) used these OECD data. The other studies that measure stocks of foreign investment estimate the total value by the various methods discussed below.

Some measure the value of foreign investment flowing into a country in a particular year, including reinvested earnings, as shown in the International Monetary Fund (IMF) *Balance of Payments Yearbook* (1950–70) (Kaufman et al. 1975; Papanek 1973; Stevenson 1972). The decision to use such a "flow" measure as opposed to a "stock" measure is quite significant, as we show below. Stock measures estimate the total cumulated value of foreign-owned capital in a country. Flow measures are based on current account inflows of foreign capital for some time period.

To measure stock value of foreign investment other than by using the OECD figures, researchers have used four methods. (1) Several studies of Latin America have used various U.S. Department of Commerce figures on the value of U.S. investment in those countries (Evans 1972; Kaufman et al. 1975; Ray and Webster 1978; Szymanski 1976). These figures are analogous to those of the OECD except that they measure only the book value of United States foreign investment. They do not, of course, take into account the value of investment in Latin America by other countries such as England, Germany, Japan, and France and are therefore a rather problematic proxy.[6] (2) Two studies use the number of subsidiaries of multinational corporations operating in each country as a measure of investment dependence (Bornschier 1975; Evans 1972). (3) Several studies use the amount of profit made by foreign-controlled firms as indicated in the IMF *Balance of Payments Yearbook* item: "debits on direct investment income" (Chase-Dunn 1975a; Rubinson 1976, 1977; Szymanski 1976), or the somewhat less specific item of "factor income paid abroad" (Alschuler 1976; Ray and Webster 1978). (4) Stoneman (1975) estimates the stock of foreign investment by cumulating yearly flows of foreign investment, including reinvested earnings from 1950, into five-year sums. He combines these sums with the 1967 OECD (OECD 1972) data to estimate stocks for earlier years.

2. *Aid dependence.*—The distinction between flows and stocks which was discussed with regard to investment dependence can also be applied

to aid dependence, although there is no aid equivalent to foreign ownership. Flows of public grants and loans to development projects are indicated on current account in the IMF *Balance of Payments Yearbook*. Some researchers have combined flows of private and public capital into a single measure of aid dependence (Griffin and Enos 1970; Kaufman et al. 1975; Ray and Webster 1978), while others examine aid flows separately from private capital flows (Papanek 1973; Stoneman 1975; Stevenson 1972).

Four studies attempt to measure overall structural aid dependence, the conceptual equivalent of stocks of foreign investment. Szymanski (1976) uses the accumulated total of U.S. aid flows to Latin American nations from 1945 to 1960. Chase-Dunn (1975a) and Rubinson (1976, 1977) use the accumulated government, or government guaranteed, foreign debt as presented by the International Bank for Reconstruction and Development (IBRD) *World Tables* (1971).

3. *Economic growth.*—Most of the studies use GNP per capita as a measure of level of economic development and study its rate of change over some time period to estimate growth. Three studies also analyze economic growth in the manufacturing sector (Chase-Dunn 1975b; Evans 1972; Szymanski 1976). Four studies employ measures of change in total GNP rather than in GNP per capita (Griffin and Enos 1970; Kaufman et al. 1975; Ray and Webster 1978; Stoneman 1975).[7] Chase-Dunn (1975a) and Bornschier (1975) use, in addition, measures of energy consumption per capita and labor force structure to measure economic development.

4. *Inequality.*—Inequality is measured in three ways in these studies: by individual or household income inequality, sectoral inequality, and land tenure inequality. Most of the studies use personal income inequality which is the relative distribution of money income across individuals or households in a country (Chase-Dunn 1975a; Bornschier 1975, 1978; Bornschier and Ballmer-Cao 1978; Rubinson 1976). Income inequality is measured either by the Gini index, the percentage of income going to the richest 5 percent and to the richest 20 percent of income recipients, or by the percentage of income to each quintile.

Sectoral inequality, the relative distribution of per worker product in eight economic sectors, is used by Chase-Dunn (1975a), Bornschier (1975) and Kaufman et al. (1975). Although some researchers use it as a proxy for income inequality, it is understood by others as an indicator of uneven economic development. Kaufman et al. (1975) also use land tenure inequality, a measure of the distribution of the geographical size of land holdings. These measures of inequality are not measured over time because of problems of data availability, and so all the analyses using inequality measures are cross-sectional.

Control Variables

The studies also differ in their use of other variables to control for spurious factors or to better specify the model. The need for proper control or specification is important because of the potential biases that could affect the relationships being studied. Four of the studies do not include any control variables (Griffin and Enos 1970; Kaufman et al. 1975; Stevenson 1972; and Szymanski 1976). And in relating the economic growth rate to the stock of foreign direct investment per capita, McGowan and Smith (1978) also do not use any control variables.

In studying the effects of foreign investment and aid on economic growth and inequality, researchers have included six types of variables to control the relationships or specify the model. First, several studies control for other types of dependence measures. Alschuler (1976) controls for trade dependence. In Stoneman's (1975) analysis of economic growth, he includes the stock of foreign investment, flows of foreign private investment capital, and flows of foreign aid in the same equation. Bornschier (1975) controls for the change in the number of multinational subsidiaries when estimating the effect of the level of penetration of multinational corporations on economic growth. The use of such controls as these allows researchers to sort out the independent effects of different types of dependence.

Second, several studies control for the effects of capital formation or domestic savings. Controlling for capital formation is important because this variable is an important cause of economic growth, and low levels of domestic capital formation may cause foreign capital to flow in to take up investment opportunities. The studies that control for this factor are those of Bornschier and Ballmer-Cao (1978), Chase-Dunn (1975a). Papanek (1973), Rubinson (1976), and Stoneman (1975).

Third, Chase-Dunn (1975a) and Rubinson (1977) control for the amount of mineral resources in a country. The possession of mineral resources has a positive effect on economic growth and also is likely to attract foreign capital to exploit these resources. This variable was controlled by including in the models the percentage of GDP in mining and petroleum production.

Fourth, several authors control for the relationship between foreign investment or aid and the prior level of economic development. This control is important in order to sort out the direction of causal effects. It is often argued that foreign investment or aid goes to countries with a relatively higher level of economic development because there are greater investment opportunities. This mechanism would produce a positive relationship between level of economic development and foreign investment at any one point in time. To study the effect of foreign investment on later economic growth, this initial positive correlation between economic growth and foreign investment must be controlled. That is, two processes may be occurring: one by which economic growth leads to more foreign investment, and another by which foreign investment reduces the rate of economic growth. Studies which control for the former relationship are Bornschier (1975), Bornschier and Ballmer-Cao (1978), Chase-Dunn (1975a), Evans (1972), Ray and Webster (1978), and Rubinson (1977).

Fifth, one study, that by Bornschier and Ballmer-Cao (1978), controls for population growth to test the hypothesis that the effects of dependence on economic growth are mediated by population growth.

Sixth, two studies specify their equations by including measures of intervening mechanisms by which foreign investment or aid is thought to affect economic growth. Thus, Bornschier and Ballmer-Cao (1978) control for income inequality, and Rubinson (1977) controls for the degree of state strength in a country.

Comparison of Results

We now turn to a comparison of the results of the studies under review. The question at issue here is, What are the effects of foreign investment and aid on economic growth and inequality? Table 17.2 contains a summary of these findings presented in terms of the direction (positive or negative) of the effect. We first discuss the findings upon which all the studies agree and then we consider the problems raised by the contradictory or inconsistent findings.

Inequality

The five studies dealing with inequality all find that the effects of dependence on inequality are positive. That is, these studies show that dependence tends to increase the amount of inequality within countries. Five studies show positive effects of measures of investment dependence on measures of inequality (Bornschier 1975, 1978; Chase-Dunn 1975*a*; Kaufman et al. 1975; and Rubinson 1976). Two studies show positive effects of measures of aid dependence on inequality (Chase-Dunn 1975*a*; Rubinson 1976). No studies find either zero or negative effects of dependence on inequality.

Given the unanimity of these results, we conclude that investment and aid dependence have the effect of increasing inequality. We note, however, that all the studies of inequality are cross-sectional because sufficient data on inequality have not been available for a longitudinal analysis. It is possible, therefore, to also argue that countries with more unequal income distributions attract more foreign investment and aid and that inequality and dependence form a mutually reinforcing pattern. Studying these reciprocal processes, then, becomes an important area for further research.[8]

Given that the evidence indicates that dependence increases inequality, there is a need for studies which research the mechanisms of this relationship. A number of theoretical discussions have already developed several hypotheses that can be tested in future research (Amin 1976; Girling 1973; Bornschier 1978). The different types of inequality studied may also reveal different processes. The effect of dependence on sectoral inequality may be due to the particularly uneven development caused by foreign direct investment, which causes growth in the immediate

Table 17.2
The Direction of Effects of Foreign Investment and Aid on Economic Growth and
Inequality as Reported in Cross-National Studies

	Economic Growth	Economic Inequality
Investment dependence:		
Positive effects......	Kaufman et al.	Bornschier (1975, 1978)
	McGowan and Smith	Chase-Dunn (1975a)
	Papanek (1973)	Kaufman et al.
	Ray and Webster	Rubinson (1976)
	Stoneman (flows)	...
	Szymanski	...
Negative effects......	Alschuler	...
	Bornschier (1975)	...
	Bornschier and Ballmer-Cao	...
	Chase-Dunn (1975a)	...
	Evans	...
	Rubinson (1977)	...
	Stevenson	...
	Stoneman	...
Aid dependence:		
Positive effects......	Kaufman et al.	Chase-Dunn (1975a)
	McGowan and Smith	Rubinson (1976)
	Papanek (1973)	...
	Ray and Webster	...
	Stoneman (flows)	...
	Szymanski	...
Negative effects......	Chase-Dunn(1975a)	...
	Griffin and Enos	...
	Rubinson (1977)	...
	Stevenson	...

enterprise or sector in which it is invested but structurally retards overall economic growth in other sectors. The effect of dependence on income inequality is most likely due to its effects on the class structure of the country and the translation of this class structure into political power. These hypotheses are promising areas for future research.

Economic Growth

Table 17.2 shows that there are contradictory findings about the effects of foreign investment and aid on economic growth.

Six studies find positive effects of investment dependence on economic growth; eight find negative effects. Six studies find positive effects of foreign aid on economic growth; four find negative effects. Using our

Table 17.3

Studies of the Effects of Foreign Investment on Economic Growth by Measurement of Foreign Investment and Direction of Effects

Measurement of Foreign Investment	Direction of Effects	
	Positive	Negative
Stocks...............	Kaufman et al.	Alschuler
	McGowan and Smith	Bornschier (1975)
	Ray and Webster	Bornschier and Ballmer-Cao
	Szymanski	Chase-Dunn (1975a)
	...	Evans
	...	Rubinson (1977)
	...	Stoneman
Flows.................	Kaufman et al.	Griffin and Enos
	Papanek (1973)	Stevenson
	Ray and Webster	...
	Stoneman	...

previous examination of the differences among the studies, we now attempt to account for these different findings.

Stocks and Flows

One difference which may account for some of these contradictory findings is suggested by our earlier discussion of studies which measure dependence by using measures of flows instead of measures of stocks. Recall that measures employing flows look at inflows of capital or aid on current account while those which employ stocks try to measure the total amount of accumulated foreign capital or aid in a country. Flow measures, then, describe the amount of foreign capital or aid coming into a country within a limited time period, while stock measures describe the accumulated amount that exists in a country. Table 17.3 lists the studies of economic growth by whether they employ flow or stock measures or both.

Table 17.3 presents an interesting set of results. Looking at the studies which employ measures of stocks, we see that seven of the 11 find negative effects on growth. Of the four studies which find positive effects, note that all of them are restricted to a single geographical area: three to Latin America and one to sub-Saharan Africa. Of the six studies which employ measures of flows, four find positive effects and only two find negative effects. This pattern of findings is the same for the effects of both investment and aid dependence.

Thus, employing the distinction between stocks and flows, we can reconcile a good number of the seemingly contradictory findings about

Table 17.4

Studies of the Effects of Stock of Foreign Investment on Economic Growth by
Sample Composition and Direction of Effects

| Sample Composition | Effects on Stock of Foreign Investment | |
	Positive	Negative
Unrestricted...........	...	Bornschier (1975)
	...	Bornschier and Ballmer-Cao
	...	Chase-Dunn (1975a)
	...	Rubinson (1977)
	...	Stoneman
Latin America.........	Kaufman et al.	Alschuler
	Ray and Webster	Evans
	Szymanski	Stoneman
Africa...............	McGowan and Smith	...
	Stoneman	...
Asia.................	Stoneman	...

the direction of effects of dependence on economic growth. The results
of Table 17.4 suggest, then, that current flows of investment capital and
aid have positive effects on growth, whereas long-term stocks of foreign
investment and aid have negative effects. The findings of Griffin and
Enos (1970) for aid and of Stevenson (1972) for investment are the only
studies of flows which do not fit this pattern.[9] These two findings may
be due to sampling error, since Stevenson uses only seven cases and
Griffin and Enos use only 12.

This difference in findings as a consequence of whether one measures
dependence by stocks or flows is more than just a measurement result.
It should be interpreted as a substantive finding. What this pattern
suggests is that the immediate effect of inflows of foreign capital and
aid is to increase the rate of economic growth, while the long-run
cumulative effects operate to reduce the rate of economic growth. This
has been suggested by Bornschier (1975) and by Bornschier and Ballmer-
Cao (1978). And there is a variety of other evidence in these studies
to support such a proposition. Stoneman (1975) includes both stock
and flow measures in the same analysis: he finds that the flow measures
are consistently positive while the stock measures are consistently
negative. He also reports that lagging the stock measure increases the
significance of the negative effect. Chase-Dunn (1975b) finds in a series
of panel analyses that stock measures tend to have zero effects on
growth over short time lags but increasingly negative effects over longer
and longer lag periods. That is, the immediate effects of stocks is zero,
but the longer-term effect is negative. This same result is shown by

Bornschier (1975) with a different measure of investment dependence. Bornschier (1975) also shows a similar result in analyses in which he includes both the level of penetration by multinational subsidiaries and the change in the level of penetration. He finds that short-term increases in penetration have positive effects on growth but become zero and then negative as the lag period is lengthened.

These results tend to confirm the hypothesis that current inflows of investment capital and aid cause short-term increases in growth due to the contribution to capital formation and demand as foreign corporations purchase land, labor, and materials and start production, while the long-run structural distortions of the national economy produced by foreign investment and the exporting of profits tend to produce negative effects over time. We conclude, then, that the effect of short-term flows of investment and aid has positive effects on growth, but that their cumulative effect over time is negative. Many of the seemingly contradictory findings of these studies can be reconciled under this proposition.

Geographic Subsamples

Distinguishing between studies using measures of flows and those using measures of stocks eliminates many of the apparent contradictions in Table 17.3, but there still remain four studies which use measures of stocks and find positive effects of foreign investment or aid on economic growth (Kaufman et al. 1975; McGowan and Smith 1978; Ray and Webster 1978; Szymanski 1976). The common feature of these studies is that each one studies only a particular geographic area. The studies by Kaufman et al. Ray and Webster, and Szymanski concern Latin America only; that by McGowan and Smith concerns black Africa only. However, in Table 17.4 there are also two studies which find negative effects of the stock of foreign investment in Latin American samples (Alschuler 1976 and Evans 1972). Stoneman (1975) also presents some separate analyses by region, and he finds negative effects in his Latin American sample and positive effects in his Asian and African samples. In this section, then, we discuss the contradictory findings that appear in studies of separate geographic regions.

Table 17.5 shows those studies which use stocks measures by the samples they use and their findings. We note first that all five studies which use samples unrestricted by geographic region find negative effects (Bornschier 1975; Bornschier and Ballmer-Cao 1978; Chase-Dunn 1975*a*; Rubinson 1977; Stoneman 1975). These five use either all countries for which data were available, including both developed and underdeveloped, or just the less developed countries. This table shows, then, that with large samples, unrestricted by region, only negative effects are found. On the other hand, of the six studies of Latin America, three find positive effects and three find negative ones. The two studies of Africa and the one of Asia find positive effects. We see, then, a clear difference:

Table 17.5

Regression Estimates of the Effects of Private Foreign Direct Investment on Economic Growth, 1960–1975, within Level of Development and Regional Categories

	Latin America	Asia	Africa
All countries within region....	-.003	-.004	-.001
Richer countries within region..	-.002	-.007	-.003
Poorer countries within region..	+.003	-.003	+.000

the studies with large unrestricted samples show consistent negative effects; conflicting findings appear in the studies of a single geographic region, Latin America.

In comparing the three studies of Latin America which find positive effects with the three that find negative effects, it is not easy to discover factors which could explain the different findings. The studies include basically the same set of countries, with the inclusion or exclusion of Venezuela being the main difference. Ray and Webster (1978) show that the including and excluding of Venezuela has little effect. Sample composition, then, is not an explanation. The measurement of foreign capital dependency, however, suffers from shortcomings in all studies except Stoneman's (1975). Evans (1972), Kaufman et al. (1975), Ray and Webster (1978), and Szymanski (1976) use U.S. figures for the stock of foreign direct capital as a proxy for the total stock. This is a problematic proxy (see n. 6). We should point out, in addition, that none of the findings are very large in a statistical sense.[10] Also, the sample size ranges from 17 to 19 cases, which is rather small for correlation and regression analysis, since differences in one or two cases can affect the magnitude and direction of estimates.

Thus, our comparison of the different studies reveals no systematic reason to explain the different findings of the studies of Latin America. Similarly, the positive effect found in the studies of the African and Asian subsamples is problematic. McGowan and Smith's (1978) finding of a positive effect of investment on growth may be due to the fact that they use a very short lag; as noted above, the longer-term effects of foreign investment are negative. Stoneman's (1975) findings, however, do not suffer from this potential drawback. The problem, then, is to explain why the studies of separate geographical regions diverge in findings from those with larger and unrestricted samples.

Thinking about the pattern in Table 17.5 we can offer four hypotheses to explain these findings from the studies of geographical regions:

Hypothesis 1.—The discrepant results in geographical regions may indicate that the relationship between foreign investment and growth actually varies by geographical region. Although the researchers who use only regional subsamples do not offer any theoretical reason why the relationship should vary by region, the possibility exists.

Hypothesis 2.—A second explanation may be that variables which should be controlled on theoretical grounds are not associated with foreign capital in world samples but are in regional subsamples. A case in point is the variable "domestic capital formation," which has a substantial correlation with the stock of foreign capital in the total sample, but quite different correlations in regional subsamples. Therefore, a more specified, but spurious "geographical-region hypothesis" may be operating. To test this hypothesis requires that the same set of variables be used in each equation that tests the effects of foreign investment in the regional samples.

Hypothesis 3.—These results may indicate that the relationship between foreign investment and growth varies with the level of development of countries. Most countries in Asia and Africa are among the most underdeveloped countries in the world, while Latin American countries are much richer. Geographical samples, then, confound the effect of region with the effect of level of development. Some evidence for this explanation is found in Bornschier and Ballmer-Cao's (1978) study. They find that the relationship between foreign investment and growth is negative for the sample of all less developed countries; but within the sample of the very small (in terms of the absolute size of the modernized segment) and poor countries (mainly African: 25 out of 38), they find a small positive effect. These effects, however, become negative after the introduction of controls (especially capital formation). The hypothesis that the effect might vary by level of development is also suggested by McGowan and Smith (1978) and by Stoneman (1975).

Hypothesis 4.—The results may be a "statistical artifact" produced by the limited range of variation and small sample sizes that naturally characterize any such subsample analysis. Since all the studies which use larger samples with greater variation find negative effects, it is possible that the studies which use smaller samples with limited variation are subject to greater sampling error. That is, if we imagine that the true regression line relating foreign investment to growth is negative, it is still possible that any limited subset of points along that line shows a different relationship between investment and growth than the entire set of points. Stoneman (1975) suggests this explanation to account for why his African and Asian subsamples differ from his much larger sample of all less developed countries.

New Analyses

Our method of comparing and contrasting the differences among the studies does not allow us to choose among these four alternatives. The effects of level of development, geographical region, and limited variation are all confounded in those studies which use only countries from a single region. Therefore we now present results from a new set of analyses to try to clarify these different findings. The new analysis is done in two ways. First, following the form of the previous studies in Table 17.4, we present analyses separately by the different regions and level of development, using the set of control variables our previous review has shown to be important. Second, we use a large sample of developing countries in an analysis of covariance model to allow us to test simultaneously for the possible interactions between foreign investment and region and between foreign investment and level of development, as suggested by the hypotheses. This analysis of a large sample also allows us to overcome the problems of small sample size and restricted variation that occur in the separate analyses by region. . . .

Table 17.5 presents the summary calculations for the effect of foreign capital penetration within the six categories of the analysis. Table 17.5 shows that the effects of foreign capital penetration are negative in all regions. The effect within Latin America is -0.003, the effect within Asia is -0.004, and the effect within Africa is -0.001. The table also shows the effect within the richer and poorer samples of each region. As we concluded above, the effect within the richer group of countries in each region is always more negative than the effect within the poorer group. The table also shows that the only non-zero positive effect occurs within the poorer countries of Latin America. As we noted above, this finding is not of substantive importance. We conclude, then, that there are no regional interactions. Hypotheses 1 and 2 are not confirmed. And we can also eliminate hypothesis 4, the hypothesis of limited variation due to small sample size because the analyses . . . are done with a large sample of countries. We conclude, then, that the effects of foreign capital penetration are negative within all regional samples, and the only substantively important interaction effect is that foreign capital penetration is significantly more negative in richer than in poorer developing countries. . . .

Discussion

Our review of the evidence has produced the following assessment of the empirical relationships with which we are concerned: (1) The effect of direct foreign investment and foreign aid has been to increase economic inequality within countries. This effect holds for income inequality, land inequality, and sectoral income inequality. (2) Flows of direct foreign investment and foreign aid have had a short-term effect of increasing the relative rate of economic growth of countries. (3) Stocks of direct foreign investment and foreign aid have had the cumulative effect of decreasing the relative rate of economic growth of countries. This effect is small in the short run (1–5 years) and gets larger in the long run (5–20 years). (4) This relationship, however, has been conditional on the level of development of countries. Foreign investment and aid have had negative effects in both richer and poorer developing countries, but the effect is stronger in the richer than in the poorer countries. (5) These relationships hold independent of geographical area.

Our review of these studies has also suggested some requirements of research design factors which should be included in future studies of these relationships: (1) Such studies must be longitudinal. This requirement arises because the short-term and long-term effects differ. We have found that short lags produce small or no effects while longer lags produce negative effects. (2) These studies must control for the initial relationship, or correlation, between foreign investment and economic wealth or growth. This is because, for a variety of reasons, foreign investment or aid is often attracted to wealthier or faster growing countries. Unless a researcher controls for this effect, the results will confound the negative effect of foreign investment or aid on economic growth with a positive effect of economic growth on attracting investment or aid. (3) Studies should also control for the initial level of savings (gross domestic investment) in a country, since savings are a major cause of economic growth and may be an inducement for the inflow of foreign capital. (4) These studies should include measures of both the stock and flow of foreign investment, since they have opposite effects on economic growth.

The confirmation of a set of empirical relationships is only a first step in understanding the effects of foreign investment and aid. Studies are needed which try to explain these relationships by explicitly designing research to uncover the structural mechanisms by which these effects occur. Few of the studies reviewed here have explicitly attempted this task. There have been some attempts, and we review them briefly here. Both Chase-Dunn (1975b) and Szymanski (1976) find that foreign investment tends to produce uneven growth across economic sectors. Such uneven development may be one mechanism by which foreign investment leads to a lowered rate of growth. Bornschier and Ballmer-Cao (1978) find that foreign investment leads to increasing income inequality, early monopolization, and structural underemployment, thus favoring early saturation of effective demand and lowering the rate of capital formation in a country. And since capital formation is a major cause of increasing growth, this reduction in capital formation is another mechanism by which foreign investment reduces growth. Finally, Rubinson (1977) finds that one of the ways in which foreign investment reduces growth is by reducing state power, and hence the ability of the state to undertake a policy of growth, independent of the class interests created by foreign capital. All these studies, however, should be seen as initial attempts to specify the mechanisms by which foreign investment and aid affect growth and inequality. Much more explicit research is needed in this area.[11]

These highly aggregated studies, however, can take us only so far in understanding these processes. Three types of studies more micro-sociological in nature are needed. First, dependency situations are not homogeneous, and there are considerable differences in the dynamics of situations such as export enclaves, national export economies, and dependent industrialization. Controlled comparisons of the effects of foreign investment and aid in these different situations should be very fruitful. Second, studies of individual countries and of the effects of foreign investment disaggregated by composition are necessary to clarify the specific mechanisms by which these processes operate. Third, direct studies of the operations of multinational corporations and of their relationships with the state are necessary. There has already been considerable research in these three areas, and an important task is to integrate the many disparate findings into a theoretically organized scheme.

Finally, we note that the empirical relationships we have found occurred during a specific time period, from 1950 to 1970. It is possible that these relationships are conditional on features of the world economy at that time. It seems possible that the effects of foreign investment and aid on growth and inequality may be conditional on whether the world economy is in a period of relative expansion or contraction. For example, Gobalet and Diamond (1977) find some evidence that the negative effects of foreign investment on economic growth are significantly greater from 1965 to 1975 than from 1955 to 1965. Since the earlier period was one of worldwide economic expansion and the later period has been one of worldwide relative economic contraction, their study suggests that foreign investment may have more negative effects in periods of economic contraction. More generally, we also note that no relationships of the type we have analyzed should be assumed to be invariant across quite different historical periods. An important theoretical task is to understand the general conditions under which all such relationships occur.

In conclusion, this paper has reviewed and summarized the findings about a particular set of relationships which are important for under-standing the process of national development. But the discovery of empirical relationships, and of the mechanisms which produce those relationships, should not be considered an end in itself. Such tasks as these are necessary because they are aids to the building of a theory of development. The findings reviewed here should be used toward this end.

Notes

1. Portions of this research have been supported by the German Society of Peace and Conflict Research (DGFK), Bonn-Bad Godesberg, Germany, through the research project, "MNC's, Economic Policy, and National Development," directed by Volker Bornschier and Peter Heintz. We would like to thank Alexandros

Kyrtsis, Dan Quinlan, and Richard Tardanico for their help on this project. The authors' names are listed alphabetically to indicate equal coauthorship.

2. For an introduction to this literature see Lall (1975), Oxaal, Barnett, and Booth (1975), Portes (1976), and Wallerstein (1974).

3. There is also an extensive cross-national empirical literature on the effects of the structure and composition of international trade on economic growth. This body of research requires its own review. For examples, see Alschuler (1976), Delacroix (1977), Galtung (1971), Quinlan (1977), Tyler and Wogart (1973), Rapkin (1976), and Walleri (1976).

4. Direct foreign investment confers rights of ownership and control to the investor. Portfolio investment, usually in government guaranteed bonds, does not legally confer control of operations to the investor.

5. GDP is gross domestic product. GDP differs from GNP (gross national product) by including "net factor income paid abroad" and inflows of factor income. GDP thus includes all transactions taking place on the national territory regardless of the citizenship of the actors. GNP includes only transactions among national citizens and excludes flows abroad or inflows from abroad. "Factor income paid abroad" is used by some researchers as a measure of dependence because it includes as one of its components the expatriated profits on foreign investments. GNP is a better measure of economic activity which is uncontaminated by the direct exchanges with foreign investors. The term "domestic" has created much confusion about GDP and GNP.

6. According to the OECD (1972) estimates of the book value of the stock of private foreign direct investment in 1967 (in developing countries), $17.4 billion was controlled by U.S. actors and $17.7 billion was controlled by actors from other developed countries. The U.S. share was not the same across regions. For example, in Africa the U.S. share was $1.4 billion and the non-U.S. share $5.2 billion. In South America the U.S. share was $7.4 billion and the non-U.S. share $4.7 billion. Nor are the relative shares of U.S. and non-U.S. investment the same across countries within regions. Within Latin America, e.g., the U.S. share in Argentina is 56 percent, in Brazil 36 percent, in Colombia 86 percent, and in Venezuela 73 percent. These figures strongly suggest that the U.S. stock of foreign investment is not a good indicator for total foreign investment.

7. Rubinson (1977) also uses total GNP rather than GNP per capita, but he estimates the equations using weighted least squares, weighting by population. This technique produces results equivalent to the use of per capita measures.

8. Chase-Dunn (1975b) performs a crude test of the hypothesis that inequality causes dependence by entering inequality in a panel model examining the causes of dependence. He finds no effects of inequality on dependence.

9. We consider the positive findings about the effects of stocks of foreign investment on growth below.

10. Only Ray and Webster (1978) find large and significant positive effects of the stock of foreign investment on growth within Latin America. But in reanalyses of their results and those of the other Latin American studies, we found that their unusually large effects resulted from their use of the GNP per capita data compiled by the United States Agency for International Development (USAID). Use of the GNP per capita data compiled by either the World Bank or the United Nations produces small positive effects similar to the findings of Kaufman et al. (1975) and Szymanski (1976). Given the extreme care with which the World Bank and the United Nations compile GNP data, we suspect that data from either of these organizations are superior to those provided by the USAID.

11. Two new studies have been done which we unfortunately have not been able to incorporate into our review. Evans and Timberlake (1977) have shown that foreign capital penetration is related to a distorted occupational structure in which there are disproportionate numbers of workers in tertiary occupations. This, they argue, is one of the ways in which foreign capital penetration affects economic inequality in a country. Gobalet and Diamond (1977) have demonstrated an interaction between state power and foreign capital penetration. The negative effects of foreign capital on economic growth are larger in countries with a relatively weak state than in countries with stronger states.

References

Alschuler, Lawrence. 1976. "Satellization and Stagnation in Latin America." *International Studies Quarterly* 20 (March):39–82.

Amin, Samir. 1976. *Unequal Development: An Essay on the Social Formations of Peripheral Capitalism.* New York: Monthly Review.

Bohrnstedt, George. 1969. "Observations on the Measurement of Change." Pp. 113–33 in *Sociological Methodology, 1969,* edited by Edgar Borgatta. San Francisco: Jossey-Bass.

Bornschier, Volker. 1975. "Abhaengige Industrialisierung und Einkommensent-wicklung." *Schweizerische Zeitschrift fuer Soziologie* 1 (November):67–105.

————. 1978. "Einkommensungleichheit innerhalb von Laendern in komparativer Sicht, *Schweizerische Zeitschrift fuer Soziologie* 4:3–45.

Bornschier, Volker, and Than-Huyen Ballmer-Cao. 1978. *Multinational Corporations in the World Economy and National Development. An Empirical Study of Income per Capita Growth from 1960–1975.* Bulletin of the Sociological Institute of the University of Zurich, no. 32. Zurich: Sociological Institute of the University of Zurich.

Chase-Dunn, Christopher. 1975a. "The Effects of International Economic Dependence on Development and Inequality: A Cross-national Study." *American Sociological Review* 40 (December):720–38.

————. 1975b. "International Economic Dependence in the World System." Ph.D. dissertation, Stanford University.

Delacroix, Jacques. 1977. "Export of Raw Materials and Economic Growth." *American Sociological Review* 42 (October):795–808.

Evans, Peter. 1972. "The Development Effects of Direct Investment." Paper read at the Annual Meeting of the American Sociological Association, New Orleans, August.

Evans, Peter, and Michael Timberlake. 1977. "Dependence, Inequality, and the 'Bloated Tertiary Sector.'" Paper read at the Annual Meeting of the American Sociological Association, Chicago, August.

Frank, André Gunder. 1972. "Economic Dependence, Class Structure, and Underdevelopment Policy." Pp. 19–45 in *Dependence and Underdevelopment,* edited by James Cockcroft, André Gunder Frank, and Dale Johnson. New York: Doubleday.

Galtung, Johan. 1971. "A Structural Theory of Imperialism." *Journal of Peace Research* 8 (2):81–117.

Girling, Robert. 1973. "Dependency and Persistent Income Inequality." Pp. 83–101 in *Structures of Dependency,* edited by Frank Bonilla and Robert Girling. Stanford, Calif.: Institute of Political Studies.

Gobalet, Jeanne G., and Larry J. Diamond. 1977. "Effects of Investment Dependence on Economic Growth: The Role of Internal Structural Characteristics." Mimeographed. Stanford, Calif.: Stanford University, Department of Sociology.

Griffin, Keith, and J. L. Enos. 1970. "Foreign Assistance: Objectives and Consequences." *Economic Development and Cultural Change* 18, no. 3 (April):313–27.

Heintz, Peter. 1969. *Ein soziologisches Paradigma der Entwicklung mit besonderer Beruecksichtigung Lateinamerikas.* Stuttgart: Enke.

Heintz, Peter, and Suzanne Heintz. 1973. *The Future of Development.* Stuttgart: Huber.

Heise, David. 1970. "Causal Inference from Panel Data." Pp. 3–27 in *Sociological Methodology, 1970,* edited by Edgar Borgatta and George Bohrnstedt. San Francisco: Jossey-Bass.

International Bank for Reconstruction and Development (IBRD). 1971. *World Tables.* Washington, D.C.: IBRD.

————. 1976. *World Bank Atlas.* Washington, D.C.: IBRD.

International Monetary Fund (IMF). 1950–1970. *Balance of Payments Yearbook.* Washington, D.C.: IMF.

Kaufman, R. H., H. Chernotsky, and D. Geller. 1975. "A Preliminary Test of the Theory of Dependency." *Comparative Politics* 7 (April):303–30.

Lall, Sanjaya. 1975. "Is 'Dependence' a Useful Concept in Analyzing Underdevelopment?" *World Development* 3 (11–12):799–810.

McGowan, Patrick, and Dale Smith. 1978. "Economic Dependency in Black Africa: A Causal Analysis of Competing Theories." *International Organization* 32, no. 1 (Winter):179–235.

O'Brien, Philip. 1975. "A Critique of Latin American Theories of Dependency." Pp. 7–27 in *Beyond the Sociology of Development: Economy and Society in Latin America and Africa,* edited by Ivar Oxal, Tony Barnett, and David Booth. London: Routledge & Kegan Paul.

Organization for European Cooperation and Development (OECD). 1972. *Stock of Private Direct Investment by DAC Countries in Developing Countries, End 1967.* Paris: OECD.

Oxaal, Ivar, Tony Barnett, and David Booth, eds. 1975. *Beyond the Sociology of Development: Economy and Society in Latin America and Africa.* London: Routledge & Kegan Paul.

Papanek, Gustav. 1972. "The Effect of Aid and Other Resource Transfers on Savings and Growth in Less Developed Countries." *Economic Journal* 82 (September):934–50.

————. 1973. "Aid, Foreign Private Investment, Savings, and Growth in Less Developed Countries." *Journal of Political Economy* 81, no. 1 (January/February):120–30.

Portes, Alejandro. 1976. "The Sociology of National Development." *American Journal of Sociology* 82, no. 1 (July):55–85.

Quinlan, Dan. 1978. "World Economic Position and National Development." Ph.D. dissertation, Johns Hopkins University.

Rapkin, David P. 1976. "Trade, Dependence and Development: A Longitudinal Analysis." Paper read at Southern Political Science Association Meetings, Atlanta, November 4–6.

Ray, James Lee, and Thomas Webster. 1978. "Dependency and Economic Growth in Latin America." *International Studies Quarterly* 22, no. 3 (September):409–34.

Rubinson, Richard. 1976. "The World-Economy and the Distribution of Income within States: a Cross-national Study." *American Sociological Review* 41 (August):638–59.

———. 1977. "Dependence, Government Revenue, and Economic Growth, 1955–1970: A Cross-national Analysis." *Studies in Comparative International Development* 12 (Summer):3–28.

Rubinson, Richard, and Dan Quinlan. 1977. "Democracy and Social Inequality: A Reanalysis." *American Sociological Review* 42 (October):611–23.

Senghaas, Dieter. 1977. *Weltwirtschaftsordnung und Entwicklungspolitik. Plaedoyer fuer Dissoziation.* Frankfurt: Suhrkamp.

Singer, Hans. 1950. "The Distribution of Gains between Investing and Borrowing Countries." *American Economic Review* 40 (May):473–85.

———. 1975. "The Distribution of Gains from Trade and Investment—Revisited." *Journal of Development Studies* 11 (July):376–82.

Stevenson, Paul. 1972. "External Economic Variables Influencing the Economic Growth Rate of Seven Major Latin American Nations." *Canadian Review of Sociology and Anthropology* 9 (4):347–56.

Stoneman, Colin. 1975. "Foreign Capital and Economic Growth." *World Development* 3 (1):11–26.

Szymanski, Albert. 1976. "Dependence, Exploitation and Development." *Journal of Military and Political Sociology* 4 (Spring):53–65.

Tyler, William, and J. Peter Wogart. 1973. "Economic Dependence and Marginalization: Some Empirical Evidence." *Journal of Inter-American Studies and World Affairs* 15 (February):36–46.

U.S. Department of Commerce. 1973. *Survey of Current Business.* Washington, D.C.: Government Printing Office.

Walleri, R. Daniel. 1976. "The Political Economy of International Inequality: A Test of Dependency Theory." Ph.D. dissertation, University of Hawaii.

Wallerstein, Immanuel. 1974. *The Modern World-System: Capitalist Agriculture and the Origins of the European World-Economy in the Sixteenth Century.* New York: Academic Press.

18. Dependence on Foreign Investment and Economic Growth in the Third World

Robert W. Jackman

With this chapter attention is turned to a series of empirical studies that take issue with those who have found evidence to support the dependency/world-system approach. Robert W. Jackman concerns himself with the impact of dependence on economic growth in developing nations. Specifically, he wants to test the proposition that the so-called "Matthew effect" is a function of a nation's position in the world economy. He reviews the literature that has supported dependency/world-system and finds two major flaws. First, Jackman argues, insufficient attention has been paid to testing the relative merits of the modernization versus dependency/world-system approaches. Second, he argues that the theory itself is ambiguous on the question of the relationship between dependency and growth. Jackman finds that although the gap between rich and poor nations is in fact widening, the gap between the West and the wealthiest of the Third World nations is narrowing. Moreover, the Matthew effect appears to be very weak. Jackman also finds that the initial level of foreign investment in a Third World country has an inconsistent relationship to growth, but contrary to the findings of the dependency/world-system research, growth in foreign investment actually speeds economic growth in the Third World.

> *For whosoever hath, to him shall be given, and he shall have more abundance: but whosoever hath not, from him shall be taken away even that he hath.*
> —*Matthew* 13:12

That there is a widening gap between rich and poor countries has become commonly accepted. International inequality is growing because industrial countries have higher rates of economic growth than do underdeveloped countries.[1]

A growing literature on dependency seeks to account for this "Matthew effect"[2] in terms of the position of countries within the world economy,

Reprinted by permission of Princeton University Press from *World Politics*, vol. 34 (January 1982): 175–197. Copyright © 1982 by Princeton University Press.

with special emphasis on the distinction between the "core" industrialized countries and the "periphery." Within this general perspective, the effect of foreign-controlled multinational corporations on capital formation and on economic growth within the periphery has been of major concern. In particular, the investments made by these corporations in underdeveloped countries are often seen as inhibiting economic growth, since they are more than offset by excessive rates of capital repatriation to the industrial core. Foreign investment thus appears to remove from the periphery even that which it hath.

Politically, these patterns are perceived as having two major sets of implications. First, they undermine the autonomy of the periphery. Multinationals and international lending agencies become major, if not dominant, forces in economic policy making, a position they maintain by means of an implicit threat of withdrawal from, and consequent loss of capital by, the host country in the periphery.[3] Second, these patterns lead to the development of new class relations and an acceleration of social inequality in the periphery; new groups emerge that are linked to the core, while the remainder of the periphery population becomes increasingly marginal, in both economic and political terms. Thus, an understanding of the relation between economic dependence and economic growth is important both for its own sake and because this relation is widely believed to have far-reaching indirect effects on patterns of political development.

In this chapter, I examine the way in which foreign investment influences economic growth in Third World countries. After briefly outlining the central issues at stake, my analysis proceeds in two steps. First, I estimate the magnitude of the Matthew effect that is said to distinguish the industrialized West from the Third World. Second, I examine the degree to which foreign investment has affected economic growth in the Third World since 1960. To summarize in advance, the results provide little evidence either for the Matthew effect as commonly propounded, or for the idea that dependence on foreign investment inhibits growth. This, in turn, implies that many of the deleterious political outcomes often attributed to economic dependence are moot.

The Issues

Since discussions of different approaches to economic growth and development are readily available elsewhere,[4] I shall confine my attention here to a brief sketch of the key issues. To simplify somewhat, two broad approaches exist: the "world-system/dependency" approach with its emphasis on forces external to the nation-state, and the "modernization" approach with its emphasis on internal mechanisms.[5] These approaches have been taken in the quantitative comparative literature[6] as providing two competing hypotheses about the impact of foreign investment on economic growth.

First, following the work of Baran, Frank,[7] and others, the dependency approach is generally taken to imply that foreign investment depresses growth. The core-periphery relationship is considered exploitative, in that profits are transferred back to the core rather than reinvested in the periphery; economic dependency thereby contributes to the "underdevelopment" of the periphery. At the same time, the external orientation of periphery economies encouraged by foreign investment is said to generate internal distortions and contradictions that retard growth. Growth is therefore slower in the periphery than it otherwise might be.

In sharp contrast, the modernization approach (which is usually taken to include neo-classical economics), implies that foreign investment promotes growth by providing external capital, which either substitutes for or supplements local capital. It is the presence rather than the origin of the capital that is considered important: capital fosters growth, and its benefits spread throughout the economy. In addition, foreign investment is thought to stimulate growth through the introduction of new technology into the less developed countries (LDCs).[8]

Although the results of earlier attempts to verify these two approaches were mixed, more recent analyses have claimed to furnish evidence for the dependency explanation or a variant of it, while they have been taken as providing little evidence for the modernization explanation. For example, Stoneman argues that direct foreign investment is associated with structural effects that retard the economic growth of poor countries.[9] Similarly, Chase-Dunn reports that foreign investment inhibits growth and exacerbates inequality, from which he concludes "that dependency theories predict the effects of inputs from advanced nations to less-developed ones better than neo-classical international economics theories or sociological modernization theories."[10] Modifying the argument slightly, Bornschier and his colleagues maintain that in the long term (5 to 20 years), the stock of foreign investment decreases the rate of economic growth; however, this pattern is especially strong within the initially richer of the developing countries. Although they properly note that "no one finding can either prove or disprove such a complex theoretical framework," they do take this result as at least "consistent with dependency theory."[11] Finally, in a related analysis that focuses more generally on "structural position" in the world economy rather than on foreign investment, Snyder and Kick report that being in the periphery inhibits economic growth; they take this as "strong support for world-system/dependency theories of structure in the post-World War II period and of the sources of differential economic growth of nations."[12]

There are at least two major problems with these studies—problems they share in varying degrees with most of the crossnational literature on this topic.[13] First, these inquiries are deficient as tests of the *relative* merits of the two approaches because they pay little attention to the factors identified in the modernization approach as important determinants of economic growth. Second, it is not at all clear that the dependency approach unambiguously implies that dependency retards economic growth.[14] I will discuss these issues in turn.

Snyder and Kick are perhaps most explicit in their dismissal of modernization theories, which they reject as "straw men" on the tenuous grounds that "an exogenetic vantage point can easily incorporate domestic factors . . . , while the converse would be conceptually more difficult."[15] The disregard of modernization explanations is less explicit in other studies. For example, the only control variables that Chase-Dunn considers are the level of domestic capital formation and the percentage of GDP originating in the mining sector.[16] Bornschier and his colleagues are careful to distinguish *levels* from *rates* of growth in their discussion of foreign investment, but make no corresponding distinction in their discussion of domestic capital formation.[17]

This neglect has led to an important lacuna. To be sure, a comprehensive attempt to specify the so-called modernization approach is perhaps impossible, given the heterogeneity of the studies commonly included under this rubric. Nonetheless, it is important to identify at least some of the critical factors addressed in this literature; if we do not, we have no way of evaluating the relative merits of the dependency and modernization approaches as explanations of growth in the Third World.

A good place to start is with domestic capital formation, in view of the central role assigned to capital invesment in standard treatments of economic growth. If it is important to distinguish levels from growth in foreign investment, as do Bornschier and his colleagues, then it is equally important to make the corresponding distinction in the specification of domestic investment. After all, if the standard view is correct, the source of investment (foreign or domestic) is not the critical factor. In addition, it is a commonplace in discussions of economic growth that high crude birth rates inhibit economic growth because they produce a disproportionately young, nonproductive population:[18] hence, the well-known argument that control of fertility rates facilitates economic growth. (If that were the case, countries with declining crude birth rates should have higher rates of economic growth.) Finally, it is often observed that, all other things being equal, larger countries should have higher growth rates because greater population size introduces economies of scale into patterns of production. Indeed, Chenery and Syrquin suggest that size may be especially important for those Third World countries *above* the lowest income levels, since these countries have sufficiently advanced economic infrastructures to be able to take advantage of economies of scale.[19]

The above points are hardly intended to exhaust the possibilities.[20] However, they do at least furnish a more reasonable background than has been provided in recent studies, against which any effects of foreign investment on growth can be evaluated.

A second general problem in the quantitative literature is the common assumption that in the dependency approach, dependence is seen as inhibiting economic growth.[21] The validity of this assumption is not at all self-evident. In this connection, it is important to remember that Marxist views of imperialism underlie the theory, and that these views imply that imperialism leads to *growth* in the periphery. Thus, in *The Communist Manifesto* we read:

> The bourgeoisie . . . draws all, even the most barbarian, nations into civilisation. . . . It compels all nations, on pain of extinction, to adopt the bourgeois mode of production; it compels them to introduce what it calls civilisation into their midst, i.e., to become bourgeois themselves. In one word, it creates a world after its own image.[22]

In his elaboration, Lenin argued that the core needed to develop markets in and acquire raw materials from the periphery, but that over time the core would stagnate while the periphery became a source of industrial growth.[23] In other words, imperialism would lead to capitalist economic growth in the periphery.

Much of the quantitative literature seems to have gone astray by relying on analyses like Frank's and Bodenheimer's.[24] The problem here, as Portes notes, is that

> These writings have created the erroneous impression that "dependency" analyses continue to be concerned with the same quasi-colonial situation of economic stagnation and foreign control of export enclaves. On the contrary, contemporary dependency studies address a situation in which domestic industrialization has occurred along with increasing economic denationalization; in which sustained economic growth has been accompanied by rising social inequalities; and in which rapid urbanization and the spread of literacy have converged with the ever more evident marginalization of the masses.[25]

Thus, contrary to the assumption made in many of the recent quantitative studies, the dependency perspective continues to be informed by and to extend Marxist views of imperialism. Cardoso and Faletto refer to the process as one of "dependent development":

> By development, in this context, we mean "capitalist development." This form of development, in the periphery as well as in the center, produces as it evolves, in a cyclical way, wealth and poverty, accumulation and shortage of capital, employment for some and unemployment for others. So we do not mean by the notion of "development" the achievement of a more egalitarian or just society. *These are not consequences expected of capitalist development*, especially in peripheral economies.[26]

The foreign investment introduced by multinationals is thus seen as entirely compatible with high rates of economic growth. However, this rapid growth is likely to be unbalanced, and therefore inegalitarian.[27] In light of this, the common argument that the dependency approach implies a negative relationship between foreign investment and growth is not as well-founded as it might appear. Although these considerations do not in themselves bear on the results reported in the recent empirical literature, they do suggest that those results cannot be correctly interpreted as providing unambiguous support for a dependency argument.

Before examining the way in which foreign investment affects economic growth rates in the Third World, I turn to the prior question: have Third World countries experienced slower rates of economic growth than the industrialized West? Although this question is generally answered affirmatively, and although such an answer is generally taken as a given in the empirical dependency literature, there has been remarkably little systematic analysis of the magnitude and form of the pattern.

How Big Is the Matthew Effect?

In one of the few studies that have directly addressed this issue, Portes examines the growing inequality between poor and advanced countries in two ways. First, he presents data showing that over the years 1963–1973, underdeveloped countries had an average annual percentage growth rate in per capita GNP of 3.2 percent, as compared with 3.9 percent for the developed countries. He also notes that these figures understate the gap because OPEC countries were included in the former category. Second, he cross-classifies countries by 1963 per capita GNP and by growth rates from 1963 to 1973. Bearing in mind the "great deal of dispersion" evident in this classification, Portes concludes that "left to themselves, economic mechanisms . . . tend to increase disparities between the wealthiest and poorest nations."[28]

I adopt a comparable approach, by regressing growth rates on initial levels of wealth. Data on annual average growth rates in per capita GNP from 1960 to 1978 are from the World Bank, as are figures on 1960 per capita GNP.[29] Since I am concerned with the comparison between the Third World and the West, I exclude countries with centrally planned economies from the analysis. In view of Portes's discussion, I also exclude the three "capital surplus oil exporters" identified by the World Bank: Kuwait, Libya, and Saudi Arabia.[30]

In the first row of the top panel of Table 18.1, growth rates are regressed on the (natural) logarithm of 1960 per capita GNP. The estimates for this regression suggest a positive relationship between initial wealth and subsequent growth (as anticipated in the literature), and the coefficient has a t-ratio of 3.4 which is statistically significant well beyond the .01 level. At the same time, however, the $\bar{R}^2$ of .101 indicates that the fit is poor: initial wealth does not account for much of the variance in growth.

The second row displays the estimates using an alternative specification. Following Chenery and Syrquin,[31] growth rates are regressed on the logarithm of 1960 per capita GNP and its square. In other words,

Table 18.1

Regressions of Average Annual Growth Rates in Per Capita GNP, 1960 to 1978, on
Per Capita GNP, 1960

[Coefficients (T-ratios)]

Cases	Dependent Variable	lnGNP per capita 1960	(lnGNP per cap. 1960)^2	Constant	$\bar{R}^2$	F-ratio
Third World and Industrial West (N=98)	GNP growth 1960-1978	.588*** (3.4)		-.492 (0.5)	.101	11.9
		5.870*** (3.3)	-.464*** (3.0)	-14.954*** (3.1)	.170	10.9
Third World Only (N=80)	GNP growth 1960-78	1.012*** (3.5)		-2.559* (1.8)	.127	12.5
		5.647 (1.6)	-.452 (1.3)	-14.189 (1.6)	.135	7.1
Third World and Industrial West (N=102)	GNP growth 1960-74	.784*** (4.4)		-1.435 (1.5)	.156	19.6
		6.292*** (3.4)	-.484*** (3.0)	-16.520*** (3.3)	.220	15.2

* p .10; ** p .05; *** p .01.

the model is quadratic in the logarithms, and allows for a possible
nonlinearity in the relationship. Comparing the $\bar{R}^2$s for the two specifications, it is clear that the nonlinear model in row 2 gives a much
better fit than does the linear model (the $\bar{R}^2$ increases by 68 percent
from .101 to .170), although the relationship can again hardly be described
as strong.

The second row also shows that the estimate for lnGNP per capita
is positive (+5.870), while that for the squared term is negative (-.464).
In addition, both estimates have highly significant t-ratios. This means
that the relationship follows an inverted "U" pattern, so that growth
rates increase with initial wealth up to an inflection point which occurs
at the 1960 per capita GNP level of $559.[32] Beyond this level, growth
rates *decrease*. When this curve is plotted as in Figure 18.1, we find
that at the lowest 1960 per capita GNP level of $44, the estimated
average growth rate is 0.6 percent. This rises to a maximum estimated
average growth rate of 3.6 percent at the inflection point in the curve,
and then declines to 2.4 percent at the highest 1960 per capita GNP
level of $2,719. In other words, the lowest growth rates are found among
the poorest Third World countries, as anticipated. Contrary to expec-

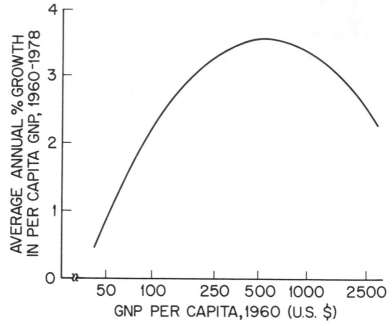

Curve plotted from the estimates in the second row of Table 18.1 (N = 98).

Figure 18.1 Relation between 1960 GNP per capita and average annual percentage growth in GNP per capita, 1960 to 1978.

tations, however, the highest growth rates are found not in the industrialized West, but in the wealthiest Third World countries.

Substantively, these estimates suggest two things. First, the Matthew effect occurs primarily *within* the countries of the Third World, defined here as those in the low- and middle-income categories identified by the World Bank.[33] Among these countries, those that were the wealthiest in 1960 had the highest growth rates between 1960 and 1978. Among the industrialized countries of the West, however, the pattern is reversed, and the relationship between initial wealth and subsequent growth is negative, although on the average these countries have higher rates of growth than the poorest Third World countries. Thus, while it is true that the gap between the West and the poorest Third World countries has been increasing, that between the West and the wealthiest Third World countries has been decreasing, which implies a Matthew effect of considerably modified form. Second, in terms of goodness of fit, the pattern is not a strong one, accounting for less than one-fifth of the variance in growth rates. This means that the strength of the Matthew effect just described should not be overstated.

In order to check this pattern further, in the second panel of Table 18.1, I re-estimate the model for low- and medium-income countries only (that is, I exclude the 18 Western countries as identified by the World Bank). If the above interpretation is correct, the pattern should be approximately linear among these Third World countries, so that adding the quadratic term should not improve the fit. The estimates in the second panel indicate that this is indeed the case: the $\bar{R}^2$ does not increase meaningfully when the quadratic term is added, and unlike the t-ratio for the linear model, those for the quadratic model are less than 2.0. At the same time, these estimates underscore the weakness of the relationship: initial wealth accounts for only about one-eighth of the variance in subsequent growth among Third World countries.

Finally, it might be argued that the period 1960 to 1978 was "unusual," in that the sharp rise in oil prices starting in late 1973 may have affected growth rates after that date so drastically (especially within the West) as to bias the overall figures for 1960 to 1978. Hence, my inverted U-shaped curve with its inflection point of $559 may simply reflect this new circumstance rather than a long-term pattern. On *a priori* grounds, there is little to commend this view, since there is every reason to believe that the rise in oil prices has affected the Third World at least as much as the West, if not more.[34] On empirical grounds, there is also little to support this argument. As the figures in the bottom panel of Table 18.1 show, the same inverted U pattern is found when average annual growth rates in per capita GNP for 1960 to 1974 are substituted for those for 1960 to 1978.[35] Whether we examine the shorter or the longer period, we find only a weak Matthew effect of the modified form described above.

The fact that the Matthew effect is weaker, and of a form different from the one that has generally been assumed, challenges a key assumption of much of the quantitative dependency literature. The observed pattern, in which parts of the periphery have experienced higher rates of growth than the core, undermines the argument advanced by Snyder and Kick,[36] among others, that the core has been successfully and invariably underdeveloping the periphery.

Foreign Investment and Growth, 1960 to 1978

The pattern of growth just described does not logically preclude the possibility that foreign investment systematically affects growth in the Third World. That is the issue to which I now turn. I begin with a simple model that expresses growth as a function of levels of, and growth in, both domestic *and* foreign investment; changes in the crude birth rate; and initial population size. This model is estimated for all Third World countries, which are defined as before to include the low- and middle-income countries identified by the World Bank,[37] but not the three capital surplus oil exporters, Kuwait, Libya, and Saudi Arabia.

The variables are defined as follows. The dependent variable is the average annual percentage growth rate in per capita GNP, 1960 to 1978, as described in the previous section. The level of domestic investment is measured by figures on gross domestic investment as a percentage of gross domestic product (GDP), 1960, as reported by the World Bank.[38] Growth in domestic investment is defined as the average annual percentage growth rate in gross domestic investment, 1960 to 1973, as calculated by the World Bank.[39] Thus, the first measure reflects initial levels of domestic investment, while the second reflects subsequent average growth or decline in domestic investment patterns. The choice of 1973 as the cutoff point for the second variable is dictated by practical considerations of data availability; as will become evident below, this year also has the advantage of coinciding with the cutoff point for available data on growth in foreign investment.

Measuring foreign investment patterns is more difficult because data are more scarce. Here I follow previous studies[40] and use the total amount of direct investments by members of the Organization for Economic Cooperation and Development (OECD) in the Third World. More specifically, this variable reflects "the net book value to the direct investor of affiliates (subsidiaries, branches, and associates) in LDCs."[41] Data on this measure are available for two years, 1967 and 1973.[42] Since figures are unavailable for the years before 1967 (and since this date is closer to 1960 than it is to 1978), I take the 1967 figures to reflect the "initial" level of foreign investment (as is done in the above studies, among others). Paralleling the treatment of the initial level of domestic investment, the 1967 level of foreign investment is taken as a percentage of 1967 GDP.[43] Thus, both levels of investment variables are expressed as shares of total domestic production. To measure growth in foreign investment, I follow conventional procedures where annual series are unavailable, by taking the logarithm of the ratio of total 1973 foreign investments to total 1967 foreign investments: this ratio approximates a compound growth figure.[44]

Initial population size is measured by figures on the total production for 1960; since this variable is badly skewed, it is transformed logarithmically prior to the analysis.[45] Changes (usually declines) in the crude birth rate are measured in the same way as the flow of foreign investment, since a continuous series is again unavailable. Thus, I take the logarithm of the ratio of 1977 crude births per 1,000 population to 1960 crude births per 1,000 population.[46]

Finally, as part of the analysis to follow, I also control for the level of initial wealth, by dividing countries according to their 1960 per capita GNP (as defined in the previous section). Of the 86 Third World countries for which data are available, 44 have a 1960 score of less than $150, while 42 have a score of $150 or more. I therefore take this point (which is close to the median value) as the basis for distinguishing initially low-income from initially medium-income countries.

To summarize, I examine the following model for Third World countries both as a whole and subdivided into low- and medium-income groups:

$$\triangle GNP60\text{-}78 = a + b_1 DomInv/GDP60 + b_2 \triangle DomInv60\text{-}73$$
$$+ b_3 ForInv/GDP67 + b_4 \triangle ForInv67\text{-}73 + b_5 Pop60$$
$$+ b_6 \triangle Birth60\text{-}77 + e \tag{1}$$

where:

$\triangle GNP60\text{-}78$ = annual average percent growth in GNP per capita, 1960–1978

$DomInv/GDP60$ = Gross Domestic Investment/GDP, 1960

$\triangle DomInv60\text{-}73$ = annual average percent growth in Gross Domestic Investment, 1960–1973

$ForInv/GDP67$ = Foreign Investment/GDP, 1967

$\triangle ForInv67\text{-}73$ = $\log_e$(Foreign Investment 1973/Foreign Investment 1967)

$Pop60$ = $\log_e$ Total Population, 1960

$\triangle Birth60\text{-}77$ = $\log_e$(Crude birth rate 1977/Crude birth rate 1960)

This simple model elaborates previous efforts[47] in two ways. First, paralleling the treatment of foreign investment, domestic investment is specified as consisting of two basic elements: levels and growth rates. Second, the model incorporates initial population size and changes in crude birth rates, to reflect the emphasis that these factors have received in the standard literature.[48]

Table 18.2 displays the estimates for equation (1). Those in the top panel are based on all 72 Third World countries for which data on all variables are available, while the second and third panels report the corresponding figures for low- and medium-income Third World countries, respectively.

For all 72 Third World countries, the figures show that both the initial level of and subsequent growth in domestic investment have a positive effect on economic growth, as expected; both estimates are significant statistically beyond the .01 level. In addition, population size has no effect for Third World countries as a whole, but declining birth rates are associated with higher growth rates, as anticipated. However, neither the size of the estimates for foreign investment nor their t-ratios are consistent with those reported in many recent studies. The level of foreign investment has a negatively-signed estimate, but with a t-ratio of only 0.7, while growth in foreign investment has a positively-signed estimate, but with a relatively high t-ratio of 2.8. Stoneman as well as Bornschier and his colleagues report highly significant t-ratios for the level of foreign investment; the latter study reports a low t-ratio for the growth coefficient of 1.4 (N = 76).[49] In contrast, the figures in the first row of Table 18.2 indicate that the level of foreign capital has *no* effect on economic growth for the Third World as a whole, one way or the other. At the same time, they suggest that growth in foreign capital (like both the level and growth of domestic capital) contributes to

Table 18.2

Regressions of Average Annual Growth Rates in Per Capita GNP, 1960 to 1978, on Stocks and Flows of
Domestic and Foreign Investment, Population Size, and Changes in Crude Birth Rates

[Coefficients (T-Ratios)]

Cases	DomInv/ GDP60	DomInv 60-73	ForInv/ GDP67	ForInv 67-73	Pop60	Birth 60-77	Constant	$\bar{R}^2$	F-ratio
All Third World countries (N=72)	.084*** (3.1)	.215*** (5.2)	-.007 (0.7)	1.020*** (2.8)	.170 (1.2)	-2.270** (2.4)	-2.376* (1.8)	.601	18.8
Poor Third World countries: 1960 GNPcap $150 (N=33)	-.019 (0.3)	.202*** (3.2)	.077** (2.6)	.340 (0.7)	.250 (1.4)	-3.934** (2.1)	-2.414 (1.4)	.666	11.6
Wealthier Third World countries: 1960 GNPcap $150 (N=39)	.083** (2.1)	.194*** (3.5)	-.011 (1.1)	1.705*** (3.1)	.413* (1.9)	-2.973** (2.5)	-4.591** (2.1)	.582	9.8

* p .10; ** p .05; *** p .01.

economic growth—which is consistent with the standard view that capital formation is generally associated with growth.

In a similar vein, the subgroup estimates of the effects of foreign investment in the second and third panels of Table 18.2 provide little support for the conclusions advanced by Bornschier and others. Among the low-income countries, I obtain a *positive* estimate for the level of foreign investment (t-ratio: 2.6), which suggests that, for these countries, foreign investment may in fact foster growth rather than retard it. Although positive, the estimate for growth in foreign investment for these countries is smaller than its standard error. Among the medium-income countries, I obtain negative coefficients for the stock of foreign investment, consistent with the results reported by Bornschier and his colleagues. However, my estimate for this coefficient is not statistically significant (t-ratio: 1.1). In addition, the effect of growth in foreign investment is much more pronounced in my analysis than it is in theirs (my t-ratio of 3.1 is almost four times the size of theirs of 0.8).

To summarize the subgroup estimates in Table 18.2, the effects of foreign investment on economic growth vary with the initial level of wealth, but not in the way suggested in previous studies. Among the low-income countries, the level of foreign investment has a positive effect, while growth in foreign investment is unrelated to economic growth. Among the medium-income countries, by contrast, the level of foreign investment has a negative but insignificant effect, while growth in foreign investment has a positive effect on economic growth.

Among the other coefficients, the subgroup estimates reinforce the earlier interpretation that both the initial level and the subsequent growth of domestic investment lead to higher growth rates, except that the level of domestic investment coefficient for the low-income countries is much smaller than its standard error. In the two subgroups, the estimates for growth in domestic investment are of similar size. Along with this, the subgroup estimates for population size show that this factor has no systematic effect among low-income countries, while it has a systematic positive effect among countries in the medium-income category. This pattern is fully consistent with the argument that among middle-income countries, size has a positive impact on economic growth because it allows for economies of scale.[50] Finally, in both low- and medium-income countries, declining birth rates are associated with growth, and the coefficients are of similar size in the two subgroups.

The most obvious, and major, difference between my analysis and earlier studies is that mine pays more attention to the specification of "internal" factors that affect economic growth.[51] Indeed, by simply excluding initial population size from the model, it is possible to increase the size of the level of foreign investment coefficients for the sample as a whole, and for the medium-income countries in particular. (Not surprisingly, since population size has no meaningful effect among low-income countries, the exclusion has little effect on the coefficient in this subgroup.) In the case of all Third World countries, the coefficient for level of foreign investment and its t-ratio double in size when the population term is excluded, although the increased t-ratio remains small (1.4). For the medium-income countries, the pattern is more dramatic: exclusion of the population term doubles the level of foreign investment coefficient and produces a t-ratio of 2.2, which is statistically significant beyond the .05 level. Thus, the inclusion of population size has a pronounced effect on the results: indeed, this inclusion shows that the apparently negative effect of stocks of foreign investment in medium-income countries is spurious.

One potential problem remains concerning the estimates of Table 18.2. For some countries, the level of foreign investment is unusually high. For all Third World countries, ForInv/GDP67 ranges from 0.6 percent to 103.7 percent, with a mean of 16.0 percent. In contrast, DomInv/GDP60 ranges from 5.0 percent to 45.0 percent, although the mean of 16.6 percent is quite close to that for the first variable. While it is in principle not unreasonable for the level of foreign investment to exceed domestic production, it is important to be sure that a few extreme scores are not responsible for the results reported above. Six countries have ForInv/GDP67 scores greater than 50 percent, a figure that is over three times the size of the mean. These (with their scores) are: Jamaica (58.4 percent), Liberia (96.4 percent), Mauritania (62.5 percent), Panama (103.7 percent), Trinidad and Tobago (84.6 percent), and Zaire (50.2 percent). All except Mauritania fall into the medium-income category. The next highest score is 38.6 percent for Venezuela, a medium-income country, while the next-highest score for a low-income country is 26.8 percent (Nigeria). To what extent are the results in Table 18.2 sensitive to these extreme values?

Table 18.3 displays estimates that correspond to those in Table 18.2, except that the six countries with extreme scores on ForInv/GDP67 are excluded. For low-income countries, the N is reduced by 1, to 32, while for medium-income countries, it is reduced by 5, to 34. For all the figures in the top and bottom panels of Table 18.3, most of the coefficients and their t-ratios are not affected substantially, when compared to Table 18.2, by the exclusion of these cases. Thus, my earlier conclusion that the level of foreign investment has no effect on growth for the sample as a whole, or for medium-income countries in particular, is not dependent on the five extreme values. However, the exclusion of just one case (Mauritania) from the low-income countries indicates that the positive and significant estimate for ForInv/GDP67 reported in Table 18.2 is not especially robust. Excluding Mauritania (a country whose ForInv/GDP67 score is more than twice the size of the next-largest score among low-income countries, and whose growth in GNP of 3.6 percent is well above average) leads to a reduction of the t-ratio for this coefficient from 2.6 to 1.5, which is not statistically significant at even the .10 level. In all, then, there is no evidence that the level of foreign investment

Table 18.3
Regressions of Average Annual Growth Rates in Per Capita GNP, 1960 to 1978, on Stocks and Flows of Domestic and Foreign Investment, Population Size, and Changes in Crude Birth Rates, Excluding Outliers on Stock of Foreign Investment

[Coefficients (T-Ratios)]

Cases	DomInv/ GDP60	DomInv 60-73	ForInv/ GDP67	ForInv 67-73	Pop60	Birth 60-77	Constant	$\bar{R}^2$	F-ratio
All Third World countries (N=66)	.061** (2.1)	.272*** (5.8)	-.011 (0.6)	.676* (1.8)	.218 (1.6)	-2.317** (2.4)	-2.622** (2.0)	.660	22.1
Poor Third World countries: 1960 GNPcap $150 (N=33)	-.032 (0.5)	.223*** (3.0)	.062 (1.5)	.280 (0.6)	.257 (1.4)	-3.545* (1.8)	-2.251 (1.3)	.662	11.1
Wealthier Third World countries: 1960 GNPcap $150 (N=34)	.074* (1.8)	.274*** (4.7)	-.033 (1.4)	1.268** (2.3)	.452** (2.1)	-2.891*** (2.4)	-4.821** (2.3)	.681	12.7

* p .10; **p .05; *** p .01.

has a consistent impact on growth in either the poor or the medium-income countries of the Third World.

Conclusions

The preceeding analyses show, first, that there is little evidence of the commonly argued Matthew effect where the core has experienced higher rates of growth than the periphery. Instead, my estimates suggest a modified Matthew effect *within* Third World countries, such that the initially wealthiest of these have grown more rapidly than the West which, in turn, has grown faster than the poorest countries of the Third World. It is important to remember, however, that even this modified Matthew effect is not a strong one.

Second, my results indicate that the impact of foreign investment on economic growth rates within the Third World is limited. In particular, the initial level of foreign investment has *no* consistent effect on growth, one way or the other, when other relevant factors are controlled. This last proviso is fundamental; it accounts for much of the difference between my results and those reported in earlier studies. I have shown here that the apparently negative effect of levels of foreign investment suggested by others is spurious, and reflects instead the effect of population size. There is no evidence that high levels of foreign investment themselves dampen economic growth in a systematic manner, as one is led to expect by much of the recent literature. This underscores the costs associated with treating conventional approaches to economic growth as straw men.

At the same time, my results show that the *growth* of foreign investment has a *positive* effect on economic growth, at least among the initially wealthier countries of the Third World. It may be tempting to conclude that these results are consistent with a dependency view. After all, as Portes and others have pointed out, dependence on foreign capital may stimulate growth. However, any such conclusion on the basis of this analysis of the available data is premature. While the positive effect of the growth of foreign investment may be consistent with some of the dependency arguments, it is also consistent with more conventional perspectives. Further analyses are required if we are to choose between these contending views.

What forms might these additional analyses take? I believe one fruitful avenue would be to address some of the *consequences* of economic growth. The pattern of dependent development suggested by Cardoso and Faletto and others implies that foreign investment fosters growth, which (because it is uneven) produces *more* inequality. Minimally, this argument requires that these three factors be statistically interrelated; its evaluation would require building on the present analysis, which addresses only foreign investment and economic growth. Failure to find a more complete pattern would lend support to more conventional arguments, which link neither foreign investment nor economic growth to inequality.

In line with most of the literature, I have treated growth as being potentially dependent on foreign investment. Consider, however, a second avenue that would recast part of the analysis in light of the following alternative:

> Direct investment is dictated almost exclusively by commercial considerations, so that its volume is a reliable index of independent opinions on the economic prospects of the local economy and on the productivity of capital in different employments in it. . . . Mistakes are made; but those providing the capital have a continuing interest in minimising the error and in taking remedial action where necessary.[52]

Such a view implies that economic growth rates (reflecting the "prospects of the local economy") and growth in foreign investment are reciprocally related. Higher growth rates attract more foreign capital, which fosters higher growth rates, and so on. Ironically, such a pattern involves a success-breeds-success Matthew effect of its own. However, that is hardly the Matthew effect anticipated in much of the dependency literature.

Taken together, additional analyses along these lines will enable us to choose between dependency and more conventional approaches to economic growth. Until we have such analyses (which will require more extensive data on foreign investment than are currently available), the results in this chapter undermine two currently popular views. They indicate that, first, the core has *not* invariably been underdeveloping the periphery in a blanket way. Second, foreign investment emanating from the industrial West has *not* served to depress growth rates in the Third World. To the extent that economic growth bears on patterns of political change and development, these results suggest that many of the negative political consequences claimed for dependence on foreign capital may be substantially overstated.

Notes

1. See, e.g., Gunnar Myrdal, *Rich Lands and Poor* (New York: Harper & Row, 1957), and Alejandro Portes, "On the Sociology of National Development: Theories and Issues," *American Journal of Sociology*, Vol. 82 (July 1976), 55–85.

2. A term coined by Robert K. Merton, "The Matthew Effect in Science," *Science*, Vol. 159 (January 1968), 56–63.

3. See Tony Smith, "The Underdevelopment of Development Literature: The Case of Dependency Theory," *World Politics*, XXXI (January 1979), 247–88, at 251.

4. For example, Christopher Chase-Dunn, "The Effects of International Economic Dependence on Development and Inequality: A Cross-national Study," *American Sociological Review*, XL (December 1975), 720–38; Chase-Dunn, "Comparative Research on World-System Characteristics," *International Studies Quarterly*, XXIII (December 1979), 601–23; Portes (fn. 1); J. Samuel Valenzuela and

Arturo Valenzuela, "Modernization and Dependency: Alternative Perspectives in the Study of Latin American Underdevelopment," *Comparative Politics*, X (July 1978), 535–57; and Smith (fn. 3).

5. This distinction is, of course, common in the recent literature. However, it is important to recognize that the labels are quite broad, since there is considerable heterogeneity of views within the dependency and (especially) the modernization approaches. Indeed, apart from this distinction (which itself only reflects a tendency), there is little that unifies the studies typically labeled as examples of the modernization perspective.

6. For example, see Chase-Dunn (fn. 4, 1975); Volker Bornschier, Christopher Chase-Dunn, and Richard Rubinson, "Cross-national Evidence of the Effects of Foreign Investment and Aid on Economic Growth and Inequality: A Survey of Findings and a Reanalysis," *American Journal of Sociology*, Vol. 84 (November 1978), 651–83; and David Snyder and Edward L. Kick, "Structural Position in the World System and Economic Growth, 1955–1970: A Multiple-Network Analysis of Transnational Interactions," *American Journal of Sociology*, Vol. 84 (March 1979), 1096–1126.

7. Paul Baran, *The Political Economy of Growth* (New York: Monthly Review Press, 1957); and Andre G. Frank, *Capitalism and Underdevelopment in Latin America* (New York: Monthly Review Press, 1967).

8. See, for example, Peter T. Bauer and Basil S. Yamey, *The Economics of Underdeveloped Countries* (Chicago: University of Chicago Press, 1957), chap. 10.

9. Colin Stoneman, "Foreign Capital and Economic Growth," *World Development*, III (January 1975), 11–26.

10. Chase-Dunn (fn. 4, 1975), 720.

11. Bornschier and others (fn. 6), 652.

12. Snyder and Kick (fn. 6), 1123. However, the analyses underlying this conclusion are not especially robust: see Jackman, "A Note on the Measurement of Growth Rates in Cross-national Research," *American Journal of Sociology*, Vol. 86 (November 1980), 604–17, at 607–11.

13. Most of this literature is listed in Bornschier and others (fn. 6).

14. However, many of these studies also draw on Wallerstein's world-system analysis, which, paralleling Frank's work (fn. 7), does imply such an outcome: see Immanuel Wallerstein, *The Modern World System* (New York: Academic Press, 1974). Nor is the view of dependency in the studies cited above unique to those analyses. A similar interpretation is clear, for example, in case studies which indicate that dependency has fostered growth and which then interpret this pattern as undermining or substantially modifying the world-system/dependency perspective: see, among others, Richard Barrett and Martin K. Whyte, "Dependency Theory and Taiwan: Analysis of a Deviant Case," *American Journal of Sociology*, Vol. 87 (March 1982), 1064–89, and Ruth Milkman, "Contradictions of Semi-Peripheral Development: The South African Case," in Walter L. Goldfrank, ed., *The World System of Capitalism: Past and Present* (Beverly Hills, Calif.: Sage, 1979), 261–84. For more general criticisms of the world-system/dependency approach, see, for example, Peter Gourevitch. "The International System and Regime Formation," *Comparative Politics*, X (April 1978), 419–38; Smith (fn. 3); and Aristide R. Zolberg, "Origins of the Modern World System: A Missing Link," *World Politics*, XXXIII (January 1981), 953–81.

15. Snyder and Kick (fn. 6), 1097.

16. Chase-Dunn (fn. 4, 1975).

17. Bornschier and others (fn. 6), 671–77.

18. See, among others, Ansley J. Coale and Edgar M. Hoover, *Population Growth and Economic Development in Low-Income Countries* (Princeton: Princeton University Press, 1958); Paul Bairoch, *The Economic Development of the Third World Since 1900*, trans. by Cynthia Postan (Berkeley: University of California Press, 1975), chap. 1; and Joan Robinson, *Aspects of Development and Underdevelopment* (Cambridge: Cambridge University Press, 1979), 7–10.

19. Hollis Chenery and Moises Syrquin, *Patterns of Development, 1950–1970* (New York: Oxford University Press, 1975), chap. 4. This is not to imply that any scale effects due to population size can be achieved through very high rates of fertility. The two factors are quite distinct. Indeed, a disproportionately young, nonproductive population is more likely to strain existing resources than to allow for economies of scale.

20. Among the factors I have not included, one of the more interesting may be agricultural productivity (see, for example, Bairoch [fn. 18], chap. 2). Unfortunately, this omission must stand here since appropriate data are unavailable.

21. Rare exceptions include Robert R. Kaufman, Daniel S. Geller, and Harry I. Chernotsky, "A Preliminary Test of the Theory of Dependency," *Comparative Politics*, VII (April 1975), 303–30, at 307–08, and James L. Ray and Thomas Webster, "Dependency and Economic Growth in Latin America," *International Studies Quarterly*, XXII (September 1978), 409–34, at 411.

22. Karl Marx and Frederick Engels, *The Communist Manifesto* (New York: Pathfinder Press, 1970), 20.

23. V. I. Lenin, *Imperialism: The Highest Form of Capitalism* (Peking: Foreign Language Press, 1965).

24. Frank (fn. 7); Susanne J. Bodenheimer, "Dependency and Imperialism: The Roots of Latin American Underdevelopment," *Politics and Society*, 11 (May 1971), 327–57.

25. Portes (fn. 1), 75. For similar arguments, see Fernando H. Cardoso, "The Consumption of Dependency Theory in the United States," *Latin American Research Review*, XII (Spring 1977), 7–24; Thomas E. Weisskopf, "Dependence as an Explanation of Underdevelopment: A Critique," mimeo (Center for Research on Economic Development, University of Michigan, 1977); and Valenzuela and Valenzuela (fn. 4), 536.

26. Fernando H. Cardoso and Enzo Faletto, *Dependency and Development in Latin America*, trans. by Marjory M. Urguidi (Berkeley: University of California Press, 1978), XXiii; emphasis added. See also, Barbara Stallings, *Economic Dependency in Africa and Latin America* (Beverly Hills, Calif.: Sage, 1972), 35–44.

27. Along with the quantitative studies of the impact of dependence on growth mentioned earlier, there has been a growing number of studies of the effects of dependence on inequality *within* countries: for example, Chase-Dunn (fn. 4, 1975); Bornschier and others (fn. 6); Volker Bornschier and Thanh-Huyen Ballmer-Cao, "Income Inequality: A Cross-national Study," *American Sociological Review*, XLIV (June 1979), 487–506; and Peter B. Evans and Michael Timberlake, "Dependence, Inequality, and the Growth of the Tertiary: A Comparative Analysis of Less-Developed Countries," *American Sociological Review*, XLV (August 1980), 531–52. With few exceptions, these analyses have provided support for the dependence-inequality relationship. Evans and Timberlake go as far as to suggest that this relationship is therefore "one of the most robust quantitative, aggregate findings available" (p. 532). There is an interesting paradox here. On the one

hand, the quantitative literature says that dependence retards growth, while on the other hand it maintains (often in the same study) that dependence increases inequality. If Cardoso and Faletto (among others) are correct, these two patterns are contradictory. They are also contradictory if we take seriously the view advanced some time ago by Olson that rapid economic growth inherently exacerbates social inequality and is therefore politically destabilizing; see Mancur Olson, "Rapid Economic Growth as a Destabilizing Force," *Journal of Economic History*, XXIII (December 1963), 529–52.

28. Portes (fn. 1), 59.

29. The former figures appear in World Bank, *World Development Report, 1980* (Washington, D.C.: World Bank, 1980), table 1; the latter are in World Bank, *World Tables, 1971* (Washington, D.C.: World Bank, 1971).

30. These three countries are identified in World Bank, *World Tables, The Second Edition, 1980* (Baltimore: The Johns Hopkins University Press, 1980), 470–71. Note, however, that the same pattern is obtained when both sets of countries are included in the analysis, and whether or not Kuwait is included (Kuwait is an outlier here, with an extremely high initial per capita GNP coupled with a negative growth rate of -2.3 percent).

31. Chenery and Syrquin (fn. 19).

32. There is, of course, considerable collinearity between logGNP per capita and its square. This, however, is not a problem in the present analysis, for two reasons. First, *despite* the collinearity, the t-ratios are high. Second, an alternative estimation procedure that reduces the collinearity gives the same results. Specifically, instead of estimating (where X = logGNP per capita):

$$\text{growth} = b_0 + b_1 X + b_2 X^2,$$

we subtract the mean of X from X and then estimate:

$$\text{growth} = c_0 + c_1(X - \overline{X}) + c_2(X - \overline{X})^2.$$

This procedure removes the collinearity for the purposes of estimation while generating the same curve, since $b_0 = c_0 - c_1\overline{X} + c_2\overline{X}^2$; $b_1 = c_1 - 2c_2\overline{X}$; and $b_2 = c_2$. For discussion on centering X around its means (or some other constant) to reduce collinearity in polynomial regression, see Ralph A. Bradley and Sushil S. Srivastava. "Correlation in Polynomial Regression," *The American Statistician*, XXXIII (February 1979), 11–14. I would like to thank Kenneth Bollen for drawing this procedure and reference to my attention.

33. World Bank (fn. 30), 470–71.

34. Compare Bairoch (fn. 18), 210.

35. The 1960 to 1974 figures are from World Bank, *World Bank Atlas, 1976* (Washington, D.C.: World Bank, 1976).

36. Snyder and Kick (fn. 6).

37. World Bank (fn. 30), 470–71.

38. World Bank (fn. 29, 1980), table 5. Here and elsewhere, I employ the most recent estimates available, since the World Bank and other agencies are continuously revising their estimates for earlier as well as for more recent years. Typically, these revisions are minor.

39. World Bank, *World Tables, 1976* (Baltimore: The Johns Hopkins University Press, 1976), Series I.

40. For example, Bornschier and others (fn. 6), and Evans and Timberlake (fn. 27).

41. OECD, *Stock of Private Direct Investment by DAC Countries in Developing Countries, End 1967* (Paris: OECD, Development Assistance Directorate, 1972).

42. Volker Bornschier and Peter Heintz, *Compendium of Data for World-System Analysis* (Zurich: Bulletin of the Sociological Institute, University of Zurich, 1979), table 3.2.1.

43. The latter data are from World Bank (fn. 30), Series I.

44. See George W. Barclay, *Techniques of Population Analysis* (New York: John Wiley, 1958), 28–33; and Charles L. Taylor and Michael C. Hudson, *World Handbook of Political and Social Indicators*, 2d ed. (New Haven: Yale University Press, 1972), 286.

45. Data are from World Bank (fn. 39), Series I.

46. The 1977 figures are from World Bank, *World Development Report, 1979* (New York: Oxford University Press, 1979), table 18; those for 1960 are from World Bank (fn. 29, 1980), table 18.

47. For example, Chase-Dunn (fn. 4, 1975); Stoneman (fn. 9); Bornschier and others (fn. 6).

48. Unlike some other recent models (e.g., Bornschier and others, fn. 6), mine does not include initial per capita GNP as an explanatory variable in equation (I). Since the model is estimated below for two groups of countries defined in terms of their initial per capita GNP, the inclusion of this variable on the right-hand side of equation (I) would have served only to control twice for the same variable.

49. Stoneman (fn. 9); Bornschier and others (fn. 6).

50. Chenery and Syrquin (fn. 19), chap. 4.

51. Some of the earlier studies also suffer from problems of heteroscedasticity, on which see Jackman (fn. 12). That is not an issue in the present analysis. Note also that Bornschier and others (fn. 6) employ a different deflator for the stock of foreign investment (the geometric mean of energy consumption and population size). However, my own checks indicate that this does not account for the differences between my results and theirs.

52. Bauer and Yamey (fn. 8), 143.

19. Some Recent Explanations of Income Inequality

Erich Weede
Horst Tiefenbach

This discussion continues the critique of empirical studies of dependency. Erich Weede and Horst Tiefenbach are concerned with various explanations of the internal gap between rich and poor. Rather than confining themselves to a test of dependency theory alone, they examine five separate explanations of internal income inequality. Using data from previous investigations, they conclude that Kuznets's inverted U-curve explanation is the most convincing; that is, income inequality is low among the poorest nations, rises among the industrializing nations, and then declines at higher levels of development. Support is also found for the egalitarian influence of a high military participation ratio (i.e., high proportion of military to the population), of communist rule, and of democracy, although the impact of each of these factors was not uniformly strong. Tests performed on three separate versions of dependency theory (including the approaches taken by Rubinson and Bornschier in previous chapters) are not supported by the data according to Weede and Tiefenbach. This article sparked an intense debate between its authors and Bornschier; the interested reader should consult the various comments and replies found in the journal from which this chapter was drawn.

Introduction

The inequality of income distribution has been treated in recent years from a variety of theoretical perspectives. This article attempts to evaluate five alternative explanations of the size distribution of income. Such an evaluation may either support or negate previous findings. Either result is bound to be provisional. However, evaluation and critique are necessary features of the scientific enterprise, and we regard them as essential in our attempt to contribute to the growth of knowledge in this area of research.

Reprinted with permission from *The International Studies Quarterly*, vol. 25 (June 1981):255–282.

Our survey of alternative approaches to explaining income inequality is restricted to a special type of research design: cross-national regression and correlation analysis. Verbal theorizing that has not yet been translated into cross-national and quantitative research, whether for reasons of theory or of data availability, is beyond the scope of this article. Moreover, we will not attempt to evaluate whether previous translations of verbal theorizing into quantitative research designs are adequate; in this regard, we will uncritically rely on previous work. In fact, our review of the literature is intended simply to produce a list of independent variables for our own analysis, and some comments on the proper specification of relationships.

We decided to review the previous literature on income inequality for the simple reason that none of the previous explanatory approaches claims to offer a complete explanation. All have omitted one or another major independent variable. Therefore, we intend to use the independent variables from each theoretical approach under consideration as control variables for evaluating the impact of explanatory variables from other theoretical approaches.

We realize, of course, that the set of independent variables surviving our tests also does not provide a complete explanation. Additional explanatory variables might easily be suggested, and, if they were put into competition with the variables which survive our tests, our variables might succumb. It is also quite possible that some of the explanatory variables which do not stand up to our tests might resurface in further research. We adhere to the view that support or rejection can only be provisional. Cross-sectional correlations and regressions can never establish causality or provide final proofs. We agree with Popper (1969), however, that in any case the certitude of possessing truth is beyond human reach.

We also realize that cross-sectional correlations and regressions may differ from longitudinal ones, not only in magnitude, but even in sign. We maintain, however, that theoretical explication should maximize rather than minimize the opportunities for empirical inquiry. All propositions about correlates or determinants of inequality should therefore be assumed to hold cross-sectionally as well as longitudinally, unless theoreticians explicitly lead us to expect different signs or orders of magnitude in different research designs. The latter, of course, would also justify cross-sectional as well as longitudinal research. In either case, empirical research is encouraged rather than discouraged, and theoreticians are forced to clarify and elaborate.

Moreover, the superiority of a cross-sectional or a longitudinal design depends on the kind of problem under discussion. Oshima (1962: 443) has argued in favor of longitudinal studies of economic determinants of income inequality because "most of the noneconomic factors can be assumed to change but slowly." If this is true, then longitudinal studies are likely to be of less help than cross-sectional designs in identifying the sociopolitical determinants, or correlates, of income inequality which constitute our focus of attention.

Theoretical Perspectives

Cross-sectional differences in income distribution have been statistically explained in various ways: First, the size distribution of income may be a curvilinear function of the level of economic development, as was first suggested by Kuznets (1963, 1976) and empirically supported by Paukert (1973), Ahluwalia (1974, 1976a, 1976b), Chenery and Syrquin (1975), Garnier and Hazelrigg (1977), and Jagodzinski and Weede (1980). According to this approach, inequality is fairly moderate at low levels as well as at high levels of economic development, but rises to a maximum somewhere in between. Inequality is thus lower in many of the poor countries of Asia and Africa and in the wealthier industrial countries, but reaches a maximum in countries at middle levels of economic development, as is the case in a number of countries in Latin America.

Second, it has often been claimed that socialist states have a more equal distribution of income than capitalist countries. Data and results published by Ahluwalia (1974, 1976a, 1976b) definitely support this claim. Arguments for the beneficial impact of centrally planned economies should be regarded with caution, however, since (for reasons to be discussed below) one may doubt the comparability of money incomes in socialist and capitalist countries.

Third, Andreski (1954) has suggested—and Lenski (1966) agreed— that the military participation ratio exerts a major influence on economic status and thereby on the size distribution of income. High involvement in international conflicts and the corresponding military value of the populace should equalize income distributions. Moreover, Andreski himself had already suggested the military participation ratio as an indicator of the population's military value. In an empirical test of this hypothesis, Garnier and Hazelrigg (1977) concluded that economic development and military participation are about equally important determinants of equality. Using a somewhat broader data base than Garnier and Hazelrigg (1977), Jagodzinski and Weede (1980) replicated the finding that economic development, as well as military participation, exerts some influence on the size distribution of income. But in the Jagodzinski and Weede (1980) study, the level of economic development definitely exceeds military participation in importance.

Fourth, Lenski (1966) and Cutright (1967) have suggested that democracies have a somewhat more equal distribution of income than other types of political systems. Older empirical studies such as Cutright's (1967) or Jackman's (1975), which have produced contradictory results, suffer from using sectoral income distribution data rather than personal or household distribution data. A recent paper by Stack (1978b: 271), however, proposes that "the most important determinant of the degree of inequality is the index of democratic performance"[1] taken from Jackman (1975). While Stack's work suffers from an improper specification of the relationship between economic development and inequality, Weede (1980), using proper controls for economic development and the same inequality data as Stack (1978b), was able to reconfirm that democracy is an important correlate of a more equal distribution of income.

Fifth, the size distribution of income may result from the modus operandi of the capitalist world economy. This has been suggested by Galtung (1971), Wallerstein (1974), Rubinson (1976), Bornschier et al. (1978), and Bornschier and Ballmer-Cao (1979). Galtung's data support his view that maldistribution is the result of vertical trade patterns, that is, the exchange of raw materials for processed goods, and of feudal interaction patterns indicated by commodity and trade partner concentrations. Further empirical support was derived by Tylor and Wogart (1973) and Walleri (1978b).

Since Wallerstein (1974), in contrast to Galtung (1971), did not translate his ideas into a quantitative research design, we will focus on Rubinson's (1976) views, which are similar and sympathetic to Wallerstein's. According to Rubinson, state strength is the major means of protection against the vicissitudes of the capitalist world economy, and therefore a determinant of less inequality. In Rubinson's (1976) research, government revenue as a percentage of gross domestic product (GDP) is the master indicator of state strength. Since it measures only domestic state strength, that is, governmental control over the economic activities of its citizens, it is supplemented by exports as a percentage of GDP. High values indicate a lack of state strength, or high dependence on the international environment and the capitalist world economy. In a recent attempt at replication, however, Weede (1980) could not reproduce Rubinson's findings about the egalitarian impact of state strength.

In a survey of cross-national evidence, Bornschier et al. (1978: 664) conclude that "investment and aid dependence have the effect of increasing inequality." Since much, though not all, of the work which they summarize improperly specifies the economic development-inequality relationship, the fact that they found a unanimity of results does not constitute a very strong case. The more recent study by Bornschier and Ballmer-Cao (1979) does, however, since they did use the right specification. They argue that multinational corporations (MNCs) dominate the world economy and that MNC penetration affects the class structure of developing countries and thereby increases income inequality. Their measure of MNC penetration is based on the total stock of foreign investment and standardized by the geometric mean of total energy consumption and population.

These five alternate approaches to the size distribution of income do not exhaust potential and meaningful approaches, nor do they exhaust those that have been used in quantitative and empirical inquiry. To cite only a few more examples: Ahluwalia (1976a, 1976b) investigated the effects of fast economic growth and of educational variables; Stack (1978a) looked for the effects of Keynesian economic policies; Hewitt (1977) enriched the study of political correlates of inequality by focusing on social democracy. These studies, in general, attempt to increase our understanding of the relationships between explanatory variables such as economic development or democracy, on the one hand, and income inequality on the other. They are primarily interested in finding possible intervening variables that would better explain these relationships. These problems, however, are beyond the scope of this article.

Data Set and Research Design

From the five basic theoretical approaches to inequality outlined above, we have taken a list of variables to test against each other. We can thus see how they perform in bivariate and multiple regression analysis. Independent variables refer to: (1) the level of economic development; (2) socialist or communist rule; (3) military participation; (4) pluralist democracy; and (5) dependency and state strength. The choice of indicators for these variables is dictated by two overlapping criteria: For reasons of comparison we want to use indicators that have been used in previous research, and we have to use the available data. This latter consideration also dictates the time period of investigation: Most of the available data on inequality of household or personal income are from the mid-1960s. Table 19.1 summarizes conceptual variables, indicators, and data sources.

We would like our analysis to cover all independent countries.[2] Unfortunately, missing values constitute a major problem in this type of research. While inequality data are much better now than they were a few years ago, the lack of such data for many societies, especially poor and/or socialist ones, brings our number of cases down to 71. Our study includes all countries which were sovereign in 1965 and for which we could find inequality data in Paukert (1973) and/or Ahluwalia (1974). Ahluwalia (1974), though, reports no Gini coefficients, and he, like Ballmer-Cao and Scheidegger (1979: 214–217), relies on Jain (1975). Because corresponding income shares reported by Ahluwalia and Ballmer-Cao and Scheidegger correlate about 0.9, we added the Gini estimates from Ballmer-Cao and Scheidegger to our data set.

Two reasons are primarily responsible for our decision to use six different inequality indicators: First, Gini, as an overall index, and top 20 percent and low 40 percent income shares measure different aspects of inequality. Second, in our research on income inequality (Weede and Tiefenbach, 1981), we were very much impressed that most of our findings lacked robustness against minor changes in data sources or operationalization. The data, even though they reflect the best judgment of their compilers, are far from perfect. Since the robustness of findings cannot be assumed, it has to be investigated.

Table 19.1
Variables, Indicators and Data Sources

Variables	Indicators	Data Sources
Dependent Inequality	Paukert's Low 40% income share High 20% income share Gini	Paukert, 1973, pp. 114-115
	Ahluwalia's Low 40% income share High 20% income share	Ahluwalia, 1974, pp. 8-9
	Ballmer's Gini	Ballmer-Cao and Scheidegger, 1979, pp. 216-217

Independent
1) Level of
   economic
   development
	GNP per capita
	(GNPC)
		Taylor and Hudson, 1972,
		pp. 314-320

2) Socialism	Communist rule dummy variable	1 for Czechoslovakia, Yugoslavia, Bulgaria, Hungary and Poland; 0 for all other nations in our sample

3) Military
   participation
   ratio
	Military personnel/
	population
		Taylor and Hudson, 1972,
		pp. 38-41

4) Democracy	Democratic performance	Jackman, 1975, pp. 216-218 where communist nations receive lowest score (18) like Franco Spain

5) Dependency	a) Government revnue
	   as a percent of GDP
	   Exports as a percent
	   of GDP
	b) Trade structure
	   (Galtung's vertical
	   trade)
	   Export commodity
	   concentration index
	   Partner concentration
	   index
	c) MNC penetration
	   (based on the stock
	   of foreign direct
	   investment, outlyers
	   recoded)
		Chenery and Syrquin, 1975,
		pp. 188-191
		Chenery and Syrquin, 1975.
		pp. 192-195
		Ballmer-Cao and Scheidegger,
		1979, pp. 111-112
		Taylor and Hudson, 1972,
		pp. 366-368
		Taylor and Hudson, 1972,
		pp. 369-371
		Ballmer-Cao and Scheidegger,
		1979, pp. 130-131

For purposes of regression analysis, our N is lower than 71. Where inequality data come from Paukert, N is equal to or less than 52; where inequality data come from Ahluwalia, N is equal to or less than 63; where inequality data come from Ballmer-Cao and Scheidegger, N is equal to or less than 64. Whether the maximum N is achieved depends on data availability for the independent variables. Using personal income data from Paukert, and household income data from Ahluwalia, or data from Ballmer-Cao and Scheidegger for slightly different sets of countries and periods of observation,[3] should at least indicate the robustness or sensitivity of our findings to measurement error, to error due to missing values or accidental sampling of contemporary countries and, to a lesser degree, invariance of patterns of association over short and adjacent periods of time.

There are no missing values for GNP per capita, for communist rule, for the military participation ratio, and for export partner concentration. There are 70 observations for MNC penetration, 63 for commodity concentration, 62 for government revenue as a percentage of GDP, and 61 for exports as a percentage of GDP and for trade structure. The data base is weakest where the effects of democracy are considered. There are only 48 cases on Jackman's (1975) democratic performance scale. While Hewitt's (1977) measure looks like another, and possibly superior, indicator of democracy, we decided not to use it because of the lack of coverage of most Third World countries.

We cannot imagine that a few missing values on one or the other of our independent variables constitute a major problem in our study, with the possible exception of democratic performance. But it seems impossible to predict with any confidence what would happen if inequality data on all or about twice as many countries were to become available. Unfortunately, our critical evaluation shares this limitation with all other cross-national studies of income inequality that have been done so far.

Data Analysis

The size distribution of income is a curvilinear function of the level of economic development. This relationship is best specified by a quadratic polynomial regression of inequality indicators on economic development indicators, *after* the latter have been logarithmically transformed:

$$\text{Gini income distribution} = b_0 + b_1 (\ln\text{GNPC}) \\ - b_2 (\ln\text{GNPC})^2 \\ + E$$

Unfortunately, many social scientists work with different specifications and conclude that economic development is of secondary importance as a determinant of inequality when compared with competing explanatory variables within the context and limitations of a cross-national

Table 19.2
Adjusted Percentages of Variance Explained in Inequality by Economic Development[a]

| | Low 40%
Income Share | | Top 20%
Income Share | | Gini | |
	Paukert	Ahluwalia	Paukert	Ahluwalia	Paukert	Ballmer-Cao
GNPC	0	7 (8)	19	18 (19)	11	21 (20)
ln GNPC	0	0 (4)	7	6 (11)	1	11 (16)
GNPC, GNPC^2	0	8 (8)	19	17 (18)	9	20 (23)
ln GNPC (ln GNPC)^2	20	23 (14)	34	31 (25)	26	29 (24)

a. N is 52 wherever inequality data come from Paukert (1973); N is 58 wherever inequality data come from Ahluwalia (1974); N is 59 wherever inequality data come from Ballmer-Cao and Scheidegger (1979); numbers in parentheses refer to regressions where five communist-ruled nations have been added.

design. Table 19.2 reports the percentages of variance in inequality indicators explained by GNPC under different linear as well as nonlinear specifications.

In general, we are most successful in accounting for top 20 percent income shares, fairly successful for the Gini index, and least successful for low 40 percent income shares. The observation of a closer relationship between economic development and the income shares of the most privileged groups rather than the poorest groups is in fair agreement with Kuznets's (1963) early findings. More relevant to the specification issue are the results of a comparison of the fourth row in Table 19.2 with the first three rows. Of the four specifications used, the polynomial regression of inequality indicators on lnGNPC provides a consistently better fit than any other specification of the relationship.[4] From line four of Table 19.2 we read that economic development typically accounts for 20 percent to 31 percent of the variance in our inequality measures. This result is robust over six operationalizations of inequality.

Unfortunately, the best-fitting specification is the least popular among sociologists. As far as we know, only Garnier and Hazelrigg (1977), Bornschier (1978), Bornschier and Ballmer-Cao (1979), and Jagodzinski and Weede (1980) controlled for economic development properly.

Table 19.3 provides information about the explanatory power of other independent variables, if used in simple bivariate regression. Where applicable, the communist rule indicator does about as well as economic development does in terms of variance explained. However, a note of caution is in order: Since only five countries in our sample are under communist rule, variance on this indicator is extremely limited, and the ensuing conclusions are weak. Nevertheless, it seems prudent to retain communist rule for the multivariate analyses to be done below.

Table 19.3

Percentages of Variance Explained in Inequality by Communist Rule, Military
Participation, Democracy, and Six Dependency Indicators in <u>Bivariate</u> Regressions[a]

	Low 40% Income Share		Top 20% Income Share		Gini	
	Paukert	Ahluwalia	Paukert	Ahluwalia	Paukert	Ballmer-Cao
Communist rule dummy	--	33**	--	22**	—	29**
ln (military participation ratio +1)	3	11**	12**	16**	12**	22**
Democratic performance	5	4	23**	4	18**	13**
Revenue as a % of GDP	0.5	3	9*	10**	5	22**
Exports as a % of GDP	3	9*	2	6*	3	4
Trade structure	3	24**	17**	25**	13**	32**
Commodity concentration	0.4	2	3	6*	1	4
Partner concentration	8*	5*	16**	9**	15**	6*
MNC penetration	7*	25**	10*	22**	11**	20**

a. Results significant at the 5 per cent level are followed by a single
asterisk, those significant at the 1 per cent level are followed by a double
asterisk; results in democratic performance row refer to non-communist nations
only; N varies between 34 and 46 in the democratic performance row, and
between 47 and 64 elsewhere.

Both democratic performance, as evaluated by Jackman's (1975) index,
and military participation correlate only moderately with income shares
or Gini. Although neither democracy nor military participation look like
major determinants of the size distribution of income, we will analyze
their impact in competition with independent variables from other
theoretical approaches.

The effect of dependency measures in our bivariate regressions is difficult to summarize. Rubinson's (1976) state strength indictors (revenue or exports as a percentage of GDP) appear weak to moderately strong. Independent variables related to Galtung's "structural theory of imperialism" perform quite unevenly. Trade structure (the import of raw materials and the export of processed goods)[5] is a fairly strong correlate of the size distribution of income. Feudal interaction patterns, that is, the restriction to a few commodities and export partners by dependent societies, seem to matter much less, although export partner concentration appears far from negligible. Investment dependence or MNC penetration again is fairly strongly related to income inequality. In bivariate regressions, therefore, all the considered approaches receive some support, albeit to a different degree.

Bivariate tests are least adequate for evaluating dependence (or state strength) approaches to inequality. According to Galtung's (1971) "structural theory of imperialism," dependence results from vertical trade *and* feudal interaction patterns as indicated by commodity concentration *and* partner concentration. Similarly, according to Rubinson (1976), inequality should be explained by the lack of domestic state strength, as indicated by revenue as a percentage of GDP, *and* by the lack of state strength vis-à-vis the international environment, as indicated by exports as a percentage of GDP. Dependency approaches, therefore, do not predict high bivariate correlations between single independent and dependent variables; they do predict high multiple correlations if we simultaneously enter various aspects of dependence.

While we calculated multiple regressions using all of our predictors relevant to Galtung's (1971) or Rubinson's (1976) theory, we do not present them in any detail. Suffice it to say that either trade structure or partner concentration alone does about as well in terms of adjusted percentage of variance explained as both of them and commodity concentration do together; and that both state strength indicators together do little better than the stronger one does. The strength of either indicator varies across equations. We will therefore represent each dependency perspective by its single most powerful predictor in the tables presented below.

Our many independent variables and the comparatively small number of observations—especially after listwise deletion for missing values— argues against the inclusion of all variables simultaneously in a single grand multiple regression. In particular, the small number of observations on democratic performance should not be allowed to reduce the data base for evaluation of all other independent variables by as much as one third. While we will return to the issue of a single grand regression later and report its essential results, we would like to emphasize that multicollinearity is not the reason why we prefer a stepwise approach to a single grand equation. Certainly, multicollinearity exists. It affects most equations once lnGNPC is entered, because more developed nations are characterized by better democratic performance, higher military participation ratios, higher revenue/GDP ratios and more favorable trade structures. Such multicollinearity makes it difficult to disentangle the effects of these variables from those of economic development.

Table 19.4 reports the results of the regressions of inequality indicators on lnGNPC, its square, communist rule, democratic performance, and the military participation ratio.

The effect of economic development is generally as expected, increasing inequality at low levels of development and decreasing it at higher levels of development.[6] The only caveat is the insignificance of the squared term in one of the six equations which is largely due to the small N and the underrepresentation of very poor societies. Where applicable, communist rule clearly promotes a more equal distribution of income. Democratic performance appears fairly useful in explaining Paukert's inequality data, but absolutely useless in explaining Ahluwalia's or Ballmer's (Ballmer is hereafter used as an abbreviation for Ballmer-Cao and Scheidegger, 1979). In the equation for Ahluwalia's top 20 percent income share, even the sign of the coeffecient is incompatible with theoretical expectations. The military participation ratio is consistently significant for Paukert's inequality data, but not elsewhere. However, at least the signs are always consistent with theoretical expectations.

Since democratic performance does worse in Table 19.4 than any other independent variable does; since it is responsible for the loss of up to 19 observations; and since doubts concerning its validity have been raised elsewhere (Hewitt, 1977), it seems best to omit it from further analysis and to simply note that it does much better in one data set than in others. The first benefit of the omission of democratic performance, which also increases the number of cases, is that military participation becomes significant in more equations. Unfortunately, we cannot document this here for reasons of space.

The first version of dependency theory to be considered is Rubinson's (1976) state strength approach. In Rubinson's research, government revenue as a percentage of GDP and exports as a percentage of GDP appeared as fairly strong predictors of the size distribution of income. Rubinson's (1976) work, however, suffers from an improper specification of the economic development/inequality relationship.

In Table 19.5, we enter Rubinson's master indicator of state strength, revenue as percentage of GDP, together with economic development and military participation. Since communist nations have been eliminated from these equations because of missing data on revenue/GDP, the impact of communist rule cannot be assessed here. Table 19.5 clearly confirms the curvilinear relationship between economic development and inequality. Military participation adds to low 40 percent incomes, subtracts from top 20 percent incomes, and thereby decreases overall inequality. Only in one of the six equations does this effect fail to be significant at the 5 percent level, but there it is a near miss. The results

Table 19.4
Regressions of Inequality on Economic Development and Political
Characteristics of Nations[a]

	Low 40% Income Share		Top 20% Income Share		Gini	
	Paukert	Ahluwalia	Paukert	Ahluwalia	Paukert	Ballmer-Cao
lnGNPC	-14.43*	-20.83*	43.78*	62.73*	0.43*	0.38*
	0.01	0.03	0.01	0.00	0.01	0.02
$(\ln GNPC)^2$	1.00	1.69*	-3.42*	-5.16*	-0.032*	-0.032*
	0.12	0.03	0.01	0.00	0.02	0.01
beta weight of $b_1(\ln GNPC)$ $+b_2(\ln GNPC)^2$	0.52	0.31	0.39	0.54	0.44	0.33
Communist rule	--	10.23*	--	-13.45*	--	-0.22*
		0.00		0.04		0.00
		0.59		-0.41		-0.67
Democratic performance	0.10	0.003	-0.23*	+0.07	-0.003*	-0.0008
	0.07	0.96	0.03	0.48	0.02	0.32
	0.35	0.01	-0.37	+0.14	-0.42	-0.19
ln (military participation ratio + 1)	2.17*	1.34	-3.09*	-1.55	-0.04*	-0.028
	0.01	0.12	0.04	0.34	0.01	0.06
	0.53	0.21	-0.35	-0.13	-0.45	-0.23
N	34	43	34	43	34	46
Adjusted percentage of variance explained	37	47	50	49	50	55
Percentage of variance explained	45	53	56	55	56	60

a. Except for the third row, first cell entries are unstandardized regression coefficients which are followed by an asterisk at the 5 per cent level; second cell entries are significance levels of regression coefficients; and third cell entries are standardized regression coefficients.

Table 19.5
Regression of Inequality on Economic Development, Military Participation, and State Strength[a]

	Low 40% Income Share		Top 20% Income Share		Gini	
	Paukert	Ahluwalia	Paukert	Ahluwalia	Paukert	Ballmer-Cao
lnGNPC	-21.48*	-21.96*	54.22*	53.88*	0.52*	0.44*
	0.00	0.00	0.00	0.00	0.00	0.00
$(\ln\ GNPC)^2$	1.69*	1.81*	-4.67*	-4.55*	-0.044*	-0.037*
	0.00	0.00	0.00	0.00	0.00	0.00
beta weight of b_1 (lnGNPC) $+b_2\ (\ln GNPC)^2$	0.56	0.49	0.62	0.55	0.53	0.45
ln (military	1.38*	1.28*	-2.54	-3.23*	-0.034*	-0.033*
participation	0.04	0.05	0.06	0.02	0.02	0.01
ratio + 1)	0.35	0.30	-0.30	-0.33	-0.39	-0.34
Revenue as a	0.00	-0.037	+0.21	+0.084	+0.002	-0.001
% of GDP	0.98	0.72	0.33	0.70	0.50	0.46
	0.00	-0.07	+0.20	+0.07	+0.15	-0.14
N	47	55	47	55	47	56
Adjusted percentage of variance explained	25	19	35	30	30	36
Percentage of variance explained	30	25	40	35	35	41

a. See note in Table 19.4.

clearly contradict Rubinson's expectations: From the second to the fifth column it appears that high government revenue as a percentage of GDP detracts from low 40 percent income shares, adds to top 20 percent income shares, and increases overall inequality. Less startling, but more important, than those four unexpected signs is the insignificance of state strength. Nor would it help Rubinson's (1976) approach if exports as a percentage of GDP were added into the equation.

Our failure to replicate Rubinson's (1976) results raises the question of why this is so. Having tried the exclusion of the military participation ratio from our list of independent variables, we found that this still does not make revenue/GDP significant. Two other differences between Rubinson's and our research design may be responsible for the differences in results: First, while he regressed indicators of inequality on lnGNPC only, we added its square for the right specification of the inequality-development relationship. Second, while we proceed as though all of our inequality data referred to 1965, Rubinson (1976) took into account the fact that inequality data refer to different years. Most of them are from the mid-1960s, but some of them are from a decade earlier or a few years later. For this reason, Rubinson time-matched[7] independent and dependent variables. On the surface, this seems more persuasive than our assumption of rough stability of income distributions over a decade or two. Elsewhere, however, one of us (Weede, 1980) has demonstrated that Rubinson's (1976) results can be reproduced using his specification even without time-matching, but not with the specification used in Table 19.5. Therefore, the issue of time-matching seems less important than the specification issue.

We will refrain from a detailed comparison of coefficients obtained here and in previous or later tables because all of them include some insignificant predictors as a potential source of bias (Goldberger, 1970). In our opinion, precisely estimating effects is of less pressing concern than improving the specification by eliminating unsuccessful predictors.

In Table 19.6, we test Galtung's (1971) "structural theory of imperialism." The effects of economic development, communist rule, and military participation remain the same. The new independent variable is trade structure. Since this index gives high values to exporters of processed goods and importers of raw materials, it should contribute positively to low 40 percent incomes and negatively to top 20 percent incomes or Gini. This occurs, but only once at a significance level of 5 percent and once more at the 10 percent level. Thus, Galtung's (1971) notion about the inegalitarian impact of vertical trade receives very weak support. If one were to replace trade structure by partner concentration in foreign trade, or even to introduce both of them together, Galtung's (1971) "structural theory of imperialism" would do no better, nor worse, than is shown in Table 19.6.

Table 19.7 again confirms the curvilinear relationship between economic development and inequality, as well as the equalizing impact of communist rule. What is new in Table 19.7 is MNC penetration, a measure of investment dependence taken from Ballmer. Contrary to what we expected after reading Bornschier and Ballmer-Cao (1979) and Table 19.3 above, MNC penetration seems to have no effect at all. In the first and fifth columns of Table 19.7, even the signs of the regression coefficients contradict expectation. Nowhere do the effects come close to significance, although we took Bornschier and Ballmer-Cao's MNC penetration data, and for the last column, their inequality data as well.

Of course, we made some different decisions that might account for our difficulty in replicating Bornschier and Ballmer-Cao's (1979) findings.

Table 19.6

Regressions of Inequality on Economic Development, Political Characteristics, and Trade Structure[a]

	Low 40% Income Share		Top 20% Income Share		Gini	
	Paukert	Ahluwalia	Paukert	Ahluwalia	Paukert	Ballmer-Cao
lnGNPC	-16.57*	-19.19*	39.13*	41.63*	0.38*	0.34*
	0.00	0.00	0.00	0.00	0.00	0.00
$(\ln GNPC)^2$	1.25*	1.53*	-3.26*	-3.43*	-0.03*	-0.028*
	0.01	0.00	0.00	0.00	0.00	0.00
beta weight of b_1 ($\ln GNPC$) $+b_2$ $(\ln GNPC)^2$	0.58	0.42	0.46	0.43	0.45	0.35
Communist rule	--	8.17*	--	-12.67*	--	-0.13*
		0.00		0.01		0.00
		0.40		-0.30		-0.31
ln (military participation ratio + 1)	1.78*	0.93	-2.36	-2.66*	-0.035*	-0.025*
	0.01	0.14	0.08	0.04	0.01	0.04
	0.47	0.20	-0.29	-0.28	-0.43	-0.27
Trade structure	0.59	3.11	-3.07	-4.82	-0.03	-0.069*
	0.74	0.08	0.40	0.19	0.43	0.04
	0.05	0.24	-0.13	-0.18	-0.12	-0.25
N	47	54	47	54	47	56
Adjusted percentage of variance explained	27	45	38	45	34	50
Percentage of variance explained	34	50	43	50	40	55

a. See note in Table 19.4.

Table 19.7

Regressions of Inequality on Economic Development, Political Characteristics, and MNC Penetration[a]

	Low 40% Income Share		Top 20% Income Share		Gini	
	Paukert	Ahluwalia	Paukert	Ahluwalia	Paukert	Ballmer-Cao
lnGNPC	-22.54*	-17.87*	43.01*	41.04*	0.46*	0.36*
	0.00	0.00	0.00	0.00	0.00	0.00
$(\ln GNPC)^2$	1.76*	1.50*	-3.66*	-3.53*	-0.037*	-0.031*
	0.00	0.00	0.00	0.00	0.00	0.00
beta weight of b_1 ($\ln GNPC$) $+b_2$ $(\ln GNPC)^2$	0.62	0.36	0.52	0.44	0.50	0.41
Communist rule	--	9.31*	--	-13.87*	--	-0.16*
		0.00		0.00		0.00
		0.50		-0.36		-0.43
ln (military participation ratio + 1)	1.68*	0.54	-1.85	-1.50	-0.031*	-0.02
	0.03	0.44	0.22	0.30	0.05	0.16
	0.42	0.11	-0.22	-0.14	-0.36	-0.19
MNC structure	+0.015	-0.022	0.004	0.047	-0.0001	0.0003
	0.38	0.17	0.92	0.17	0.80	0.32
	+0.15	-0.18	0.02	0.18	-0.04	0.12
N	51	62	51	62	51	64
Adjusted percentage of variance explained	24	50	33	49	29	53
Percentage of variance explained	30	54	39	53	35	57

a. See note in Table 19.4.

If one replaces the MNC penetration data by time-matched data, or if one omits military participation ratios from the equations, or if one does both, then the relationship between MNC penetration and inequality in Ahluwalia's and Ballmer's data becomes significant.[8] But omission of military participation ratios does not help MNC penetration to achieve significance in any of the three equations using Paukert's data. By contrast, omission of MNC penetration makes two of the four effects of military participation, which are not significant in Table 19.7, significant at the 5 percent level, and makes another effect significant at the 10 percent level. Their lack of robustness places the harmful effects of MNC penetration or investment dependence in doubt. The closer one sticks to Bornschier and Ballmer-Cao's (1979) original design, the more similar the results, while our minor deviations in design cause major discrepancies in results.

Military participation is significant in merely two out of six equations, both of which refer to Paukert's data. As noted above, it gains some explanatory power if one excludes the Bornschier and Ballmer-Cao (1979) measure of investment dependence. For reasons of space we cannot document this here. According to Goldberger (1970), it is preferable to rely on equations where unsuccessful predictors, such as MNC penetration in our case, have been eliminated. Nevertheless, military participation is obviously not comparable to economic development or communism, whose significance is unaffected by minor changes in the specification of equations.

The question may arise whether a single grand regression for each indicator of inequality would produce results different from those reported above. Under listwise deletion for missing values, communist countries are excluded from our equations. In order to minimize the loss of observations, we therefore exclude the democratic performance variable from the equations as well. Having done so, we retain 43 observations to account for Paukert's inequality data, 48 for Ahluwalia's, and 49 for Ballmer's. The list of independent variables includes lnGNPC, its square, the military participation ratio, MNC penetration, trade structure and revenue/GDP. Instead of presenting another table, we will simply summarize the major results.

While lnGNPC and its square are significant at the 1 percent level in all of our six equations, neither MNC penetration, nor trade structure, nor revenue/GDP is ever significant at the 10 percent level. The military participation ratio (MPR) fails to pass the 10 percent significance threshold twice (for Ahluwalia's low 40 percent and top 20 percent income shares), but exceeds that elsewhere. Moreover, in three out of six equations (for Paukert's data) the significance level of MPR is better than 5 percent, twice even better than 1 percent. By and large, we take these grand regression results for a confirmation of our previous findings.

Conclusions

Of the five alternative explanations of income inequality evaluated in this article, only two received strong support in our analysis of the data, one received moderate support, another weak or ambiguous support, and one received no support whatsoever. Below, we will summarize the evidence from our analysis and attempt to provide an interpretation.

First, the level of economic development, as measured by gross national product per capita, is a strong correlate or determinant[9] of income inequality. This finding concurs with Kuznet's (1963, 1976) early propositions and with the results of other quantitative research on the size distributions of income that use the proper specification of the relationship between the level of economic development and income inequality (Paukert, 1973; Ahluwalia, 1974, 1976a, 1976b; Chenery and Syrquin, 1975; Garnier and Hazelrigg, 1977; Weede, 1980; and Jagodzinski and Weede, 1980). According to this substantial body of evidence, the distribution of income is rather egalitarian at low levels of economic development, then becomes less egalitarian and reaches a maximum of inequality at middle levels before it becomes more egalitarian again at higher levels of development. If one were to make an inferential leap from cross-sectional relationships to cross-time processes, then the outlook for the poorest countries clustered in South Asia and sub-Saharan Africa would be rather bleak, while improvements could be expected in Latin America.[10] Although we did not intend to argue that such an inferential leap is justified, it would be rather difficult to find a better basis for extrapolation and prognosis.

With regard to the influence of economic development on income inequality, the literature contains three cross-sectional findings which provide some consolation within the framework of a generally bleak outlook for the poorest developing countries:

1. Our results support Kuznets's (1963) finding that the poorest income groups are much less affected by economic development than are middle or upper income groups. Therefore, they are unlikely to suffer much of a decline in their income shares in the early phases of economic development.
2. Fast-growing economies do not appear to have a worse income distribution than slow-growing nations at similar levels of development (Ahluwalia, 1976a, 1976b). Therefore, one should not be wary of fast-growing Third World economies. While fast- and slow-growing economies are likely to experience a period of movement toward less egalitarian distributions, the fast growers are likely to reach the equalizing branch of the curve quicker than the slow growers.

3. Most important of all, Ahluwalia (1976a, 1976b) could find no evidence at all to support the pessimism expressed by Adelman and Morris (1973) about tendencies toward absolute impoverishment during some phases of economic growth.

Second, the impact of communist rule also appeared fairly strong in our regressions. Our results thus concur with Ahluwalia's (1974, 1976a, 1976b) findings that socialist countries have a more equal distribution of income than capitalist ones. The evidence for this claim, however, rests on a much weaker data base than the one for the level of economic development, since it is based on a comparison of only five communist countries with 58 or 59 noncommunist ones. Given such a skewed distribution of our communist rule variable, these results deserve less trust than others.

Moreover, other substantial considerations suggest a more cautious interpretation of the relationship between socialism and less inequality. For one thing, the argument about the impact of socialism on equality cannot be extended from centrally planned economies to mixed economies. If it could, we would expect some equalizing impact of government revenue as a percentage of GDP on the size distribution of income which, however, we could not find. For another, one may have reasonable doubts about whether the inequality of monetary income is as important a type of inequality in communist countries as it is in capitalist countries and mixed economies. Perhaps an extreme version of this argument might be: Communist countries may enjoy a more equal distribution of monetary incomes precisely because political power and possibly other sources of privilege are less equally distributed and also more important. Finally, the communist advantage in income distribution may be counterbalanced by capitalism's reverse advantage in resource allocation. According to Bergson (1971), there is reason to doubt the efficiency of resource allocation in communist countries.

Third, the evidence about the impact of military participation ratios on income inequality is moderate. Andreski's (1954) claims about its causal importance may be exaggerated, but they are not without substance. Garnier and Hazelrigg (1977) and Jagodzinski and Weede (1980) also provide supporting evidence for this finding. Israel, Taiwan, and South Korea[11] illustrate the particularly equal distributions of income in countries with high military participation. Of course, one may argue that military participation ratios are a somewhat narrow and indirect measure of threats to national security, the consequent increase of the military participation of the populace, and the willingness of the wealthy to share income with them.

If the military participation ratio is a less valid measure of the underlying latent variable (threats to national security) than GNPC is of the level of economic development (as we are inclined to believe), then we should expect some diminution of the estimated impact of threats to national security relative to that of economic development.[12]

An attempt by Jagodzinski and Weede (1980), who worked with measurement models that do not implicitly assume equally valid independent variables, still demonstrated a definitely stronger relationship between economic development and inequality than between threats to national security and inequality.

Fourth, our analysis permits weak support for the attribution of relatively egalitarian distributions of income to democracy. The results depend on the inequality data set used. Democratic performance looks fairly useful in accounting for Paukert's (1973) personal income data, but absolutely useless in accounting for Ahluwalia's (1974) household income data or Ballmer's data. Previous research helps little in bridging this discrepancy. Earlier studies (Cutright, 1967; Jackman, 1975) were done with sectoral income data only, while later work (Hewitt, 1977; Rubinson and Quinlan, 1977; Stack, 1978b; Weede, 1980) utilized only Paukert's (1973) data. While there certainly is a body of research to support the claim of a more equal distribution of income in democracies, our inability to uphold that claim when changing the inequality data set is a severe warning against premature conclusions.

Fifth, three types of dependency approaches have been considered in this article: Wallerstein's (1974) world-economy approach as explicated and operationalized by Rubinson (1976), Galtung's (1971) "structural theory of imperialism," and Bornschier and Ballmer-Cao's (1979) investment dependence or MNC penetration approach. Our data do not support the claims of these three versions of dependency theory, but they permit a fairly clear evaluation. Rubinson (1976) was able to find empirical support for his approach only because he misspecified the relationship between economic development and inequality, as is demonstrated in detail by Weede (1980). Using the proper specification of the relationship, our analysis casts serious doubt on the validity of Rubinson's (1976) approach. Our evidence suggests that state control of the economy and little dependence on external markets do not affect the size distribution of income.[13]

Galtung's (1971) "structural theory of imperialism" also receives little support. Vertical trade, that is, the export of raw materials and the import of processed goods, performed quite poorly although it is the central mechanism producing underdevelopment in Galtung's theory. So-called feudal interaction patterns fare no better. There is absolutely no evidence to demonstrate any supposed harmful effects of commodity concentration. One could illustrate this by pointing to some oil-exporting welfare states in the Gulf region which, however, are not included in our data set. There is little evidence to support the negative effects attributed to export partner concentration. Neither Galtung's (1971) own positive results, nor those of Tylor and Wogart (1973), or Walleri (1978b), are acceptable evidence to the contrary, since none of these studies properly controlled for economic development, and some of them use sectoral rather than individual or household income data.

Two previous surveys of quantitative studies on the links between dependency and inequality (Bornschier et al., 1978; Walleri, 1978a) are extremely optimistic about the potential contribution of dependency theory to our understanding of income inequality. Unfortunately, neither of these surveys discusses such problems as the necessity to control properly for economic development when evaluating the impact of dependency variables on inequality. Since proper controls are still the exception rather than the rule in this area of research, a summary of mostly misspecified regressions can prove little. Neither Walleri's (1978a: 619) "mounting evidence in support of dependency theory," nor the contention that "dependence tends to increase the amount of inequality within countries," as maintained by Bornschier et al. (1978: 664), appears valid.

The best evidence in support of some kind of dependency approach so far comes from the carefully designed studies by Bornschier (1978) and Bornschier and Ballmer-Cao (1979). There, MNC penetration or investment dependence appears to be a major determinant of income inequality. In our analysis, however, we found this relationship difficult to replicate over different inequality data sets or after introducing additional control variables.

While we could not support any of the three versions of dependency theory evaluated in this article, we do not want to argue that dependency approaches to explanations of income inequality should be abandoned entirely. Even if our results imply a setback for dependency theory, we cannot exclude the possibility that future research will be able to make a better case than has been made so far for dependency explanations. Furthermore, new types of dependency explanation may be developed and tested. Perhaps they will be more successful than the three versions of dependency theory evaluated here.

Notes

1. Rubinson and Quinlan (1977) argue that democracy might be less a cause than an effect of an egalitarian income distribution. This possibility certainly deserves further study. Since the Rubinson and Quinlan paper misspecifies the relationship between economic development and inequality, however, it cannot be admitted as evidence. Weede (1980) could replicate neither the finding that government revenue/GDP is a determinant of inequality after economic development was properly controlled, nor the finding that economic development lacks any influence on income inequality. Therefore, government revenue/GDP is not an appropriate instrumental variable for estimating the effect of inequality on democracy, nor is economic development appropriate for estimating the impact of democracy on inequality.

2. Countries which in 1965 were still legally dependent territories had to be excluded from our analysis because some of our independent variables, such as democratic performance, military participation and state strength, are either unavailable, or meaningless, or both, for such societies.

3. In general, most of Paukert's observations are from 1965 or some year before 1965, whereas those of Ahluwalia or Ballmer-Cao and Scheidegger are from 1965 or the late 1960s.

4. The superiority of second order polynomial regression on lnGNPC over other specifications is even more clear-cut when the socialist countries are excluded from the equations than when they are included. The results obtained after excluding the socialist countries are more meaningful for reasons discussed below.

5. As operationally defined, negative values on trade structure indicate dependence.

6. Since standardized regression coefficients for simple and squared terms do not permit a meaningful interpretation in polynomial regression, we do not report them. Instead, a single standardized coefficient is reported in the third row, which summarizes the impact of lnGNPC and its square. This coefficient is calculated in a second run, where the dependent variable is regressed on a weighted sum of lnGNPC and its square as well as on the other independent variables in the corresponding equation. The weights of lnGNPC and its square are the unstandardized regression coefficients from the first run, which are reported in the first and second rows, respectively.

7. In a time-matched design, independent variables refer to the same year as dependent variables. Measurements for different nations, however, do not necessarily refer to the same year.

8. The major effect of time-matching is all the more startling since ordinary and time-matched data correlate 0.945. If the reliability of investment dependence or MNC penetration were as high, this would be a better than usual achievement in macrosociological or macropolitical research.

9. In our view, determination is always hypothetical. Assuming determination, one may derive expectations about correlations which either support or falsify causal propositions. Support, however, is necessarily weak, because any pattern of observed correlations is compatible with a multitude of causal explanations.

10. The prediction of improvements in Latin America depends on using information about the level of economic development only. If one were also to take into account the absence of threats to national security from foreign powers (because of Pax Americana) and correspondingly low military participation ratios as well as unsatisfying democratic performance, the prognosis would become worse.

11. The fast growing Korea-Taiwan duo presents a fascinating test case. On the basis of their level of economic development one should expect the income distribution to become less equal. On the basis of threats to national security and military participation ratios, however, one should expect income distributions to remain among the most egalitarian in the world. In our view, the latter expectation appears to be more realistic.

12. If there is multicollinearity and measurement error in independent variables simultaneously, the weight of more reliably measured predictors is likely to be overestimated, and of less reliably measured predictors to be underestimated (Namboodiri et al., 1975: 545).

13. We cannot rule out the possibility that some other independent variables from Rubinson's study do have the attributed impact, since we did not include in our study what we consider to be his secondary explanatory variables. None of Rubinson's results can be admitted as evidence, however, because of specification error.

References

Adelman, I. and C. T. Morris (1973) Economic Growth and Social Equity in Developing Countries. Stanford, CA: Stanford Univ. Press.

Ahluwalia, M. S. (1976a) "Inequality, poverty and development." J. of Development Economics 3 (December):307–342.

—————— (1976b) "Income distribution and development: some stylized facts." Amer. Econ. Rev. 66 (May):128–135.

—————— (1974) "Income inequality: some dimensions of the problem," 3–37 in H. Chenery et al. (eds.) Redistribution with Growth. London: Oxford Univ. Press.

Andreski, S. (1954) Military organization and society. London: Routledge & Kegan Paul. (2nd ed. 1968). Stanford, CA: Stanford Univ. Press.

Ballmer-Cao, T.-H. and J. Scheidegger (1979) Compendium of Data for World System Analysis. Zürich: Soziologisches Institut der Universität.

Bergson, A. (1971) "Development under two systems: comparative productivity growth since 1950." World Politics 23 (July): 579–617.

Bornschier, V. (1978) "Einkommensungleichheit innerhalb von Ländern in komparativer Sicht." Schweizerische Zeitschrift für Soziologie 4 (March):3–45.

—————— and T.-H. Ballmer-Cao (1979) "Income Inequality: A Cross-National Study of the Relationships Between MNC-Penetration, Dimensions of the Power Structure and Income Distribution." Amer. Soc. Rev. 44 (June):487–506.

——————, C. Chase-Dunn, and R. Rubinson (1978) "Cross-national evidence of the effects of foreign investment and aid on economic growth and inequality: A survey of findings and a reanalysis." Amer. J. of Sociology 84 (November):651–683.

Chenery, H. and M. Syrquin (1975) Patterns of Development 1950–1970. London: Oxford Univ. Press.

Cutright, P. (1967) "Inequality: a cross-national analysis." Amer. Soc. Rev. 32 (August):562–578.

Galtung, J. (1971) "A structural theory of imperialism." J. of Peace Research 8, 2:81–117.

Garnier, M. A. and L. E. Hazelrigg (1977) "Military organization and distributional inequality: an examination of Andreski's thesis." J. of Pol. and Military Sociology 5 (Spring):17–33.

Goldberger, A. S. (1970) "On Boudon's method of linear causal analysis." Amer. Soc. Rev. 35 (February):97–101.

Hewitt, C. (1977) "The effect of political democracy and social democracy on equality in industrial societies: a cross-national comparison." Amer. Soc. Rev. 42 (June):450–464.

Jackman, R. W. (1975) Politics and Social Equality. New York: John Wiley.

Jagodzinski, W. and E. Weede (1980) "Weltpolitische und oekonomische Determinanten einer ungleichen Einkommensverteilung—eine international vergleichende und quantitative-empirische Studie." Zeitschrift für Soziologie 9 (April):132–148.

Jain, S. (1975) Size Distribution of Income. A Compilation of Data. Washington: World Bank.

Kaufman, R. R., H. I. Chernotsky, and D. S. Geller (1975) "A preliminary test of the theory of dependency." Comparative Politics 7 (April):303–330.

Kuznets, S. (1976) Modern Economic Growth: Rate, Structure and Spread. (7th ed.) New Haven, CT: Yale Univ. Press.

_____ (1963) "Quantitative aspects of the economic growth of nations. VIII: The distribution of income by size." Economic Development and Cultural Change 11 (January):1–80.

Lenski, G. (1966) Power and Privilege: New York: McGraw-Hill.

Namboodiri, N. K., L. F. Carter, and H. M. Blalock (1975) Applied Multivariate Analysis and Experimental Designs. New York: McGraw-Hill.

Oshima, H. T. (1962) "The international comparison of size distribution of family incomes with special reference to Asia." Rev. of Economics and Statistics 44 (November):439–445.

Paukert, F. (1973) "Income distribution at different levels of development: a survey of evidence." Int. Labour Rev. 108 (2–3):97–125.

Popper, K. R. (1969) Logik der Forschung. Tübingen: Mohr.

Rubinson, R. (1976) "The world-economy and the distribution of income within states: a cross-national study." Amer. Soc. Rev. 41 (August):638–659.

_____ and D. Quinlan (1977) "Democracy and social inequality: a reanalysis." Amer. Soc. Rev. 42 (August):611–623.

Stack, S. (1978a) "The effect of direct government involvement in the economy on the degree of income inequality: a cross-national study." Amer. Soc. Rev. 43 (December):880–888.

_____ (1978b) "Internal political organization and the world economy of income inequality." Amer. Soc. Rev. 43 (April):271–272.

Taylor, C. L. and M. C. Hudson (1972) World Handbook of Political and Social Indicators. (2nd ed.) New Haven, CT: Yale Univ. Press.

Tylor, W. G. and J. P. Wogart (1973) "Economic dependence and marginalization." J. of Interamerican Studies and World Affairs 15 (February):36–46.

Walleri, R. D. (1978a) "The political economy literature on North-South relations: alternative approaches and empirical evidence." Int. Studies Q. 22 (December):587–624.

_____ (1978b) "Trade dependence and underdevelopment: a causal analysis." Comparative Pol. Studies 11 (April):94–127.

Wallerstein, I. (1974) The Modern World System: Capitalist Agriculture and the Origins of the European World Economy in the Sixteenth Century. New York: Academic Press.

Weede E. (1980) "Beyond misspecification in sociological analyses of income inequality." Amer. Soc. Rev. 45 (June):497–501.

_____. and H. Tiefenbach (1981) "Correlates of the size distribution of income in cross-national analysis." J. of Politics 43 (November):1029–1041.

20. Financial Dependence in the Capitalist World Economy and the Distribution of Income Within Nations

Edward N. Muller

In this original contribution, Edward N. Muller seeks to test the hypothesis derived from the dependency/world-system perspective that the financial dependence of developing countries is responsible for increasing income inequality within them. His approach is to examine the hypothesis alongside of the contrary view that suggests that the distribution of income within states is largely the result of internal noneconomic forces. Muller reviews the cases of Canada and Taiwan and finds evidence refuting the dependency/world-system perspective. He then turns to the cross-national data and finds four serious flaws with the income inequality data employed in virtually all previous studies. He corrects for three of those and seeks again to determine the influence of financial dependence on income distribution. Using transnational corporation penetration and the size of a country's external public debt as measures of financial dependence, he finds that there is little support for the dependency/world-system perspective and suggests that future research concentrate on the autonomous role of the state.

The developed "core" countries in the capitalist world economy are not only much wealthier than the less developed countries of the "periphery," they are also much more egalitarian. Data on income distribution from the most recent *World Development Report* (World Bank, 1982) show that during the 1970s the upper quintile of households in 14 countries of the core (industrial market economies) received, on the average, 40.5 percent of total household income, with a range of 36.8 (Finland) to 45.8 (France). By contrast, among 23 countries of the periphery, the average income share of the upper quintile was 52.6 percent, and the range was 38.7 (Yugoslavia) to 66.6 (Brazil).

This discussion was first presented at the 1983 Annual Meeting of the American Political Science Association in Chicago, Illinois. Support for this research was provided by the National Science Foundation, Grant SES83-20281.

The highly unequal distribution of income that prevails in many countries of the periphery is explained by dependency theory as a result in large part of the fact that the accumulation and expansion of capital is controlled by powerful foreign economic actors (for general reviews of dependency theory see, e.g., O'Brien, 1975; Portes, 1976). The few (employers and workers alike) who become linked with the international sector of the economy are thought to profit from the infusion of foreign capital at the expense of the majority of the population, which remains or becomes increasingly "marginalized," since the superior resources of transnational corporations retard the emergence of a national industrial bourgeoisie, while the advanced capital intensive technology that is imported from abroad fails to absorb labor surpluses, and in some sectors increases them.

The *bête noire* of contemporary dependency theorists—whether they stem from the Economic Commission for Latin America (ECLA) structuralist perspective, the Marxist perspective, or straddle both (see O'Brien, 1975: 10–16)—is the transnational corporation (TNC), which is regarded as the fundamental causal mechanism of dependency in the post–World War II period. The core-headquartered TNC fosters dependence in the periphery: (1) indirectly, by causing a net outflow of capital from the periphery to the core, thus creating balance of payments deficits that must be financed by foreign loans, which in turn entail a loss of national political autonomy since core financial institutions gain the right to participate in the policymaking process of debtor countries; and (2) directly, by using its advantages of capital and technology to acquire a position of dominance among medium and large firms within the most dynamic sectors of private economic activity, thereby, in Sunkel's (1972: 526) phrase, seizing "control of the commanding heights of the economy."

Dependency theorists postulate a variety of specific mechanisms to relate TNC penetration to income inequality (representative writings in English are Dos Santos, 1970; Sunkel, 1972; Cardoso, 1973; Furtado, 1973). The general argument, as stated by one of the more prolific empirical theorists of dependency, Volker Bornschier,[1] runs as follows:

Due to the links with the world economy [through the presence of transnational corporations] one may argue that the political actor of a dependent country is less likely to be willing or able to act in favor of income equilibration via the redistribution of incomes. . . .The sociopolitical basis of such an inaptitude of the peripheral State is a specific class composition underlying the social formation process, namely a class coalition within the integrated [into the world economy] segment against the marginalized majority of the population. . . . The integrated segment strives after the bourgeois life style of this reference system [the bourgeois lifestyle that exists in the core countries]. This is likely to contribute to income privileges with regard to the average life situation in their specific less developed countries. A higher income gap and a more intense marginalization in poor countries than in richer ones is thus likely to occur.

In the rich countries, however, affluence acts as a break on such a mechanism. Also multinational corporations in the wealthy countries are not interested in income inequality. Their market chances—given a very high average income in these countries—are larger the higher the mass incomes. . . . [Thus] the degree of penetration by multinational corporations as a central aspect for the structural position within the world economy is expected to go together with higher income inequality within peripheral countries and tends to have an opposite effect for core countries. [Bornschier 1983: 12–13.]

The essence of the argument is: (1) that the interest of transnational corporations is inequality in the periphery (since elite demand is thought to be the only effective market for TNC-produced goods); but (2) equality in the core (where the wealthier masses can afford to purchase TNC-produced goods); (3) that the peripheral state is powerless to control the behavior of TNCs (the power of the core state vis-à-vis TNCs is a moot point, since core states, as headquarters of TNCs, benefit from their global economic activities); and (4) that inequality is in the interest of the dominant social class formation in the periphery (the workers and elements of the bourgeoisie who benefit from the presence of TNCs); with the logical result that the political elite in peripheral countries is unable (due to assumptions 1 and 3) and unwilling (due to assumption 4) to carry out egalitarian policies, whereas the political elite in core countries is encouraged—or at least not discouraged—by TNCs to pursue egalitarian policies (due to assumption 2).

Bornschier (1983: 12) places his version of dependency theory within the world-system paradigm, which asserts that the transnational corporation is the central institution of the modern capitalist world economy, structuring the world division of labor such that distinctions between core and periphery (the core specializing in technologically sophisticated industrial production and control over capital; the periphery specializing in production of raw materials and routinized industrial production) "reflect the organizational domination of the multinational corporation." Thus, in the world-system paradigm, as in Marxist analyses, economic processes of northern capitalism, currently manifested through the institution of the transnational corporation headquartered in the core, are history's locomotive.

The most compelling counter hypothesis is certainly not the "modernization" approach (often taken to include neoclassical economics), which posits an inverse relationship between foreign investment and income inequality (Chase-Dunn, 1975: 724–726, gives a review of the literature). Rather, it is an approach sensitive to the possibility that internal often noneconomic forces, instead of external economic variables representing the logic of capitalist imperialism, may decisively shape social and economic development—including the distribution of income—not only in the periphery but in the core as well.

Consider Canada. Of all countries for which data are available, Canada's economy is the most highly penetrated by transnational corporations (see Ballmer-Cao and Scheidegger, 1979, Table 3.2.5). Yet Canada ranks among the most egalitarian capitalist countries in the world. How is it that Canada can be at once so extraordinarily dependent on foreign capital and yet have such an egalitarian distribution of income? According to Bornschier's world economy model, transnational corporations are interested in promoting equality of income in rich core countries like Canada; therefore, Canada's egalitarian income distribution is explained by its wealth and high penetration by TNC-controlled capital.

However, it would appear that Canada's egalitarian income distribution predated the "quantum leap" in foreign investment (mostly by U.S.-headquartered TNCs) that occurred after World War II. Thus, the income share of the upper quintile was 42.9 percent in 1951 (Sawyer, 1976: 26), while U.S. direct investment was increasing from $2.6 billion in 1945 to $8.5 billion in 1957 (Watkins, 1975: 84). By 1967 total TNC-controlled capital stood at $10.6 billion and the total of foreign direct investment was $20.7 billion (Ballmer-Cao and Scheidegger, 1979, Tables 3.2.2 and 3.2.1). But during this massive build-up of foreign investment in Canada, income distribution showed virtually no change.[2] From a longitudinal time-series perspective, then, the postulated inverse relationship between degree of TNC economic penetration and income inequality does not appear to hold in the case of Canada. One cannot help but suspect that the real causes of Canada's income distribution have much more to do with the form of her government, the nature of land tenure, the size of her population, not to mention the quality of her "human resources" (with respect to tangibles such as education, as well as intangibles such as achievement motivation), than with the force of capitalist imperialism (even in reverse!).

Indeed, Bornschier's novel twist to the standard imperialism argument, standing it, so to speak, on its head for core countries, is *theoretically* plausible only if one assumes that the transnational corporation is the *primum mobile* (to borrow a phrase from Tony Smith, 1981b) of the post–World War II First and Third World. Such an extreme emphasis on the power of transnational corporations is not unique to Bornschier,[3] but he is the first to propose TNC economic penetration as a *cause* of greater income equality in the core countries of the First World.

With respect to the periphery, the criticism made by Smith (1981b; also see Smith, 1979; 1981a) of dependency theory in general is relevant to the world economy model of Bornschier.

> Too much emphasis is placed on the dynamic, molding power of capitalist imperialism and the socioeconomic forces in league with it locally; too little attention is paid to political motives behind imperialism or to the autonomous power of local political circumstances in influencing the course of change in Africa, Asia, and Latin America. . . . Nowhere in this literature do we find, for example, recognition that local physical, social, or political forces might for their own autonomous reasons have been simply unable

to generate industrial development, so that imperialism is only partially and secondarily, if indeed at all, responsible for the present predicaments of many countries in the Third World. By contrast, nowhere do we find any recognition of . . . the positive, substantial uses these countries can make and have made of their contacts with the international system. [Smith, 1981b: 757.]

A contemporary case in point is Taiwan. As a dependent territory of Japan, Taiwan before the end of World War II was subject to relations of traditional colonial economic dependency. From 1945 until the early 1960s, Taiwan was highly dependent on foreign economic aid, ranking fourteenth in the world in U.S. economic aid per capita during 1958–65 (Taylor and Hudson, 1972, Table 6.4). Direct foreign investment in Taiwan accelerated rapidly in the 1960s, but while the penetration of Taiwan's economy by TNCs was "taking off," income distribution was becoming markedly more egalitarian. The share of the richest quintile in national income declined from 61.8 percent in 1953 to 51.8 percent in 1961 (Jain, 1975, Table 70); and by 1971 the income share of the upper quintile had dropped to below the 40 percent mark, rendering it comparable in size to that of Denmark, Norway, Sweden, and the United Kingdom—the most egalitarian countries of the core. On the basis of a detailed case study of the Taiwan experience, Barrett and Whyte (1982: 1086) observe that "the presence in Taiwan of a strong state bureaucracy able to maintain separation from, and dominance over, powerful economic interests seems to have been a major determinant of the form development took on that island." Thus the assumption of dependency theory that domestic governments are pawns of *comprador* elites allied with transnational corporations does not hold for Taiwan.

Nor is Taiwan merely a deviant case. Among other semi-industrial countries of the periphery, the income share of the upper quintile in Spain is similar to that in Taiwan, despite an even higher degree of TNC penetration of the Spanish economy; and Argentina registers a moderately egalitarian income distribution (the income share of the upper quintile in 1970 was 50.3), which has remained virtually unchanged since the early 1950s (the upper quintile income share was 50.1 percent in 1953 and 51.6 percent in 1961 according to data from Table 1 of Figueroa and Weisskoff, 1980), despite a quite high degree of TNC economic penetration. As in Taiwan, so would it seem in Spain and Argentina that autonomous domestic political forces (the Franco regime in Spain; Peron's rule in Argentina from 1946 to 1955) had far more influence on the distribution of income than the force of international capitalist imperialism operating through the guise of the transnational corporation.

The prototype of inegalitarian dependent development is, of course, Brazil, which *dependencistas* such as Cardoso, Dos Santos, Furtado, and Sunkel had prominently in mind during the initial flourishing of the dependency school in the late 1960s. Brazil indeed has a very high level of TNC penetration, and as foreign investment poured into Brazil in the 1960s—encouraged mightily by the military-dominated authoritarian regime that was established in 1964—the distribution of personal income became increasingly concentrated in the hands of the few (the income share of the upper quintile rose from 56.9 in 1960 to 66.6 in 1970—see Table 1 of Figueroa and Weisskoff, 1980). But in generalizing from a particular country such as Brazil, the student of economic development in the periphery risks the fallacy of the special case (see Seers, 1963). Is inegalitarian dependent development an inevitable consequence of the "laws of motion" of capitalist imperialism or does the Brazilian case reflect the operation of internal possibly idiosyncratic forces?

Previous cross-national research purports to have shown that inegalitarian dependent development is a general phenomenon. These studies, however, have been subject to flaws of research design, compounded by unreliable measurement of income distribution. As I will show in the next section, they cannot be regarded as at all conclusive. In this chapter, I will correct these flaws and perform a reliable test of the dependency/world-system hypothesis. If the null hypothesis cannot be confidently rejected, I will interpret this as support for the rival "internal dynamics" hypothesis.

Previous Research

The initial cross-national investigation of the association between financial dependence and the distribution of personal income was performed by Chase-Dunn (1975), who reported positive but nonsignificant relationships between inequality and two indicators of financial dependence, debits on investment income per capita and external public debt per capita, for a sample of 31 less developed countries (LDCs). This was followed by a global analysis of 41 countries by Rubinson (1976), who reported a positive, statistically significant effect of investment dependence on inequality and a positive but nonsignificant effect of debt dependence on inequality. For an expanded global sample (N = 50), Bornschier and Ballmer-Cao (1979) also found a positive, statistically significant relationship between investment dependence and inequality, while Evans and Timberlake (1980) found such a relationship in their analysis of an expanded sample of less developed countries (N = 49). (The latter two studies further investigated intervening mechanisms between investment dependence and income inequality: indicators of the distribution of power and growth of the service sector of the labor force.)

Weede and Tiefenbach (1981) challenged the growing consensus on the existence of a cross-nationally valid, positive relationship between investment dependence and income inequality (see the review article by Bornschier, Chase-Dunn, and Rubinson, 1978). They pointed out that all previous investigations except that of Bornschier and Ballmer-

Cao had failed to control for the correct specification of the relationship between income inequality and economic development, a nonmonotonic quadratic polynomial function (see Ahluwalia, 1974, 1976). Upon controlling for the nonmonotonic economic development relationship, Weede and Tiefenbach (1981: 273) showed that across three different data sets (Paukert, 1973; Ahluwalia, 1974; Ballmer-Cao and Scheideggar, 1979) investment dependence—as measured by a variable constructed by Bornschier (1978) called multinational corporation (MNC) penetration—was estimated consistently to have a nonsignificant effect on inequality. Although Bornschier and Ballmer-Cao (1979) had taken the nonmonotonic economic development relationship into account, Weede and Tiefenbach were unable to replicate the statistically significant positive result reported by Bornschier and Ballmer-Cao, even for Bornschier and Ballmer-Cao's own data (Bornschier and Ballmer-Cao had analyzed only 50 cases of their data; Weede and Tiefenbach used the full sample of 64 cases with information on both income distribution and MNC penetration).

The response of Bornschier (1981) to the results of the Weede and Tiefenbach analysis entailed two points, one related to research design, the other to measurement. In regard to research design, Bornschier (1981: 283–284) claimed that Weede and Tiefenbach had misunderstood his argument:

> The key point of the argument [of a positive relationship between MNC penetration and inequality] is that this relationship holds for LDC's only. For the group of richest countries, which are the headquarter countries of MNC's, there is a tendency toward an opposite association between MNC's and income inequality. . . . When this was combined with the positive relationship between MNC penetration for peripheral countries, one effect cancels out the other, and hence Weede and Tiefenbach find no effect in their particular world sample.

Bornschier (1981: 284) also stated that he had in the meantime developed an improved MNC penetration indicator. Theoretically, the ideal measure of the concept of penetration of an economy by transnational (or "multinational" in Bornschier's terminology)[4] corporations would be a ratio of the stock of capital controlled by transnationals to the total stock of domestically owned capital and the size of the labor force. Bornschier's first MNC penetration indicator (used in Bornschier and Ballmer-Cao, 1979) had employed proxies for all terms, i.e., TNC-controlled capital was estimated by the stock of foreign direct investment, domestic capital was estimated by total energy consumption, and the size of the labor force was estimated by total population. Bornschier's theoretically more appropriate MNC Penetration indicator drew upon recently available data on the stock of capital invested by the world's largest 400 transnationals in order to measure TNC-controlled capital directly. A much more direct estimate of the total stock of capital was constructed (see Bornschier, 1980: 197), and total population was retained as a proxy for size of labor force. MNC penetration then is defined as the ratio of TNC-controlled capital to the geometric mean of total domestic capital and population.

On the one hand, it is indisputable that the research design and measurement points raised by Bornschier represent significant improvements upon much of the earlier empirical work. A basic characteristic of dependency theory is rejection of what Hirschman (1981: 3–5) calls the *monoeconomics claim* of orthodox economic theory. The monoeconomics claim is simply the belief in the existence of universal economic laws. In rejecting this claim, dependency theorists draw a fundamental distinction between countries that occupy a central or "core" position in the capitalist world economy and those on the periphery. The economic "laws of motion" of countries on the periphery are regarded as being substantially different from those of core countries. With respect to income distribution, dependency theory predicts only that within countries of the periphery, the greater the financial dependence on the core, the greater the inequality in the distribution of income. Therefore, correct specification of the financial dependency hypothesis requires explicit differentiation between core and periphery.

Operational definition of the concept of TNC economic penetration has been problematic in all previous research. More or less indirect proxies have been used as indicators of the stock of TNC-controlled capital; but the most serious limitation has been failure to measure the stock of TNC-controlled capital as a proportion of the total stock of domestic capital—a procedure essential to accurate representation of the degree to which TNC-controlled capital "penetrates" the economy.

However, on the other hand, Weede and Tiefenbach should not be faulted for failing to correct problems of research design and measurement present in the Bornschier and Ballmer-Cao analysis of 1979. In any event, the corrected reanalysis of Bornschier (1981; also see Bornschier, 1983) reports a statistically significant positive effect of MNC penetration on income inequality in LDCs and a statistically significant negative effect of MNC penetration on income inequality in developed countries, independent of the nonmonotonic relationship between income inequality and level of economic development.

Although Bornschier's current results are more convincing than those of previous analyses, they nevertheless still are subject to certain flaws of research design and measurement. The remaining research design problem is that of temporal ordering between presumed cause and effect variables. MNC penetration scores are for 1967. In order not to violate the logic of causal inference, income distribution should be observed at least circa 1967 and preferably somewhat later. Among the developed countries income distribution scores are for various years between 1967 and 1973 (except Denmark, which is 1966), so the temporal ordering of MNC penetration and income distribution is appropriate. But in the sample of LDCs, of which there are 48, income distribution in 18 instances (38 percent of the total) is measured before 1967, and in 12 LDCs the measurement of income distribution is very old, i.e., 1960 or earlier. Thus, in a nonnegligible number of LDCs, Bornschier is correlating MNC penetration with income distributions that existed well before the observation of penetration of the economy by TNC-controlled capital. Moreover, 7 of the 12 very old measurements are for African countries before (or during the year of) independence. It requires a considerable leap of faith (and logic) to assume that an MNC penetration score assessed nearly a decade after a dependent territory has become a self-governing state could have been a major cause of the distribution of income that prevailed under colonial status.[5]

To further exacerbate the temporal ordering problem, 4 of the 12 very old measurements (Burma, 1958; Chad, 1958; Niger, 1960; Nigeria, 1959) and 1 of the 6 measurements between 1961–65 (Morocco, 1965) were considered by their compiler (Paukert, 1973: 125), in a note of caution to the user, to be of "rather doubtful value." Another very old measurement, the 1957 income distribution for Greece, appears to be for urban areas only, which is not a reliable basis for estimating country-wide distribution. Consequently, the likelihood of measurement error is correlated with inappropriate temporal ordering.

In light of these potential sources of error, one's confidence in Bornschier's current findings is reduced. A reinvestigation sensitive to the temporal ordering of cause and effect observations and to the quality of measurement of income distribution obviously is called for.

Data

Information on income distribution and on the extent to which the economy is penetrated by capital controlled by transnational corporations is available in Ballmer-Cao and Scheidegger (1979: Tables 3.2.5 and 5.3) for 64 countries. MNC penetration scores are for 1967, derived from the formula:

$$\text{MNC Penetration} = \frac{\text{Stock of Capital Invested by MNCs}}{\sqrt{\text{Stock of Capital * Population}}} \tag{1}$$

MNC penetration thus is defined as the ratio of capital controlled by transnational corporations to the geometric mean of domestic capital and population, a procedure that affords an indicator of the relative weight (or penetration) of TNC-controlled capital in an economy.

With respect to the data on income distribution, I have where necessary updated, revised, or deleted information as follows:

1. data for Argentina, Denmark, Spain, and Trinidad and Tobago have been updated from pre-1967 to post-1967 measurements;
2. data for Brazil, Canada, Chile, Ecuador, Honduras, Ivory Coast, Japan, Kenya, Malawi, Netherlands, Norway, Panama, Peru, Sweden, Taiwan, Tanzania, United States, and Venezuela have been revised according to more recent calculations;[6]
3. data for Sierra Leone (1968) have been deleted because they do not cover the Western Province;
4. data for Greece (1957) have been deleted because they do not include rural areas and are too old;
5. data for Austria (1967) have been deleted because they were judged unreliable by Sawyer (1976: 22);
6. data for Burma (1958), Chad (1958), Morocco (1965), Niger (1960), and Nigeria (1959) have been deleted because they were judged unreliable by Paukert (1973: 125) and, except for Morocco, are too old;
7. data for Benin (1959), Iraq (1956), Jamaica (1958), Madagascar (1960), Senegal (1960), and Zambia (1959) have been deleted because they are too old.

The result of these emendations and deletions is the data listed in Table 20.1, which I divide into a restricted sample of 45 countries and an extended sample of 50. The extended sample allows income distribution measurements up to five years prior to observation of MNC penetration and includes data from a "secondary source" (Roberti, 1974) used by Ballmer-Cao and Scheidegger (1979).

The income share accruing to the highest 20 percent of recipients is a standard measure of inequality, often used in preference to the Gini coefficient (see, for example, the discussion in Ahluwalia, 1976), which is unduly sensitive to the middle of the distribution (e.g., Allison, 1978: 868). The dependency hypothesis predicts a concentration of income at the upper end of the distribution as a result of MNC penetration (or other indicators of financial dependence) in peripheral economies; therefore, the income share of the upper quintile is the most appropriate inequality measure.

Countries are grouped in Table 20.1 by core versus peripheral status in the world capitalist economy and, within the periphery, by their trade structure (following the classification in World Bank, 1981, Table 6.1). Core countries are defined as the 17 members of the Development Assistance Committee (DAC) of the Organization for Economic Cooperation and Development (OECD). Coverage of this group is comprehensive (only Austria and Belgium are missing). Among countries of the periphery, the sample contains 70 percent of the semi-industrialized group;[7] 40 percent of the capital-deficit oil exporters (but none of the capital surplus oil exporters); 41 percent of the primary producing (other than oil) group; and 8 percent of the least developed group.

Table 20.1 Distribution of Scores on MNC Penetration and Share of National Income Accruing to the Upper Quintile: 50 Nations

CORE			PERIPHERY: SEMI-INDUSTRIAL			PERIPHERY: PRIMARY PRODUCING AND LEAST DEVELOPED		
COUNTRY	1967 MNC PENETRATION	INCOME SHARE OF UPPER QUINTILE c.1970, % (SOURCE/YEAR)	COUNTRY	1967 MNC PENETRATION	INCOME SHARE OF UPPER QUINTILE c.1970, % (SOURCE/YEAR)	COUNTRY	1967 MNC PENETRATION	INCOME SHARE OF UPPER QUINTILE c.1970, % (SOURCE/YEAR)
Australia	186.4	38.8 (W:67)	Argentina	63.0	50.3 (W:70)	Oil Exporters:		
Canada	215.7	41.0 (W:69)	Brazil	64.4	66.6 (W:72)	Ecuador	28.3	73.5 (A:70)
Denmark	34.2	37.5 (W:76)	Colombia	56.4	59.4 (A:70)	Indonesia	9.9	52.0 (J:71)
Finland	5.4	49.1* (R:67)	India	11.3	53.1 (J:68)	Trinidad	69.4	50.0 (W:75)
France	61.5	46.9 (W:70)	Mexico	45.8	64.0 (A:69)	Venezuela	98.6	54.0 (W:70)
Germany (FRG)	51.8	45.6 (S:70)	Pakistan	16.2	41.5 (J:71)	Mean	51.6	57.4
Italy	38.1	46.5 (W:69)	Philippines	24.7	53.9 (W:71)	Other Primary:		
Japan	12.8	41.0 (W:69)	South Africa	107.7	62.0* (J:65)	Bolivia	8.1	61.0 (P:68)
Netherlands	71.6	42.9 (W:67)	South Korea	3.5	43.4 (J:71)	Chile	27.2	51.4 (W:68)
New Zealand	58.3	41.0 (A:71)	Spain	56.8	42.2 (W:74)	Costa Rica	26.6	50.6 (A:71)
Norway	34.1	37.3 (W:70)	Taiwan	41.5	39.2 (W:71)	El Salvador	31.8	61.4* (J:61)
Sweden	57.9	37.0 (W:72)	Turkey	38.6	60.6 (A:68)	Ghana	64.4	47.8* (R:68)
Switzerland	92.5	45.9 (B:68)	Uruguay	26.3	47.4 (A:67)	Honduras	4.9	67.8 (W:67)
United Kingdom	73.1	39.4 (S:72)	Yugoslavia	0.4	41.5 (A:68)	Ivory Coast	32.2	57.2 (A:70)
United States	18.0	42.8 (W:72)	Mean	39.8	51.8	Kenya	49.7	68.0 (A:69)
Mean	67.4	42.2				Malaysia	48.9	56.6 (W:70)
						Panama	185.6	61.8 (W:70)
						Peru	47.8	61.0 (W:72)
						Sri Lanka	9.4	43.4 (W:70)
						Thailand	11.1	57.7* (A:62)
						Tunisia	18.5	55.0 (A:70)
						Zimbabwe	91.9	69.1 (J:68)
						Mean	43.9	58.0
						Least Developed		
						Malawi	14.8	50.6 (W:68)
						Tanzania	20.0	50.4 (W:69)

SOURCES: A-Ahluwalia, 1976; B-Ballmer-Cao and Scheidegger, 1979; J-Jain, 1975; P-Paukert, 1973; R-Roberti, 1974; S-Sawyer, 1976; W-World Bank, 1979, 1980, 1981, 1982

*Extended sample.

The economies of the core countries are by far the most highly penetrated by TNC-controlled capital; but they also, as noted previously, have the lowest mean inequality. In the periphery, the economies of primary producing countries are on the average more highly penetrated by TNC-controlled capital than the semi-industrialized group, and the former also have higher mean inequality than the latter. One cannot generalize about the least developed countries of the periphery on the basis of this sample.

MNC Penetration

A general model for testing the dependency/world-system explanation of variation in income distribution within nations can be stated as:

$$\text{Income Share}_{T20} = a + b_1 \text{MNC Penetration} + b_2 \text{ Core} + b_3 \text{ (MNC*Core)} + b_4 Z_i + E \tag{2}$$

where:

Income Share$_{T20}$ is the share of personal income accruing to the upper quintile of recipients;
MNC Penetration is given by (1);
Core is a dummy variable scored "1" for DAC countries of OECD, "0" otherwise;
MNC*Core is the product of MNC Penetration and Core;
Z_i represents other possible determinants of Income Share$_{T20}$, e.g., level of economic development;
E is an error term.

Bornschier's world-system version of dependency theory predicts a positive b_1 parameter estimate and a negative b_3 parameter estimate. Versions of modernization theory or neoclassical economics might be construed as predicting a negative b_1 parameter estimate and estimates approximately equal to zero for the b_2 and b_3 parameters.[8] The argument of the internal dynamics approach is, in regard to indicators of financial dependence, the null hypothesis. The internal dynamics prediction thus is for estimates of b_1 and b_3 to be approximately zero, while b_2 should be negative simply because of the known fact that core countries are on the average more egalitarian—for whatever reasons—than countries of the periphery.

Prior to full-sample estimation of the parameters of (2) it is useful to examine scatterplots of the relationship between MNC Penetration and Income Share$_{T20}$ within core and periphery subsamples. Given the presence of extreme MNC penetration scores for Canada and Australia in the core and for Panama in the periphery, it is not surprising that Income Share$_{T20}$ scores show a better fit to a natural log (increment of

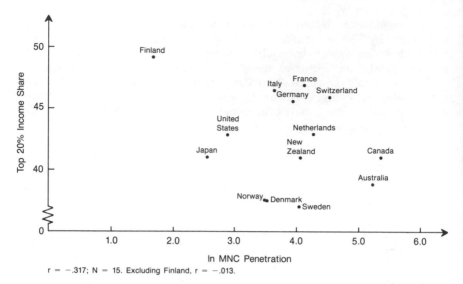

Figure 20.1 Relationship between MNC penetration and top 20 percent income share; extended sample of the core.

"1" added to Yugoslavia) function of MNC penetration ($r = -.317$ and .323 in core and periphery, respectively) than a linear function ($r = -.223$ and .283 in core and periphery, respectively); therefore the abscissa of the plots shown in Figures 20.1 and 20.2 is lnMNC Penetration.

From Figure 20.1 it is apparent that no systematic relationship of any form exists between lnMNC penetration and Income Share$_{T20}$ in the restricted sample of the core, which does not include Finland. The Finnish data are excluded from the restricted sample because they are based only on tax statistics. As Sawyer (1976: 23) observes, this results in:

1. The exclusion of nontaxable income from the income concept. Thus "social" (as opposed to "occupational") pensions are excluded. In 1969 they represented as much as 6 percent of total income.
2. The separate assessment of many young people who are still living with their parents. Thus, nearly 20 percent of individuals receiving an income of less than 2,000 markkaa (the boundary of the lowest income class) were in this category.

The Finnish data consequently are not considered by Sawyer to be comparable with the income data for the other core countries because the distribution is downwardly biased among lower percentiles and upwardly biased among higher percentiles. Data for 1977, prepared to conform with the standards of the Conference of European Statisticians,

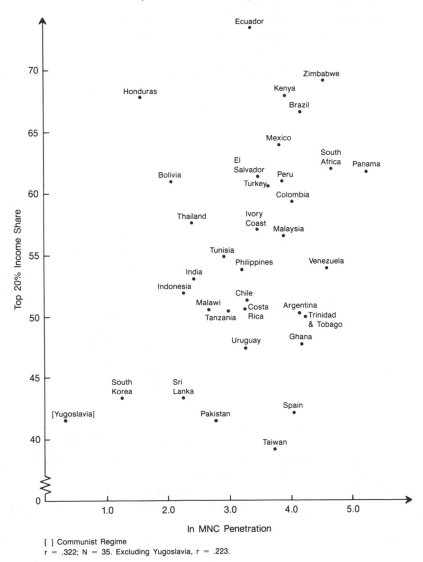

[ ] Communist Regime
r = .322; N = 35. Excluding Yugoslavia, r = .223.

Figure 20.2 Relationship between MNC penetration and top 20 percent income share; extended sample of the periphery.

show an income share of 36.8 percent accruing to the upper quintile of households (World Bank, 1982, Table 25); this amount is 12.3 percentage points less than that calculated by Roberti (1974, Appendix Table II) from 1967 tax statistics. Thus, the negative correlation of −.317 in the extended sample is due entirely to the presence of noncomparable data for Finland.

Table 20.2. Bivariate Correlations (r) for the General MNC Penetration Model:
Extended Sample (N=49) Below Diagonal; Restricted Sample (N=45) Above Diagonal

	Income Share$_{T20}$	lnMNC Penetration	Core	MNC*CORE
INCOME SHARE$_{T20}$:	---	.007	-.627	-.612
lnMNC PENETRATION:	.013	---	.336	.418
CORE:	-.630	.310	---	.976
MNC*CORE:	-.616	.388	.978	---

A slight positive trend is discernible in the plot of Income Share$_{T20}$ by lnMNC Penetration for the extended sample of the periphery (Figure 20.2), but the correlation of .322 is not significant at the .05 level (two-tailed test with 33 degrees of freedom). The magnitude of the correlation is also quite sensitive to the presence of a single case, Yugoslavia, the only country under communist rule. Presumably, the ideology of Yugoslavia's political system has had far more influence on income distribution than the absence of TNC economic penetration. If the absence of TNC economic penetration is indeed the relevant factor, instead of the presence of communist rule, then one should observe at least a slight rise in inequality following any substantial rise in the stock of foreign investment. Between 1967 and 1973 the stock of foreign investment in Yugoslavia registered a sharp increase, growing from zero to $70 million; yet five years later, the income share of the upper quintile stood at 38.7 percent (World Bank, 1982, Table 25), a *decrease* of 2.8 percentage points from 1967. In light of this trend, there seems to be no firm basis for asserting a causal connection between Yugoslavia's extremely low 1967 MNC penetration score and the highly egalitarian distribution of income that prevails there (and in other countries under communist rule).

If Yugoslavia is excluded on the grounds of being a special case because of its type of regime, the relationship between lnMNC Penetration and Income Share$_{T20}$ in the periphery is reduced to a randomly distributed cloud of data points. Moreover, these results do not change for the restricted sample of 31 cases, where r = .341—a value again not significant at the .05 level—and drops to .241 upon exclusion of Yugoslavia.

Bivariate correlations for the variables in the general model of TNC economic penetration given by (2) are listed in Table 20.2. One should note, first, the very strong correlation—almost unity—between the Core

Table 20.3. Regressions[a] of the Income Received by the Highest Quintile on Logged MNC Penetration, Core Dummy, and MNC*CORE Interaction Term

	Intercept	lnMNC PENETRATION	CORE	MNC*CORE	R^2	F
I. Extended Sample:						
(1)Income Share$_{T20}$=	46.19**	+2.71*	-4.27	-2.77	.42	12.58**
	(10.82)	(2.20)	(-0.37)	(-0.94)	(N=49)	
(2)Income Share$_{T20}$=	47.80**	+2.23	-15.02**		.42	18.47**
	(12.23)	(1.99)	(-6.08)		(N=49)	
(Excluding Yugoslavia)						
(3)Income Share$_{T20}$=	48.48**	+2.09	-6.56	-2.14	.42	12.18**
	(9.67)	(1.46)	(0.55)	(-0.71)	(N=48)	
(4)Income Share$_{T20}$=	50.09**	+1.61	-14.86**		.42	18.23**
	(11.28)	(1.29)	(-6.01)		(N=48)	
II.Restricted Sample:						
(5)Income Share$_{T20}$=	45.31**	+2.94*	-3.39	-3.00	.42	11.59**
	(10.09)	(2.24)	(-0.29)	(-1.00)	(N=45)	
(6)Income Share$_{T20}$=	47.18**	+2.37	-14.96**		.42	16.89**
	(11.55)	(2.00)	(-5.81)		(N=45)	
(Excluding Yugoslavia)						
(7)Income Share$_{T20}$=	47.50**	+2.34	-5.58	-2.39	.41	11.41**
	(8.85)	(1.52)	(-0.45)	(-0.78)	(N=44)	
(8)Income Share$_{T20}$=	49.46**	+1.75	-14.79**		.42	16.59**
	(10.54)	(1.32)	(-5.73)		(N=44)	

[a] t ratio in parenthesis.
* p<.05 **p < .01

dummy variable and the MNC*Core interaction term and, second, the correlation of almost exactly zero between lnMNC Penetration and Income Share$_{T20}$.

OLS (ordinary least squares) regression estimates of the parameters of the general model are given in Table 20.3 for the extended and restricted samples with and without Yugoslavia. The F test for the first equation indicates statistical significance at a high level of confidence, but of the explanatory variables, only the parameter estimate for lnMNC Penetration is significant at better than .05. The implication is that Core and MNC*Core are irrelevant variables and can be deleted from the equation; yet, if they are deleted, Income Share$_{T20}$ becomes a function only of lnMNC Penetration, with which it is uncorrelated. This non-sensical result reflects the presence of extreme multicollinearity between Core and MNC*Core, a condition that typically prevents the calculation of reliable parameter estimates. The third, fifth, and seventh equations also have relatively high R^2s, but unreliable parameter estimates, due to the problem of multicollinearity.

The additive equations, I(2), I(4), II(6), and II(8) afford as high a level of predictive accuracy as the interactive equations, I(1), I(3), II(5), and II(7). Since the additive equations are not affected by multicollinearity and are more parsimonious without loss of predictive accuracy, they are to be preferred to the interactive specification.

The t ratios for equations I(2), I(4), II(6), and II(8) show that the Core parameter estimates are significantly different from zero at a high level of confidence, whereas one cannot confidently reject the null hypothesis in the case of the parameter estimates for lnMNC Penetration. Also, with respect to accuracy of prediction, there is little to be gained from including the MNC Penetration variable, since Core alone can account for 40 percent of the variance of Income Share$_{T20}$. Moreover, inclusion of the MNC Penetration variable in the additive specification implies a positive *global* effect on inequality, which is a misrepresentation of the world economy paradigm and an empirical misrepresentation to boot.

The results of bivariate scatterplots and multivariate regression thus support the internal dynamics argument, at least with respect to cross-sectional variation in income inequality. It is possible to further investigate the dependency thesis from the perspective of longitudinal variation, using short-duration time series data that are available for a limited but heterogeneous sample of countries of the periphery.

Change in the income share of the upper quintile between c. 1970 and c. 1976 (data from World Bank, 1982, Table 25) is plotted in Figure 20.3 by change in the stock of foreign direct investment between 1967 and 1973 (data from Ballmer-Cao and Scheidegger, 1979, Table 3.2.1) for five peripheral countries from the semi-industrial group (ranging from relatively poor India to relatively rich Spain) and two from the primary producing group. In every case but one, the income share of the upper quintile declined by a not insubstantial margin (from 2.6 to 6.3 percentage points) subsequent to sizable (especially in terms of percentage change) increases in the stock of foreign investment. In South Korea, the exceptional case of an income distribution becoming less egalitarian after an increase in the stock of foreign investment, the gain in the upper quintile income share was less than 2 percentage points. These longitudinal data thus run counter to the prediction of dependency theory; and in conjunction with the support for the null hypothesis from the cross-sectional analysis, it would seem to be correct to infer that economic penetration of the periphery by the core, through the

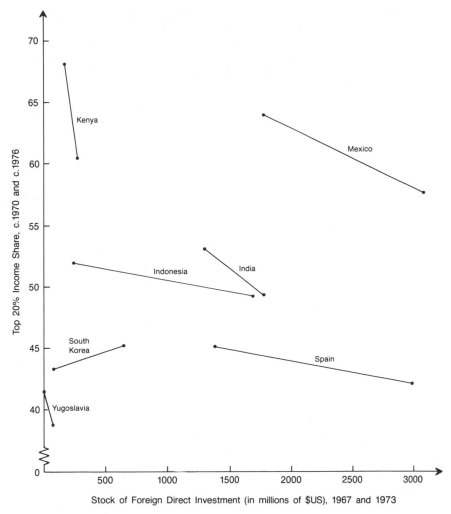

Figure 20.3 Time series of foreign investment and top 20 percent income share.

institution of the transnational corporation, is not a systematic or general cause of inequality in the distribution of income within peripheral countries.

Debt Dependence

An alternative indicator of financial dependence within the capitalist world economy is a country's level of external public indebtedness.

Dependency theorists regard debt dependence as a result of TNC economic penetration. Thus, Dos Santos (1970: 234) writes:

> Foreign capital retains control over the most dynamic sectors of the economy and repatriates a high volume of profit; consequently, capital accounts are highly unfavorable to dependent countries. . . . An important deficit is produced in the total balance of payments. . . . The result is that "foreign financing" becomes necessary, in two forms: to cover the existing deficit, and to "finance" development by means of loans for the stimulation of investments and to "supply" an internal economic surplus which was decapitalized to a large extent by the remittance of part of the surplus generated domestically and sent abroad as profits.

And Bornschier (1982: 51) reiterates and expands upon this argument:

> The acute infrastructure requirements in the periphery for the capital-intensive mode of core corporation production are likely to increase the external debt of the state. . . . Moreover, the class coalition which is favored by the operatives of core corporations is likely to increase social cleavages and thus the sharpness of social conflict; the state will consequently need increasing resources to control and suppress such conflict. . . . Furthermore, at the level of the system as a whole, the World Bank also acts like a "fire brigade" to stave off bankruptcy: highly indebted governments are therefore likely to receive World Bank support.

The core-headquartered TNC is considered by Bornschier (1982: 52) to be the "backbone in the entire system of economic dependencies"; variation in TNC economic penetration is postulated to cause variation both in external public debt and in World Bank debt/aid, and variation in external public debt is postulated to cause variation in World Bank debt/aid. A panel regression analysis of mid-1960s to mid-1970s data from 66 peripheral countries is cited as empirical support for the postulated causal linkages.

Since debt dependence is thought to be a result of TNC economic penetration, its causal status logically is that of an intervening variable between TNC economic penetration and income inequality. Therefore, one should investigate the possibility that debt dependence, because it is a more direct antecedent, might have a stronger effect on income inequality than TNC economic penetration.

Data on external public debt as a percentage of GNP in 1970 are available from the World Bank (1980, Table 15) for countries of the periphery only.[9] When 1970 scores on the External Debt variable are correlated with 1967 lnMNC Penetration, the positive relationship expected from dependency theory does not appear. For the extended sample the correlation between lnMNC Penetration and External Debt is $-.281$ (not significant at the .05 level); excluding Yugoslavia raises the correlation to $-.409$ (significant at .05). The respective correlations for the restricted sample are $-.310$ (not significant at .05) and $-.467$ (significant at .01).

The reason for the inverse relationship is that countries with high External Debt scores such as Bolivia, Malawi, and Tunisia have low MNC penetration scores, while many countries with low External Debt scores, e.g., Argentina, Brazil, South Africa, Spain, and Venezuela, have high scores on MNC penetration.

Since the expected positive relationship between MNC Penetration and External Debt is not present in these data, it is not surprising to find that Income Share$_{T20}$ is uncorrelated with External Debt, as can be seen from the scatterplot in Figure 20.4. The correlation is quite close to zero in the extended sample, with and without Yugoslavia, and the same is true for the restricted sample (r = .012 and −.033, with and without Yugoslavia).

Conclusion

A basic tenet of dependency theory is the proposition that among less developed countries on the periphery of the capitalist world economy, international relations of financial dependence on the core are a major cause of intranational inequality within the periphery. Core-headquartered transnational corporations are assumed to control the "commanding heights" of peripheral economies in an alliance with local elites and a small "labor aristocracy" of workers that favors concentration of income in the hands of the few. Confronted with the overwhelming economic power of this unholy alliance, national political elites are unwilling and/or unable to act in favor of income redistribution. Penetration of the peripheral economy by transnational corporations thus reduces the peripheral state to the role of willing captive or helpless pawn in a process of uneven exchange that results in economic development and relative equality in the core and underdevelopment and extreme inequality in the periphery.

Generally sympathetic reviews of the writing of dependency theorists in the late 1960s and early 1970s called attention to certain empirical weaknesses such as the overlooking of countries like Australia and Canada, which, in the description of Portes (1976: 78), "are profoundly 'dependent,' in the sense of penetration of their economies by foreign-owned subsidiaries, and yet exhibit a much higher per capita income, a better distribution of wealth, and more efficient health and educational services than most 'Third World' countries." And O'Brien (1975: 19) cautioned that, in general, "the empirical evidence offered in support of these hypotheses is admittedly somewhat casual."

The challenge of empirical verification of dependence theory has been taken up since the mid-1970s by scholars who have sought to cast dependency hypotheses into scientifically testable propositions subject to cross-national falsification. The culmination of this endeavor is a global model formulated by Bornschier, based on the world-system paradigm, which assumes that the driving force or "backbone" of the

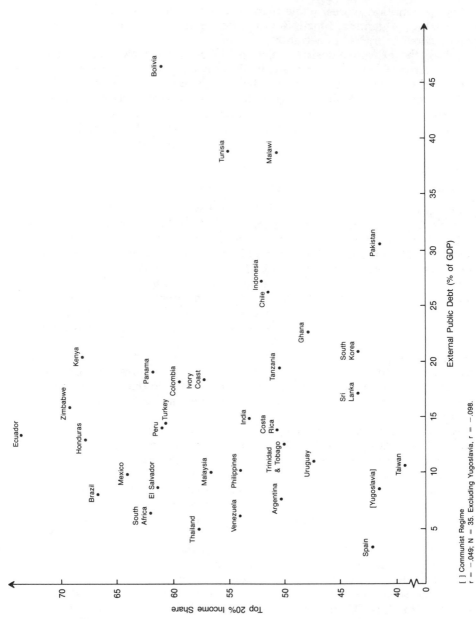

Figure 20.4 Relationship between external public debt and top 20 percent income share; extended sample of

capitalist world economy is the transnational corporation, an economic actor whose interest is continued or enhanced concentration of income in the poorer countries of the periphery, where elite demand is presumed to be the only effective market for the products of TNCs, but less concentration of income in the rich countries of the core, where mass consumption constitutes the effective market. Thus does Bornschier's world-system approach explain the anomaly of egalitarian income distribution in financially dependent countries such as Australia and Canada, while preserving the dependency theory hypothesis of a positive relationship between financial dependency and inequality in the periphery, all within the context of a global model sensitive to the general dependency claim that the "laws of motion" in the periphery are fundamentally different from those in the core.

The major counter hypothesis to dependency theory and the world-system paradigm stems from an "internal dynamics" approach to explanation of income distribution. This approach does not necessarily reject the claim of different laws of motion for core and periphery, but it emphatically rejects the claim that the laws of motion are those of capitalist imperialism operating as an international economic force that determines the distribution of income within nations. In rejecting the economic determinism of the dependency/world-system paradigm, the internal dynamics approach counters with the specific prediction that the cross-national relationship between indicators of financial dependence in the capitalist world economy and distribution of income within nations will conform to the null hypothesis.

It should be stressed here that the internal dynamics perspective is not an argument for historical uniqueness. The distribution of income within nations is not *necessarily* considered to be the result of *idiosyncratic* internal forces; quite to the contrary, internal characteristics of an economic, political, sociological, or psychological nature certainly could exert a systematic effect, cross-nationally on income distribution. But it is assumed that any such general determinants, should they exist, are not externally conditioned.

In this analysis of mostly cross-sectional data on international financial dependence and intranational income distribution, I have sought to perform a methodologically rigorous test of predictions from the dependency/world-system model. In this regard, I have rejected data on the distribution of income that suffer from one or more of the following limitations:

1. only partial coverage of income distribution;
2. unreliable coverage of income distribution;
3. measurement of income distribution that predates the observation of financial dependence by a substantial margin;
4. measurement of income distribution for dependent territories.

These problems affect, by my estimation, about 30 percent of the observations of income distribution from Ballmer-Cao and Scheidegger (1979, Table 5.3) used in the various analyses of Bornschier; about 40 percent of the observations of income distribution used by Evans and Timberlake (1980, Appendix A, Column 1b); and about 50 percent of the observations of income distribution used by Rubinson (1976, Appendix 3). Therefore, the results of previous research, which claim to show support for the dependency/world-system approach to explanation of income distribution, are open to question. The data on income distribution that I use obviously are not flawless; but they are not subject to the first, third, and fourth problems mentioned above; and as for their reliability, they are the best currently available information from World Bank sources, given the caveat that the monitoring of income distribution data according to standardized procedures has not yet been integrated into the official statistical accounting system in many countries.

The most straightforward way to approach the empirical question of a relationship between international financial dependence and intranational income distribution, given a relatively reliable data base, is to begin by inspecting scatterplots, an elementary procedure that has been bypassed in previous research (which rarely even reports bivariate correlations). A scatterplot reveals that the negative relationship between MNC penetration and income inequality in the core, previously reported by Bornschier, is not strong and, more importantly, is almost completely an artifact of an unreliable observation of income distribution for Finland. For the sample of countries of the periphery, which includes reasonably comprehensive coverage only of those in the middle income range, a positive relationship between MNC penetration and income inequality is indeed observed, but it again is not very strong and in this instance is quite sensitive to the special case of Yugoslavia, where there is good reason to believe that the *political* factor of communist rule is responsible for the egalitarian distribution of income. Short-duration time-series data reinforce the speculation about the irrelevance of MNC penetration (specifically, the lack thereof in 1967) for income distribution in Yugoslavia; and they more generally do not support the prediction of dependency theory, although the sample of countries is very small. Finally, an alternative indicator of international financial dependence, the size of a country's external public debt, shows a virtually zero correlation with income inequality in a cross-sectional analysis of the periphery. These findings indicate that it is pointless to carry the investigation further, introducing additional control variables, since the basic bivariate results (and a multivariate test of a core-periphery interaction specification) point consistently in the direction of the null hypothesis.

It is possible to boost the correlation between MNC penetration and income inequality to statistical significance by including more countries under communist rule in the periphery (and arbitrarily assuming approximately zero MNC penetration, in the absence of actual data) and/

or by introducing very old income distribution data from dependent territories into the analysis. The former procedure does not "save" dependency theory, however, because the alternative political hypothesis is so obvious, and the simple inclusion of a dummy communist rule variable reduces the MNC penetration effect to statistical nonsignificance. The latter procedure is not justifiable methodologically; but if more comprehensive data on income distribution become available for the group of least developed countries, and if they raise the MNC penetration effect beyond that observed currently for predominantly middle-income countries of the periphery, then the income inequality hypothesis of dependency theory might be saved (with a twist of irony, since it was not formulated with the poverty-stricken countries of Africa and Asia in mind).

In global comparative perspective, then, the Brazilian "model," a major source of inspiration for the hypothesis that dependence on TNC-controlled capital leads to income inequality in the periphery, does not appear to be representative of any general trend characteristic of middle-income developing countries as a group. And even in the case of Brazil, an argument can be made that it was not dependence on foreign capital which caused the income-concentrating policies of the late 1960s and 1970s, but rather decisions taken independently by the Brazilian military rulers, after the *golpe de estado* of 1964, to follow the "wisdom" of neoclassical economics that redistributive policies would retard economic growth and that, in accordance with the "law" of the Kuznets inverted U curve of inequality and development, the best way to benefit all classes of society would be to pursue short-run income-concentrating policies in order to stimulate rapid economic growth, which would lead automatically to greater income equality in the long run (see the discussion in Wright, 1978: 63–66). Thus, with respect to future cross-national investigation of the causes of income inequality within nations, the more promising avenue of approach would seem to be one that leads away from external "world-system" economic determinism and toward the consideration of internal dynamics, with particular attention to the autonomous role of the state.

Notes

1. I describe Bornschier as an *empirical* theorist because he states concepts and propositions in testable form and confronts them with data.
2. The income share of the upper quintile hovered at about the 41 percent mark during the 1950s and 1960s (see Sawyer, 1976: 26).
3. For example, Sunkel (1972: 523) cites approvingly the following passage from a 1969 Harvard University Division of Research paper by Vaupel and Curham:

> The international corporation is acting and planning in terms that are far in advance of the political concepts of the nation-state. As the Renaissance of the fifteenth century brought an end to feudalism, aristocracy and the dominant

role of the Church, the twentieth-century Renaissance is bringing an end to middle-class society and the dominance of the nation-state. The heart of the new power structure is the international organization and the technocrats who guide it. Power is shifting away from the nation-state to international institutions, public and private.

And Cardoso (1973: 149) describes the transnational corporation as the "moving force" behind his model of associated dependent development.

4. "Transnational" corporation is the usage adopted by the United Nations in order to avoid confusion about the ownership of these enterprises, which is not in any sense multinational. Their operations are across political frontiers; hence the term "transnational."

5. Arrighi (1970: 223–225) observes that since decolonization in Africa a new pattern of foreign investment, in which transnational ("oligopolistic") corporations play a major role, has replaced the small-scale enterprises of colonial capitalism. Therefore, it would be a mistake to attribute long-term retroactive temporal stability to 1967 MNC Penetration scores for newly independent African nations.

6. The upper quintile income share for these countries differs from that reported in Ballmer-Cao and Scheidegger (1979) by more than 1 percentage point; trivial revisions of less than a single point also have been made for other countries.

7. Unlike the World Bank (1981, Table 6.1), which excludes Taiwan from all consideration, I include it in the semi-industrialized group; I also place Ireland in this group, as well as India and Pakistan, which are considered to be partially industrialized by the World Bank, despite having low per capita income. Countries under communist rule and dependent territories are not included.

8. The negative effect on inequality presumably would occur as the result of a positive relationship between foreign investment and economic growth, the benefits of which would eventually "trickle down" through the mass of the population, increasing the size and wealth of the middle class.

9. The World Bank does not collect data on external debt for other than developing countries; also, according to the World Bank (1980: 161), comparable data do not exist for other countries.

References

Ahluwalia, Montek S. 1974. "Income Inequality: Some Dimensions of the Problem." Pp. 3–37 in Hollis Chenery et al. (eds.), *Redistribution with Growth.* New York: Oxford University Press.

———. 1976. "Inequality, Poverty, and Development." *Journal of Development Economics* 3: 307–342.

Allison, Paul D. 1978. "Measures of Inequality." *American Sociological Review* 43:865–879.

Arrighi, Giovanni. 1970. "International Corporations, Labor Aristocracies, and Economic Development in Tropical Africa." Pp. 220–267 in Robert I. Rhodes (ed.), *Imperialism and Underdevelopment.* New York: Monthly Review Press.

Ballmer-Cao, Thanh-Huyen and Jürg Scheidegger. 1979. *Compendium of Data for World System Analysis.* Zürich: Soziologisches Institut der Universität.

Barrett, Richard E. and Martin King Whyte. 1982. "Dependency Theory and Taiwan: Analysis of a Deviant Case." *American Journal of Sociology* 87: 1064–1089.

Bornschier, Volker. 1980. "Multinational Corporations and Economic Growth." *Journal of Development Economics* 7: 191–210.

——. 1981. "Comment." *International Studies Quarterly* 25: 283–288.

——. 1982. "The World Economy in the World-System: Structure, Dependence and Change." *International Social Science Journal* 34: 37–59.

——. 1983. "World Economy, Level Development and Income Distribution: An Integration of Different Approaches to the Explanation of Income Inequality." *World Development* 11: 11–20.

Bornschier, Volker and Thanh-Huyen Ballmer-Cao. 1979. "Income Inequality: A Cross-National Study of Relationships between MNC-Penetration, Dimensions of the Power Structure and Income Distribution." *American Sociological Review* 44: 487–506.

Bornschier, Volker, Christopher Chase-Dunn, and Richard Rubinson. 1978. "Cross-National Evidence of the Effects of Foreign Investment and Aid on Economic Growth and Inequality." *American Journal of Sociology* 84: 651–683.

Cardoso, Fernando Henrique. 1973. "Associated Dependent Development: Theoretical and Practical Implications." Pp. 142–176 in Alfred Stepan (ed.), *Authoritarian Brazil.* New Haven: Yale University Press.

Chase-Dunn, Christopher. 1975. "The Effects of International Economic Dependence on Development and Inequality: A Cross-National Study." *American Sociological Review* 40: 720–738.

Dos Santos, Theotonios. 1970. "The Structure of Dependence." *American Economic Review* 60: 231–236.

Evans, Peter and Michael Timberlake. 1980. "Dependence, Inequality, and Growth in Less Developed Countries." *American Sociological Review* 45: 531–552.

Figueroa, Adolfo and Richard Weiskoff. 1980. "Viewing Social Pyramids: Income Distribution in Latin America." Pp. 257–294 in Robert Ferber (ed.), *Consumption and Income Distribution in Latin America.* Organization of American States, ECIEL.

Furtado, Celso. 1973. "The Post-1964 Brazilian 'Model' of Development." *Studies in Comparative International Development,* 115–127.

Hirschman, Albert O. 1981. *Essays in Trespassing.* New York: Cambridge University Press.

Jain, Shail. 1975. *Size Distribution of Income.* Washington, D.C.: World Bank.

O'Brien, Philip J. 1975. "A Critique of Latin American Theories of Dependency." Pp. 7–27 in Ivar Oxaal et al. (eds.), *Beyond the Sociology of Development.* Boston: Routledge & Kegan Paul.

Paukert, Felix. 1973. "Income Distribution at Different Levels of Development." *International Labor Review* 108: 97–125.

Portes, Alejandro. 1976. "On the Sociology of National Development: Theories and Issues." *American Journal of Sociology* 82: 55–85.

Roberti, Paolo. 1974. "Income Distribution: A Time Series and a Cross-Section Survey." *The Economic Journal* 84: 629–638.

Rubinson, Richard. 1976. "The World Economy and the Distribution of Income Within States: A Cross-National Study." *American Sociological Review* 41: 638–659.

Sawyer, Malcolm. 1976. "Income Distribution in OECD Countries." *OECD Economic Outlook,* 3–36.

Seers, Dudley. 1963. "The Limitations of the Special Case." *The Bulletin of the Institute of Economics and Statistics, Oxford* 25: 77–98.

Smith, Tony. 1979. "The Underdevelopment of Development Literature." *World Politics* 31: 247–288.

———. 1981a. *The Pattern of Imperialism*. New York: Cambridge University Press.

———. 1981b. "The Logic of Dependency Theory Revisited." *International Organization* 35: 755–761.

Sunkel, Osvaldo. 1972. "Big Business and 'Dependencia.'" *Foreign Affairs* 50: 517–531.

Taylor, Charles L. and Michael C. Hudson. 1972. *World Handbook of Political and Social Indicators*, 2nd ed. New Haven: Yale University Press.

Watkins, Mel. 1975. "Economic Development in Canada." Pp. 72–96 in Immanuel Wallerstein (ed.), *World Inequality*. Montreal: Black Rose Books.

Weede, Erich and Horst Tiefenbach. 1981. "Some Recent Explanations of Income Inequality." *International Studies Quarterly* 25: 255–282.

World Bank. 1979. *World Development Report 1979*. New York: Oxford University Press.

———. 1980. *World Development Report 1980*. New York: Oxford University Press.

———. 1981. *World Development Report 1981*. New York: Oxford University Press.

———. 1982. *World Development Report 1982*. New York: Oxford University Press.

Wright, Charles L. 1978. "Income Inequality and Economic Growth: Examining the Evidence." *The Journal of Developing Areas* 13: 49–66.

21. Some Questions on the Validity of Income Distribution Data

William Loehr

In the previous chapter, Muller raised a number of questions about the validity of data used to measure income inequality. In this selection, drawn from a longer essay on the relationship between development and income distribution, William Loehr discusses the weaknesses of the data. He points out the serious limitations of family income data that have been used in nearly all prior studies and suggests that a more reliable measure of income distribution would be based upon the individual. Studies using such a measure would probably reveal even greater levels of inequality in developing countries than have existing studies, Loehr says. He then discusses the utility of examining sectoral income distribution data and concludes by looking at a number of policy instruments that can be employed in developing countries to reverse the trend toward greater income inequality.

Almost all empirical studies of income distribution . . . rely upon income data related to families. Most censuses collect data in this way, and thus the largest samples for cross-sectional work can be obtained by dealing with family data. This approach has serious shortcomings, however. First, definitions of "family" differ. Some censuses may not include groups of unrelated adults in this category; others do. Some include income information for people who normally live within the family unit but who are temporarily absent at the time of census; others include only those persons in residence at the time. Perhaps more intractable are the differences in the concept of "family" which exist among nations. For income purposes, it is important to know whether we are dealing with a society in which the traditional extended family predominates or whether the nuclear family is the norm. The former, of course, is of much greater relevance in less developed countries (LDCs), while in developed countries (DCs) the (more easily dealt with)

Reprinted with permission from "Economic Underdevelopment and Income Distribution: A Review of the Literature," in *Economic Development, Poverty, and Income Distribution* edited by William Loehr and John P. Powelson. Boulder, CO: Westview Press, 1977.

nuclear family is most often observed. In the extended family system, it may be completely irrelevant that individuals are not members of the same household, in the sense that they do not dwell together. For income purposes, such individuals may be just as interdependent as if they lived together. The fact that persons living and working in urban areas support parents living in rural areas complicates any real measurement of "household" income. (For a theoretical analysis in which these factors play an important role, see Sen, 1975.) Further complications arise when we attempt to compare household incomes in societies which are monogamous with incomes in those which are not. Moreover, the limits of the extended family differ; in some societies only parents and siblings are included, while others include uncles, cousins, etc.

Distributions of income based upon the individual may, therefore, be of greater relevance than those relying on the household concept. Unfortunately, such data are difficult to come by, and few censuses collect them.[1] In general, income distributions by individuals are likely to show greater inequality than those compiled on a family basis. To the extent that poorer families in LDCs tend to be larger and more "extended" than richer families, there is likely to be greater inequality in those countries. The nuclear family is the norm in the DCs, and a nuclear family tends to include a smaller number of individuals than the extended family that prevails in LDCs. The larger household incomes of DC families support relatively few individuals, while the smaller household incomes in LDCs must be shared by more people. Thus, the income gap between LDCs and DCs is even wider when distributions are based on individual income.

Sectoral Income Distribution

If different sectors in an economy have different intrasectoral income distributions, and if a major shift in population takes place from a sector with low inequality to one with greater inequality, overall inequality will be seen to rise. This is true even if inequality within each sector is constant. Increasing inequality in LDCs, accompanied by economic growth, can be at least partially explained by this arithmetic truism. We can generally observe in LDCs that inequality tends to be greater in the urban (industrial) sector than in the rural (agricultural) sector (Weisskoff, 1970; Swamy, 1967). Rapid growth usually proceeds in a dualistic fashion, so that growth in the industrial sector is more rapid than growth in the agricultural sector (Adelman and Morris, 1973). In addition, rapid population growth and rural-to-urban migration occur. These factors alone are enough to ensure that, *ceteris paribus*, income distribution will become more unequal overall during the early stages of development and then more equal later on (Robinson, 1976).

Oshima (1970), in a study of inequality in Asian countries, found that changes in income distribution are not a result of economic growth per se. Using his quantile deviation measure, he was able to calculate the share of inequality attributable to each economic sector. He noted that changes in economic structure—i.e., shifts from a rural to an urban focus of economic activity as growth proceeds—were more important than growth per se in explaining changing income distribution. His main conclusion (p. 34) was that undue policy emphasis on industrialization can lead to unemployment, excessive urbanization, regional imbalance, and widening inequality. Thus, he laid the blame for inequality squarely in the lap of dualistic development.

Weisskoff (1970) examined the shift from agriculture to nonagricultural economic activities and also found a resulting overall increase in inequality. Swamy (1967), in a study of inequality in India, was able to separate the increase in inequality into two parts: one attributable to intersectoral inequality, the other to intrasectoral inequality. He found that changes in intrasectoral equality between 1951 and 1960 were small. No observable change took place in the agricultural sector, while the income distribution in the nonagricultural sector became slightly more unequal. Only 15 percent of the overall increase in Indian income inequality could be attributed to changes in the intrasectoral income distribution; the remaining 85 percent was the result of increased intersectoral inequality—i.e., shifts in population from the low-inequality (agricultural) to the higher-inequality (nonagricultural) sector.

Variables which relate the overall personal distribution of income to sectoral distributions are (a) the relative size distribution of income within each sector, (b) the weight of each sector in terms of the number of people it represents, and (3) the intersectoral differences in income per person (Kuznets, 1963, p. 22). Kuznets found it useful to array sectors by increasing product per worker—just as one would array families by ascending income levels—and then calculate concentration ratios, where the relevant Lorenz curve has as many segments as there are sectors.[2] His data clearly show much wider sectoral inequality in LDCs than in DCs. Furthermore, although in countries at all levels of development the agricultural sector's product per capita is lower than the countrywide average, it is close to the average in DCs and far below the average in LDCs. In general, relative differences in the sectoral levels of product per worker are inversely related to levels of economic development (Kuznets, 1957, p. 45). Over the long-run development of a country, the relative product per person in the agricultural sector rises toward the countrywide average, while the same relative product gradually declines toward the average in other sectors.

Berry's work (1974) . . . was based on an analysis of the sectoral distribution of income in Colombia. By examining wage information across sectors, he could imply changes in the incomes of workers across sectors. His conclusions were somewhat at odds with Kuznets's, however, in that he found continually increasing inequality between the agricultural sector and the rest of the Colombian economy since the 1930s, despite growth in overall product per capita.

Regional Income Distribution Within Countries

Clearly, to the extent that such sectors as industrial production and agriculture are location specific, one should expect differences in income levels between regions of any given country. But one would also expect differing degrees of income inequality within regions, since the preponderance of region-specific types of production implies the generation of income in a region-specific manner as well. Geographic limitations as well as occupational immobility would tend to accentuate whatever tendencies there are for income inequality to develop within some regions. In a very limited sample of countries where data were available (Italy, the U.S., and Brazil), Kuznets (1963) found that income tended to be much more unequally distributed in poorer regions of the countries examined. In Italy, the shares of income in the lower brackets were distinctly lower than the shares for those groups nationwide, and the shares of upper groups were distinctly higher. Data by states in the United States showed a similar pattern. There appeared a negative association between the share of the top income group and the per capita income of a state *despite* lower property income in poorer states. In 1957, the Gini concentration ratios were .22 for the poorest states and .12 for the richest. Allowing for the effect of the progressive income tax, we see a greater equalizing effect in rich states than in poor, since the rich groups in rich states have higher absolute incomes than the same groups in poor states, and are thus subject to a higher marginal tax rate.[3]

Policy Analyses

Studies of income distribution become purely academic exercises if attention is not paid to the impact of public policy upon income distribution and to the policy recommendations which may be made to change that distribution in one way or another. Studies of public policy and income distribution fall into two very general categories. The first, and by far the most often studied, is the effect of the fiscal system on distribution. Analyses of this type are very common for almost all developed countries, and methods for delving into tax/expenditure incidence are fairly well formulated (Meiszkowski, 1969; Blinder et al., 1976). The second category deals with the distributional impact of such specific public programs as educational services, agricultural development, and construction projects.

Although studies of fiscal systems in developing countries are few, generally they can be used to exert favorable redistributive pressures within the economy. Snodgrass (1974), for example, indicates that progressiveness within the Malaysian fiscal system has increased noticeably since 1958. McLure (1975) indicates that, overall, the fiscal system of Colombia exhibits mild progressiveness. On the whole, surveys of general tax/expenditure incidence in LDCs (De Wulf, 1974) indicate that benefits from government expenditures received by upper income groups represent a smaller portion of their incomes than do the benefits received by low income groups. Both conceptual and methodological problems, however, cast serious doubt on the adequacy of these studies in determining whether or not public policy is "pro poor." Usually what is measured is the amount of public expenditure for such items as teachers and irrigation projects, rather than the value of education to those being taught or the marginal value of agricultural products to producers. Since the recipients of public benefits at the low end of the income scale rarely have any say about the quantity or quality of the services they receive, we cannot be sure that their evaluation of such services would correspond to that of public officials.

Many public expenditures provide public goods and services which add particular difficulties to the evaluation of benefit incidence.[4] Because there are no generally accepted ways of allocating these benefits, assumptions about their value must be used only as rules of thumb. One assumption is that all persons benefit equally (since all consume equally); others are that benefits are received in proportion to income or wealth or that benefits are received and valued in some impressionistic way. Unfortunately, the proportion of public goods in most government budgets is large, and assumptions about how benefits are to be assigned largely determine the outcome of studies concerned with overall incidence of public expenditures (De Wulf, 1974, p. 22).

Students of tax/expenditure incidence are further thwarted by poor-quality data. The excellent study by Krzyzaniak and Ozmucur (1972) offers a good illustration. Their analysis of the incidence of taxes in Turkey resulted in estimates of tax burdens for thirty-five income categories and demonstrated that, under varying assumptions, Turkish taxes, overall, probably are proportional. However, the many adjustments needed to make the data comparable (and to force them into a format which allowed a study of this type) introduce the potential for a wide range of errors, thus weakening the validity of their results.

Studies of specific public policies generally show that lower income segments of the population receive benefits which represent a larger portion of their incomes than richer segments. Studies cited by De Wulf (1974, p. 23) indicate, however, that, because of the extreme inequality of income existing in the first place, the absolute benefits received by upper income groups are far in excess of those accruing to the poor. Colombian data on the distribution of educational benefits, for example, show that the lowest income classes receive benefits (measured by expenditure) equivalent to 13.1 percent of their incomes and that the highest income group receives as little as 0.8 percent. In absolute terms, however, the latter group receives more than six times the educational benefits of the poor. Fields's (1975) study of higher education in Kenya indicates that there is a "systematic process operating against the poor," tending to perpetuate inequities existing there.

Employment programs have captured the attention of many economists of late, and proposals for attacking the problems of unemployment and inequitable income distribution decorate almost any development plan. While most of these efforts can probably be recommended to improve the employment situation, they cannot be seen as panaceas for solving distribution problems. Too many other factors, in addition to employment, affect distribution. Webb (1972), for example, points to the effect of nonlabor income, which appears much more inequitably distributed in Peru than labor income. Jarvis (1974) points to this factor as well as to the distribution of capital ownership and the effect of dualism before concluding that employment programs, as a means of achieving income redistribution, are likely to be of only marginal benefit. Like many other critics of employment policy, Jarvis advocates a more direct government role in income redistribution.

Stabilization policies seem to have been associated with sharply increased inequality. Arndt (1975) analyzed post-Sukarno Indonesia and the stabilization and growth policies pursued there after 1966. With per capita income growing at a rapid 4 percent per year, ever larger shares were accruing only to the upper income groups. While the poorest income groups lost part of their relative share, it was Arndt's judgment that they were at least holding their own in absolute terms. The severe stabilization program in Brazil, begun in 1964, also resulted in rapid economic growth and a deterioration in economic equity (Wells, 1974). The data presented by Wells, however (Table 8), show that the poorest decile of the working population could not possibly have been holding its own on an absolute scale, since its relative share dropped by more than 40 percent. Informal reports from Chile indicate that current trends there are mostly along Brazilian lines. Unfortunately, the cases cited present such a mixture of economic and political confusion that few clear economic forces can be observed.

Often, where data permit, simulation exercises can help determine the impact of specific programs upon income distribution. Weisskoff's 1973 study of growth in Puerto Rico, plotting the path of employment and income distribution, probably could not have been done in many developing countries because of data limitations. Via simulation, Thirsk (1972) examined the Colombian policy of subsidizing the mechanization of agriculture. He showed explicitly the changes in income distribution which resulted from the relative changes in prices of productive factors and the changes in gross domestic product (GDP) which resulted from improvements in efficiency. He was able to show that withdrawing the subsidy both improved income distribution (by increasing labor intensiveness and decreasing the income share of capital owners) and increased GDP (through more optimal allocation of resources).

Occasionally, reference is made in economics literature to policies for improving income distribution as part of an overall development strategy. Development plans are replete with statements about combining distributional objectives with other goals, such as growth and export expansion.[5] Often, however, no analytical framework exists which links distribution with other considerations. Thus, one cannot easily determine whether multiple objectives are consistent with one another or, if there are trade-offs among them, define those trade-offs. In the Chilean case, for example, Foxley and Munoz (1974) indicate that the objectives of the Allende government for 1970–1976—to increase economic growth and employment and reduce foreign indebtedness—were not consistent, given internal savings propensities. Their evaluation of the Chilean situation could generally be applied in other cases: "The way to promote a sustained redistribution effort must . . . make direct redistributive efforts compatible with the savings and investment efforts, and also [compatible] with an increase in efficiency." (Foxley and Munoz, 1974, p. 29).

Overall studies of specific policies or sets of policies usually are deficient in that they do not single out the specific groups which are to benefit or pay the cost. It is insufficient to merely indicate which income classes will feel some impact, since each income class usually consists of a variety of people with different behavioral patterns. What is needed is more information about such specific functional groups as small farmers, shopkeepers, skilled labor, and entrepreneurs. These groups often span several income categories, but all are nevertheless tied together in a set of economic activities which eventually determine what the overall income distribution will be. Since each of these groups operates in a slightly different economic area, their motivations and needs will differ. Studies must, therefore, be designed to analyze the specific needs of each group so that policies can be derived to effectively meet those needs.

Notes

1. Household data are easier to collect, since once a definition of "household" is determined the census is faced with a population which is much smaller and much more fixed in location than is the population of individuals.

2. Kuznets's (1957) measure of weighted relative inequality among sectors is calculated as follows: If agriculture produces .3 of total national product and employs .4 of the labor force, the difference (i.e., .1) is really the difference between the relative per worker product (i.e., $.3/.4 = .75$) and the countrywide average (i.e., 1.00). That difference $(.75 - 1.00 = -.25)$ is then weighted by the share of that sector in the total labor force (i.e., .4). The sum of these differences is a measure of relative inequality among sectoral products per worker, weighted by the share of each sector in the labor force. The index ranges from 0 (complete equality) and approaches infinity as production becomes entirely concentrated in one sector which employs fewer and fewer people.

3. It is interesting to note that Kuznets (p. 41) found that when the 12 highest nonwhite population states were separated from the others, income inequality was shown to be clearly greater in the nonwhite states and greatest in the poorest 6 nonwhite states.

4. Public goods are those which (1) once provided, no one can be excluded from consuming and (2) the consumption of them by one person does not reduce the supply available to others. The classic example of a "pure" public good is defense. However, rarely are public goods "pure" in the sense of meeting the definition precisely.

5. For an example, see Republic of Kenya (1974).

References

Adelman, I. (1975). "Development Economics—A Reassessment of Goals." *American Economic Review* 65, no. 2 (May 1975): 302–309.

Adelman, I., and C. T. Morris (1973). *Economic Growth and Social Equity in Developing Countries*. Stanford, Calif.: Stanford University Press.

Adelman, I., and C. T. Morris (1967). *Society, Politics and Economic Development*. Baltimore: Johns Hopkins Press.

Adelman, I., and C. T. Morris (1974). "Who Benefits from Economic Development," in OECD, *Planning, Income, Distribution, Private Foreign Investment*. Paris: OECD, 1974.

Ahluwalia, M. S. (1974). "Income Inequality: Some Dimensions of the Problem," in Chenery et al.

Arndt, H. W. (1975). "Development and Equality: The Indonesian Case." *World Development* 3, nos. 2 and 3 (February/March 1975).

Berry, A. (1974). "Changing Income Distribution under Development: Colombia." *Review of Income and Wealth* 20, no. 3 (September 1974).

Blinder, A., et al. (1974). *The Economics of Public Finance*. Washington: The Brookings Institution.

Chenery, H., et al. (1974). *Redistribution with Growth*. London: Oxford University Press.

De Wulf, L. (1974). "Do Public Expenditures Reduce Inequality?" *Finance and Development* (September 1974).

Fields, G. (1975). "Higher Education and Income Distribution in a Less Developed Country." *Oxford Economic Papers* 27, no. 2 (July 1975).

Fishlow, A. (1972). "Brazilian Size Distribution of Income." *American Economic Review* 62, no. 2 (May 1972).

Foxley, A., and O. Munoz (1974). "Income Redistribution, Economic Growth and Social Structure: The Case of Chile." *Oxford Bulletin of Economics and Statistics* 36, no. 1.

Jain, S. (1974). "Size Distribution of Income: Compilation of Data." IBRD, Bank Staff Working Paper no. 190 (November 1974).

Jarvis, L. S. (1974). "The Limited Value of Employment Policies for Income Inequality," in Edgar O. Edwards, ed. *Employment in Developing Nations*. New York: Columbia University Press.

Kravis, I. (1960). "International Differences in the Distribution of Income." *Review of Economics and Statistics* 42, no. 4 (November 1960).

Kumar, D. (1974). "Changes in Income Distribution and Poverty in India: A Review of the Literature." *World Development* 2.

Krzyzaniak, M., and S. Ozmucur (1972). "The Distribution of Income and the Short Run Burden of Taxes in Turkey, 1968." Program of Development Studies, Rice University, Houston, Paper no. 28.

Kuznets, S. (1963). "Quantitative Aspects of the Economic Growth of Nations: Distribution of Income by Size." *Economic Development and Cultural Change* 11, no. 2 (January 1963).

————. (1957). "Quantitative Aspects of the Economic Growth of Nations: Industrial Distribution of National Product and Labor Force." *Economic Development and Cultural Change*, no. 4 (July 1957).

McLure, Jr., C. E. (1975). "The Incidence of Colombia Taxes: 1970." *Economic Development and Cultural Change* 24, no. 1 (October 1970).

Meiszkowski, P. (1969). "Tax Incidence Theory: The Effects of Taxes on the Distribution of Income." *Journal of Economic Literature* 7, no. 4 (December 1969), 1: 103–124.

Oshima, H. T. (1970). "Income Inequality and Economic Growth: The Postwar Experience of Asian Countries." *Malayan Economic Review* 15, no. 2 (October 1970).

————. (1962). "The International Comparison of Size Distribution of Family Incomes with Special Reference to Asia." *Review of Economics and Statistics* 44, no. 4 (November 1962): 439–445.

Paukert, F. (1973). "Income Distribution at Different Levels of Development: A Survey of Evidence." *International Labor Review* 108, nos. 2 and 3 (August/September 1973).

Roberti, P. (1974). "Income Distribution: A Time-Series and A Cross-Section Study." *Economic Journal* 84, no. 335 (September 1974).

Robinson, S. (1976). "A Note on the U Hypothesis Relating Income Inequality and Economic Development." *American Economic Review* 66, no. 3 (June 1976).

Sen, A. (1975). *Employment, Technology and Development.* Oxford: Clarendon Press.

Snodgrass, D. R. (1974). "The Fiscal System as an Income Redistributor in West Malaysia." *Public Finance* 29, no. 1.

Sonquist, J. A. and J. N. Morgan (1964). *The Detection of Interaction Effects.* Ann Arbor: Institute of Social Research, University of Michigan.

Swamy, S. (1967). "Structural Change in the Distribution of Income by Size: The Case of India." *Review of Income and Wealth* 13, no. 2 (June 1967).

Thirsk, W. R. (1972). "Income Distribution, Efficiency and the Experience of Colombian Farm Mechanization." Program of Development Studies, Rice University, Houston, Paper no. 33.

Tokman, V. E. (1974). "Redistribution of Income, Technology and Employment: An Analysis of the Industrial Sectors of Ecuador, Peru and Venezuela." *World Development* 2.

Webb, R. C. (1972). "The Distribution of Income in Peru." Research Program in Economic Development, Woodrow Wilson School, Princeton University, Princeton, N.J., Discussion Paper no. 26.

Weisskoff, R. (1970). "Income Distribution and Economic Growth in Puerto Rico, Argentina, and Mexico." *Review of Income and Wealth* 16, no. 4 (December 1970).

Wells, J. (1974). "Distribution of Earnings, Growth, and the Structure of Demand in Brazil during the 1960s." *World Development* 2, no. 1 (January 1974).

22. Assessing Progress Toward Greater Equality of Income Distribution

Gary S. Fields

In this chapter, Gary S. Fields raises more doubts about the income inequality data used in many studies and challenges the interpretation of those data. He begins by pointing out a number of flaws in the inequality data, noting that the approach to studying the question has almost always been to examine relative inequality. Through a series of numerical examples, Fields shows that relative inequality can increase while absolute poverty declines. He believes that the relative approach is fixated on subjective conditions, and he thinks it preferable to study the objective conditions under which the world's poor live. Fields presents evidence to show that there is very little support for the inverted U curve first suggested by Kuznets. Further doubts are cast on the U curve through a brief examination of some historical trends in distribution. Finally, Fields reinterprets the Brazilian and Indian cases, showing that in spite of worsening relative inequality in Brazil, absolute poverty declined, whereas in India absolute poverty worsened significantly even though the distribution of income did not.

Income as an Indicator of Economic Well-Being

The usefulness of income equality as a criterion for assessing progress and commitment toward economic development hinges on the assumption that income is a meaningful indicator of economic position. Two standards for gauging the usefulness of the income measure are conceptual suitability, on the one hand, and data availability on the other.

Economic well-being is related to the goods and services one consumes; and consumption, in most cases, depends on income.

It is easy to think of exceptions to these generalizations: the cripple who derives less satisfaction from goods and services than the fortunate who are well-endowed physically; the young couple who receives large and frequent gifts from their parents; the rich with large asset holdings who finance their consumption out of their wealth rather than from their earnings; and the peasant family that grows and consumes its own food and has little or no cash income deriving from the sale of a marketable surplus. In all these cases, cash income is an inaccurate measure of the individual's or family's command over economic resources. At issue is the severity of the inaccuracies, some of which are undoubtedly more worrisome than others.

Income-distribution statistics in less developed countries (LDCs) take only some of these considerations into account. Health status and intrafamily gifts are examples of a broad range of considerations that never enter into income-distribution data. The costs of worrying about these factors far outweigh the benefits. On the other hand, adjustments for home-produced consumption and income from wealth are often made, and with good reason, since these factors together affect the economic position of large numbers of income recipients.

Income-distribution figures typically measure money income received during a month or a year. For example, the U.S. census asks for income received in the previous year, but since the census is conducted only at ten-year intervals, in the interim the census bureau regularly reports income data derived from the Current Population Survey (CPS) of some 47,000 households. Income is defined as follows:

Data on income collected in the CPS are limited to money income received before payments for personal income taxes and deductions for Social Security, union dues, Medicare, etc. Money income is the sum of the amounts received from earnings; Social Security and public assistance payments; dividends; interest; and rent; unemployment and workmen's compensation; government and private employee pensions; and other periodic income. (Certain money receipts such as capital gains are not included.) Therefore, money income does not reflect the fact that many families receive part of their income in the form of non-money transfers such as food stamps, health benefits, and subsidized housing; that many farm families receive non-money income in the form of rent-free housing and goods produced and consumed on the farm; or that non-money incomes are also received by some nonfarm residents which often take the form of the use of business transportation and facilities, full or partial payments by business for retirement programs, medical and educational expenses, etc. [U.S. Bureau of the Census 1976.]

Many economists have questioned the conceptual suitability of such figures. Taussig (1973), for instance, cites nine reasons why the standard annual money-income statistics published in the United States fail to provide an adequate measure of economic well-being; he computes alternative measures based on these adjustments. The factors considered are:

1. The census money-income measure excludes nonmonetary income receipts.
2. These figures are reported on a before-tax rather than an after-tax basis.
3. No account is taken of price differences in various cities or regions of the country.
4. Income is reported for family units defined by the census, generally with no allowance made for variations in family size or composition.
5. The figures contain no information on the distribution of net worth.
6. Data are presented for a single year; a longer time horizon might distinguish permanent from transitory components.
7. No account is taken of differences in leisure.
8. These income figures exclude capital gains, benefits from government services, and other supplements to one's income and consumption.
9. The figures are reported for the census-defined family unit rather than for a "pooling consumer unit."

In studies of LDCs, researchers have wrestled with these and other issues in seeking to arrive at a "correct" distribution of income for a less developed country. The most eminent researcher in this area is Kuznets (1963, 1976); see also the work of Bronfenbrenner (1971, pp. 31–38) and Szal (1975).

From these and other writings emerge three points of consensus:

1. When appropriately defined, measured, and adjusted, income is an analytically valuable guide to economic status.
2. The family is a more appropriate recipient than the individual.
3. A number of adjustments to annual (or monthly) cash income are in order.

Of course, statistics on income (whether national, sectoral, or individual) are often seriously inaccurate. A particularly negative view is expressed by Averch, Denton, and Koehler (1970) with respect to income data in the Philippines. A less pessimistic assessment is presented by Altimir (1975) for Latin American income data, although he does point to tendencies for income reported in censuses and surveys to understate national income by 10-20 percent or more. These and other reviews of data reliability should serve as a warning to those who unquestioningly accept the authority of respected scholars and who uncritically utilize data compilations.

The usual types of figures on incomes, although less than ideal in many respects, may serve as a useful guide to changes in the economic position of the poor. The remainder of this chapter suggests ways to take income-distribution considerations into account, within the limits of existing data.

Alternative Approaches to the Study of the Size Distribution of Income

Income distribution is not the same thing as income equality or inequality. "By *personal distribution* we mean division of income (or wealth) by size, or more precisely, by size brackets of the income or wealth of economic units" (Bronfenbrenner 1971, p. 27; emphasis in the original). Bronfenbrenner carefully distinguishes between the personal distribution of income and statistics such as the coefficient of variation that *"measure* the degree of *inequality* of a personal income distribution" (p. 43; emphasis added).

The distinction between income distribution and income equality (or inequality) is an important one. Contrast the way we usually think about income distribution with the way we are accustomed to think about the distribution of other economic or social data, such as the distribution of education.

When we consider education, our concern is with how many people have attained how high a level. If a larger fraction of a population achieves literacy, for example, we are inclined to regard that country's education system as having done "better." In making such a judgment, we usually do not think to ask whether more people have also completed university; nor do we compute a statistical measure of inequality of educational attainments, such as the variance or a Gini coefficient. Rather, our strategy is to pinpoint a target group whose upgrading we care most about and then to measure the rate of absolute improvement within that target group.

In studies of income distribution, the approach is ordinarily quite different. Most studies ask: "Did income distribution worsen?" Typically, that question is answered by examining either (1) how the income shares of particular deciles (or other groupings) changed; (2) how the Lorenz curve shifted; or (3) whether measures such as Gini coefficients, variance of incomes or their logarithms, and so on, exhibit greater or lesser inequality. All these are relative-inequality measures. In effect, then, by beginning with relative-inequality measures rather than with absolute levels, the approach to studies of the distribution of income reverses the approach to studies of the distribution of other economic and social goods.

Relative Inequality Approach

Most studies of income distribution in LDCs measure *relative* income inequality, conveniently illustrated by a Lorenz curve in Figure 22.1. The Lorenz curve depicts the income share of any cumulative percentage of the population, ordered from lowest income to highest. All relative-inequality measures in current use are based on the Lorenz curve. The Gini coefficient, being most directly related, is the ratio of the area between the Lorenz curve and the 45 ° line (area A in Figure 22.1) to

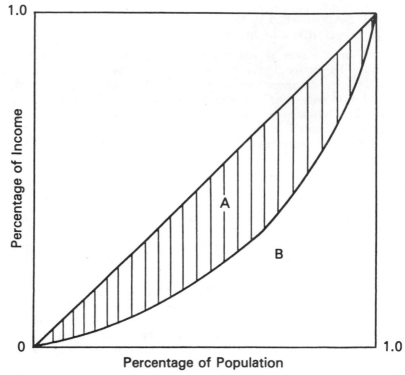

Figure 22.1 Lorenz diagram.

the total area (A + B). The Gini coefficient varies between zero and one. The higher the coefficient, the greater the degrees of relative inequality. The fractile measures in common use, such as the income share of the poorest 40 percent or the richest 10 percent, can be read directly from the Lorenz curve. A class of relative-inequality measures may be calculated from the data contained in Lorenz curves. These include many familiar indexes such as the variance (or standard deviation) of income or its logarithm, the coefficient of variation, the Kuznets ratio, the Atkinson index, the Theil index, and many others (Sen 1973).

In using one or more of these inequality measures, the judgment is typically made that *social welfare (W)* depends positively on the *level* of national income (Y) and negatively on the *inequality* in the distribution of that income (I). For example, taking the share of income of the poorest 40 percent of the population (S) as an index of equality and the Gini coefficient (G) as an index of inequality, these studies would hold that W is positively related to Y and S and negatively related to G. The terminology of these studies is indicative—falling S or rising G are given the nonneutral term "worsening of the income distribution," and rising levels of measured inequality are generally considered a bad thing.

A numerical example shows how these judgments are brought to bear in practice.

Example 1

Country	Rate of Growth (%)	Share of Lowest 40 Percent:		Gini Coefficient:	
		Level	Percentage Change	Level	Percentage Change
Both countries initially		0.363		0.082	
Country A later	9	0.333	− 8	0.133	+62
Country B later	18	0.307	−15	0.162	+97

Country B grew twice as fast as country A. However, its income distribution, as measured by the Gini coefficient and income share of the lowest 40 percent, seems to be "worse" than that found in country A; that is, it would appear that the rich benefited at the expense of the poor, whose relative income share deteriorated. A development economist might question whether the higher rate of growth in country B was "worth it" in terms of income distribution, and a well-meaning development planner seeking to give very high weight to alleviation of inequality might go so far as to choose country A's policies over those of country B.

Absolute-Poverty Approach

An alternative approach directly examines a country's progress in alleviating poverty among the very poorest. Absolute-income studies of LDCs are the exception rather than the rule. Economists at the Institute of Development Studies, University of Sussex, have been taking an absolute-income approach for some time (International Labour Office 1970). More recently, the World Bank has begun to shift its focus as well (Ahluwalia 1974). These studies are noteworthy precisely because they do differ from the usual approach.

We must first define poverty: an individual is poor if his or her income falls below a specified dollar amount, with analogous figures for families of different sizes. The U.S. Agency for International Development (AID), for example, uses the figure U.S. $150 per capita (1969 dollars) in LDCs; in the United States, the official poverty line in 1976 was $5,500 for a nonfarm family of four. The poverty lines used in different countries and the ways they are determined are discussed in subsequent sections. Let us denote this poverty line, which we will hold constant in real terms, by P^*. "The poor" are those whose incomes are less than P^*.

Most observers would share the following judgments about the extent of poverty (P):

1. P is positively related to the number of income recipients with incomes below the poverty line P*.
2. The larger the average income of those below the poverty line, the lower is P.
3. If other things are unchanged, the more unequal the distribution of income among the poor, the more severe is P.

In most studies, measures entering into these three judgments are computed separately. However, Sen (1976) combines these measures and argues elegantly for the use of a composite index.

Absolute-poverty measures like those just presented have been used in research in the United States for many years; see, for example, Bowman (1973) or Perlman (1976). The main advantage of absolute-poverty indexes is that they provide *direct* measures of changes in the numbers of the poor and the extent of poverty among them. Note, in contrast, that although poverty indicators can be computed from Lorenz curves or Lorenz-curve-based inequality measures, this information is obtained only indirectly and often with considerable computational difficulty.

To see how the absolute-poverty approach is applied, let us consider now another numerical example for two countries in an early and a later stage of their economic development. Assume the following hypothetical figures, where the poverty line is somewhere between $1 and $2:

Example 2

Country	Percentage of Labor Force in:		Rate of Growth of Modern Sector ("Modern Sector Labor Absorption Rate") (%)
	High Wage Jobs (Real Wage = 2) (%)	Low Wage Jobs (Real Wage = 1) (%)	
Both countries initially	10	90	
Country C later	20	80	100
Country D later	30	70	200

The poor in both countries received the benefits of growth, but in country D twice as many of the poor benefited. Other things being equal, development economists would almost certainly rate country D as superior, and development planners would seek to find out what had brought about that country's favorable experience and to adopt those policies in their own countries. In this second example the preference is clear-cut, while in the previous example the issue was open to doubt.

Relative-Poverty Approach

The relative-inequality and absolute-poverty approaches are the two main ways in which distributional aspects of economic development have been considered. In addition, there is now a newer approach being promulgated by researchers at the World Bank and elsewhere, known as the relative-poverty measure (Chiswick 1976). This figure is the absolute income (in constant dollars) received by the poorest 40 percent of the population. The choice of poorest 40 percent is purely arbitrary. What matters in this approach is the constancy of population share along with income variability among members of that group.

Consider now a third example:

Example 3

Country	Absolute Income of Poorest 40 Percent of Population
Both countries initially	$40
Country E later	40
Country F later	40

Using the relative-poverty measure, it appears that there was *no* improvement in absolute income of the poorest 40 percent in either case. One might ask: Why grow if the poor do not share in the benefits of growth? In this third example, E and F both seem to have failed to alleviate poverty.

Comparison of the Three Approaches

In point of fact, countries A, C, and E are the same country, as are countries B, D and F! Real-world economic-development histories and policy projections are often presented in these different ways. Yet, as these examples make clear, how income distribution is studied—whether in terms of relative income inequality (as in example 1), absolute incomes and poverty (example 2), or relative poverty (example 3)—may dramatically influence our perceptions of the outcome.

Specifically, we have encountered the following differences in our examples. According to the absolute-poverty criterion, B-D-F clearly dominates A-C-E on both growth and distribution grounds. Using the relative-inequality criterion, it is difficult to judge; although B-D-F grew faster than A-C-E, its income distribution seems to have worsened. Finally, by the relative-poverty criterion both appear unsatisfactory; neither country seems to have made progress in alleviating poverty, although in fact poverty was being alleviated in both, at different rates.

The relative-poverty measure fails to record an income-distribution change. These countries were alleviating poverty, yet the relative-poverty measure is totally insensitive to the change. Relative-poverty measures are unsuited for gauging the distributional consequences of the growth illustrated in this two-country comparison. Difficulties with the relative-poverty measure arise in cross-sectional data, where we look at those who are the poorest 40 percent ex post at different times, disregarding the movement of specific individuals into and out of the poorest 40 percent. Longitudinal data would permit tracing the progress of individuals who rose out of the poorest 40 percent. Unfortunately in the real world, we do not have longitudinal data for LDCs.

The relative-inequality and absolute-poverty approaches yield somewhat different answers as to whether a pattern of growth is desirable. Whether poverty is relative or absolute is a value judgment. Statistical patterns that in some respects are artifacts also affect comparison of these approaches.

- What is it about the process of economic development that produces a discrepancy between the different approaches?
- Do we give greater weight to the alleviation of absolute poverty or to the narrowing of relative income inequality?

The answer to the first question is that the discrepancy is produced by the unevenness of economic development itself. An economy grows by enlarging the size of its modern sector. Incomes and wages within the modern and traditional sectors remain far apart, and neither rises. This type of growth affects only some of the poor—those who shift from the traditional to the modern sector. Those whose situations are not improved by this type of growth remain as poor as before, receiving the same income, which is now, however, a smaller part of a larger whole. The absolute incomes of the poorest 40 percent may be unchanged. The Lorenz curve shifts downward at its lower end. Lorenz-curve-based measures of relative income inequality that are sensitive to the lower end of the income distribution register a "worsening" of the income distribution.

The pattern of growth illustrated is widely regarded as an essential ingredient of development. In their famous *Development of the Labor Surplus Economy* (1964), Fei and Ranis wrote: "The heart of the development problem may be said to lie in the gradual shifting of the center of gravity of the economy from the agricultural to the industrial sector . . . gauged in terms of the reallocation of the population between the two sectors in order to promote a gradual expansion of industrial employment and output" (1964, p. 7). This characterization is echoed by Kuznets (1966). Empirical studies, such as that of Turnham (1971), document the absorption of an increasing share of the population into the modern sector as growth continues. In a case study of Indian economic development in the 1950s, Swamy (1967) found that 85 percent of the change in the size distribution of income was due to intersectoral shifts (namely, growth in importance of the urban sector and growing per-capita-income differential between the urban and rural sectors) and only 15 percent to changing inequality within the two sectors. Modern-sector enlargement comprises a large and perhaps predominant component of the growth of currently developing countries.

The choice between absolute- and relative-income measures depends on basic ethical considerations. The plight of the poor in LDCs is objective; they do not command sufficient resources to feed and clothe themselves and avoid disease. Poverty is an absolute condition, requiring analysis in absolute terms. The predominant emphasis must be given to data on changes in the number of poor people, the average extent of their poverty, and the degree of inequality among them.

Others have different concerns and make different judgments, giving great weight to the subjective feelings of the poor, who may feel relatively worse off if the economic positions of others are improving while theirs are not. Observers who feel strongly about such relative-income considerations are justified in using relative-inequality measures.

What may not be justified—and there are many examples of this in the development literature—is the coupling of a concern about the absolute economic misery of the poor with a reliance on calculations of changes in relative inequality over time. This approach may be mistaken, misleading, and logically inconsistent. For just as in the numerical example above, the assignment of heavy weight to changes in the usual indexes of relative income inequality and the interpretation of these increases as offsetting the economic well-being brought about by growth, may lead to the overlooking of important tendencies toward the alleviation of absolute poverty.

Many observers would contend that the goal of economic development is to alleviate absolute poverty. If that is the goal, it seems logical to measure progress toward that goal directly, using absolute-poverty criteria, rather than indirectly, with relative-inequality or relative-poverty indexes. The numerical example in this section showed how differences among the various approaches may arise. If students of economic development or policy makers use relative-inequality measures when they really care about absolute poverty, they may be misled.

Income Inequality and Level of Development

The initial work on size distribution of income across countries is that of Nobel Prize-winning economist Simon Kuznets (1955). Comparing India, Ceylon, Puerto Rico, the United Kingdom, and the United States, he observed greater inequality in the developing countries. The pattern of greater relative income inequality in the LDCs than in the developed countries was confirmed in a subsequent paper by Kuznets (1963) for eighteen countries.

Based on that evidence, Kuznets formulated the "inverted-U hypothesis," which states that relative income inequality rises during the early stages of development, reaches a peak, and then declines in the later stages. Kuznets assumed that LDCs had greater equality in their earliest stages of development, because all were equally poor. No data were available to test this speculation. Even today, suitable data do not exist; see Kravis et al. (1973, p. 71).

In the late 1960s and early 1970s, Adelman and Morris gathered new data for forty-three developing countries. In their 1973 book, they presented considerable evidence on the correlates of relative income inequality. By means of analysis of variance, they found six factors to be important in explaining variations in relative income inequality. Included among these was the level of economic development.

A short while later, Paukert (1973) tried to refine the Adelman and Morris estimates. He discarded information that he considered particularly unreliable, added some new countries for which good data had recently become available, and presented summary information on the size distribution of income in fifty-six countries. For each of several alternative relative-inequality measures, Paukert found that inequality begins at a comparatively low level, reaches a peak in the $301–500 per-capita-income countries, and then diminishes at higher incomes. Thus, the inverted-U pattern is reconfirmed.

From this evidence, many development economists arrived at the view that "income distribution must get worse before it gets better." There was considerable pessimism over the supposed trade-off between growth and income equality. This interference is based on cross-section data, not on historical trends. In their introduction, Adelman and Morris used such words as "preliminary," "exploratory," and "tentative" to describe their caution in interpreting results. Few countries offer direct evidence on income-distribution change over time.

A second problem with the inverted U is that we are dealing with averages among *groups* of countries and not, for the most part, with the information on individual countries themselves. Figure 22.2 presents Paukert's data in graphic form (Paukert 1973, table 6). Individual data are indicated by asterisks, and averages for each income class of countries by heavy circles. There appears to be much more variation in relative inequality *within* country groups than *between* them. Before regarding the inverted-U pattern as inevitable, therefore, even in the cross section, we need to know how well the inverted U fits the data.

By means of multiple-regression analysis on individual-country data, we may determine (1) whether an inverted U is the appropriate characterization of the inequality-income relationship, and (2) whether any particular pattern of inequality change over time is inevitable. On both accounts, the evidence suggests that income distribution need *not* get worse before it gets better.

In the individual-country data collected by Paukert, we can define six dummy variables denoting income class, the first for gross domestic product (GDP) per capita between $101 and $200, the second between

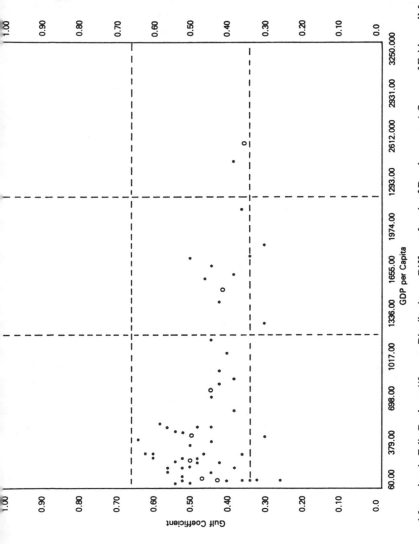

Figure 22.2 Gini coefficient and gross domestic product per capita, 56 countries.

Source: Computed from data in Felix Paukert, "Income Distribution at Different Levels of Development: A Survey of Evidence," *International Labor Review*, August-September 1973.

$210 and $300, and so on. (The reason for defining only six dummy variables when there are seven categories is to avoid perfect multicollinearity in the regression equation reported below.) For each, we assign the value 1 if the country's GDP places it in that category, 0 otherwise. If we then run a multiple regression with the Gini coefficient of inequality as the dependent variable and these six dummies as independent variables, the coefficients on the dummy variables may be interpreted as the effect on the Gini coefficient of being in that income group rather than in the $0-100 per-capita-income group. If the inverted-U hypothesis is correct, these coefficients will be positive and increasing up to some point, declining thereafter.

The results of the regression based on the figures for fifty-six countries were:

$$GINI = 0.418 + \underset{(0.042)}{0.50Y_{\$101-200}} + \underset{(0.039)}{0.080Y_{\$201-300}}$$

$$+ \underset{(0.040)}{0.076Y_{\$301-500}} + \underset{(0.045)}{0.019Y_{\$501-1,000}} - \underset{(0.039)}{0.019Y_{\$1,000-2,000}}$$

$$- \underset{(0.057)}{0.052Y_{\$2,001}}$$

$$R^2 = 0.22$$

where Y denotes GDP per capita (standard errors in parentheses). The pattern of regression coefficients is consistent with the pattern predicted by the inverted-U hypothesis, that is, rising at first and then falling. However, the initial stage of rising inequality is not statistically significant at any of the conventional levels. (Compare, say, the first three regression coefficients with their standard errors.)

Worse still for Kuznets, Paukert, and other adherents of the inverted-U hypothesis are the results of a simple parabolic regression. The inverted-U hypothesis may be tested by regressing the Gini coefficient on GDP per capita and GDP per capita squared. If the relationship is in fact of the inverted-U form, GDP per capita would have a positive coefficient, and GDP per capita squared a negative coefficient. The regression results were:

$$GINI = 0.473 - \underset{(0.56)}{0.00003GDP} - \underset{(0.34)}{0.00000GDP^2} \quad R^2 = 0.11$$

(t statistics in parentheses).

The negative coefficient on GDP in Paukert's data is contrary to the initial-worsening hypothesis.

This result is not suited to the choice of inequality measure or data set. Cline (1975) reports the results of a similar regression using Adelman and Morris's data rather than Paukert's, and using as the measure of inequality (I) the ratio of the income share of the top quintile to the share of the bottom quintile. His results, with t statistics reported in parentheses, were:

$$I = 7.23 + 0.0258\text{GNP} - 0.000014\text{GNP}^2 \quad R^2 = 0.12$$
$$(0.7) \quad (2.8)$$

In any case, the initial-worsening hypothesis receives at best only limited support in the data.

Concerning the inevitability issue (the view that "income distribution must get worse before it gets better"), we should note how little of the variance in relative inequality is explained by income level. In the dummy-variable regression, income level can explain only 22 percent of the intercountry variation in inequality as measured by the Gini coefficient, and in the parabolic regression, only 11 percent. The inverted U is avoidable. Income distribution may be determined as much by development style and public policies as by the level of development. Appropriate public policy can be designed to avoid a deterioration in the relative distribution of income and to effect an improvement in the economic status of the poor.

Causes of Relative Inequality

How do a country's economic characteristics determine its income distribution? Three particularly noteworthy studies address this question.

Adelman and Morris (1973) base their investigation on cross-sectional observations for forty-three LDCs. To measure income inequality, they used three alternative indicators: the income share of the lowest 60 percent, the income share of the middle quintile, and the income share of the richest 5 percent. They report six variables as important in determining the distribution of income in a country:

1. rate of improvement in human resources;
2. direct government economic activity;
3. socioeconomic dualism;
4. potential for economic development;
5. per-capita GNP;
6. strength of labor movement.

Interestingly, no significant relationship is found between relative income inequality and short-term economic-growth rates, short-term improvements in tax and financial institutions, or short-term increases in agricultural or industrial productivity. The interested reader is referred to their book for the proxy variables used and their specific definitions.

The Adelman-Morris exercise has been subjected to a great deal of criticism, including doubts about the quality of the underlying data, discomfort over the lack of a well-defined theoretical framework, and skepticism about the appropriateness of the statistical methods employed. These criticisms encourage hesitancy in accepting Adelman and Morris's conclusions on the importance of the six factors listed above and the unimportance of others not in that list.

A second study of causes of relative inequality, somewhat earlier but less well-known than that of Adelman and Morris, is that of Chiswick (1971). Using an elementary human-capital model, Chiswick deduced that variability in earned income should be functionally related (positively) to four factors:

1. the inequality of investment in human capital;
2. the average level of investment in human capital;
3. the average level of the rate of return to human-capital investment;
4. the inequality in the rate of return to human-capital investment.

He then subjected these hypotheses to empirical testing in a cross section of nine countries, four of which are LDCs.

Unfortunately, there are two problems: (1) there is a scarcity of data to test the model, and (2) what data there are (from Lydall 1968) prove inconclusive. In Chiswick's regressions, the variable measuring inequality of educational attainments is statistically significantly related (with the correct sign) to earnings inequality in two out of three cases. The variables for average per-capita GNP and rate of growth of GNP prove, with one exception, to be insignificant. Thus, the hypotheses derived from the human-capital model of earnings inequality receive only limited empirical support. Whether this weakness is due to limitations of the data or of Chiswick's specific formulation is an open question awaiting additional examination.

Finally, recent work at the World Bank by Ahluwalia (1976) draws on data from sixty-two countries. For alternative indicators of relative income inequality, he used the income shares of the top 20 percent, middle 40 percent, lowest 40 percent, and lowest 60 percent. He found a statistically significant relationship between income shares and per-capita GNP consistent with the inverted-U pattern. However, there does not appear to be an independent short-term relationship between the level of inequality and the rate of growth of GNP.

The explanatory variables associated with income inequality are: (1) the rate of expansion of education, (2) the rate of decline of demographic pressures, and (3) changes in the structure of production in favor of the modern sector. More specifically, improvement in literacy, reduced rate of growth of population, reduced share of agriculture in national product, and shifting of population to the urban sector are found to reduce relative income inequality.

The Ahluwalia study is carefully done and offers a reasonable set of stylized facts about the patterns of relative income inequality and their correlates.

The usual concomitants of economic development (particularly improved education, reduction in the importance of agriculture, and growth of the urban sector) significantly lower relative income inequality. The evidence is mixed on the level of economic development: Both Ahluwalia and Adelman and Morris find a significant relationship between relative inequality and per-capita GNP, while Chiswick finds these effects insignificant. None of these studies finds a statistically significant relationship between the level of inequality and the rate of economic growth. They also fail to establish the importance of tax systems and agricultural-productivity improvements.

These cross-section analyses follow a long tradition, pioneered at Harvard University in the last decade, of deriving conclusions about the process of economic development by looking at countries at different stages of development (Chenery 1960; Chenery and Taylor 1968; Chenery and Syrquin 1975). Such analyses are based on the assumption that currently developing countries will follow much the same pattern in their development experiences as is found in the cross-section. Many, myself included, reject this assumption. It would be better to investigate the direct evidence on changes in income distribution within a given country at two or more points in time in that country's development history.

Evidence on Historical Trends
Within a Country Over Time

The evidence on historical trends in income distribution within a country over time is scattered and has not yet been synthesized in a multicountry study. Much of the research is as yet unpublished, and many more studies are now in progress. In this section we will survey the major multicountry studies on this question.

The pathbreaking contribution in the field is that of Kuznets, who in his 1963 paper reviewed the available evidence for a number of now-developed countries. For two countries (Prussia and Saxony in the late 1800s), the income share of those at the top of the income distribution rose or remained the same. In the United Kingdom, Germany, the Netherlands, Denmark, Norway, Sweden, and the United States, the data show a steady decline in relative inequality, as measured by the income shares of the top 5 percent and the lowest 60 percent.

Interestingly, this is not the usual lesson drawn from Kuznets's research. He wrote, "It seems plausible to *assume* that in the process of growth, the earlier periods are characterized by a balance of counteracting forces that may have widened the inequality in the size distribution of income for a while" (1963, p. 67; emphasis added). One looks in vain for statistical evidence documenting the plausible assumption in the actual historical experiences of any of the nine countries named above. Nevertheless, these two papers are among the best known and most widely cited as supporting the inverted-U hypothesis.

Kuznets's writing stimulated development economists to study the facts in countries that were still less developed. The first multicountry historical study of the patterns of income-distribution change in LDCs was the paper by Weisskoff (1970) for Puerto Rico, Argentina, and Mexico. Weisskoff's paper includes a brief discussion of the traditional measures of relative income inequality, including the Gini coefficient, the Kuznets ratio, the coefficient of variation, variance of the logarithms of income, and standard ordinal shares. "In each of the three developing countries," he writes, "we noted that equality of income declined as the level of income rose over time" (1970, p. 317).

In contrast to Weisskoff's interpretation of his own numbers, the numerical results are in fact quite mixed. In each country at least one of the relative-inequality measures shows an increase and at least one other measure shows a decline. Thus, the effects of economic growth on relative income inequality were ambiguous in these three cases.

The reported findings of Kuznets and Weisskoff as well as growing bodies of evidence from cross-sectional studies led many observers in the early 1970s to the view that there may be a conflict between the rate of growth of income and equality in the distribution of that income. If so, this would be a harsh dilemma. Further investigation was in order, and it was soon forthcoming.

In an influential paper in an equally influential volume, Ahluwalia (1974) presented evidence relating the growth of income shares of the lower 40 percent to the overall rate of growth of the economies of eighteen countries, all but a few of which are LDCs (see Figure 22.3).

> The scatter suggests considerable diversity of country experience in terms of changes in relative equality. Several countries show a deterioration in relative equality but there are others showing improvement. . . . *There is no strong pattern relating changes in the distribution of income to the rate of growth of GNP.* In both high-growth and low-growth countries there are some which have experienced improvements and others that have experienced deteriorations in relative equality. (Emphasis added.)[1]

In his work, Ahluwalia did not attempt to relate the observed changes to countries' economic-development strategies, such as import substitution or export promotion. Evidence on this question would be welcome.

The data presented by Kuznets, Weisskoff, and Ahluwalia shows that the supposed "harsh dilemma" of growth versus equality might be avoidable.

Relative-inequality studies suggest the following stylized facts:

- In a cross section of countries, the bulk of the evidence indicates an inverted-U pattern in the relationship of relative income inequality with the level of economic development.
- However, countries' income levels explain only a small part of variability in measured inequality. Other characteristics of the economy also play a role.

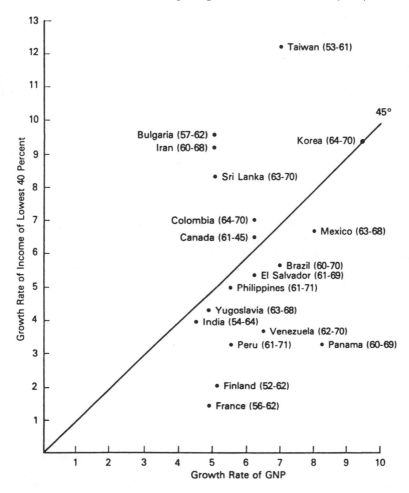

Source: M.S. Ahluwalia, "Income Inequality: Some Dimensions of the Problem," *Redistribution with Growth*, ed. Hollis Chenery et al. (London: Oxford University Press, 1974), p. 14.

Figure 22.3 Growth and the lowest 40 percent.

- Among the variables associated with cross-sectional patterns of relative inequality are improved education, growth of the urban sector, and the decline of agriculture. The evidence on the level of national income is mixed. Tax systems and agricultural productivity have not been shown to be important determinants of the cross-sectional pattern.
- In the cross section, no systematic relationship is found between the rate of growth of the economy and relative inequality.

- Similarly, changes in the relative income share of the poorest 40 percent of the population in the historical experience of a given country exhibit no marked association with the economy's growth rate.
- It may be that certain economic-development strategies, such as export promotion versus import substitution, tend to be related to
  changes in the relative income distribution; however, no systematic evidence has been gathered on this point.

Absolute Poverty versus Relative Inequality: Two Case Studies

Do figures on relative income inequality provide suitable poverty indicators? May we instead approach the question of changing income distribution from an absolute-poverty perspective? The relevant questions must address the determinants of incomes and of poverty and how these determinants have changed over time.

The relative-inequality and absolute-poverty approaches may differ in assessing the distributional consequences of growth; whether or not they do is an empirical question. The available data permit intensive examination of two countries, Brazil and India.

Brazil

One of the most interesting and controversial cases of economic development is that of Brazil. Over the decade of the 1960s, the real rate of economic growth was 79 percent. After allowing for a high population-growth rate, real income per capita grew 32 percent over the decade, a substantial achievement by LDC standards. In the late 1960s and early 1970s, Brazil experienced rates of growth approaching 10 percent per year. On this basis, the Brazilian case was widely heralded as an "economic miracle."

Then a cloud appeared on the horizon. In an exceptionally influential paper, Fishlow (1972) examined the distributional question of who received the benefits of this growth. Using the Gini coefficient of inequality and the income share received by the richest 3 percent of the population, Fishlow observed a worsening of the relative income distribution during the 1960s, despite the rapid economic growth of the latter years. A similar qualitative conclusion was reached subsequently by Adelman and Morris (1973, p. 1) based on the income share of the poorest 40 percent. Some of the data underlying these conclusions are presented in Table 22.1.

The finding that income inequality in Brazil had increased gave pause to many. As a result, there is now widespread disagreement about the desirability of taking Brazilian economic and social policies as a model for other developing countries to follow. It is probably fair to say that, because of Fishlow's paper, most observers no longer regard the Brazilian experience as "miraculous."

Table 22.1
Data on Income Distribution in Brazil

	1960	1970
Gini coefficient of inequality, total economically active population[a]	0.59	0.63
Income share of richest 3.2 percent[a]	27%	33%
Income share of poorest 40 percent[b]	10%	8%

a. Source: Albert Fishlow, "Brazilian Size Distribution of Income," American Economic Review 62(1972): 391–402.
b. Source: I. Adelman and C. T. Morris, Economic Growth and Social Equity in Developing Countries (Stanford, Calif.: Stanford University Press, 1973).

Some economists, although not Fishlow himself, inferred from this evidence that the growth that had taken place had been at the expense of the poor (Foxley 1975). A softer inference is that the poor did not share in the benefits of Brazilian growth. Both inferences are incorrect. They arise from the use of relative-inequality rather than absolute-poverty measures (Fields 1977).

Absolute-poverty comparisons require data on changes in the number of persons with incomes below a constant real-poverty line, in this case the minimum wage in the poorest region of the country, the northeast. The cumulative percentage of population was lower in 1970 than in 1960 for every income bracket. The economic growth that took place in Brazil over the decades of the 1960s reached persons at all income levels, not just those at the top.

The percentage of the economically active population with incomes below the Brazilian poverty level declined during the decade; those who remained poor were not as poor as before; and the rate of growth of income among the poor was at least as great as the rate of growth among the nonpoor.

The entire income distribution shifted in real terms, benefiting every income class. There was a small decline, from 37 to 35.5 percent, in the fraction of the economically active population below the poverty line. Those who remained "poor" experienced a marked percentage increase in real income (from one-third to as much as two-thirds higher).

The percentage increase in income for those below the poverty line was greater than the increase for those not in poverty, and may well have been twice as high or more.

The income gap between poor and nonpoor persons narrowed in terms of ratios, although the absolute gap widened. The bulk of the income growth over the decade accrued to persons above the poverty line. A similar pattern is observed for the United States, an allegedly more egalitarian society. The poverty gap in Brazil, the sum of the differences between each poor person's income and the poverty line, was reduced by 41 percent between 1960 and 1970. The United States reduced its poverty gap by exactly the same percentage over the same decade.

The poor in Brazil *did* benefit from the economic growth that took place during the 1960s. This conclusion can be stated with no intention of condoning the persistence of the severe poverty that remains, the apparent lack of a strong commitment by the Brazilian authorities to alleviate the current plight of the poor in this generation, or some of the more authoritarian measures reputed to have been used to ensure social stability. Rising Gini coefficients and income shares of the very rich are consistent with nontrivial improvements in the economic position of the poor. Relative-inequality comparisons led many to overlook important tendencies toward the alleviation of absolute poverty.

India

In India, on the other hand, the situation is very different. India is poor and growing slowly, with per-capita income under U.S. $100. During the 1960s, per-capita private-consumer expenditure grew by less than 0.5 percent per annum (Dandekar and Rath 1971, p. 40). India offers abundant data on the distribution of income and consumption dating back to the 1950s. Given the richness of the data in so poor a country with so large a research establishment, it is not surprising that we find a multitude of income-distribution studies. The remarkable feature about the relative-inequality data is that no clear pattern of change emerges.

Overall, as measured by the Gini coefficient, relative income inequality shows no particular trend. The Gini coefficient within the urban sector may have risen somewhat, suggesting greater inequality, but the evidence is mixed. The Gini coefficient within the rural sector seems to have declined, suggesting lesser inequality; but as with the urban Gini coefficient, no strong tendency is found. Possibly the income share of the bottom 20 percent rose while the share of the top 20 percent fell nationwide, together suggesting diminished inequality; but both changes are small.

Given the inconclusiveness of the individual findings, the contradictory indications as to whether inequality increased or decreased, and the small magnitudes of the changes as compared with probable errors in sampling and measurement, the conclusion seems warranted that the pattern of relative inequality in India remained essentially unchanged.

A leading Indian economist, P. K. Bardhan, takes issue with relative-inequality measurements of income distribution. "For a desperately poor country like India," he writes, "there are many who believe that no measure of inequality which is in terms of relative distribution and is independent of some absolute poverty standard can be entirely satisfactory" (1974, p. 119). Accordingly, he calculated estimates of the percentage of the population below a constant absolute-poverty line:

Year	Rural	Urban
1960–1961	38	32
1964–1965	45	37
1968–1969	54	41

Absolute poverty worsened greatly in India between 1960–1961 and 1968–1969, even though relative inequality did not.

As in the case of Brazil, relative-inequality measures suggest one set of conclusions with respect to changing income distribution while absolute-poverty comparisons suggest another. The discrepancy is exactly reversed: more absolute poverty despite apparently constant relative inequality in India, alleviation of absolute poverty despite rising relative inequality in Brazil.

The choice of a relative or absolute approach does make an important qualitative difference. Data from Brazil suggest a worsening of the income distribution: The Gini coefficient was noticeably higher in 1970 than in 1960, the share of income received by the very richest rose, and the share received by the very poorest fell. Focusing on absolute rather than relative incomes, we find that the poor in Brazil shared in economic development, albeit to a limited extent. Incomes of those below the Brazilian poverty line increased by possibly double the percentage of those above the line.

In India, relative income inequality did not change noticeably. Some inferred that India had at least held the line on income distribution. From an absolute-poverty perspective, however, India did not hold the line at all: Absolute-poverty increased considerably.

Relative-income measures disguise changes in absolute poverty among the poor in developing countries. They may lead to inaccurate assessments of commitment and progress in reducing poverty. To measure alleviation of absolute poverty, it is more appropriate to use absolute-poverty measures: the number of individuals or families with incomes below a constant real-poverty line, or the average gap between the incomes of the poor and the poverty line.

Implementing the Absolute-Poverty Approach

A country's progress in alleviating poverty is best gauged by a measure designed especially for that purpose. In this section we describe what is needed; demonstrate how the approach has been applied in

Brazil; outline the present availability of data in LDCs; and, finally, explore ways to close the gap between data needs and data availability.

The absolute-poverty approach requires definition of a time-invariant real-income figure called the poverty line. Next comes information on the number of persons (or families) with incomes below that line and the average income among them. It may also be useful to know the degree of income inequality among the poor. To measure poverty alleviation in a particular country's economic development requires comparable and detailed figures on the size distribution of income for at least two time periods, and preferably more.

Conceptually, the absolute-poverty line should be defined in such a way that we would not hesitate to regard an individual or family with income below that figure as poor (Webb 1976). A straightforward way of doing this is to establish a dollar-income figure, chosen as scientifically as possible. In the United States, for example, the poverty line was derived by ascertaining the amount of money needed to purchase a nutritionally adequate diet consistent with the food preferences of the poorest groups in the population, and then multiplying this figure by a factor of three, since the poor spend about one-third of their incomes on food (Orshansky 1965). As one LDC example, in Brazil the poverty line is taken as the minimum wage in the northeast (Brazil's poorest region), adjusted in other parts of the country for cost-of-living differences (Fishlow 1972). Another LDC example, based on consumption rather than income, is found in Ferber and Musgrove (1976). In both cases, the specific income figure depends on family size.

In India, the Planning Commission used a figure of 20 rupees (Rs.20) per month (in 1960–1961 prices) per capita as the nutritionally minimal standard. This figure was modified by other researchers: Dandekar and Rath (1971) took Rs.15 per capita per month for rural poverty and Rs.22.5 for urban, while Bardhan (1970, 1974) used Rs.15 and Rs.18, respectively (1974, pp. 119–123). The World Bank has estimated the population below U.S. $50 per capita, and AID has suggested an international per-capita figure of $150 per capita.

Provided that the poverty line chosen bears a reasonable relationship to living standards in the country in question, there is little advantage in worrying about what the exact dollar figure should be. Absolute-income standards such as $150 per capita or the minimum wage in the country are reasonable benchmarks.

What is important, indeed crucial, about the absolute-poverty line in a dynamic-development context is that it be held constant in real terms, that is, after adjusting for inflation. No other adjustment (for example, an adjustment for productivity growth) is appropriate (Bacha 1976).

In empirical research, as a check on the arbitrariness of any given poverty line, one might experiment with simple multiples of that line, as Bardhan did in India, to test whether similar changes in the incidence and severity of poverty are found. In this way, disputes over the correctness of any specific poverty-line definition are minimized; and attention is directed where it should be, namely, at the constancy of the line itself and the distribution of the population around it.

Application of the Absolute-Poverty Approach to Brazil

For Brazil, figures on the size distribution of income are available for 1960 and 1970 from a variety of sources. The published figures need to be adjusted for inflation. Taking the poverty line as new Cruzeiros (NCr.) 2,100 in 1960 units, and allowing for an overall inflation factor of 3.53, we need data on the percentage of population below NCr. 7,413 ($2,100 x 3.53) in 1970 and on the incomes of those persons.

Approximating income distributions is a tricky business when data are missing. A simple linear-interpolation procedure or a log-linear or some other approximation shows that the qualitative conclusions about changes in absolute poverty are robust to *any* assumption that one might make that is consistent with the data (Fields 1976).

These problems could easily be resolved by recourse to the underlying microeconomic data. All that would be required would be to tabulate the population into income groups after first adjusting for an inflation factor; for example, in the case of Brazil, by dividing all 1970 incomes by 3.53 so as to make them comparable with 1960 incomes, or equivalently, by multiplying all 1960 incomes by this same factor. This is something the Central Statistical Office in Brazil could easily do.

Availability of Data in Less Developed Countries

Recent years have witnessed extensive gathering of data on the size distribution of income in less developed countries. The most important compilations include those by:

1. Jain (1975) at the World Bank;
2. Adelman and Morris (1973);
3. Paukert (1973) at the International Labour Office;
4. Altimir (1974), reporting on work under a joint Economic Commission for Latin America–World Bank project;
5. a compendium of six papers—by Choo (1975), Meesook (1975), Rajaraman (1975), Phillips (1975), Urrutia (1975), and Langoni (1975)—commissioned by the Princeton University–Brookings Institution project on income distribution in less developed countries;
6. Musgrove (1976), reporting on work under the auspices of the Program of Joint Studies of Latin American Economic Integration (ECIEL) in conjunction with the Brookings Institution.

These sources are described in appendix 2A. [See original.—Ed.]

Income-distribution data for two or more points in time are available for only twenty less-developed countries: Bangladesh, Brazil, Colombia,

Costa Rica, El Salvador, Gabon, India, Ivory Coast, Korea, Malaysia, Mexico, Pakistan, Panama, Peru, Philippines, Sri Lanka, Taiwan, Thailand, Tunisia, and Venezuela. Availability of data alone is not sufficient to permit income-distribution comparisons. At a minimum, definitions of income and coverage of the consensus or surveys must be directly comparable. None of the compilations offering income-distribution data for more than one point in time ensure comparability. Even in the best of circumstances, where the data appear reasonably comparable over time, cost-of-living adjustments and interpolations of the income distribution must be made. No LDC publishes the kind of income-distribution data adjusted for inflation that permit application of absolute-poverty measures without further adjustments.

For only a handful of countries can we look back and reconstruct figures on income distribution and poverty for more than two years. The possibility of monitoring the progress made by countries toward alleviating poverty (in the same way that we can monitor annual GNP growth rates, for instance) looks bleak indeed.

Closing the Gap Between Data
Needs and Data Availability

Four specific steps can make more data on changes in income distribution and poverty alleviation available:

1. The Jain data should be used for income-distribution and absolute-poverty calculations, both at a point in time and over time in those countries for which the intertemporal data are reasonably comparable.
2. This same process should be followed using the microeconomic data in the original questionnaires or computer tapes and avoiding interpolation.
3. New censuses and surveys should be designed and financed, and ongoing ones should be encouraged to provide data that are comparable with respect to definition, scope, and coverage.
4. As the results of income-distribution and absolute-poverty studies become available, an international agency could usefully process these figures and issue the results in periodic reports.

One finding from this review of the available data and their limitations is the virtual impossibility of regularly monitoring the progress and commitment of one hundred or so LDCs on the income-distribution front. The data do not permit it, nor will they soon do so. There are nationwide income-distribution data for just forty-seven of these countries and data on changes in income distribution for only twenty. It will be many years before information on changes in income distribution and poverty become available for even a majority of these countries. Over the next several years, information will trickle in on progress in improving the economic position of the poor and on the determinants of that progress or lack thereof. In the interim, some other basis must be used to decide where progress is taking place.

Conclusions

This chapter is a response to interest in greater equality of income distribution as a goal of economic development. Greater equality of income distribution may be thought of as demonstrable improvement in the economic position of the poor. How rapidly poverty is being alleviated is very much worth knowing, but there is little information on the subject at present.

There is very real danger in using any measure as an indicator of a country's commitment to alleviating poverty. These measures cannot tell us what was possible nor how well the country did in relation to how well it might have done. Countries that show little progress in alleviating poverty may find themselves in this sorry state because they have so very far to go and so very little to do it with, rather than because they have not tried.

The state of the art is not far enough advanced to provide guidance on how to take these factors into account in deriving an adequate measure of progress relative to potential. This point applies not only to income distribution; it pertains also to improvements in agricultural productivity and nutrition and to reductions in unemployment and infant mortality as criteria for assessing a given country's commitment to improving the economic position of its poor.

In gauging commitment to the poor as a criterion for receipt of aid, simple screening processes would help avoid those countries in which the aid funds are clearly being funneled into the hands of the rich or of corrupt government officials. Beyond that, in choosing which countries merit assistance, donors might do well to continue to identify the large groups of poor and to channel resources accordingly. For this purpose, data on income distribution, despite their limitations, are invaluable.

Notes
1. M. S. Ahluwalia, "Income inequality: Some dimensions of the problem." In *Redistribution with Growth* ed. Chenery et al. (Oxford University Press, 1974). Reprinted with permission.

References

Adelman, I., and Morris, C. T. 1973. *Economic growth and social equity in developing countries.* Stanford, Calif.: Stanford University Press.

Ahluwalia, M. S. 1974. Income inequality: Some dimensions of the problem. In *Redistribution with growth,* ed. Hollis Chenery et al. London: Oxford University Press.

――――. 1976. Inequality, poverty and development. *Journal of Development Economics*, December, 3:307–342.

Altimir, O. 1974. A data file on income distribution based on household surveys in Latin American countries. Economic Commission for Latin America, and Development Research Center, International Bank for Reconstruction and Development.

Averch, H. A.; Denton, F. H.; and Koehler, J. E. 1970. A crisis of ambiguity: Political and economic development in the Philippines. K-473-AID. Santa Monica, Calif.: Rand Corporation.

Bacha, E. 1976. On some contributions to the Brazilian income distribution debate. I. Discussion Paper no. 11. Cambridge, Mass.: Harvard Institute for International Development.

Bardhan, P. K. 1970. On the minimum level of living and the rural poor. *Indian Economic Review*.

――――. 1974. The pattern of income distribution in India: A review. In *Poverty and income distribution in India*, ed. T. N. Srinivasan and P. K. Bardhan. Calcutta: Statistical Publishing Society.

Bowman, M. J. 1973. Poverty in an affluent society. In *Contemporary economic issues*, ed. E. Chamberlain. Homewood, Illinois: Irwin.

Bronfenbrenner, M. 1971. *Income distribution theory.* Chicago: Aldine Publishing Company.

Chenery, H. B. 1960. Patterns of industrial growth. *American Economic Review*, September.

Chenery, H. and Syrquin, M. 1975. Patterns of development, 1950–1970. London: Oxford University Press, a World Bank Publication.

Chenery, H. B. and Taylor, L. 1968. Development patterns among countries and over time. *Review of Economics and Statistics*, November, 50:391–416.

Chiswick, C. U. 1976. Measuring poverty income distribution in Thailand. IBRD Research Project no. 671–36, Working Paper series A-1. Washington, D.C.: Development Research Center, World Bank.

Choo, H. 1975. Review of income distribution data: Korea, the Philippines, and Taiwan. Discussion paper no. 55. Princeton, N.J.: Research Program in Economic Development, Wodrow Wilson School of Public and International Affairs.

Cline, W. R. 1975. Distribution and development: A survey of the literature. *Journal of Developing Economics*, February, pp. 359–400.

Dandekar, V. M., and Rath, N. 1971. Poverty in India. *Economic and Political Weekly*, January, 2.

Fei, J.C.H. and Ranis, G. 1964. *Development of the labor surplus economy.* Homewood, Illinois: Irwin.

Ferber, R. 1976. Distribución de ingreso y desigualdad de ingresos en algunas area urbanas. *Ensayos Eciel* 3:67–125. Rio de Janeiro: Program de estudios conjuntos sobre integración economica latinoamericana.

Fields, G. S. 1976. More on changing income distribution and economic development in Brazil. Discussion Paper no. 244, New Haven, Conn.: Economic Growth Center, Yale University.

――――. 1977. Who benefits from economic development?—A reexamination of Brazilian growth in the 1960s. *American Economic Review*, September.

Fishlow, A. 1972. Brazilian size distribution of income. *American Economic Review* 62:391–402.

Foxley, A. 1975. *Distribution of income.* Cambridge: Cambridge University Press.

International Labour Office. 1970. *Towards full employment: A programme for Colombia.* Geneva: International Labor Office.

Jain, S. 1975. Size distribution of income: Compilation of data. Bank Staff Working Paper no. 190. Washington, D.C.: World Bank.

Kravis, I.; Kenessey, Z.; Heston, A.; and Summer, R. 1975. *A System of international comparisons of gross product and purchasing power.* Baltimore, Md.: Johns Hopkins University Press.

Kuznets, S. 1955. Economic growth and income inequality. *American Economic Review,* March, pp. 1–28.

————. 1963. Quantitative aspects of the economic growth of nations: VIII. Distribution of income by size. *Economic Development and Cultural Change,* January, part 2, pp. 1–80.

————. 1966. *Modern economic growth.* New Haven, Conn.: Yale University Press.

————. 1976. Demographic aspects of the size distribution of income: An exploratory survey. *Economic Development and Cultural Change* 25:1–95.

Langoni, C. G. 1975. Review of income distribution data: Brazil. Discussion Paper no. 60. Princeton, N.J.: Research Program in Economic Development, Woodrow Wilson School of Public and International Affairs.

Lydall, H. B. 1968. *The structure of earnings.* Oxford: Clarendon Press.

Meesook, O. A. 1975. Review of income distribution data: Thailand, Malaysia and Indonesia. Discussion Paper no. 56. Princeton, N.J.: Research Program in Economic Development, Woodrow Wilson School of Public and International Affairs.

Paukert, F. 1973. Income distribution at different levels of development: A survey of evidence. *International Labour Review,* August-September.

Perlman, R. 1976. *The economics of poverty.* New York: McGraw Hill.

Phillips, A. O. 1975. Review of income distribution data: Ghana, Kenya, Tanzania, and Nigeria. Discussion Paper no. 58. Princeton, N.J.: Research Program in Economic Development, Woodrow Wilson School of Public and International Affairs.

Rajaraman, I. 1975. Review of income distribution data: Pakistan, India, Bangladesh, and Sri Lanka. Discussion Paper no. 57. Princeton, N.J.: Research Program in Economic Development, Woodrow Wilson School of Public and International Affairs.

Sen, A. K. 1976. Poverty: An ordinal approach to measurement. *Econometrica,* March.

Swamy, S. 1967. Structural changes and the distribution of income by size: The case of India. *Review of Income and Wealth,* June.

Szal, R. J. 1975. A methodology for the evaluation and adjustment of income distribution data. Discussion Paper no. 54. Princeton, N.J.: Research Program in Economic Development, Woodrow Wilson School of Public and International Affairs.

Taussig, M. 1973. Alternative measures of the distribution of economic welfare. Industrial Relations Section, Princeton University.

Turnham, D. 1971. The employment problem in less developed countries: A review of evidence. Development Centre Employment Series no. 1. Organization for Economic Cooperation and Development. Paris: Development Centre.

United States. Bureau of the Census. 1976. Money income and poverty status of families and persons in the United States: 1975 and 1974 revisions. Series P-60, no. 103.

Urrutia, M. 1975. Review of income distribution data: Colombia, Mexico and Venezuela. Discussion Paper no. 59. Princeton, N.J.: Research Program in Economic Development, Woodrow Wilson School of Public and International Affairs.

Webb, R. 1976. On the statistical mapping of urban poverty and employment. Bank Staff Working Paper, no. 227. Development Economics Department, Development Policy Staff. Washington, D.C.: World Bank.

Weisskoff, R. 1970. Income distribution and economic growth in Puerto Rico, Argentina and Mexico. *Review of Income and Wealth*, December, pp. 303–332.

23. The Vicious Circle of Poverty

P. T. Bauer

In this chapter, P. T. Bauer takes a critical look at a version of the "Matthew effect" discussed by Jackman in Chapter 18. In the 1950s and 1960s, it was a frequently stated proposition among those concerned with development that there exists a "vicious circle of poverty" in which poverty breeds further poverty, making it impossible for poor nations to break out of the circle. Bauer disputes this perspective on both logical and empirical grounds, arguing that the widening international gap between rich and poor has been exaggerated because, among other things, it is based upon international exchange rates rather than on a comparison of domestic purchasing power. Bauer goes on to consider the impact of population growth on development.

The Vicious Circle[1]

The widely held notion that poor countries are caught in a vicious circle of poverty and stagnation, or, as the late Professor Ragnar Nurkse put it, that a country is poor because it is poor, is not true; this chapter explains why. This chapter also challenges the popular idea that there is an ever-widening gap between per capita incomes in rich and poor countries and explains why this assertion is either untrue or meaningless.

The great upsurge of interest during the last twenty years in the economics of poor countries and in their development has not so far yielded many illuminating generalizations. The thesis usually known as the vicious circle of poverty claims to be a principal one. It is not quite so dominant now as it was a few years ago but it is still prominent in academic, official and popular literature. It also serves as the background or even as the basis for important policy proposals and measures, notably the suggestion that appreciable economic progress in poor countries requires drastic sacrifices at home, supplemented by large-scale aid from abroad.

Reprinted with permission from *Dissent on Development: Studies and Debates in Development Economics,* by P. T. Bauer, pp. 31–37, 51–62. Cambridge, MA: Harvard University Press, 1976.

The Thesis Outlined

The thesis states that it is poverty itself which sets up well-nigh insurmountable obstacles to its own conquest. The thesis is presented in several distinct and different formulations, which are not exclusive but cumulative. The most usual is that the low level of income makes saving impossible, thus preventing the capital accumulation necessary for an increase in income. Others include the suggestion that narrow markets in poor countries obstruct the emergence and extension of the specialization necessary for higher incomes; that demand is too small to permit profitable and productive investment; that government revenues are insufficient for the establishment of effective public services; and that malnutrition and poor health keep productivity low, which prevents a rise in income. International private investment cannot, on this argument, alleviate the situation, since one aspect of the vicious circle is a lack of profitable opportunities for private investment.

I shall first quote at some length from influential sources to show the importance of the thesis in the literature, to illustrate the reasoning behind it and to forestall criticism that I am quoting out of context. A succinct formulation can be quoted from an early edition of Professor Samuelson's textbook:

> They [the backward nations] cannot get their heads above water because their production is so low that they can spare nothing for capital formation by which their standard of living could be raised.[2]

The next example is from a study submitted to a United States Senate Committee by the Center for International Studies of the Massachusetts Institute of Technology, a well-known and influential organization in this field:

> . . . the general scarcity relative to population of nearly all resources creates a self-perpetuating vicious circle of poverty. Additional capital is necessary to increase output, but poverty itself makes it impossible to carry out the required saving and investment by a voluntary reduction in consumption.[3]

The emphasis on the impossibility of a voluntary reduction in consumption is notable. If it is the low level of incomes which prevents capital formation it is not clear how the exercise of compulsion would secure the required resources.

Yet another formulation, which has often been quoted, is by the late Professor Nurkse, whose book *Problems of Capital Formation in Underdeveloped Countries* is one of the best-known and most influential of the writings in this field. He writes under the heading "The Vicious Circle of Poverty":

In discussions of the problem of economic development, a phrase that crops up frequently is "the vicious circle of poverty." . . .

A situation of this sort [of the vicious circle of poverty], relating to a country as a whole, can be summed up in the trite proposition: "a country is poor because it is poor." Perhaps the most important circular relationships of this kind are those that afflict the accumulation of capital in economically backward countries. The supply of capital is governed by the ability and willingness to save; the demand for capital is governed by the incentives to invest. A circular relationship exists on both sides of the problem of capital formation in the poverty-ridden areas of the world.

On the supply side, there is the small capacity to save, resulting from the low level of real income. The low real income is a reflection of low productivity, which in its turn is due largely to the lack of capital. The lack of capital is a result of the small capacity to save, and so the circle is complete.

On the demand side, the inducement to invest may be low because of the small buying power of the people, which is due to their small real income, which again is due to low productivity. The low level of productivity, however, is a result of the small amount of capital used in production, which in its turn may be caused, or at least partly caused, by the small inducement to invest!

The low level of real income, reflecting low productivity, is a point that is common to both circles.[4]

Parts of this formulation are vague and indeed slipshod in their shift between what will, may, or is likely to occur. But the general conclusion is clear. Such quotations could easily be multiplied from the writings of such well-known authors as Professor Gunnar Myrdal, Dr H. W. Singer, and others.

This thesis can also be expressed in the form of a model, that is, an analytical device setting out the crucial variables in the explanation of particular phenomena. The crucial variables and relationships in most growth models are these: the growth of income is a function of the rate of capital accumulation, that is, of investment; investment depends on saving; and saving is a function of income. Hence the growth of income depends on the growth of capital and the growth of capital depends on the growth of income. The model behind the thesis of the vicious circle of poverty pivots on the notion that the low level of income itself prevents the capital formation required to raise income. It is designed to explain the continuation through time of a zero or negligible rate of economic growth.

The Thesis Invalid

The thesis is demonstrably invalid in that it is conclusively refuted by obvious empirical evidence. The model behind it is defective in that the variables specified or implied in it are either relatively unimportant as determinants of development, or they do not interact in the fashion implied. If the thesis were valid, for instance, innumerable individuals, groups and communities could not have risen from poverty to riches as they have done throughout the world, in both rich and poor countries. This in itself should be sufficient to disprove the thesis as a general proposition. But the thesis is also refuted by the very existence of developed countries, all of which started poor, with low incomes per head and low levels of accumulated capital, that is, with the economic features which now define underdeveloped countries. Yet they have advanced, usually without appreciable outside capital and invariably without external grants, which would have been impossible according to the thesis of the vicious circle of poverty and stagnation. As the world is a closed system, the thesis is inconsistent with the phenomenon of development. The thesis of a general vicious circle of poverty thus conflicts with the most elementary empirical evidence.

Empirical Evidence

The thesis is also refuted by the rapid economic advance of many poor countries in recent decades, a phenomenon which is of obvious interest in this general context.

According to statistics of the Economic Commission for Latin America the gross national product in Latin American countries increased over the period 1935 through 1953 at an annual rate of 4.2 percent, and output per head by 2 percent.[5] Over the period 1945 through 1955 the rate of growth was even faster, as total output increased by about 4.9 percent annually and output per head by 2.4 percent, an appreciably higher rate than in the United States.[6]

Latin America is largely pervaded by the money economy, so that statistics of the gross national product are more meaningful than for most underdeveloped countries. The record of the substantial growth rates in the publications of the Economic Commission for Latin America is of special interest, because economists connected with that organization have been prominent exponents of the thesis of the vicious circle of poverty.

Southeast Asia, particularly Malaya (broadly, the present Malaysia), and West Africa are other underdeveloped regions which have achieved rapid and readily demonstrable progress since the latter part of the nineteenth century. However, there are no series of national income figures going back before World War II in these areas and the present figures are unreliable. The national income per head in Malaya (gross domestic product per head per year) was about £100 in 1961,[7] the latest year for which official figures are available, and in Ghana about £75 in 1962, again the latest available figures. These are low figures by Western standards, but they nevertheless represent substantial advances since the beginning of the century, when these countries were largely subsistence economies. The conventional statistics, moreover, much exaggerate income differences between the developed and underdeveloped countries. This is discussed at length later in this chapter.

Apart from national income statistics there is much information about the rapid progress of these economies in recent years. The rubber industry of Southeast Asia began only around 1900. In 1963 it produced about two million tons of rubber annually (in spite of the disorganization in Indonesia, the country with the largest area under rubber), worth about £400 million. More than two-thirds of the output is from Asian-owned properties. In 1900 there were no exports of plantation rubber from Malaya; in 1963 they exceeded 800,000 tons. In 1900, total domestic exports from Malaya were worth about £8 million annually; in 1963 they were about £300 million.[8]

West Africa is another major region of the underdeveloped world where there has been large-scale material progress since the end of the nineteenth century. The progress of Gold Coast–Ghana[9] and Nigeria in particular has been rapid and is well documented; and in these areas, especially Gold Coast–Ghana, statistics are somewhat more reliable and meaningful than elsewhere in Africa. By the mid-1950s national income per head was about £70 to £75, approximately four times what it had been in 1890. The population also approximately quadrupled between 1890 and 1960.[10] Material advance is reflected, too, in statistics of foriegn trade, government revenues, literacy rates, school attendance, public health, infant mortality, and so on.

Statistics of foreign trade are of particular interest for West Africa because well over 99.5 percent of the population is African: all agricultural exports (the bulk of exports) are produced by them and practically all imports are destined for their use. In 1890 there were no exports (or production) of Gold Coast cocoa; by the mid-1930s these were about 300,000 tons annually, and by the early 1960s they were over 400,000 tons, all from farms established, owned and operated by Africans; there are no foreign-owned cocoa farms. In 1890 combined imports and exports were less than £1 million annually; by the 1930s both imports and exports were in tens of millions; since the mid-1950s imports and exports have been about £100 million annually. Over this period there was a spectacular increase in imports of both consumer and capital goods. In 1890 there were no imports, or only negligible imports, of flour, sugar, cement, petroleum products, or iron and steel. In recent decades most of these have been on a massive scale. In the early 1890s there were about three thousand children at school; by the mid-1950s there were over half a million. In the 1890s there were neither railways nor roads, but only a few jungle paths, and transport of goods was entirely by human porterage or by canoe. By the 1930s there was considerable railway mileage and a good road system; and journeys by road required fewer hours than they had required days in 1890.

Substantially the same applies to Nigeria between the end of the nineteenth century and 1960, when Nigeria became independent. Around 1900 exports and imports were each about £2 million annually; by the 1930s they were in tens of millions, and by the late 1950s they were about £150–200 million annually. Here again practically all exports are produced by Africans and practically all imports are destined for their use. In 1900 there were no exports (or production) of cocoa from Nigeria, and exports of oil palm products were one-tenth of their volume in the late 1950s. There was also a phenomenal increase in imports of mass consumer goods and capital goods over this period; in recent years there has also been a substantial increase in the local production of commodities previously imported.

To take one more example. In the first half of the nineteenth century Hong Kong was an empty, barren rock. By the end of the century it was a substantial port and a minor entrepôt center. It has now become a major manufacturing center, exporting manufactures on a massive scale. Throughout the Western world severe barriers have had to be erected to protect the domestic industries of the United States, Great Britain, Germany and France against imports from the unsubsidized competition of the industries of Hong Kong, an underdeveloped country, eight thousand or more miles away. This rapid progress has occurred in spite of the presence in Hong Kong of three features often said to reinforce the vicious circle of poverty, namely lack of natural resources, extremely severe population pressure, and a very restricted domestic market. . . .

The notion of the gap in per capita incomes between rich and poor countries and the suggestion of its increase encounter certain basic problems of concept which often go unrecognized.

A clear distinction needs to be drawn between differences in the absolute magnitude of per capita (that is average) incomes in developed and underdeveloped countries and in the ratios between these per capita incomes which denote the proportionate or relative differences. This distinction is obviously important because the two types of difference invariably change at different rates and often in opposite directions.

A simple numerical example will illustrate this obvious but widely overlooked point. Assume two groups of people whose average incomes are 100 and 50 units in the first period and 1,000 and 900 units in the second period. The absolute gap in incomes has doubled, but the relative difference has contracted by four-fifths.

Although the term gap suggests differences in absolute magnitudes, in most contexts it is relative or proportionate differences which are usually regarded as interesting or relevant.

In Britain in 1970 a difference between annual incomes of say £10,000 and £8,000 is regarded as less significant than that between £1,000 and £500, though the absolute gap (the difference in absolute magnitudes) between the former is four times that of the gap between the latter.

Further, when incomes increase at a uniform rate over time, the gap between the absolute level of average income between, say, the top 10 percent of income earners and the bottom 10 percent will increase, even though both groups are better off. Thus the absolute difference between the per capita incomes of the highest and the lowest decile of the population in Britain today is almost certainly larger than it was two hundred years ago because of the rise in the absolute levels in income, but the proportionate or relative difference has almost certainly narrowed with the improvement of the position of unskilled labor. The main influences which promote long-term increases in world incomes (especially the spread of skills and the accumulation of capital) normally widen absolute differences in per capita incomes between randomly chosen groups but simultaneously tend to reduce the relative differences between certain major groups by reducing the relative scarcity of the resources of the more prosperous categories compared with those of the poorer categories.

The allegations of the ever-widening gap do not usually specify whether they refer to changes in absolute differences in per capita incomes or to changes in relative differences. Nor is it possible to examine either the significance or the validity of these allegations, since they are rarely, if ever, supported by statistical evidence, least of all by statistics about the movement in the ratio of per capita incomes between rich and poor countries.

Distinction Between Developed and Underdeveloped Countries

The notion of the gap implies a distinct and substantial discontinuity in per capita incomes of developed and underdeveloped countries. In fact, there is no such appreciable gap. There is continuous graduation in per capita incomes between different countries. There is no significant difference between the per capita income of the poorest developed country and the richest underdeveloped country—certainly any such difference would be a fraction of the errors and biases of these figures as they are given. And because the line of distinction is arbitrary, and countries are not homogeneous entities, there are groups and regions in many poor countries with higher per capita incomes than the per capita incomes of many countries classed as developed or rich, and *a fortiori* than per capita incomes of many groups and regions within developed countries.

The absence of a wide gap between per capita incomes in the poorest developed country and the richest underdeveloped country and the arbitrariness of the line of division between the two categories affects crucially this area of discourse. The gap in per capita incomes (both absolute and relative differences) of the two global categories, the developed world and the underdeveloped world, depends on where the line is placed. And in the absence of a clear discontinuity between the per capita incomes in the poorest developed countries and the richest underdeveloped countries any line of division on the basis of per capita incomes is arbitrary. Yet the extent of the difference in incomes (the gap) between the two categories depends on where it is placed.

The placing of the line of division depends quite often on accident, or on personal preference, but primarily on political pressures. For instance, in current discussion the underdeveloped world is largely equated with countries whose populations are mainly of non-European origin, a grouping which reflects the operation of political pressures. Again, communist countries are not usually included in the under-developed world, though on the basis of per capita incomes or living standards several of them could appropriately be classified as under-developed. Their omission again illustrates the play of political forces.

The arbitrary nature of the current distinction between developed and underdeveloped countries on the basis of per capita incomes is compounded by the fact that per capita income is in itself a seriously inadequate index of development. This inadequacy is at times recognized. For instance, some of the oil states of the Middle East, habitually and appropriately classified as underdeveloped, have per capita incomes which are among the highest in the world. In many, perhaps most contexts, it is permissible to use interchangeably the terms developed and rich on the one hand, and underdeveloped and poor on the other. But this practice, as the above example shows, is inappropriate in discussions on an allegedly wide and widening gap in incomes.

The distinction between developed and underdeveloped countries on the basis of per capita incomes is not only arbitrary but is also shifting. Quite obviously all developed countries began as underdeveloped. And some countries, such as Japan and Italy, which until recently were classified as underdeveloped, are no longer so regarded. These changes in categories through time preclude any simple assessment of the long-term changes of difference in average incomes between developed and underdeveloped countries.

As a corollary of this situation, a widening difference in per capita incomes between two groups can always be established spuriously by changing the composition of the groups. Thus, any worthwhile discussion of differences in average incomes and of changes in these differences depends crucially on the composition of the two categories.

The suggestion of a wide and widening gap between the developed and the underdeveloped world implies not only a clear distinction between the two categories but also substantial homogeneity within them. It implies that the underdeveloped countries are a substantially uniform mass. Such worldwide aggregation and averaging is meaningless. The aggregates are extremely heterogeneous, arbitrary and shifting categories whose composition is unstable and which are comprised of component elements which are themselves heterogeneous collectivities. One aspect of this diversity is the presence of wide differences in rates of material progress within both aggregates. As a result of these differences in rates of material progress, differences in average incomes (both absolute and relative) often move differently between significant groups within the two categories.

I have already noted some United Nations statistics according to which per capita output in Latin America as a whole grew faster between 1945 and 1955 than in the United States of America, so that over this period the relative difference in per capita incomes between these collectivities narrowed.[11] Such statistics could readily be multiplied from the publications of the international agencies. Other familiar examples of recent rapid material progress and substantial rise in per capita income in poor countries outside Latin America include Japan, South Korea, Taiwan, Hong Kong, Thailand, the Ivory Coast, Kenya, the oil states of the Middle East and Israel. Indeed in recent years per capita incomes over large parts of the underdeveloped world have increased faster than in many developed countries, including the United Kingdom and the United States.

Four countries, India, Indonesia, Pakistan and Brazil, account for about three-fifths of the population of the underdeveloped world outside China; India alone, with a population of 550 million, accounts for well over one-third. Thus a slow rate of economic progress in these countries can mask the rapid progress of a score or more of other countries when their performance is aggregated. And since about 1960 the material progress of India, Indonesia and Brazil has been relatively sluggish. Once again the divergent experience of underdeveloped countries is obscured by worldwide aggregation.[12]

The choice of the period under review is also fundamental to discussions of a trend in the differences in incomes because the rate of change of incomes varies through time. Thus the period over which the gap is supposed to widen needs to be specified. The relevance of this simple conclusion is also clear from the changes in the relative economic position of different countries and populations in the course of history, changes which include economic decline, both absolute decline and decline relative to other countries. These phenomena, often noted by historians, are inconsistent with the supposedly ever-widening gap between rich and poor as a general trend. The allegations of a supposedly ever-widening gap between rich and poor countries do not usually mention either the period envisaged or the phenomenon of economic decline.

The argument of this section is not affected by the wide margins of error in international comparisons of national income, notably the general undervaluation of national income in underdeveloped countries, which is noted subsequently in this chapter. And much additional evidence could be produced to show that the ratio of per capita incomes between every rich and every poor country has certainly not widened in recent decades. But the foregoing should suffice to show that the allegation of an ever-widening difference in incomes between the developed and the underdeveloped world is at best unsubstantiated; as it is usually presented it is meaningless, and in so far as it can be evaluated it is largely untrue.

If it is felt useful to divide the world into two categories on the basis of differences in stages of development (an exercise of debatable usefulness); then differences in demographic patterns, notably in birth rates, which reflect differences in attitudes and institutions and which are often correlated with ethnic differences, would seem to provide a basis which would be potentially more illuminating than the present basis of conventionally measured per capita incomes. For instance, as part of this suggested basis, a distinction between societies in which fertility rates are close to the fecundity rate and those in which fertility rates are significantly below the fecundity rate, might prove useful; it has a certain amount of precision, it is more stable in time, and it could give a measure of insight into the underlying determinants of material progress.

Problems of International Income Comparisons

Estimates of differences in per capita incomes and living standards in rich and poor countries (that is the magnitudes between which the gap is supposed to be widened) are subject to very wide margins of error which are far larger than is usually recognized. On balance, however, the result is usually an underestimate of incomes in poor countries and an overestimate in rich ones, thus exaggerating the difference in incomes and living standards between the two groups.

To begin with, even the population statistics of underdeveloped countries, which underlie calculations of per capita incomes and which are free from conceptual problems, are exceedingly unreliable. For instance, according to the official statistics, the population of Nigeria in 1963 was 55.6 million. Professor Peter Kilby, a prominent scholar of Nigerian affairs, estimated it at 37.1 million. Again, the Second Indian Five-Year Plan estimated the population growth at about 1.25 percent per annum over its duration; the figure was subsequently found to be over 2 percent, thus exceeding the estimate by more than four-fifths.

Quantitatively even more important than the margins of error in statistics of population, are the huge margins of error and statistical bias in the estimates of the national income of poor countries and in the comparisons between the national incomes of rich and poor countries. There are many reasons for these errors and biases. This matter is so fundamental to this area of discussion and so little appreciated that it warrants extensive consideration.

One major reason for the underestimate of the national income of poor countries and the consequent exaggeration of the difference in incomes between rich and poor countries is the use of rates of exchange in comparing national incomes which greatly understate the domestic purchasing power of the currencies of underdeveloped countries relative to those of developed countries. Other reasons include the much greater quantitative importance of intra-family services and also of subsistence and near-subsistence output in poor compared to rich countries, categories, which are either ignored or substantially undervalued in national income statistics.[13] Further, many goods and services conventionally included in national income are more nearly costs of production than income, for instance the journey to work, and these are relatively more important in rich than in poor countries.

These problems of international comparison have been known for some time.[14] But their most thorough and methodical examination has come only comparatively recently from Professor Dan Usher, who has closely studied the extent of the major errors and biases and the reasons behind these. The following passages from Professor Usher's recent book, *The Price Mechanism and the Meaning of National Income Statistics*, epitomize his position.[15]

Our picture of economic life in poor countries is influenced significantly by statistics showing many countries to have incomes of as little as $50 per year and by estimates of the productivity of labour in agriculture of less than a tenth of the productivity of labour elsewhere in the economy. Using Thailand as an example, this book shows that statistics like these may contain errors of several hundreds percent. . . . The discrepancy is not due primarily to errors in data. . . . The fault lies with the rules [of national income comparisons] themselves . . . [which] generate numbers that fail to carry the implications expected of them.

In Thailand I saw a people not prosperous by European standards but obviously enjoying a standard of living well above the bare requirements of subsistence. Many village communities seemed to have attained a standard of material comfort at least as high as that of slum dwellers in England or America. But at my desk I computed statistics of real national income showing people of underdeveloped countries including Thailand to be desperately if not impossibly poor. The contrast between what I saw and what I measured was so great that I came to believe that there must be some large and fundamental bias in the way income statistics are compiled. . . . Something is very wrong with these statistics. For instance, if the figure of $40 for Ethiopia means what it appears to mean, namely that Ethiopians are consuming per year an amount of goods and services no larger than could be bought in the United States for $40, then most Ethiopians are so poor that they could not possibly survive, let alone increase their numbers. . . . National income statistics are the principal medium through which we see the process of economic growth. We characterise countries as developed or underdeveloped according to their national incomes. Income statistics are also components of measures of the productivity of industries and of the equality of the income distribution. The main point of this book, brought out both by the theory and by the numbers, is that the picture conveyed by national income statistics is often distorted, not because the statistics themselves are inaccurate, nor because they fail to reflect accepted canons of statistical method, but because we attribute to income statistics a social meaning that they do not necessarily possess. Higher income is supposed to mean better off; higher productivity is supposed to mean contributing more to the economic welfare of the community. The theoretical part of the book shows how this association can fail. The empirical part of the book shows that there can be a very great discrepancy between conventional statistics and revised statistics designed to reflect more closely the appropriate social facts.

The statistics of incomes examined by Professor Usher refer to per capita figures, as for instance the figure of $40 for Ethiopia, that is, they refer to averages. Accordingly, a large proportion of the population would have significantly lower incomes, a consideration which reinforces Professor Usher's case about the utterly meaningless nature of these compilations. Professor Usher's reference to the contrast between what he saw and what he measured provides specific and remarkable confirmation of the importance of direct observation in this area and of the misleading nature of the results which emerge when direct observation is neglected.

Professor Usher writes elsewhere:

> For example, the conventional comparison shows that the per capita national income of the United Kingdom is about fourteen times that of Thailand. Recomputations made by the author to allow for various biases in the comparison suggest that the effective ratio of living standards is about three to one. Even if the recomputed ratio is doubled, the change in order of magnitude is large enough to affect our way of thinking about the underdeveloped countries.[16]

Biases and errors of orders of magnitude must strike at the root of international statistics as indices of productivity or of economic development or of comparative living standards. These limitations and errors of comparison are distinct from the inevitable inaccuracies of national income computations in poor countries where even such comparatively straightforward information as population statistics is incomplete.

In the light of the evidence assembled and analyzed by Professor Usher, it seems doubtful whether international comparison of national incomes retains any meaning at all, except when restricted to groups of countries which already have roughly the same standard of living.[17]

It is necessary to insist on the presence of these huge margins of error and of bias in national income compilations of poor countries and in international comparisons. It is the conventionally measured per capita incomes which serve as usual or principal bases for classifying countries as developed or underdeveloped, rich or poor, and as a major criterion for the allocation of foreign aid.

International comparisons of per capita incomes, living standards and requirements are significantly affected further by differences in age composition. If per capita incomes of the same age group are equal between two populations, the average for the two populations as a whole will differ if the age composition is different. In underdeveloped countries the age composition usually differs significantly from that in developed countries because of the much higher proportion of children, who usually have appreciably lower incomes and requirements than have adults. Comparisons in per capita incomes unadjusted for differences in age structure confuse differences in levels of income with differences in age.[18]

This complication is again ignored in the standard international comparisons. The adjustment required to correct for differences in age composition are not marginal. The differences in age structure between poor and rich countries are substantial and so are the resulting understatements of per capita incomes in the latter, compared with computations on an age-standardized basis.

Comparisons of living standards, as distinct from per capita incomes, are affected by differences in requirements, for instance in the (generally lower) requirements of food and clothing, and in the (generally higher) availability of leisure in underdeveloped countries. On the other hand, life expectation is generally higher in rich than in poor countries. Attempts to compare relative welfare conditions run into further, more deep-seated, problems. For instance, different economic processes have widely different effects in promoting or inhibiting people's capacities and opportunities for enjoying their incomes.

We may conclude this discussion of the problems of comparison of incomes by forestalling a possible reservation or objection. Most of these problems and limitations of international comparisons affect calculations and estimates of both the *levels* and the *changes* in incomes and living standards. It may be objected that if the errors and biases of comparison remain constant through time, their presence would not affect the suggestions of a widening gap in incomes. Such an objection would be invalid. First, the extent of the biases and errors could not remain constant because of changes in social and economic conditions, including the organization and pattern of production and consumption within the huge aggregates under comparison. Obvious examples include changes in rates of growth, and in the relative importance of subsistence production. Second, when errors and biases are so wide that they even affect the orders of magnitude, quantified discussion about international differences in incomes and about changes in these differences loses much of its interest and meaning. Third, if the gap is thought of in terms of absolute differences in incomes, its movement through time is affected by the presence of biases and errors, even if these remain constant as a proportion of estimated per capita incomes.

Population Growth and the Widening Gap

Estimates and comparisons of changes in per capita incomes and living standards are also complicated by certain fundamental problems of concept and measurement (besides those already discussed) arising from changes in rates of population growth in underdeveloped countries, and also from differences between rates of population growth in developed and in underdeveloped countries.

Over the last fifty to eighty years the population of most underdeveloped countries has increased greatly, mostly by a factor of between two and five. This increase has come about as a result of a fall in death rates, especially among children, which implies a longer life expectation. The position of those who have failed to die has certainly improved, as has the situation of those whose children continue to live, an improvement not reflected in conventional statistics compiled on a per capita basis. Indeed, as we shall shortly see, these population statistics often register as deterioration changes which are clearly an improvement. Thus the usual way of drawing conclusions from income per head obscures important conceptual problems in the definition and measurement of income in that the satisfactions derived from living longer and from having children are ignored.

Over considerable periods in recent times, notably since about 1930, rates of population growth in many underdeveloped countries have been higher than in most developed countries. A differential rate of increase in population in rich and poor countries brings about a change in relative numbers, which directly affects the measurement of international differences in incomes and of changes in these differences. Both absolute and proportionate differences in per capita incomes[19] between rich and poor countries can widen even when per capita incomes in poor countries grow faster than in rich countries, if the rate of population increase is fastest in the poorest countries within the poor countries' group.

Again, if population increases faster in poor than in rich countries, per capita income may fall in the world as a whole even if it has increased in every single country rich or poor. Further, within any one country, the per capita income can fall, even if the incomes of all individuals and groups have risen, if the relative numerical importance of the poorer groups increases. In the absence of changes in attitudes and in methods of production, per capita income also falls as a result of an increase in the proportion of children in a population, since the income of children is generally below the overall national average.

These considerations underline again the need for care when referring to underdeveloped *countries*. What matters is the position and prospects of people, not of the country: as we have just noted, the average income in the country can fall even if everybody is materially better off than before, and the converse result is also possible, though in practice rather improbable. These considerations derive from familiar statistical results of a change in the relative importance of the components of an aggregate.

Thus when birth rates and death rates change, special care needs to be exercised in comparisons and interpretations of the movement through time of per capita incomes and of differences in incomes. An increase in the survival rate of the poorest groups usually promotes both a fall in per capita incomes and an increase in absolute and relative differences in incomes between rich and poor. Conversely, an increase in mortality among the relatively poor, or enforced reduction in their birth rates through government fiat would raise average incomes and reduce income differences. Yet the latter types of change could hardly be interpreted as an improvement in the conditions of the relatively poor.

The improved health, longer life expectation and the increase in the rate of population growth in underdeveloped countries have come about largely as a result of contacts established by the West. There are thus many more people alive in poor countries than there would have been in the absence of these contacts. It is only in this sense that the widely publicized notion is true that the West has caused the poverty of the underdeveloped world: it has enabled many relatively poor people to live longer.

The fall in death rates in many underdeveloped countries has come about largely through the suppression or reduction of famine, disease, infant mortality, slave raiding and tribal warfare. Some of these changes in turn reflect far-reaching changes in the conditions of existence which have occurred in many parts of the underdeveloped world in recent decades. Conventional statistics of national income accounting cannot adequately reflect such far-reaching and pervasive changes.[20] This limitation is quite apart from the conceptual and statistical problems, only some of which have been noted in this chapter, which arise when the concept, derived largely from the study of societies pervaded by a money economy, is applied to societies in which subsistence production and intra-family transactions are important; or when it is applied to comparisons between such economies and largely monetized or industrialized economies, or is used as an index of change in such economies. . . .

Notes

1. The original version of this essay was published as "The Vicious Circle of Poverty: Reality or Myth?," in *Weltwirtschaftliches Archiv,* September 1965.

2. Paul A. Samuelson, *Economics: An Introductory Analysis* (2nd ed.), New York, 1951, p. 49.

3. *Study submitted by the Center for International Studies of the Massachusetts Institute of Technology to the State Committee investigating the operation of Foreign Aid,* Washington, 1957, p. 37.

4. Ragnar Nurkse, *Problems of Capital Formation in Underdeveloped Countries,* Oxford, 1953, p. 4, et seq.

5. United Nations, Department of Economic and Social Affairs, *Analyses and Projections of Economic Development. I: An Introduction to the Technique of Programming,* New York, 1955, p. 10.

6. United Nations, Department of Economic and Social Affairs, *Economic Survey of Latin America 1955,* New York, 1956, p. 3.

7. The statistics of national income per head in this paragraph are calculated from the figures of the gross domestic product presented in the United Nations' *Year Book of National Accounts Statistics 1963,* New York, 1964, pp. 85 and 107; and from the population figures in the United Nations' *Monthly Bulletin of Statistics,* vol. XVIII, New York, December 1964. More up-to-date figures are, of course, available since this essay was written, but they do not affect the argument.

8. The external trade of Malaya and Singapore in 1963 is derived from data in the official *Monthly Statistical Bulletin of the States of Malaya,* Kuala Lumpur, October 1964, and from the Singapore *Monthly Digest of Statistics,* vol. III, October 1964.

9. In this chapter we refer to this territory as Gold Coast, Ghana, or Gold Coast–Ghana, according to the period covered by the context.

10. Details will be found in R. E. Szereszewski, *Structural Changes in the Economy of Ghana 1891–1911*, London, 1966; and in P. T. Bauer, *West African Trade*, Cambridge, 1954.

11. These particular United Nations statistics refer to output, not to income per head, but the difference is immaterial in this context. Indeed, because of favorable changes in the terms of trade of the major Latin American countries over this period it is probable that the growth in per capita output understates the improvement in the position of Latin America compared to that of the United States between 1945 and 1955.

12. I am indebted to Dr F. A. Mehta for this particular example.

13. Subsistence production and intra-family services are not marketed, so that all prices placed on these must be largely arbitrary. There is an element of self-contradiction in pricing non-marketed output. The various methods adopted tend in practice to impart a strong downward bias to estimates of incomes and living standards in underdeveloped compared to developed countries.

14. A pioneer work in this area is A. R. Prest and I. G. Stewart, *The National Income of Nigeria 1950–1951*, London, 1953; another important contribution is A. R. Prest, *Public Finance in Underdeveloped Countries* (Appendix I: The Valuation of Subsistence Output), London, 1962; other studies which note some of the conceptual and statistical problems of national income estimates of underdeveloped countries, and of international comparisons of income, include A. R. Prest, *The Investigation of National Income in British Tropical Dependencies*, London, 1957; Stephen Enke, *Economics for Development*, Englewood Cliffs, N.J., 1963; and also the important collection of essays by Professor S. Herbert Frankel, *The Economic Impact on Underdeveloped Societies*, Oxford, 1953.

15. Oxford, 1968, introduction and summary.

16. "The Transport Bias in National Income Comparisons," *Economica*, May 1963, p. 140.

17. Professor Usher's arguments and the supporting evidence behind them not only expose the invalidity of international comparisons of per capita incomes between widely different societies, they also put into perspective such notions as the widely publicized suggestion by Professors Max F. Millikan and Walt W. Rostow (in *A Proposal*, New York, 1957) that if per capita incomes in an underdeveloped country rise by between 1 and 2 percent annually for five years, that country can be assumed to be on the point of take-off (whatever that means) and thus qualify for as much foreign aid as it can absorb (in practice, unlimited amounts). Thus, changes of 1 percent in per capita incomes are supposed to serve as bases for the most far-reaching policies when the statistics of those incomes are subject to errors of several hundred percent; and when these errors are compounded by the huge margins of error in estimates of population and population growth in underdeveloped countries. Quite apart from the other fundamental criticisms to which the suggestion of Professors Millikan and Rostow is subject, the notion that the increase in per capita national incomes in these countries can be assessed within 1 percent reveals total unfamiliarity with their conditions.

Substantially the same criticism applies to major recommendations of the *Report of the Commission on International Development* (Pearson Report), New York, 1969, which also proposes to link foreign aid to specified rates of growth of the national income of the recipients.

18. Quantification of the effects of age composition on differences in per capita incomes is difficult because of statistical and conceptual problems which

include among others the interrelations of differences in age composition with differences in the length and effectiveness of education and in the period over which the returns from education are enjoyed.

Some of these difficulties are discussed by Professor Anne Krueger in an important article "Factor Endowments and Per Capita Income Differences among Countries," *Economic Journal*, September 1968. Professor Krueger shows that in spite of a number of complications it can be established that differences in age composition explain an appreciable part of the differences in per capita incomes between the United States and some twenty underdeveloped countries examined in her article.

19. The technical reader will note that this conclusion applies whether average is interpreted as arithmetic mean, median or mode.

20. A bias which often overstates the material progress of underdeveloped countries needs to be briefly noted. Economic progress in poor countries is usually accompanied by a reduction in the importance of subsistence output, which is often undervalued in national income statistics. Accordingly, a relative growth in production for the market and a corresponding relative decline in subsistence production can overstate material progress. The bias is not significant over the periods considered in the text and does not invalidate its argument.

24. Is There a Tradeoff Between Growth and Basic Needs?

Norman L. Hicks

In Chapter 22, Fields argued that more attention needs to be paid to absolute poverty reduction if we truly wish to study the gap between rich and poor. In this chapter, Norman L. Hicks questions whether policies directed toward meeting basic human needs, and hence toward reducing absolute poverty, will result in slowed growth. In other words, are developing nations faced with a cruel choice between growth and basic needs? Hicks discusses the limitations of using the available data to answer this question, pointing out that many basic needs indicators are not sensitive to distribution questions, but merely report averages that can obscure important differences between rich and poor sectors of a population. Selecting life expectancy at birth and adult literacy as two reasonable measures of the progress of a nation in meeting basic human needs, he finds that meeting such needs actually contributes to growth, even among developing countries with good records in meeting basic needs but unexceptional growth rates. Although Hicks says that these conclusions are tentative and require better data for confirmation, the data presented make it seem reasonable to believe that the dual goals of absolute poverty reduction and economic growth are not incompatible. These findings, therefore, reinforce Fields's suggestion that the focus of research should be on the reduction of absolute poverty.

While the developing countries have had substantial increases in output during the past 25 years, it has been widely recognized that this growth has often failed to reduce the level of poverty in their countries. Various alternatives have been proposed to redress this problem—including strategies aimed at increasing employment, at developing rural areas, at redistributing the benefits of growth in favor of low income groups, and at meeting the basic needs of the poor. An approach that concentrates on meeting basic needs emphasizes improvements in health, nutrition, and basic education—especially through improved and redirected public services, such as rural water supplies, sanitation facilities, and primary schools. It has been argued that the direct provision of such goods and services affects poverty more immediately than those approaches that

Reprinted with permission from *Finance and Development*, vol. 17 (June 1980):17–20.

rely on raising the incomes and the productivity of the poor (see Paul Streeten's article, "From growth to basic needs," in the September 1979 issue of *Finance & Development*).

The critical question for the individual country is: Will the provision of basic goods and services slow down a country's growth rate? In other words, is there a tradeoff between growth and basic needs? From a theoretical standpoint there may be no necessary reason for such a tradeoff; but the evidence is not conclusive. Countries which have emphasized basic needs, such as Burma, Cuba, Sri Lanka, and Tanzania, may be seen to have done so at the cost of lower growth rates of output. On the other hand, one can point to countries such as Taiwan, Korea, and Singapore, which have both grown relatively rapidly and made commendable progress in providing social services, reducing poverty, and improving the distribution of income. The issue is complicated by the many factors which affect growth other than the elements emphasized in theory; that is, the allocations of national resources between savings and consumption or between social services and other "productive" sectors. The true impact of an investment program oriented toward basic needs thus becomes very difficult to evaluate.

The Debate

Proponents of a basic needs approach argue that the direct provision of essential goods and services is a more efficient and more rapid way of eliminating poverty than an approach based on hopes that the benefits of increased national growth will eventually reach the poor. While supporting efforts to raise productivity and income, they emphasize that these alone may be neither sufficient nor efficient. Their case rests on their experience that:

- the poor tend not to spend incremental income wisely or efficiently, since they may not be good managers or are not sufficiently knowledgeable about health and nutrition;
- there is serious maldistribution of incomes within households which cannot be overcome by raising family incomes but which can be corrected by the direct provision of goods and services to the neglected members;
- some basic needs—such as water supplies and sanitation—can only be met efficiently through public services; and
- it is difficult to formulate policies or investment strategies to increase the productivity of all of the poor in a uniform way.

The argument against directly providing for basic needs is based on two main contentions. First, transfers of essential goods and services result in increasing the consumption level of the poor at the cost of eventually reducing the net level of investment and saving in the economy and therefore the welfare of everybody. Second, the poor would be better provided for in the long run through the higher incomes realized by greater overall investment under a more conventional, growth-oriented development strategy. Meeting basic needs is seen as a strategy providing for a temporary consumption transfer to the poor, and not as a transfer of capital resources that would result in a permanent improvement in their condition.

The concept that basic needs can be better met in the long run through increased output appears faulty for two important reasons. First, the basic needs of the poor can be met in ways that have little or no direct effect on national levels of investment and growth—by reducing the consumption expenditures on nonessentials of the poor and the rich or by redirecting the expenditures of the public sector from nonbasic to basic needs activities. Second, it seems quite likely that expenditures on basic needs improve the productivity of human resources, and can therefore be considered a form of long-term investment in human capital. The question then becomes one of identifying the degree to which expenditures on basic needs actually result in permanent improvements in human capital, and whether economic returns to this form of human investment are higher than those from other kinds of investments available to developing countries.

Conflicting Evidence

There is a considerable body of literature which attempts to identify the economic returns from improvements in human capital. In developed countries, considerable attention has been given to the concept of "growth accounting." In this approach, the growth of total output (measured by gross national product [GNP]) is broken down into components relating to the growth of factor inputs (land, labor, and capital) and an unexplained "residual" which captures productivity changes of an unidentified origin. While the earliest efforts in growth accounting can be traced back to George Stigler (1947), the definitive work remains that of Edward Denison (1967, 1974, 1979).

Denison's latest estimates show that less than 60 percent of the growth in GNP in the United States can be attributed to the increase in traditional factor inputs—labor and capital primarily—while the re-mainder is the result of economies of scale, improvements in resource allocation, and a large residual attributed to human capital, which is labeled "advances in knowledge." Education is considered by Denison to be a factor input which alone accounts for 14 percent of the growth of GNP between 1929 and 1976. If education is combined with the residual advances in knowledge, then the contribution of human capital to growth would be about 38 percent. Attempts to apply the same technique to developing countries (Krueger, 1968) tend to show similar results.

There is some question, however, whether the residual can be attributed to improvements in the stock of human capital. It could represent errors in the calculations of other variables, the omission of other important factors, or simply a faulty assumption about the nature of the underlying production function. While growth accounting attributes an important role to human capital in explaining growth, it does not necessarily *prove* that human capital is important. Thus it is not a completely reliable way to measure the contribution of human capital to the growth process.

An alternative way of assessing the impact of improvements in human capital is to measure the rate of return from education. This can be done by estimating the lifetime earnings of people with various levels of education, compared to the private and social costs of education, which include earnings forgone while at school. In general, these kinds of studies have found high rates of return from investment in education particularly from primary education in developing countries. A survey of 17 developing countries by George Psacharopoulos (1973) found an average return of 25 percent for primary education. These returns range, however, from a low of 6.6 percent (Singapore, 1966) to a high of 82 percent (Venezuela, 1957).

There are considerable conceptual difficulties in measuring such rates of return on investments in human capital. The returns may be overstated because they capture the "screening" effect of higher education, which means that more highly educated people receive better paying jobs regardless of any true differentials in productivity. The high unemployment rate often found among highly educated people in some developing countries suggests that investments in education may not always raise productivity, particularly in those countries already possessing a large supply of educated persons. Several studies have questioned the utility of education investments in development. For instance, Héctor Correa (1970) found in a study of a group of Latin American countries that while health and nutrition were very important factors in GNP, improvements in education appeared to have no impact at all. M. Ishaq Nadiri (1972) concluded from a survey of the published literature that education was not very useful in explaining differences in growth rates between developing countries, although it did seem to explain variations in productivity within countries over time. Thus, the evidence on the role of human capital, particularly education, in affecting the growth of output in developing countries is not definitive or measurable. Furthermore, the concept of human capital improvements covers areas (higher education is an example) which are not considered to be as relevant to a basic needs approach, and vice versa.

Another way of measuring the importance of human capital is to look at the statistical correlations between the provision of basic needs and the growth rates in a large number of countries. The problem with simple correlations is that they cannot identify the links between basic needs that have been met and growth. Better provision of basic goods and services is just as likely to be a result of higher incomes, as its cause. At the same time, growth in income is clearly going to be affected by factors other than those related to the provision of basic needs. Thus, one has to isolate the meeting of basic needs from other factors which can be considered important determinants of growth, in order to avoid giving too much weight to the basic needs variables.

Measurement Problems

We have no easy measure, however, of progress in meeting basic needs. A variety of social indicators can be used, but using them often presents conceptual problems. Some indicators reflect results, while others—such as population per doctor and school enrollments—measure inputs. Some indicators measure the average level of social progress for the whole society, while others are based on a "have, have-not" principle. Thus, the percentage of households with access to clean water can accurately capture the numbers without such service. By contrast, an average of the calories consumed per capita as percent of requirements is quite misleading, since it combines the overconsumption of the rich and the underconsumption of the poor. Likewise, figures on average life expectancy, or average infant mortality, do not give us any idea of the range between the rich and the poor. Two countries with identical average statistics for infant mortality, for instance, could have quite different infant mortality rates for their least favored groups. It would be more useful if social indicators provided data separately for different income groups within a population. There is no reason why we could not construct distribution statistics for social indicators similar to our measures of income distribution.

Until better indicators are produced, however, we are forced to use what we have readily available. It seems appropriate to use life expectancy at birth as one crude measure of the effectiveness of a country's success in providing for basic needs. This single measure can encompass the combined effects on mortality of health care, clean water, nutrition, and sanitation improvements, although it is admittedly an average of country experience with no feel for how well these have been provided for different groups within the population. Progress in meeting needs for primary education can be measured by adult literacy—a better indicator than primary school enrollment, since it is oriented toward effects rather than efforts. These two indicators—life expectancy and adult literacy— give crude but fairly useful measures of progress in meeting basic needs. Both indicators are generally available for most developing countries on a fairly reliable basis, which is not true for some alternative measures, such as infant mortality.

But even if we use these selected social indicators to measure progress in meeting basic needs, the problem of identifying causality remains. Is the progress in meeting basic needs shown by these indicators a

Table 24.1
Economic Growth, Life Expectancy, and Literacy for Selected Countries

Country	Growth rate 1960-77[1] (in percent)	Life expectancy 1960 (in years)	Deviation from expected levels of life expectancy[2]	Adult literacy 1960 (in percent)	Deviation from expected levels of literacy, 1960[3]
Singapore	7.7	64.0	3.1	--	--
Korea	7.6	54.0	11.1	71.0	43.6
Taiwan	6.5	64.0	15.5	54.0	14.2
Hong Kong	6.3	65.0	6.5	70.0	6.4
Greece	6.1	68.0	5.7	81.0	7.5
Portugal	5.7	62.0	4.7	62.0	1.7
Spain	5.3	68.0	1.8	87.0	1.2
Yugoslavia	5.2	62.0	4.7	77.0	16.7
Brazil	4.9	57.0	3.0	61.0	8.6
Israel	4.6	69.0	2.0	--	--
Thailand	4.5	51.0	9.5	68.0	43.5
Tunisia	4.3	48.0	-0.5	16.0	-23.8
Average top 12 countries	5.7	61.0	5.6	64.7	12.0
Average all countries[4]	2.4	48.0	-.0	37.6	-.0

Source: World Bank, World Development Indicators, 1979.
1. Growth rate of real per capita GNP.
2. Deviations from estimated values derived from an equation where life expectancy in 1960 (LE) is related to per capita income in 1960 (Y) in the following way: LE = 34.29 + .07679 Y - .000043 Y^2 (R^2 = .66)
3. Deviations from estimated values derived from an equation where literacy in 1960 (LIT) is related to per capita income in 1967 (Y) in the following way: LIT = 9.23 + .1595 Y- .0000658 Y^2 (R^2 = .44)
4. Data for average growth rates and life expectancy refer to a sample of 83 countries, while that for literacy covers 63 countries.

result of growth in output, or is it one of the causes? One way to overcome this problem is to look at the data for growth rates of different countries compared to the levels of basic needs at the beginning of a particular period. If past achievements in meeting basic needs now require high levels of consumption expenditures, the data then should show that good basic needs performance has been associated with low growth. On the other hand, if provision of basic needs leads to an improvement in people's productivity, the indicators should show that basic needs are related to higher growth.

Comparative Evidence

The simplest way of identifying the relationship between the provision of basic needs and growth is to examine the record of countries that have grown very rapidly in the past and to compare their basic needs performance—measured by life expectancy and adult literacy—with that of the average country. Table 24.1 presents data for the 12 fastest growing countries between 1960 and 1977 (excluding the oil exporting countries and those with populations of under one million). The average per capita growth rate of these countries—5.7 percent per annum—was substantially higher than the average of all 83 countries in our sample. Further, the populations of this group of countries clearly had above-average life expectancy at the beginning of this period: 61 years, compared with an overall average of 48 years in all 83 countries.

This would seem to demonstrate that improving the provision of basic needs can augment the rate of growth. While this may be true, the data in the table contain a considerable bias. The countries that grew the fastest in the 1960–77 period were also countries which already had above-average levels of income. Since levels of income and life expectancy tend to be closely (but not perfectly) correlated, it is not surprising to find that the statistics for our 12 countries show above-average life expectancy.

To overcome this bias, an equation was established to relate life expectancy to income and to establish the "expected" level of life expectancy for every country. Better than normal performance on life expectancy could then be measured by the deviation between the actual and the expected levels. In a sense, this formula adjusts the level of life expectancy for the level of income. These deviations are shown in the third column of Table 24.1. The 12 countries in the sample have life expectancies that are, on average, 5.6 years higher than what normally would have been expected on the basis of their relative income level. Consequently, there does seem to be a positive association between life expectancy and growth, even when allowing for the fact that some of the more rapidly growing countries are also those at more advanced stages of development.

Adult literacy is another useful measure of a basic needs performance. Table 24.1 shows that in the rapidly growing countries, about 65 percent of adults were literate in 1960, compared with about 38 percent for the sample of 63 countries. Even when adjusted for income differences, literacy levels in the rapidly growing countries were about 12 percentage points higher than in the other countries at the beginning of the period.

The preceding analysis suggests that meeting basic needs may contribute significantly to growth, but it does not prove that the approach is a sufficient condition for high growth. In Table 24.2, we turn the question around and look at the 12 countries that have the highest deviation from expected levels of life expectancy. Many of the same countries shown in Table 24.1 appear here, namely, Taiwan, Korea, Thailand, Hong Kong, and Greece. In addition, there are a number of other countries which have done well in terms of life expectancy but have not had exceptionally high growth rates during the period, such as Sri Lanka, Paraguay, the Philippines, Burma, and Kenya. Nevertheless, the average growth rate for this second group of 12 countries—4.0 percent per annum—is still considerably higher than the average for the larger group.

Table 24.2
Growth and Life Expectancy, Selected Countries

Country	Deviation from expected level of life expectancy (in years)	Growth rate, 1960–77 (in percent)
Sri Lanka	22.5	1.9
Taiwan	15.5	6.5
Korea	11.1	7.6
Thailand	9.5	4.5
Malaysia	7.3	4.0
Paraguay	6.9	2.4
Philippines	6.8	2.1
Hong Kong	6.5	6.3
Panama	6.1	3.7
Burma	6.0	0.9
Greece	5.7	6.1
Kenya	5.5	2.4
Average, 12 countries	9.1	4.0
Average, all countries	0	2.4

Source: World Bank, World Development Indicators, 1979.
Note: For explanation of variables, see Table 24.1

One might argue, however, that the simple statistical analysis presented here is inadequate for drawing firm conclusions. The growth performance of countries is dependent on a variety of factors, such as the level of investment, export earnings and capital flows, and the general nature of development policies pursued.

The influence of these factors, as well as the emphasis on basic needs, can be combined and analyzed using multiple regression techniques on the cross-country data. This has been done for the period 1960–73 (see Hicks, 1979), regressing the growth rate of per capita GNP on the investment rate, the growth rate of imports, and the levels of either literacy or life expectancy in 1960. (The growth rate of imports combines the effects of export growth and capital flows.) This analysis concluded that the basic needs variables were significantly related to the growth rate, even after allowing for the influence of the other variables. It was found that countries which had life expectancies ten years higher than expected tended to have per capita growth rates 0.7 to 0.9 percentage points higher. Thus the more sophisticated techniques confirm the simpler ones shown here, which already concluded that those countries which do well in providing for basic needs tend to have better than average performance in terms of economic growth. This would also seem to suggest that a basic needs emphasis in development, far from reducing the rate of growth, can be instrumental in increasing it.

It would appear that economists who formerly focused on human capital may have concentrated too narrowly on one aspect of human capital, namely education. It seems possible that other aspects of a basic needs approach to development, which aim to improve the health and living conditions of the poor, should also be considered as building up a country's human capital. Exactly how health and related basic needs improvements help increase productivity and growth in the economy is difficult to pinpoint. The most obvious relationship is that healthy workers can produce more, work harder and longer, and so on. In addition, healthy students are apt to learn more. Improved health conditions reduce the waste of human and physical resources which results from the bearing and raising of children who die before they reach productive ages. The prospect of a short life expectancy reduces the potential gain from long years of schooling. These kinds of gains in productivity from investments in health and education are now being recognized as important as the returns from investments in the more standard forms of physical capital. In other words, investing in people may be a good way to both eliminate the worst aspects of poverty and to increase the growth rate of output.

Related Reading

M. S. Ahluwalia, and H. B. Chenery, "A Model of Distribution and Growth," in Chenery, et al., *Redistribution with Growth* (Oxford: Oxford University Press, 1974).

Mark Blaug, "Human Capital Theory: A Slightly Jaundiced Survey," *Journal of Economic Literature*, Vol. XIV (September, 1976), pp. 827–56.

Héctor Correa, "Sources of Growth in Latin America," *Southern Economic Journal*, Vol. 37 (July 1970), pp. 17–31.

E. F. Denison, *Why Growth Rates Differ: Postwar Experiences in Nine Western Countries* (Washington, D.C.: The Brookings Institution, 1967). *Accounting for United States Economic Growth, 1929–1969* (Washington, D.C.: Brookings Institution, 1974). *Accounting for Slower Growth* (Washington, D.C.: Brookings Institution, 1979).

Norman Hicks, "Growth vs. Basic Needs: Is There a Trade-Off?" *World Development*, Vol. 7 (November/December 1979), pp. 985–94.

Norman Hicks, and Paul Streeten, "Indicators of Development: The Search for a Basic Needs Yardstick," *World Development*, Vol. 7 (June 1979), pp. 567–80.

Anne O. Krueger, "Factor Endowments and Per Capita Income," *Economic Journal*, Vol. 78 (September 1968), pp. 641–59.

David Morawetz, *Twenty Five Years of Economic Development* (Washington, D.C.: The World Bank, 1977).

M. Ishaq Nadiri, "International Studies of Factor Imports and Total Factor Productivity: A Brief Survey," *Review of Income and Wealth*, Series 18 (June 1972), pp. 129–54.

George Psacharopoulos, *Returns to Education* (San Francisco/Washington: Jossey-Bass, 1973).

F. Stewart, and Paul Streeten, "New Strategies for Development: Poverty, Income Distribution and Growth," *Oxford Economic Papers*, 28 (1976).

G. J. Stigler, *Trends in Output and Employment* (New York, National Bureau for Economic Research, 1947).

Paul Streeten, "Basic Needs: Premises and Promises," *Journal of Policy Modeling*, 1 (1979), pp. 136–46.

Paul Streeten, and S. J. Burki, "Basic Needs: Some Issues," *World Development*, Vol. 6 (March 1978), pp. 411–21.

PART 4
CASE STUDIES AND
CONCLUSIONS

25. "Trickle-up" Income Redistribution and Development in Central America During the 1960s and 1970s

John A. Booth

In this case study, John A. Booth looks at the impact of foreign investment and economic growth on inequality in Central America. He briefly traces the economic history of the five nations that are the subject of his investigation, placing particular emphasis on the role of the Alliance for Progress and the Central American Common Market as stimulators of foreign investment and growth. In three of the countries, Booth is led to conclude, wealth was transferred out of the hands of the poor during the course of economic growth. In the other two, however, some redistribution in favor of the lower income sectors occurred. The principal difference between these two outcomes of development, argues Booth, is governmental policy. In those cases where the poor benefited from development, public policies had been implemented to promote that goal. Booth's evidence reinforces the argument made by Adelman and Taft in Chapter 15 that public policy can mitigate the pernicious impact of development on the poor. Moreover, it suggests that dependency does not invariably foster inequality, but only does so when governments do not implement redistributive programs. Finally, the chapter makes a direct connection between the exacerbation of inequality on the one hand and the social unrest, violence, and revolution that have emerged in the region on the other.

Latin America has been characterized by persistently high concentrations of income and wealth, and by limited transfers to the poor of the material gains of output growth. In a recent article, David Felix argues that development strategies that have relied on rapid industrial growth within free-market contexts to reduce inequality (i.e., to cause wealth to "trickle down") have generally failed. He attributes this failure to consumption patterns in Latin American culture that tend to increase rather than decrease inequality.[1] Only public policies of redistributive

---

This is an original contribution to this volume.

taxation and expenditure (such as practiced in the Southern Cone of South America and in Costa Rica) have succeeded in reducing income disparities.[2]

This chapter explores the impact of Central American economic development and growth stimulation policies as promoted by the Central American Common Market (CACM) and by the Alliance for Progress. It finds that the rapid economic growth achieved in several Central American economies since 1960 has actually caused income and wealth to trickle not down, but up—away from the poor—in both relative and absolute terms.

Introduction

Economic and political forces cannot be separated in Central America's developmental history. The five states of Central America share a historical experience that has given their economies common features and problems. When Mexico won independence in 1821, the five hastily formed Central American states declined to join the Mexican Empire and in 1823 formed the federated Central American Republic; but liberal-conservative strife over economic and political issues eventually destroyed the republic in the late 1830s. Militarized liberal and conservative elites then fought over political control of the separate states in subsequent decades. These partisan landed-elites from both parties continued the colonial-era practice of coercing Indians to produce agricultural or mineral resources. Central America has specialized in agricultural exports since the colonial era, but during the later nineteenth century, coffee became the major export for each nation in the region. The growth of coffee cultivation and export created new concentrations of both capital and political power for Central America's coffee barons.

Foreign investment in the banana industry came to most of Central America in the early twentieth century; other commodities (cacao, cotton, sugar, beef) also became or remained important. All of the region's export commodities were subject to great price swings on the international market, swings that brought Central America cyclical depressions that retarded both economic growth and the diversification of production. Industrialization was very slow, and class systems marked by extreme inequality developed and persisted in each Central American nation. National economic elites, aptly characterized as "reactionary despots,"[3] employed political and military power to maintain their privileged positions in Central America and (except in Costa Rica) tended to repress rather than to accommodate popular demands for reform.

Following World War II, a recovery of commodity prices spurred a vigorous capitalization of agriculture in each Central American nation. Both national and foreign investors stepped up the cultivation of grains for the Central American market and cotton for the international market.

Except for Honduras, where agrarian colonizations and expanding employment in the modern, capitalist sector of agriculture continued to absorb much of the agrarian labor force, by the end of the 1960s Central American nations had developed immensely expanded migrant wage-labor forces in agriculture and growing surpluses of rural labor.[4] Unemployable *campesinos* swelled cityward migration rates as the continued capitalization of agrarian production reduced the number of subsistence farms, reduced domestic food production, and greatly concentrated land ownership and agricultural production. National dependency on food imports rose regionwide, as did the number of citizens thus directly affected by imported inflation and changing import prices.

These unpropitious trends in agriculture were aggravated by rapid population growth throughout Central America, which led many observers to expect the region's poverty to worsen rather than to improve. Annual per capita income for the region as a whole was only about $250 in the late 1950s, barely two-thirds the average for Latin America overall. Pessimism about prospects for improvements in Central American economies and worries about the sociopolitical implications of such poverty grew among Central American political and economic leaders. These worries, however, coincided with the spread of a new developmentalist ideology among Central American policymakers. The new ideology promoted regional economic integration and rapid industrialization as tools for breaking out of the agro-export economic trap and for gradually increasing the wealth of the poor.

Worry turned to action when Fidel Castro's success in Cuba in 1959 and depressed export prices in the late 1950s spawned a wave of unrest in Central America. Confronted with the prospect of socialist revolution if they failed to act, Central American policymakers rather quickly decided that integration and industrialization were preferable, in terms of their own interests, to Castro's policies. Central America thus embarked, with the substantial aid of the U.S. Alliance for Progress, upon the promotion of economic integration and industrialization through the Central American Common Market.

From the outset CACM enjoyed strong U.S. support. Containment of communism had dominated U.S. policy toward Latin America since World War II and economic policy had received scant attention. But the shock of Castro's overthrow of Batista quickly brought economic matters quickly to the fore in U.S. Latin American policy. U.S. security interests were redefined to include the active promotion of capitalist economic development. Seeking, like Central American policymakers, to undermine the appeal of socialism to the poor, the alliance promoted heavy public and private investment to stimulate economic development and growth that would filter wealth down to the poor by expanding overall economic activity, employment, and markets.[5]

The Central American Common Market and Economic Growth

Formed in 1961, CACM reduced barriers to trade and investment within Central America and thus speeded up industrialization. Roughly $1.4 billion was invested in Central America between 1961 and 1969.[6] Throughout Central America much of the new domestic and foreign investment went into the capital-intensive production of consumer goods. Regionwide, foreign investment rose from $388.2 million in 1959, 3.8 percent in the manufacturing sector, to $755.3 million in 1969, 30.8 percent in manufacturing.[7] Foreign investment between 1959 and 1969 grew fastest in Nicaragua, where its absolute and relative presence had previously been the lowest in the region; foreign investment grew slowest in Guatemala and Honduras, where its absolute levels had previously been the highest. By 1969, foreign investment in manufacturing had risen greatly, rising from nominal levels in 1959 in every country to 11.2 percent in Honduras, 21.1 percent in Costa Rica, 38.1 percent in El Salvador, 43.6 percent in Guatemala, and 54.4 percent in Nicaragua.[8]

The effects of this investment surge were marked increases in Central American gross domestic products (GDPs) from the decades of the 1950s to the 1960s (see Table 25.1). Per capita changes in GDP also rose from an average annual increase of 1.7 percent from 1950–1961 to an average of 2.7 percent for the 1961–1972 period. The highest average rates of per capita GDP growth during the 1960s were in Nicaragua (3.5 percent), Guatemala, and Costa Rica (3.2 percent each); El Salvador (2.2 percent) and Honduras (1.4 percent) did less well. Guatemala and Costa Rica sustained their higher growth rates into the late 1970s (2.6 and 2.2 percent means per year, respectively); Nicaragua (0.6 percent per annum) and Honduras (0.4 percent per annum) performed poorly in the 1970s. Despite national differences, analysis of each of the five Central American nations reveals that manufacturing increased its share of overall economic activity, but that imported technology accounted for much of the growth in production.[9]

Impact of Growth on Income and Wealth Inequalities

Income

Studies of CACM's first decade reveal that capital-intensive investment in industry increased industrial employment opportunities only modestly in comparison to the rapid increase in the number of economically active people in Central America. Moreover, while productivity in the industrial sector rose sharply and contributed greatly to the overall growth of production registered during the decade, workers' real wages and their share of the increased production actually declined in all nations except Costa Rica.[10]

In 1973, the OPEC oil embargo and subsequent rapid escalation of oil prices caused a wave of inflation in consumer prices that continued

Table 25.1
Percent Growth in Per Capita Gross Domestic Product

Year	Costa Rica	El Salvador	Guatemala	Honduras	Nicaragua
Pre-CACM					
1950	-1.0	--	-3.0	0.5	13.6
1951	-2.4	-0.9	-1.9	2.7	3.8
1952	7.0	4.6	-1.2	1.1	13.9
1953	10.6	4.3	0.4	5.2	-0.6
1954	-4.3	-1.8	-1.4	-8.4	6.3
1955	6.5	2.2	-0.8	-0.1	3.7
1956	-8.0	5.0	5.8	5.4	-3.1
1957	3.4	2.4	2.3	1.9	5.4
1958	7.3	-0.7	1.4	0.5	-2.6
1959	0.2	1.6	1.6	-0.2	-1.5
1960	5.2	1.2	-0.9	3.0	-1.3
1961	0.7	-0.2	1.8	-0.6	4.8
CACM Era					
1962	2.6	8.3	1.0	2.6	8.2
1963	5.1	0.6	7.0	0.5	8.2
1964	1.4	5.6	2.1	2.0	9.0
1965	5.6	1.7	1.9	5.4	6.8
1966	4.3	3.4	3.0	2.6	0.6
1967	2.6	1.7	1.6	2.4	4.3
1968	4.2	-0.5	6.3	2.7	-1.4
1969	3.2	-0.2	2.2	-2.4	4.0
1970	4.1	-0.7	2.7	-1.1	-2.5
1971	4.1	1.5	2.6	0.1	1.4
1972	-1.7	2.6	4.3	0.2	0.3
1973	5.5	2.1	3.5	1.0	1.7
1974	3.0	3.5	3.1	-3.2	9.0
1975	-0.3	2.5	-1.2	-5.2	-1.1
1976	3.0	1.0	4.2	2.6	1.6
1977	6.3	2.8	4.6	2.0	2.8
1978	3.3	1.4	2.4	4.1	-10.2
1979	1.8	-5.9	1.9	1.4	-27.2

Source: James W. Wilkie and Stephen Haber, Statistical Abstract of Latin
America, Vol. 21 (Los Angeles: University of California Latin American
Center Publications, 1981), Table 22-3.

Table 25.2
Percent Change in Consumer Prices, 1963-1979

Year	Costa Rica	El Salvador	Guatemala	Honduras	Nicaragua
1963	3.0	.9	.1	2.9	.8
1964	3.3	1.8	-.2	4.6	9.6
1965	-.7	1.4[a]	-.7	3.2	3.9
1966	.2	-.9	.6	.2	3.9
1967	1.1	1.8	.5	1.2	1.6
1968	4.0	1.8	1.8	2.6	3.1
1969	2.8	3.2[a]	2.2	1.8	2.0[b]
1970	4.6	2.6	2.4	2.9	5.9
1971	3.1	.3	-.5	3.1	5.6
1972	4.6	1.7	.5	3.4	3.3[b]
1973	15.2	6.4	14.4	4.7	16.8[b]
1974	30.1	16.9	15.9	12.9	20.5[b]
1975	17.4	19.1	13.1	8.1	1.8
1976	3.5	7.0	10.7	5.0	2.9
1977	4.2	11.9	12.6	8.6	11.4
1978	6.0	13.3	7.9	5.7	4.6
1979	9.2	15.0	11.5	8.8	48.5

Source: Wilkie and Haber, op cit., Tables 2505, 2508, 2509, 2511, 2513.
a. Assigned mean value of other four nations as estimate.
b. Estimates based on Central Bank or other data; see John A. Booth, The End and the Beginning: The Nicaraguan Revolution (Boulder, CO: Westview Press, 1982).

throughout the decade (see Table 25.2). In Guatemala, for example, the average annual change in the consumer price index (CPI) from 1963 through 1972 was only 0.7 percent, but it zoomed to 12.3 percent annually for the 1973–1979 period. In Costa Rica for the same two periods, the CPI changes averaged 2.6 percent and 13.2 percent, respectively. Similarly drastic changes affected consumer prices in the other three Central American nations.

The effects of this inflationary spiral on workers' wages varied sharply within the region due to regime policy.[11] In all countries, real wages (wage rates in agriculture, construction, manufacturing, and communications and transportation, corrected for changes in consumer prices) declined because of the mid-1970s inflationary spiral (Table 25.3) or continued downward trends begun earlier. (Note that the values in Table 25.3 are index numbers for each nation; they are not comparable cross-nationally nor do they imply comparable purchasing power.) In the three countries with the most repressive labor policies, real wages eroded rapidly. The real wage decline in Guatemala was rapid and steady. In El Salvador and Nicaragua, real wages recovered somewhat in 1976,

Table 25.3
Real Working-class Wage Indices (1973=100)

Year	Costa Rica	El Salvador[a]	Guatemala[b]	Honduras[c]	Nicaragua[d]
1963	80	90	--	--	92
1967	--	105	112	--	137
1970	96	96	113	--	121
1971	107	94	115	--	119
1972	103	98	115	96	114
1973	100	100	100	100	100
1974	108	92	91	71	100
1975	91	90	84	82	106
1976	103	95	81	94	106
1977	113	88	78	88	97
1978	--	87	--	103	--

Based on Wilkie and Haber, op. cit., Tables 1400, 1401, 1402, 1403 and consumer price data in Table 25.2. Values of the indices represent an unweighted average of wages in manufacturing, construction, transport, storage and communication, and in agriculture, corrected for consumer price changes.

a. Includes wages in agriculture (mean for men and women), manufacturing, and construction.
b. Includes wages in manufacturing only.
c. Includes wages in manufacturing and construction only.
d. Includes wages in manufacturing, transportation (only), and construction.

then plunged again lower. Wages in El Salvador dropped still further in 1980 and 1981. Costa Rica, with its mildly redistributive social democratic policies, and Honduras, with a populist military regime and powerful labor unions, however, present a sharp contrast to the other three nations' real wage patterns. Despite early 1970s real wage declines, wages in the late 1970s recovered much of previous purchasing power.

Distribution of Compensation

During the 1970s, the CACM development model also brought increased income distribution inequality. One measure of income distribution within a society is the share of national income paid out as employee compensation, for which there are data on three nations. A decrease in the level of income paid as employee compensation indicates a shift of wealth away from salaried and wage-earning workers and toward investors and entrepreneurs.

In Costa Rica and Honduras from 1970 to 1975 employee compensation fluctuated somewhat, but overall remained relatively stable or tended to increase (Table 25.4). In contrast, Nicaraguan employee compensation

Table 25.4
Compensation of Employees as Percent of National Income[a]

Year	Costa Rica		Honduras		Nicaragua	
	Percent	Index	Percent	Index	Percent	Index
1962	45.0	100	46.2	100	57.5	100
1965	51.0	113	42.4	92	65.0	113
1967	52.2	116	41.8	90	65.3	114
1968	51.6	115	42.5	92	65.3	114
1969	51.3	114	42.0	91	65.6	114
1970	50.8	113	42.1	91	65.3	114
1971	52.0	116	43.7	95	65.5	114
1972	52.5	117	44.6	97	65.6	114
1973	49.4	110	45.0	97	69.7	121
1974	48.6	108	42.8	93	58.9	102
1975	49.8	111	--	--	59.1	103

Source: Wilkie and Haber, op. cit., Table 1404.
a. Base year of index is 1962.

dropped steeply in 1974. Although it is risky to estimate changes beyond our 1975 data, the working-class wage trends reported for Nicaragua for the late 1970s (Table 25.3) strongly suggest that employee compensation there most likely diminished still further. On the assumption that 1976–1979 real wage data for Costa Rica and Honduras (Table 25.3) also suggest trends in employee compensation, one can speculate that wage and salary earners in Costa Rica and Honduras at least held on to their extant share of the national income pie during the last years of the decade.

Wealth

Another measure of inequality involves the concentration of wealth. Though indices of wealth distribution are sadly imprecise,[12] partial data nevertheless suggest some clues.

During the 1960s, Nicaragua's three major capitalist factions, centered around the Banco de America, the Banco Nicaraguense, and the Somoza family interests, began to converge. Once clearly separate entities, these investor groups began to engage in joint ventures so that their distinctiveness declined rapidly during the first decade of the Common Market industrialization boom. They also prospered greatly, profiting from increasing worker productivity and from the Somoza regime's policy of depressing working-class wages and controlling labor unions. Following the 1972 Managua earthquake, however, the increasingly aggressive expansionism of the Somoza interests began to undermine the other investor groups' relative positions and profits by encroaching upon enterprises or economic sectors once reserved mainly to other capitalists. Anastasio Somoza Debayle's previously growing backing among the upper classes thus began to break down during the mid-1970s, and the development of a unified national bourgeoisie was arrested.

Nicaragua's middle class, beneficiary of a decade of improving economic status during the 1960s, suffered a sharp reversal in its status in 1973.[13] The Managua earthquake wiped out many small businesses and commercial jobs in the central *barrios* of the capital and markedly shrank middle-class employment opportunities. Those who remained employed found their salaries subjected to a stiff surtax for reconstruction and an increase in the work week by as much as 25 percent. Working-class groups also suffered declines in well-being. In the Nicaraguan agricultural sector, land concentration continued, especially in the country's populous Pacific zone, displacing subsistence cultivators into an already oversupplied wage-labor market and swelling the ranks of the rural and urban unemployed. Overall unemployment rates rose steadily in Nicaragua throughout the 1970s (Table 25.5), from less than 4 percent in 1970 to 13 percent in 1978. In sum, large numbers of Nicaraguans from the middle and lower classes suffered dramatic declines in their wealth, living conditions, and control over their economic well-being during the mid-1970s.[14]

In El Salvador during the 1970s, wealth also became more concentrated in fewer hands.[15] During the 1950s and 1960s much of the nation's best agricultural land had been converted to capital-intensive cultivation of export crops (in particular cotton) at the expense of access to land by subsistence tenants, squatters, and smallholders. The 1965 agricultural minimum wage law caused the number of *colonos* and *aparceros* (rural workers provided a plot of subsistence-cultivation land by their employers) to drop to one-third of 1961 levels by 1971, and the share of landless *campesinos* among rural Salvadorans to rise from 12 percent to 41 percent. In contrast, the coffee aristocracy, which had long dominated agriculture, both increased the size of its landholdings and its control over the fast-expanding industrial sector. The coffee barons invested in high technology, capital-intensive industries which generated enormous profits. Industrial workers' productivity grew rapidly while real industrial wages declined and new employment opportunities in manufacturing, albeit increasing, fell far behind the demand for new jobs. Unemployment in El Salvador thus rose during the 1970s, both in the countryside and in the cities.[16]

While the number of unemployed grew during the 1970s and Salvadoran workers' apparent share of the burgeoning national income and their real wages deteriorated, production and investment became more centralized. The coffee-growing elite had invested roughly four times

Table 25.5
Unemployment Trends (percentages)

Year	Costa Rica	Guatemala[a]	Honduras[b]	Nicaragua
1970	--	4.8	--	3.7
1971	--	--	8.8	3.6
1972	--	--	7.7	6.0
1973	--	--	7.4	9.1
1974	--	--	6.9	7.3
1975	--	--	9.7	--
1976	4.4	--	9.4	--
1977	4.7	--	8.9	13.0[c]
1978	4.6	--	9.2	20.0[c]
...				
1982	--	8.5	--	--

Source: Unless otherwise noted, data are drawn from Wilkie and Haber, op cit., Table 1308.

a. From data reported by the Guatemalan Ministry of Labor, cited in La Nación Internacional, 26 August-1 September, 1982, p. 12.
b. Figures given are based upon projections of economically active population from base years 1974 and 1977 (from Wilkie and Haber, Table 1301). Values are number of unemployed as percent of economically active population.
c. From Booth, op. cit.

as much in industry as any other Salvadoran group, and had attracted about 80 percent of the foreign capital invested in the country. Moreover, while the total output of Salvadoran industry more than doubled and the number of employees in industry doubled between 1967 and 1975, the number of firms actually producing diminished by as much as 10 percent. "The old saying that 'money follows money' was never truer than in El Salvador. . . . These investment patterns not only contributed to an ever greater concentration of wealth, but confirm that the traditional developmentalist assumption that wealth . . . will 'trickle down' in developing nations is groundless."[17]

Although data on Guatemalan wealth distribution are more difficult to obtain than for Nicaragua and El Salvador, certain inferences can be drawn from recent studies.[18] Land ownership in the densely populated northern and central areas of the nation as well as in the southern coastal plains became progressively more concentrated during the 1950s and 1960s.[19] Surplus agricultural population from the Indian highlands was absorbed by the dynamically expanding cotton industry in the south through the 1960s, but by the 1970s that region's capacity to absorb new workers diminished. In the late 1970s, then, Indian agrarian unemployment began to rise, and communally and privately held land in the Indian highlands was being taken over by Ladinos. The overall impact of this process of land concentration was the development of two migrant flows among the growing number of landless campesinos—to urban centers and to newly opened public lands in the Peten and Izabal. Numerous reports, however, suggest that many of the smallholders in Peten and Izabal have been dispossessed of their plots, especially by military officers and politicians who have amassed much land in these areas. The 1976 Guatemalan earthquake hit the Indian zones very hard, greatly harming the living conditions of thousands of rural poor.

Worker productivity in manufacturing in Guatemala has grown steadily since the 1950s, yet both real wages and the apparent working-class share of national income declined during the 1970s.[20] The main beneficiaries of increasing productivity have been both foreign and national capitalists. The ownership of industrial production in Guatemala has become steadily more concentrated among a decreasing number of large firms, while private-sector pressure groups' organization has become steadily more extensive and sophisticated. Capital-intensive industrialization has created far too few new jobs to absorb the growing number of workers, and in some industries modernization and concentration of ownership have actually displaced many workers. Unemployment roughly doubled from 4.5 percent in 1970 to 8.5 percent in 1982. In sum, broad sectors of Guatemala's working classes appear to have lost, both relatively and absolutely, income, wealth, and economic self-control.

Honduras and Costa Rica stand in sharp contrast to the marked increases in class inequality occurring in Nicaragua, El Salvador, and Guatemala during the 1970s. Although both nations were members of CACM and experienced the devastating effects of energy price increases in the mid-1970s, data reveal that these factors affected Honduran and Costa Rican distributions of income and wealth much less than in neighboring nations.

Costa Rica's social democratic political system and low military expenditures had permitted after 1948 the development of an extensive social welfare system that considerably eased the impact of inflation on popular living conditions. As noted, real wages were permitted by the government to recover in fairly short order from the energy-cost-driven inflationary spiral of the mid-1970s (Table 25.3). The distribution of income within Costa Rica actually became slightly *less unequal* during the 1970s (Table 25.4). Overall, a policy toward organized labor that was quite generous (in comparison to other Central American nations) plus redistributive and social welfare policies altered the flow of wealth so that both middle and lower sectors in Costa Rica were actually increasing their income share in the 1960s and 1970s.[21] In addition, unemployment levels in Costa Rica remained lower than in other Central American nations.

In Costa Rican agriculture, land concentration displacing smallholders took place rather steadily in the 1960s and early 1970s, but the availability of colonizable land until the late 1960s and the still growing banana industry absorbed much of the surplus agricultural work force. Moreover, during the 1974–1978 period Costa Rica developed an aggressive and successful land reform program that provided land to many rural dwellers and staved off the deterioration of living standards for many peasants.[22]

Honduras, the least successful in CACM, during the 1970s underwent wealth and income inequality increases far smaller than those affecting Guatemala, El Salvador, and Nicaragua.[23] Working-class wages largely recovered from inflation in the late 1970s, and income distribution, though fluctuating, did not markedly disfavor wage and salary earners. Indeed, there is evidence that the income distribution among wage and salary earners in the urban sector became slightly more egalitarian between 1950 and 1968. Unemployment appears to have cycled between about 9.5 percent and 7.5 percent several times between 1971 and 1978, but did not exceed that range (Table 25.5).

In Honduras, the growth of capitalist agriculture as an employment generator and the continued availability of colonizable agricultural land absorbed most of the surplus agricultural population until the early 1970s. Moreover, a major agrarian reform program was conducted during the 1970s:

> Government policies to redistribute farmland and colonize unoccupied areas have altered the face of Honduran agriculture and rural society during the last two decades. By the end of 1982, approximately 55,000 peasant families had been granted legal occupation of some 245,000 hectares . . . under a variety of reform measures. These totals represent roughly 14 percent of the country's rural population . . . and about 9 percent of its farmland.[24]

The Crisis of the 1980s

The Nicaraguan insurrection of 1977–1979 had several negative effects on CACM: It interfered with intraregional commerce, caused foreign investment to decline, initiated a process of capital flight that accelerated with the Sandinistas' 1979 victory over the Somoza regime, and sharply reduced tourism. Beginning in the late 1970s, then, production in Central America began to drop and by the early 1980s negative growth rates plagued El Salvador, Costa Rica, and Guatemala. Unemployment levels in most Central American countries increased sharply due to these production declines.

Added to these negative influences was a decline in coffee prices, the cruelest cut Central American economies could suffer. Severe shortages of foreign reserves and huge international debts forced Nicaragua to renegotiate its international loans in 1980. Similar difficulties caused a currency crisis and an 80 percent devaluation, foreign debt renegotiation, and a severe austerity program in Costa Rica in 1981, and edged Honduras toward comparable problems. El Salvador averted a currency-debt crunch only by dint of massive infusions of U.S. financial aid since 1980.

Despite years of accelerated industrialization in Central America, CACM had not created a strong economic infrastructure. The region continued to be highly dependent upon foreign capital and imported raw materials. Despite considerable industrialization, CACM economies remained commodity-price dependent and suffered from extreme vulnerability to external factors beyond their control. "The common market project never went beyond . . . being a free trade zone, and also failed . . . to achieve productive integration."[25] Central American countries thus entered the 1980s in the grip of a severe economic crisis that appeared would worsen substantially before improving.

Conclusions

The CACM-Alliance for Progress development model brought Central American nations massive amounts of new investment during the 1960s and 1970s, but created import-dependent, capital-intensive manufacturing that failed to absorb a rapidly growing labor supply. In Costa Rica and Honduras, with mildly redistributive public policies and available agricultural land and agrarian employment, some trickling down of wealth to the lower classes was induced. However, where policymakers combined free-market capitalism with repressive labor policies, as in Nicaragua, Guatemala, and El Salvador, wealth was redistributed in favor of the wealthy.

> The social costs of the process defy quantification. . . . Underemployment and low incomes translate into the perpetuation and even deterioration of truly deplorable living conditions. The real results of integration are found in . . . infant mortality, malnutrition, the extremely slow decline in illiteracy, the accelerated increase in underemployment, deterioration in housing, lack of opportunities for getting ahead, and last, even the actual physical degradation of the population.[26]

Two decades of the Common Market integration-industrialization development model brought Central American nations rapid growth but little real or positive development. Albeit more productively diversified, the Central American economies remain highly vulnerable to external economic forces. The working classes (except in Costa Rica and perhaps Honduras) are both relatively and absolutely worse off than before integration began. Moreover, the increasing impoverishment of much of the Central American populace has been linked to recent high levels of popular frustration in Nicaragua, El Salvador, and Guatemala.[27] The political turmoil and revolutionary movements that this frustration has engendered, ironically, are the products of the very developmental model

364	John A. Booth

adopted by Central American policymakers in order to forestall revolutionary pressures.

Notes

1. David Felix, "Income Distribution and the Quality of Life in Latin America: Patterns, Trends, and Policy Implications," *Latin American Research Review* 18 (no. 2, 1983):3–34.
2. Ibid., 3; Edelberto Torres Rivas, "The Central American Model of Growth: Crisis for Whom?," in Stanford Central America Action Network, ed., *Revolution in Central America*, Boulder, Colo.: Westview Press, 1983, 140–153.
3. Enrique A. Baloyra, "The Deterioration and Breakdown of Reactionary Despotism in Central America," paper presented at the 44th International Congress of Americanists, Manchester, England, September 6–10, 1982.
4. Daniel Camacho et al., *El fracaso social de la integración centroamericana*, San José, Costa Rica: Editorial Universitaria Centroamericana, 1979, passim.
5. James W. Wilkie, "The Alliance for Progress and Latin American Development," in *Statistics and National Policy: Supplement 3 (1974), UCLA Statistical Abstract of Latin America*, Los Angeles: UCLA Latin American Center, 1974, 409–431.
6. Rafael Menjívar, "Prólogo," in Rafael Menjívar, ed., *La inversión extranjera en Centroamérica*, San José, Costa Rica: Editorial Universitaria Centroamericana, 1974, 14–15.
7. Ibid., 15.
8. Ibid., 16.
9. Camacho et al., *El fracaso social de la integración centroamericana*, passim.
10. Ibid.
11. Note that the indices for wages are not identical across national lines, nor are they fully representative of all wages and salaries. See the details in Table 25.3. Unfortunately Central American nations report such data in different ways—if at all.
12. Some Central American governments, including El Salvador and Guatemala, often do not publish key socioeconomic or political data that reflect badly upon a regime. Data resources from Guatemalan censuses remain very limited.
13. John A. Booth, *The End and the Beginning: The Nicaraguan Revolution*, Boulder, Colo.: Westview Press, 1982, Chapters 5–6.
14. Data drawn mainly from Ibid.; and Mario A. de Franco and Carlos F. Chamorro, "Nicaragua: Crecimiento industrial y desempleo," in Camacho et al., *El fracaso social de la integración centroamericana*, 94–133.
15. Data drawn mainly from Tommie Sue Montgomery, *The Salvadoran Revolution: Origins and Evolution*, Boulder, Colo.: Westview Press, 1982, passim; and James Dunkerley, *The Long War: Dictatorship and Revolution in El Salvador*, London: Junction Books, 1982, 87–118.
16. See also Hugo Milina, "Las bases económicas del desarrollo industrial y la absorción de fuerza de trabajo en El Salvador," in Camacho et al., *El fracaso social de la integración centroamericana*, passim.
17. Montgomery, *The Salvadoran Revolution*, 94–95.
18. See Thomas P. Anderson, *Politics in Central America: Guatemala, El Salvador, Honduras, and Nicaragua*, New York: Praeger Publishers, 1982, 19–67; *Mesoamérica*, May 1982.

19. Richard Hough et al., *Land and Labor in Guatemala: An Assessment*, Washington, D.C.: Agency for International Development-Development Associates, 1982, passim.

20. Gustavo A. Noyola, "Integración centroamericana y absorción de mano de obra en Guatemala," in Camacho et al., *El fracaso social de la integración centroamericana*, 276–319.

21. Menjívar et al., *La inversión extraniera en Centroamérica*, passim; Daniel Camacho "Integración centroamericana y desempleo: El caso de Costa Rica," in Camacho et al., *El fracaso social de la integración centroamericana*, 21–94.

22. Mitchell A. Seligson, *Peasants of Costa Rica and the Development of Agrarian Capitalism*, Madison: University of Wisconsin Press, 1980, 122–170; Francisco Barahona Riera, *Reforma agraria y poder político*, San José, Costa Rica: Editorial Universidad de Costa Rica, 1980, 221–422.

23. José Rafael del Cid, "Honduras: Industrialización empleo, y explotación de la fuerza de trabajo," in Camacho et al., *El fracaso social de la integración centroamericana*, 134–200; Anderson, *Politics in Central America*, 109–135; and *Mesoamérica*, nos. 1–5, 1981–1982.

24. Douglas Kincaid, "Honduras: Rural Politics and Agrarian Reform," *Mesoamérica* (May 1983): 7.

25. Torres Rivas, "the Central American Model," 151.

26. Ibid., 151.

27. John A. Booth, "Toward Explaining Regional Crisis in Central America: The Socioeconomic and Political Roots of Rebellion," paper presented to the 44th International Congress of Americanists, Manchester, England, September 6–10, 1982.

26. Sugar Dependency in Cuba: Capitalism versus Socialism

John T. Smith

According to many theorists, one of the clearest manifestations of dependency is a concentration on agricultural exports. In many ways Cuba represents the archetypical case; for most of this century Cuban sugar exports have dominated that nation's economy, an economy in which slow growth and a yawning gap between rich and poor seemed like parts of an unalterable pattern. Fidel Castro's coming to power resulted in a dramatic reduction of income inequality. It has not, however, according to John T. Smith, reduced dependency. Smith argues that in terms of the income derived from the export of sugar, Cuba was probably better off when its trade was with the capitalist economies than today, when most of its sugar goes to socialist economies. The dramatic reduction in income inequality, as well as other changes in the economy of Cuba, cannot therefore be attributed to a reduction of dependency, but rather to internal policy decisions made by Castro. It could be argued that even though trade with the socialist powers is not necessarily more profitable, nations that have joined the socialist orbit seem able to escape from the income inequality effects of dependency whereas those nations remaining within the capitalist orbit cannot. This hypothesis can be tested with reference to the Taiwanese case reported on in Chapter 27.

Many critics of capitalism have argued that developing nations experience slowed economic growth and exacerbated income inequality as a result of their dependency on the world capitalist system. Dependent capitalist development is seen as having particularly pernicious effects on the monoculture export economies of the tropics. These critics also argue that socialist economies operate in a fundamentally different fashion from capitalist ones in that they place human concerns above industrial expansion; socialism, unlike capitalism, is not a system in which each side of the worker-manager conflict is conditioned by the struggle of one over the other. Developing nations that are tied to socialist rather than capitalist powers are seen, from this perspective, as largely removed from the exploitative effects of capitalist dependency. As such, these

---

This is an original contribution to this volume.

countries are likely to experience rapid growth and reduced income inequality.

Although numerous statistical studies have been conducted on cross-section data gathered to test the above propositions, some of which have been included in this volume, these studies face numerous problems in their attempts to control extraneous factors which may influence the results. Rarely do researchers have the opportunity to control for virtually all the relevant factors and focus exclusively on the impact of socialism versus capitalism on growth and inequality. Fortunately, the case of Cuba offers one such opportunity because it is possible to compare capitalist Cuba with socialist Cuba.

Surprisingly, despite the wealth of research that has been conducted on Cuba since the 1959 Revolution, most scholars seeking to test dependency theory have not sought to use the Cuban case as a test. The one major exception is William LeoGrande's (1980) seminal study. LeoGrande's (1980:10) evidence led him to conclude that owing to the "nonmarket character of trade relations within the socialist camp," Cuba has benefited materially from its shift out of the capitalist orbit. He suggested that there was a fundamental difference between capitalist and socialist trade relations. In a capitalist market, "dependency of an economy on foreign trade makes it vulnerable to external economic forces because domestic actors have no control over the size of their markets or the world prices of their export commodity. Monoculture accentuates that vulnerability by tying the health of the economy to the market fluctuations" (LeoGrande, 1980:10).

Cuba's dependency has been altered in a number of key respects according to LeoGrande. First, socialist trade differs from capitalist in that the export volume and price are set by negotiation rather than market forces. Second, "Cuba has also had the added advantage of the Soviet Union's willingness to pay premium prices for Cuban sugar, and to reopen trade when the world market price of sugar has increased substantially over the price being paid by the USSR" (LeoGrande, 1980:11). Third, Cuba has reduced its trade dependency, because trade as a proportion of the Cuban economy has declined. Fourth, there has been an improvement in trade composition; whereas, in the past Cuba's trade was almost exclusively sugar, or sugar-related, since the revolution this pattern has been altered. Fifth, Cuba no longer relies so heavily on one partner for trade, as it did when it was dependent upon the United States. Finally, Cuba's greatest success in altering the pernicious pattern of dependency, according to LeoGrande, has been in the area of direct foreign investment (DFI), which prior to socialism in Cuba signified the ownership of the means of production by foreigners: "The difference . . . is that while U.S. DFI meant U.S. ownership of key economic sectors in Cuba, investment aid from the Soviet Union does not result in Soviet ownership" (LeoGrande, 1980:18).

In examining this argument by LeoGrande, I will make a comparison of U.S.-Cuban trade and Soviet-Cuban trade. The argument of this chapter will be developed on two interrelated levels. At the international level, I will compare socialist and capitalist markets, as well as the potential income derivable from Cuban sugar trade. Then I will briefly discuss the issues of diversification, Cuban foreign debt, and trade partner concentration.

The International Level

Capitalist Trade

The United States preferential sugar market was created in an attempt to stabilize the price the United States paid for sugar. It was designed to guarantee a sugar supply "at prices reasonable to consumers and fair to producers" (Tacke, 1968:167). This was to be accomplished by establishing quotas and quota prices.

The pricing procedure consists of several steps. Basically, each year the U.S. Secretary of Agriculture estimates how much sugar the United States will consume in the following year. Then, 55 percent of this figure is designated to be produced domestically, while the remaining 45 percent is divided by a set formula among the United States' foreign suppliers. The foreign suppliers are paid at prices arrived at by the Secretary of Agriculture (Grissa, 1976:83), which are normally well above the world market price.

In order to ensure its supply of sugar, the U.S. created a penalty for failure to fill quotas:

> When in any year any foreign country with a quota or proration thereof more than 10,000 short tons fails to fill its quota by more than 10 percent, and at any time during such year the world price of sugar exceeds the domestic price, the quota or proration thereof for such country for subsequent years shall be reduced by an amount equal to the unfilled quantity. [Tacke, 1968:168.]

Since the U.S. sugar import price averaged above the world market price during the 1945–1975 period, nearly all import quotas have been filled. Between 1948 and 1973, the world price topped the U.S. price only three times. During this same period, the world price averaged only 69.8 percent of the United States' subsidized price. Even when the world price rose above the U.S. price most producers realized that it was not in their best interest to jeopardize their U.S. quota; the profits gained during a short period when the world price surpassed the U.S. price were lost many times over when the world market returned to normal (i.e., the world price falls below the U.S. price).

Socialist Trade

By 1961 the Soviet Union had replaced the United States as Cuba's main trading partner. The Soviet decision to import vast quantities of

Cuban sugar was based on political rather than economic considerations. One need only consider that many of the COMECON (Soviet bloc) countries were, and many continue to be, net exporters of sugar and often *re-export* the Cuban imports at a substantial loss.[1]

In spite of the political nature of trade relations between Cuba and the USSR, the former is not freed from the fluctuations of the world price of sugar. This comes as a direct result of the agreement by which trade was, and is, conducted between the Cubans and Soviets. The agreement states that 20 percent of the Cuban sugar imported by the Soviets is to be paid in U.S. dollars and the remaining 80 percent in Soviet products (Grissa, 1976:32). This means that in order for Cuba to obtain sufficient dollar currency, it needs to sell its sugar on the world market.

The data presented in Figures 26.1 and 26.2 demonstrate the sensitivity of Cuba's sugar exports to the world price. Point A on Figure 26.1 shows that in 1966 when the world market price of sugar was 1.86 cents per pound and the Soviet price was 6.17 cents per pound the Cubans had a large proportion of their trade with the socialist bloc and a small proportion of trade with the world market. Point B on Figure 26.1, in contrast, shows that in 1974 when the world market price increased to 29.96 cents per pound and the Soviet price was only 19.70 cents per pound, trade between Cuba and the socialist blocs moved lower while trade with the market economies moved higher.

A curious side effect of Cuba's continued dependency upon the fluctuating world sugar market is that the Soviet Union itself is in part responsible for the continued disparity between the U.S.-USSR support prices and the world price. This comes about as a result of the re-exportation of Cuba's sugar from the COMECON countries. For example, during the 1966–1970 period, COMECON countries plus China re-exported to the world market about 52 percent of the sugar they imported from Cuba. Since the world market is not a preferential market, supply and demand sets the prices; thus when large volumes of Cuban sugar are re-exported or made available on the world market to obtain convertible currency, world prices are driven down by the re-exportation of Cuba's own sugar by its socialist trading partners.

Potential Income Derivable from Sugar Trade

It has been shown that the Cuban economy, despite having severed its dependency relationship with the U.S., is still sensitive to the capitalist world market price of sugar. The central issue, according to LeoGrande, is the purported advantage to Cuba from shifting the bulk of its trade from the capitalist to the socialist countries. Does such an advantage really exist? To determine this, I calculated a "potential value" for Cuba's sugar crop; the quantity of sugar produced/exported multiplied by the dollar equivalent price per metric ton for both the U.S. and the Soviet preferential market.

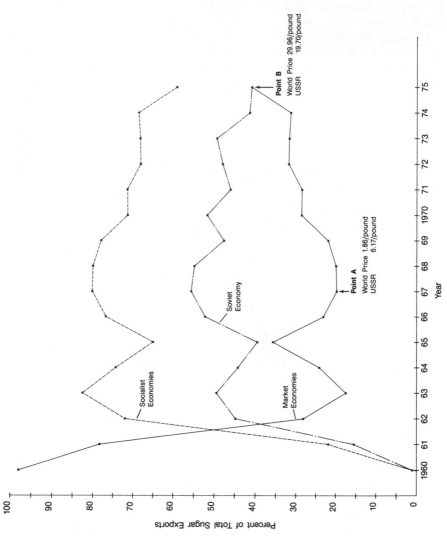

Figure 26.1 Sugar exports to market and socialist economies.

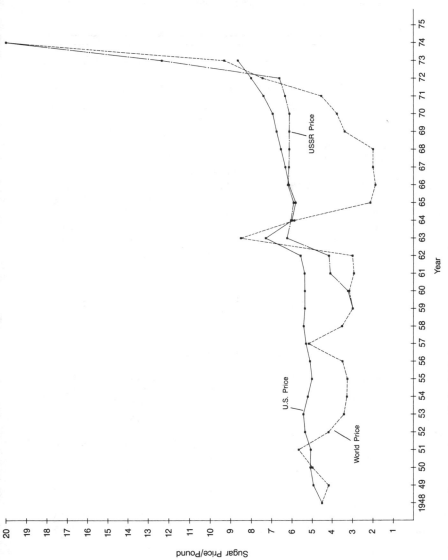

Figure 26.2 Sugar prices, 1948–1975 (in cents per pound).

Table 26.1
Potential Income Derivable from Sugar Trade with the Soviet Union and the United States

Year	Sugar Produced (1000s m.t.)	Sugar Exported (1000s m.t.)	Price (dollars) per metric ton of sugar	Potential value of total crop*	Potential value of exports*
			Exports to the United States		
1948	6353	5521	$102.29	$649.85	$564.74
1949	6752	4638	108.91	735.36	505.12
1950	6997	4818	112.21	785.13	540.63
1951	8776	5116	111.77	980.89	571.82
1952	6267	4716	117.95	739.19	556.25
1953	6030	5113	119.71	721.85	612.08
1954	5511	3947	114.86	632.99	453.35
1955	5762	4392	110.23	635.15	484.13
1956	6890	5059	112.43	774.64	568.78
1957	7105	5084	116.84	830.15	594.01
1958	7301	5234	119.27	870.79	624.26
Totals	73744	53638	$113.31	$8355.99	$6075.17
			Exports to the Soviet Union		
1962	4641	6233	$91.27	$423.58	$568.89
1963	4849	4277	139.40	675.95	596.21
1964	6832	5073	133.16	909.75	675.52
1965	5455	6457	130.07	709.53	839.86
1966	6832	4435	136.02	927.29	603.25
1967	6061	5683	135.36	820.42	769.25
1968	5730	4613	134.92	773.09	622.39
1969	10365	4799	134.92	1398.40	647.48
1970	7196	6906	134.70	968.63	931.76
1971	5330	5511	137.35	732.08	756.94
1972	5716	4140	145.72	832.94	603.28
Totals	69007	58127	$132.08	$9173.66	$7614.83

* Millions of U.S. dollars.

During the period 1948–1958, when Cuba was dependent upon the U.S. for the bulk of its sugar sales, the "potential value" of the total Cuban crop was $8.4 billion (See Table 26.1). The "potential value" of Cuban sugar exports for that same period was $6.1 billion. Hence, during the pre-socialist period of Cuban history there is clear evidence that Cuban trade dependency on the U.S. yielded substantial dividends for the island.

What of the socialist period? The potential income the Cubans could have received from the Soviets for their total sugar production during the years 1962 until 1972 was $9.2 billion, and the potential income for their exported sugar was $7.6 billion. The average Soviet price (in U.S. dollars) per metric ton over this period was $132.08. As these data show, Cuba had a potential earnings of $.8 billion more under the Soviets in the 1967–1972 period than it had when it was dependent on the U.S. during the 1948–1958 period, or a difference of 9.5 percent. This potential higher earnings must be considered, however, in light of a drop in the world market price (averaged over the two time periods) of 2 percent.

Even this comparison is strained, however, because of the differing time periods under consideration. A more meaningful comparison emerges from Table 26.2, which employs the Cuban sugar production figures from 1962 until 1972 and calculates the potential income derivable by the Cubans if they had traded with the U.S. rather than the Soviets. The assumption here is that the United States would have paid the Cubans the same amount that it did to those who replaced Cuba in the U.S. preferential sugar market. The average price per metric ton, paid by the U.S., was $145.53. The potential value of Cuba's entire sugar crop would have been $10 billion, and the potential value of exports would have been $8.4 billion. Had Cuba, during this same period, been able to sell its entire crop to the Soviet Union at the Soviet preferential market price as was shown in Table 26.1, the total income to Cuba would have been $9.2 billion or $800 million *less than it would have received from the U.S.* Making the same assumptions, the potential income of Cuba's exports to the Soviets would have totaled $7.6 billion dollars vis-à-vis $8.4 billion if sold to the U.S., yielding an $800 million dollar loss to Cuba.

The relevance of these calculations becomes clearer when they are placed within the context of the economy as a whole. During the 1962–1972 period, Soviet sugar trade could have potentially accounted for a 2.8 percent average yearly increase in Cuba's gross national product,[2] while trade with the U.S. could have accounted for a 3 percent increase. The net difference to Cuban growth, therefore, was very small (.2 percent annually). Consequently, even if the calculations presented above contain inaccuracies or faulty assumptions, it is difficult to see how a significant reversal of the findings reported could have had a substantial impact on Cuba's growth. LeoGrande's optimism regarding the value of socialist trade seems unwarranted.

Table 26.2
Potential Income Derivable from Sugar Trade with the United States

Year	Sugar Produced (1000s m.t.)	Sugar Exported (1000s m.t.)	Price (dollars) per metric ton of sugar	Potential value of total crop*	Potential value of exports*
		"Exports" to the United States			
1962	4641	6233	$123.46	$572.98	$769.53
1963	4849	4277	160.28	777.20	685.52
1964	6832	5073	131.84	900.73	668.82
1965	5455	6457	127.87	697.53	825.66
1966	6832	4433	132.94	908.25	589.59
1967	6061	5683	139.33	844.48	791.81
1968	5730	4613	144.18	826.15	665.10
1969	10365	4799	148.81	1542.40	714.14
1970	7196	6906	153.00	1101.00	1056.60
1971	5335	5511	162.92	868.36	897.85
1972	5716	4140	176.15	1006.90	729.26
Totals	69007	58127	$145.53	$10045.98	$8393.88
		Exports to the Soviet Union			
1962	4641	6233	$91.27	$423.58	$568.89
1963	4849	4277	139.40	675.95	596.21
1964	6832	5073	133.16	909.75	675.52
1965	5455	6457	130.07	709.53	839.86
1966	6832	4435	136.02	927.29	603.25
1967	6061	5683	135.36	820.42	769.25
1968	5730	4613	134.92	773.09	622.39
1969	10365	4799	134.92	1398.40	647.48
1970	7196	6906	134.70	968.63	931.76
1971	5330	5511	137.35	732.08	756.94
1972	5716	4140	145.72	832.94	603.28
Totals	69007	58127	$132.08	$9173.66	$7614.83

* Millions of U.S. dollars.

Other Areas of Dependency

Although diversification of production, the foreign debt, and trade partner concentration were not emphasized in this study, it would be helpful to briefly discuss each of these areas. The general concensus is that in order for Cuba to reach self-sustained growth, it will need to diversify its economy away from sugar. As is the case with all developing nations, Cuba needs to increase hard currency income, but if it wants to break its dependency, it must be able to control its foreign debt. In addition, Cuba, in its quest for economic and political independence, should not rely on one country for trade as overreliance on one nation for trade can be tantamount to surrendering a degree of sovereignty.

Diversification

One of Castro's goals was to eliminate sugar monoculture through rapid industrialization and agricultural diversification (Mesa-Lago, 1981:47). To achieve this goal, the Cuban government nationalized the means of production and reduced the amount of cultivated land by 25 percent. However, the reduced revenue from a smaller sugar crop was not made up for by other sectors and the entire economy shrank. The end result was that Cuba's heavy dependence on sugar continued after the revolutionary government took power.

Cuba's failure to diversify becomes painfully clear when studying the distribution of their exports. Over the period 1957–1976, sugar averaged 82 percent of Cuba's exports; tobacco, 5 percent; minerals, 8 percent; and other products including seafoods, fruit, and rum, 5.3 percent (Mesa-Lago, 1981:83). Sugar as a percentage of exports fluctuated a bit, but for the most part, its percentage was not reduced from pre-revolutionary levels.

Foreign Debt

Under U.S. "guidance," the Cuban economy was to grow at a very slow pace, but to those given to optimism, there were signs of hope. Cuban cities, such as Havana, where U.S. investment and technology transfers helped sustain growth, did develop into modern industrial cities. But these cities were growing on investments from foreign countries, mainly the United States; in 1959, Cuba's foreign debt stood at about $45 million.

For the first few years the new government, with Soviet aid, tried desperately to break the island's dependency on sugar. The Soviet Union spent enormous sums of money trying to aid Cuba in this effort, but the final outcome was a decision to reemphasize sugar. During this period, the foreign debt grew to about $6 billion. "The anti-sugar-pro-diversification strategy of the early stages of the revolution, combined with other factors, provoked a sharp decline in sugar output in 1962–1963, which in turn rapidly expanded the balance of trade deficit and made unfeasible the ambitious program of industrialization" (Mesa-Lago, 1981:18).

Trade Partner Concentration

During the period 1945 to 1975, Cuba remained the largest exporter of sugar in the world. From 1950 to 1959, 53.6 percent of Cuba's sugar was traded with the United States. More importantly, 73 percent of Cuba's total trade was conducted with the U.S. Few dispute the fact that Cuba was deeply dependent on the United States.

From 1961 to 1975, Cuba's main trading partner was the Soviet Union. During this period, an average of 39.6 percent of Cuba's sugar exports were traded with the Soviets. Over the same time period, the Soviet Union accounted for an average of 48 percent of Cuba's total trade. LeoGrande suggested that because the percentages are smaller than when Cuba traded with the U.S. that Cuba is less dependent now. But the trade conducted between Cuba and the COMECON countries, the Soviet Union included, averaged 71.8 percent. As was previously mentioned, many of the COMECON countries were, and are, sugar exporters. COMECON importation of Cuba's sugar reflects a Soviet attempt to minimize its losses by spreading them out among the members rather than an effort to diversify trade partner concentration. Thus, this trade should be counted together.

Conclusion

Dependency theory's assertion that there is a fundamental difference between capitalist and socialist trade has not been sustained. This discussion has shown that Cuba's dependency on sugar has not been reduced, and, perhaps more importantly, it has contradicted the frequently made assertion by dependency thinkers that there is a qualitative difference in capitalist and socialist trade relations. Specifically, I have not uncovered evidence to support the notion that the Cubans are materially better off exporting their sugar to socialist rather than capitalist countries.

Cuba has made major strides in its social development since joining the socialist camp. Improvement in education, social security, housing, health care, etc., has been well documented (Mesa-Lago, 1981). However, Cuba's advances in these and other areas cannot be attributable to increased income from sugar trade. Rather, they seem much more clearly a function of policy decisions made by Fidel Castro. These improvements cannot be dismissed lightly, as they have resulted in major improvements in the lives of the Cuban people. However, the benefits are not, it would appear, a result of Cuba's severance of ties with the capitalist countries, but a result of domestic policies, and to some extent, cold war politics.

Notes

1. G. B. Hagelberg, in an article entitled "Cuba's Sugar Policy," described Cuba's trade with the COMECON countries in the following manner: "This accommodation was all the more remarkable because Eastern Europe presented no natural outlet for Cuban sugar at that point. Czechoslovakia and Poland were and still are net exporters every year. . . . Bulgaria was a net exporter from 1955–1960. . . . An excellent harvest in Cuba in 1961 provided enough sugar to raise total exports to a record level, not surpassed until 1970, and the amount purchased by socialist countries in 1961 in fact greatly exceeded the amount previously purchased by the United States in any one year."

2. This potential annual increase was calculated using Cuba's last reported GNP from 1959.

References

Brunner, Heinrich. *Cuban Sugar Policy from 1963 to 1970.* Pittsburgh: University of Pittsburgh Press, 1977.

Cuban Economic Research Project of the University of Miami, Florida. Coral Gables, Fla.: University of Miami Press, 1965.

Emery, Walter (ed.). Commodity Yearbook. New York: Commodity Research Bureau, Inc., 1980.

Grissa, Abdessatar. *Structure of the International Sugar Market.* Paris: Organization for Economic Cooperation and Development, 1976.

Guevara, Ernesto. *Venceremos: The Speeches and Writings of Ernesto Che Guevara,* John Gerassi (ed.). New York: The Macmillan Co., 1968.

Hagelberg, G. B. "Cuba's Sugar Policy." In Martin Weinstein (ed.) *Revolutionary Change in the World Arena.* Philadelphia: Institute for the Study of Human Issues, 1979.

Horowitz, Irving Louis. *Cuban Communism.* London: Transaction Books, 1981.

Illan, Jose. *Cuba: Facts and Figures of an Economy in Ruins.* Miami, 1964.

Johnson, D. Gale. *The Sugar Program.* Washington, D.C.: American Enterprises for Public Policy Research, 1974.

LeoGrande, William. "Cuban Dependency: A Comparison of Pre-Revolutionary and Post-Revolutionary International Economic Relations." *Cuban Studies/ Estudios Cubanos* 9, No. 2 (July 1980):1–28.

Mesa-Lago, Carmelo. "Availability and Reliability of Statistics in Socialist Cuba." *Latin American Research Review* 4 (Spring/Summer, 1969).

_____. "Cuban Statistics Revisited." *Cuban Studies/Estudios Cubanos* 9 (July 1979).

_____. *The Economy of Socialist Cuba: A Two-Decade Appraisal.* Albuquerque: University of New Mexico Press, 1981.

Nelson, Lowry. *Cuba: The Measure of a Revolution.* Minneapolis: University of Minnesota Press, 1972.

Reynolds, Paul D. *International Commodity Agreements and the Common Fund: A Legal and Financial Analysis.* New York: Praeger Publishers, 1978.

Ritter, Archibald R. M. *The Economic Development of Revolutionary Cuba: Strategy and Performance.* New York: Praeger Publishers, 1974.

Roberts, Paul (ed.). *Cuba 1968: Supplement to the Statistical Abstract of Latin America.* Los Angeles: University of California, 1970.

Schroeder, Susan. *Cuba: A Handbook of Historical Statistics.* Boston: G. K. Hall and Co., 1982.

Swerling, Boris Cyril. *International Control of Sugar, 1918–1941.* Stanford: Stanford University Press, 1949.

Thomas, Hugh. *Cuba: The Pursuit of Freedom.* New York: Harper and Row, 1971.

The World Sugar Economy, Structure and Policies, Volumes 1 and 2. International Sugar Council. London: Brown, Knight, and Truscott, 1963.

27. Rapid Growth with Improved Income Distribution: The Taiwan Success Story

Shirley W. Y. Kuo
Gustav Ranis
John C. H. Fei

The Taiwanese case seems to contradict both the inverted U-curve theory and the dependency/world-system perspective. At the outset of the dramatic growth process which began in Taiwan after World War II, the typical signs of underdevelopment were much in evidence—income distribution was badly skewed, illiteracy was high, and life expectancy was short. In marked contrast to many other developing nations, however, Taiwan's growth was accompanied by a large reduction in income inequality. Major strides were made in improving education, health, and housing conditions. These feats were accomplished during a period in which the trade dependency of the Taiwanese economy increased significantly, with exports increasing from 9 percent of the GNP in 1952 to 49 percent in 1980. In addition, there were massive infusions of foreign investment and aid. Adherents of Kuznets's thesis would have predicted an increase in inequality during the growth phase, while followers of dependency thinking would have predicted that increased trade dependency, foreign investment, and aid would have had the same impact. In this discussion, drawn from a book on the subject, some of the basic data are presented along with an effort to explain Taiwanese exceptionalism. Primary emphasis is placed upon the public policies that served to stimulate growth while promoting equity.

At the close of World War II, per capita income in Taiwan was about US$70. Such a low per capita income has increased rapidly to reach US$2,280 by 1980. During this period, population grew at the high rate of 3.5 percent until the 1960s and at about 2 percent thereafter. Real gross national product, however, grew at the much higher annual

Reprinted with permission from *The Taiwan Success Story: Rapid Growth with Improved Distribution in the Republic of China, 1952–1979*, Shirley W. Y. Kuo, Gustav Ranis and John C. Fei, pp. 7, 38–60. Boulder, CO: Westview Press, 1981. Some tables have not been reproduced here.

rate of 9.2 percent on the average over the past three decades: 8.2 percent in the 1950s, 9.4 percent in the 1960s, and 9.9 percent in the 1970s. Due to the acceleration of growth in the later periods, real GNP doubled every seven years after 1963. As a result, real GNP in 1980 was eleven times the real GNP of 1952; that is, the amount of goods and services produced in the year 1980 in Taiwan was eleven times greater than that produced in 1952. This explains the particular phenomenon in Taiwan today that its people have not only an abundance of food and clothing for their own consumption, but also a surplus of products, which must be sold in the international market. For Taiwan, the Republic of China, rapid growth over the past three decades has meant significant improvement of people's lives. . . .

Although some education was available to the people of Taiwan when the island was under Japanese occupation, it was usually limited to the primary level. Advanced education was rare and almost always limited to medical science. After Taiwan was restored to Chinese sovereignty, the government of the Republic of China made an effort to promote education. Not only was a large portion of government money spent on education, but equal opportunity for education was also emphasized. As a result, the level and rate of education increased greatly.

The illiteracy rate of persons 6 years old and older decreased from 55 percent in 1946 to 11.2 percent in 1978. Over the same period, the percentage of school-age children in primary schools increased from 78.6 percent to 99.6 percent. In 1968 nine years of education was made compulsory; this policy has been gradually implemented since then. Over the period 1966–78, the percentage of junior high-age youth (12–14 years old) in junior high schools increased from 48.3 percent to 89.8 percent; the percentage of senior high-age youth (15–17 years old) in senior high and vocational schools increased from 28.3 percent to 51.8 percent; and the percentage of junior college- and university-age youth (18–21 years old) in colleges and universities increased from 11.3 percent to 25.5 percent. The promotion of education on the island greatly contributed to the rapid growth of the economy by providing higher-quality labor for advanced production.

The crude death rate and life expectancy are considered to be two typical indicators of the level of sanitation. The crude death rate in Taiwan decreased from 9.9 per thousand in 1952 to 4.7 per thousand in 1979, and life expectancy increased from 58.6 years to 70.7 years over the same period. Over the same time, the per capita daily calorie intake increased from 2,078 calories to 2,845 calories, and per capita protein intake increased from 49 grams to 79 grams.

Transportation in Taiwan has met with increasing difficulties because land on the island is limited and population is very dense. Particularly in the 1960s, the speed of industrialization greatly exceeded the speed of construction of highways and harbors. However, construction for transportation was intensified during 1975–78. Transportation has been greatly facilitated since then, although the situation is still far from satisfactory. The number of automobiles, motorcycles, and telephones also increased rapidly as the economy grew.

Housing construction during the past three decades has been quite successful. About 90 percent of the houses in Taipei City and 80 percent of the houses in Taiwan Province were built after World War II. Living space per head increased from 4.6 square meters in 1949 to 16.9 square meters in 1979. The share of dwelling investment in GNP increased from 1 percent in 1952 to 3.6 percent in 1979.

The rising standard of living is particularly reflected in the more extensive use of modern facilities. In 1979 there were 1,007 television sets per 1,000 households. Refrigerators, gas stoves, washing machines, flush toilets, and the like also became quite common facilities. These are tangible evidence of the improved standard of living throughout the country, which is the ultimate purpose of economic development.

Growth, Distribution, and Government Policies, 1953–54

Despite considerable wartime destruction, the physical and institutional infrastructure established under colonial rule in Taiwan was instrumental in the rapid growth of agriculture during the 1950s. The irrigation system, which extended over more than half of Taiwan's cultivated area, proved valuable in ensuring the equitable distribution of the benefits of green-revolution technology. Linkages between agriculture and the rural-based food processing industry led to a marked spatial dispersion of economic growth. This pattern later made possible the provision of substantial nonagricultural employment to farmers. Progress in public health and education during the colonial period provided the basis for a highly productive labor force in both agriculture and industry. In addition, the overwhelmingly Japanese ownership of manufacturing enterprises contributed to a more equal distribution of income in two ways: It reduced the concentration of industrial assets in private Taiwanese hands in the period immediately after World War II, and it provided a source of industrial assets that could be distributed as compensation to landowners under the program of land reform. The preconditions for rapid economic growth and an improved distribution of income thus were considerably more favorable in Taiwan than in the typical developing country.

This chapter proves the reasons for the apparent absence of conflict between growth and equity in Taiwan, especially during the 1950s. Contrary to the experience in most less developed countries (LDCs), the family distribution of income substantially improved during the subphase of primary import substitution in Taiwan.[1] The following sections examine the distribution of assets and the conditions of production during this period, first in agriculture, then to a limited extent in other sectors of the economy. This chapter concludes with a discussion

Table 27.1
Measures of Equity of Family Distribution of Income, 1953, 1959, and 1964

Item	1953[a]	1959[b]	1964[c]
Distribution of income by percentile of households (%)			
0-20 (the poorest 20%)	3.0	5.7	7.7
21-40	8.3	9.7	12.6
41-60	9.1	13.9	16.6
61-80	18.2	19.7	22.1
81-95	28.8	26.3	24.8
96-100 (the richest 5%)	32.6	24.7	16.2
Mean income per household (NT$ in 1972 prices)	22,681	31,814	32,452
Per capita GNP in market prices (NT$ in 1972 prices)	6,994	8,629	10,875
Ratio of income share of top 10% to that of the bottom 10%	30.40	13.72	8.63
Gini coefficient	0.5580	0.4400	0.3280

a. Data are based on a sample of 301 families, or a sample fraction of 2/1,000.
b. Data are based on a sample of 812 familes, or a sample fraction of 4/1,000.
c. Data are based on a sample size of 3,000 families, or a sample fraction of 14.6/1,000.
Sources: See original.

of inferences about the course of income distribution in the 1950s and early 1960s. In subsequent chapters, because of the superior, detailed data available after 1964, we can analyze more rigorously the interplay of economic growth and income distribution during the subphase of export expansion after 1960. [See original.—Ed.]

Income Distribution During 1952-64

Information about family distribution of income in Taiwan is meager before 1964, when the Directorate-General of Budget, Accounting, and Statistics (DGBAS) began to conduct regular surveys. One investigator conducted sample surveys of overall income distribution for 1953 and 1959.[2] The Joint Commission on Rural Reconstruction (JCRR) conducted sample surveys of the income of farm families in 1952, 1957, 1962, and

1967.[3] The pattern of overall income distribution for 1953, 1959, and 1964 (see Table 27.1) shows a striking improvement by almost every measure. In 1953 the Gini coefficient, a measure of income inequality (the greater the coefficient, the greater the inequality) was about 0.56, which is comparable to patterns of income distribution now prevailing in Brazil and Mexico. By 1964 the Gini coefficient dropped to 0.33, a level comparable to that of the best performers anywhere.[4] This substantial improvement in overall income distribution during the 1950s can be traced primarily to the rapidly improving rural income distribution and secondarily to the distribution of nonagricultural income, which probably did not worsen and may even have improved slightly.

Agricultural Development During the 1950s

Land reform alone could not solve the primary constraint facing Taiwan's agriculture: the shortage of land for rapidly growing agricultural population. Although an ever-increasing number of farmers left agriculture to live and work in Taiwan's expanding urban areas, the population pressure on farmland was severe, especially during the early 1950s. The agricultural population rose from 4.3 million in 1952 to 5.8 million in 1964, an increase of 33 percent. During the same period the total area of cultivated land remained nearly fixed, culminating in a decline in the average size of a family-holding from 1.29 hectares to 1.06 hectares. Taiwan overcame these pressures in three ways: by the achievement of substantial increases in agricultural productivity at the intensive margin; by the diversification of agricultural production into more profitable crops; and by the part-time reallocation of labor to nonagricultural activities, including off-farm employment for many members of agricultural families.

The growth of the agricultural sector during the 1950s was impressive. The real net domestic product of agricultural origin increased by about 80 percent during the 1952–64 period, an average rate of 5 percent a year, even though agriculture's share in net domestic product declined from 36 percent to 28 percent. Because the agricultural population increased by only one-third, an agricultural surplus was assured. Although this 5 percent annual increase in net agricultural output during the subphase of import substitution is considerably smaller than that of the industrial sector, it still is an impressive figure by any international standard of comparison. It is even more impressive when two additional factors are considered: The natural fertility of the soil is low, and the land frontier on the mountainous island had essentially been already reached. The growth in agricultural output can only be called dramatic. Between 1952 and 1964 total agricultural production, including forestry, fishing, and livestock, rose by 78 percent; the production of crops alone rose by 59.7 percent. These production increases were the result primarily of increased yields of traditional crops, but they were also the result of the introduction of new crops. The yields of such traditional crops as rice increased 50 percent, but the yields of relatively new specialty crops, such as cotton and fruits, increased more than 100 percent.[5]

Fixed capital in agriculture expanded by about 34 percent between 1952 and 1964. Much of this expansion was in irrigation and flood control facilities, which had deteriorated during the war and were rebuilt and expanded during the 1950s. Farm buildings and other structures were added to and improved. The water buffalo was gradually replaced by small tillers and other small mechanical devices. Working capital increased even more dramatically than fixed capital, growing by 140 percent between 1952 and 1964. The continuous introduction of new seed varieties that were responsive to intensive fertilizer applications and the gradual reduction in fertilizer prices and government restrictions enabled Taiwan's total fertilizer use to grow by 91 percent over the same period.[6] As livestock production grew by nearly 120 percent, more and more commercial feeds were imported. Further increases in working capital included widespread use of pesticides, a major postwar innovation that helped to reduce high losses caused by disease and insects.

Taiwan's impressive success in agriculture can be attributed to many factors. Main factors contributing to the growth and improved income distribution in the agricultural sector are land reform, reorganization of institutional infrastructure, and agricultural pricing policy.

Land Reform

The land reform that the government instituted between 1949 and 1953 was probably the most important factor in improving the distribution of income before the beginning of the subphase of export expansion in the early 1960s.[7] Although much of the reform took place before 1952, the first year for which sample data on the distribution of income exist, it continued to have an impact well into the 1950s. The reform thus remained an important factor in explaining improvements in income distribution during that decade.

Land reform was initiated for several reasons. Although the Japanese had developed a substantial agricultural infrastructure in Taiwan, they had paid relatively little attention to the distribution of land. Given the large class of tenants, competition for the scarce land was so fierce that the average lease was less than one year. As a result, rents were often equal to 50 percent of the anticipated harvest, especially in the more fertile regions. Contracts frequently were oral; rent payments had to be made in advance; and no adjustments were made for crop failures. These conditions and practices left the typical tenant helpless in any dispute with his landlord. The record of landlord abuse and the need to meet the food demands of postwar Taiwan—which, in addition to its own increased population, included hundreds of thousands of mainland Chinese—laid the groundwork for reform.[8] In addition, the principle of land ownership by the tiller, although it never received much attention, had always been part of the ideology of the Chinese Nationalists. The loss of the mainland and the social unrest threatening in Taiwan made the redistribution of wealth a particularly important issue for the government. Land reform was also considered to be an essential ingredient of agricultural growth and economic recovery. Moreover, it could be imposed by a government that was free of obligations and ties to the landowning class.

The government's conception of land reform was broad. Strengthening farmers' associations and other elements of the organizational and financial infrastructure in rural areas was considered to be important. Moreover, the repair of the physical infrastructure, begun as soon as Taiwan was retroceded to China and almost completed by 1952, increased the effect of land reform on both growth and equity. But the main component of the successful reorganization of the agricultural sector clearly was the three-pronged package of land reform: the program to reduce farm rents, the sale of public lands, and the land-to-the-tiller program.

The first step taken to promote agricultural incentives and output was to reduce farm rents and thereby increase the tenant farmers' share of crop yields. Promulgated in 1949, this program had five basic provisions: First, farm rents could be fixed at no more than 37.5 percent of the anticipated annual yield of the main crops; second, if crops failed because of natural forces, tenant farmers could apply to local farm-tenancy committees for a further reduction; third, tenant farmers no longer had to pay their rent in advance; fourth, written contracts and fixed leases of three to six years had to be registered; and fifth, tenants had the first option to purchase land from its owners. The reform affected about 43 percent of the 660,000 farm families, 75 percent of the 410,000 part owners and tenants, and 40 percent of the 650,000 hectares of private farmland. Prices of farmland immediately dropped—paddy field prices by 20 percent and dry field prices by more than 40 percent by December 1949 and a further 66 percent by 1952.[9] Equally important, the requirement for written contracts and the fixing of standard reduced rents enabled tenants to benefit from their own increased efforts for the first time. This incentive was a primary ingredient of the sustained increase in Taiwan's agricultural productivity during the early 1950s. With higher yields and lower rents, the average income of tenant farmers rose by 81 percent between 1949 and 1952.[10] These rising incomes enabled tenants to purchase land put up for sale by their landlords; about 6 percent of private farmland changed hands.

Given the success of the program to reduce farm rents, the government decided to accelerate the program initiated in 1948 to sell public land to tenant farmers. About 170,000 hectares of public land that had formerly been owned by the Japanese—about 25 percent of Taiwan's arable land—were suitable for cultivation. Taiwan Sugar Corporation owned most of this land and leased part of it to tenant farmers. The program gave priority in land purchases to cultivators of public land and landless tenants. The size of parcels was limited according to predetermined fertility grades, and the average size was 1 chia (1 chia = 0.97 hectares). Selling price were 2.5 times the value of the annual yield of the main crops; payments in kind were set to coincide with the harvest season over a ten-year period. In all, 35 percent of Taiwan's arable public land was sold during 1948–53, and 43 percent during 1953–58.

With the government setting the example of returning land to the tiller, the stage was set for the most dramatic component of the three-pronged package: the compulsory sale of land by landlords. This program stipulated that privately owned land in excess of specified amounts per landowner had to be sold to the government, which would resell that land to tenants.[11] The purchase price was set at 2.5 times the annual yield of the main crops. Landlords were paid 70 percent of the purchase price in land bonds denominated in kind and 30 percent in industrial stock of four public enterprises previously owned by the Japanese. The selling prices and conditions of repayment were the same as for the sale of public lands. This third program had a dual objective. The new owner-cultivators were encouraged to work harder because they would benefit from any increases in agricultural output. The landlords, deprived of the privilege of living comfortably off the land, were encouraged to participate in the industrial development of Taiwan through ownership of four large-scale industrial enterprises. Between May and December of 1953, tenant households acquired 244,000 hectares of farmland, 16.4 percent of the total area cultivated in Taiwan during 1951–55. . . .

Because of the reform, the distribution of land-holdings changed dramatically between 1952 and 1960. The rising share of families owning medium-sized plots of land, ranging from 0.5 to 3 chia, reflects this change: Their share increased from 46 percent in 1952 to 76 percent in 1960. The largest rise was in the share of families owning between 0.5 and 1 chia. What is even more dramatic, the average size of holdings in all categories of less than 5 chia increased. The combined share in total land of families owning less than 3 chia increased from 58 percent in 1952 to 85 percent in 1960. The proportion of land cultivated by tenants fell from 44 percent in 1948 to 17 percent in 1959. The proportion of tenant farmers in farm families fell from 38 percent in 1950 to 15 percent in 1960. The ratio of owner-cultivators to total farm families increased from 36 percent in 1949 to 60 percent in 1957. Part-owner farmers and owner-cultivators owned more than 83 percent of the total farmland in 1957.

The incentive to make extra efforts in cultivation was great after land reform. First, after rent reduction, the tenant was able to benefit not only by the reduction in rent, but also by any increase in production beyond the standard production. This was a motivating force in promoting multiple cropping. Second, the superiority of an owner-farmer system over a tenancy system was obvious on a per family, per person, or even per hectare basis. The farm income of the tenant had been only three-fourths of the income of the other two categories. Therefore, a major change in tenancy conditions provided a great incentive to produce more and made possible more efficient utilization of the agricultural labor force.

After the land reform, farmers had a freer choice of crops, because, as owner-cultivators, they were under no obligation to produce rice for rental payment. Thus, the land reform tended to reduce the relative share of rice production and to increase the share of other crops, vegetables, fruits, livestock, and poultry. Moreover, the technological change in agriculture after land reform was largely centered on the intensive use of land with more labor input.

Although the government compensated landlords for the land they were forced to give up, this compensation was only 2.5 times the standard annual yield; market values of land ranged between 5 and 8 times the annual yield. The policy thus represented a substantial redistribution of wealth. The total value of wealth redistributed as a result of this price difference was equivalent to about 13 percent of Taiwan's gross domestic product in 1952.[12] Furthermore, bonds used to reimburse landowners paid an interest rate of only 4 percent, substantially less than the prevailing market rates. Because of the landlords' lack of experience in nonagricultural matters, most landlords did not place much value on the 30 percent of their compensation received as industrial stocks. They promptly sold the stocks at prices far below value. Most of their proceeds went to consumption; some went to investments in small businesses. The majority of landlords thus ended up being not much better off than the new owner-cultivators.[13]

Through the reduction of rents and the redistribution of assets, the land reform had a marked effect on the functional distribution of income. Between 1941 and 1956 the combined share of property in total agricultural income fell from 63.7 percent to 44.3 percent. The sharp reduction in the share of property income was thus accompanied by a broader distribution of that income. Two investigators have estimated the shares of farm income by type of recipient before the land reform, using the 1936–40 average, and after the land reform, using the 1956–60 average.[14] According to these estimates, the cultivators' share of farm income increased from 67 percent to 82 percent; the share of government and public institutions, which received repayments from new landowners, increased from 8 percent to 12 percent; but the share of landlords and moneylenders declined from 25 percent to 6 percent.

Reorganization of the Institutional Infrastructure

The institutional infrastructure of Taiwan's agriculture was extensively reorganized and improved during the 1950s. The farmers' associations and credit cooperatives, set up by the Japanese to facilitate agricultural extension programs and rice procurement, were top-down institutions dominated by landlords and nonfarmers. As a result, most farmers did not directly benefit from them. In 1952, the government consolidated those institutions in multipurpose farmers' associations restricted to farmers and serving their interests. In addition to the original function of agricultural extension, the activities of farmers' associations expanded to include a credit department, which accepted deposits from farmers and made loans to them, and to provide facilities for purchasing, marketing, warehousing, and processing agricultural produce.[15] The associations thus became clearinghouses for farmers, who controlled and maintained them and viewed them as their own creatures.

The other major institutional reform affecting agriculture during the 1950s was the establishment of the Joint Commission on Rural Reconstruction (JCRR) by the U.S. Congress in 1948. Its main functions were to allocate U.S. aid, to provide technical assistance, and to help the government plan and coordinate programs for agricultural extension, research, and experimentation. Thus, although the farmers' associations provided the much-needed organizational structure at local levels and facilitated the efficient flow of agricultural surpluses to the industrial sector, the JCRR was a major catalyst. It funded and initiated many new farming techniques, and it introduced new crops and new markets. For example, the JCRR was behind the introduction of asparagus and mushroom cultivation, which led to the highly successful production and export performance of those commodities in the 1950s.

Technological change, introduced mainly by such government-supported research agencies as the JCRR, clearly was a significant factor in generating the increased agricultural output.[16] In 1960 Taiwan had 79 agricultural research workers for every 100,000 persons active in agriculture, compared with 60 in Japan, 4.7 in Thailand, 1.6 in the Philippines, and 1.2 in India.[17] The research agencies successfully introduced new strains of rice and sugar and such new crops as asparagus and mushrooms, as well as pesticides, insecticides, and new agricultural tools and machinery. In the Hayami-Ruttan terminology, most of the technological change was of the chemical variety, not the mechanical.[18]

Agricultural Pricing Policy

The agricultural pricing policies were implemented mainly through the following actions. First, by various methods of compulsory rice collection, the government controlled the supply of rice and kept a large part of rice consumption from going through the market mechanism. Thus, it contributed to the stabilization of the price of rice. Second, through collection of land tax in kind, the rice fertilizer barter system, and the purchase and collection of rice at a price relatively lower than the market price, the government made huge profits from the rice collection operation. These profits are really a form of "hidden rice tax." Third, by offering guaranteed prices for sugar cane, corn, mushrooms, asparagus, and so on, the government encouraged the production of crops other than rice.

Thus, as a result of the agricultural pricing policies, rice production underwent a relative decline and other higher-value agricultural products increased instead. This change of agricultural structure and intense agricultural diversification provided a fundamental basis for the development of food processing manufacturing and export expansion in the 1960s.

Given the physical and organizational improvement of the environmental infrastructure and the pervasive package of land reform, farmers had the incentives and the tools to improve their situation during the subphase of primary import substitution, during which government policies usually discriminate against agriculture. Moreover, the technological change seemed to be of a type that generally used labor and saved land and capital. Although the number of persons employed in agriculture increased by 12 percent between 1952 and 1964, the number of man-days increased by 17 percent. Consequently, the number of working days per worker steadily increased. In 1965 the average worker had 156 days of farm employment, compared with 90 days in 1946 and 134 days in 1952.[19] As a result, the number of working days per hectare of land increased from approximately 170 in 1948–50 to about 260 in 1963–65.[20]

Larger labor inputs to the cultivation of traditional crops and the diversification into new crops resulted in more intensive cultivation of land. Between 1952 and 1964 the multiple-cropping index increased from 172 to 188; the diversification index increased from 3.54 to 5.75. The shift toward such labor-intensive crops as vegetables and away from the complete dominance of the traditional crops of rice and sugar was continuous. As an indication of the labor intensity of vegetable cultivation, the cultivation of one hectare of asparagus requires 2,900 times the labor input of the cultivation of one hectare of rice.

Despite the substantial increase in the absorption of labor in agriculture between 1952 and 1964, rural underemployment continued during the 1950s and has been estimated to be about 40 percent during that decade.[21] The smaller, poorer farms were especially unable to generate sufficient income or to keep the entire family fully employed. This pattern led to a small amount of net physical migration out of the agricultural sector, estimated at less than 1 percent annually during the 1950s. Mostly, however, farmers increasingly sought off-farm employment in the rapidly growing rural industrial sector. Consequently, underemployment did not develop into as serious a problem as it has in most other LDCs.[22] The pattern of agricultural growth and the participation in that growth by rich and poor farmers were the basic ingredients of the dramatic improvement in the distribution of income in Taiwan during the 1950s.

Notes

1. Kowie Chang, "An Estimate of Taiwan Personal Income Distribution in 1953: Pareto's Formula Discussed and Applied," *Journal of Social Science*, Vol. 7 (August 1956); National Taiwan University, College of Law, "Report on Pilot Study of Personal Income and Consumption in Taiwan" (prepared under the sponsorship of a working group of National Income Statistics, Directorate-General of Budget, Accounting and Statistics [DGBAS]; processed in Chinese).

2. Chang, "Estimate of Taiwan Personal Income Distribution in 1953"; National Taiwan University, "Report on Pilot Study."

3. Joint Commission on Rural Reconstruction, "Taiwan Farm Income Survey of 1967: With a Brief Comparison with 1952, 1957, and 1962," *Economic Digest Series*, no. 20 (Taipei: Joint Commission on Rural Reconstruction, 1970).

4. The quality of the data, particularly for the 1950s, is suspect. Calculation of total personal income in 1953 by aggregating the product of average family income and the number of households in each income group gives a figure 20 percent lower than that of the national accounts data. A similar calculation found that the 1953 data underestimated the total family income given in the national accounts data by 16.7 percent, but that the 1959 data overestimated total family income by 15.3 percent. The 1964 DGBAS data were found to underestimate total family income by only about 5 percent.

Although more than half of Taiwan's population in 1953 was in agriculture, 84 percent of the 1953 sample group came from the more urbanized and industrialized areas; 58 percent of that group lived in Taiwan's four largest cities. If rural income was better distributed than urban income, as was seen earlier, any overweighting of urban income may have resulted in a low estimate of total personal income and a high estimate of the Gini coefficient. In turn, although DGBAS data for 1964 did not include an appropriate number of families with income exceeding NT$200,000, the downward bias in the Gini is probably too small to be of much importance. Nevertheless, the survey results for the 1950s must be accepted with caution.

With respect to the underestimation of income distribution inequality—the 1964 Gini coefficient based on decile groups is 0.328—households with income exceeding NT$200,000 accounted for only 0.1 percent of the population and 1.15 percent of total income. Even if the income share of these households is increased by 1 percentage point, which would almost double their income share, and if the 1 percent loss is equally assigned to the first nine decile groups, the Gini coefficient would increase by only 3.1 percent to 0.3307. The increase really is not that large. To give an idea of the effect of the underestimation of the Gini coefficient, again for the 1964 data, suppose the income share of the top decile group to be increased by 2, 3, and 4 percentage points. Then the Gini coefficients would rise by 6.2 percent, 9.3 percent, and 12.4 percent to 0.3406, 0.3505, and 0.3604, respectively. Thus, the smaller the population, income share, underestimation of the wealthiest households, or any combination of these elements, the smaller the downward bias of the Gini coefficient.

5. Economic Planning Council, *Taiwan Statistical Data Book, 1975* (Taipei: Economic Planning Council, 1975), pp. 48, 53–55.

6. Ibid., p. 58.

7. The discussion of land reform draws heavily on Samuel P. S. Ho, *Economic Development in Taiwan: 1860–1970* (New Haven: Yale University Press, 1978), and Chao-Chen Cheng, "Land Reform and Agricultural Development in Taiwan"

(paper read at Conference on Economic Development of Taiwan, June 19–28, 1967, Taipei; processed).

8. In 1945 and 1946, 640,000 mainlanders moved to Taiwan. Kuang Lu, "Population and Employment," in *Economic Development of Taiwan*, ed. Kowie Chang (Taipei: Cheng Chung Books, 1968), p. 532.

9. Chao-Chen Cheng, *Land Reform in Taiwan* (Taipei: China Publishing, 1961), p. 310.

10. Ibid., p. 309.

11. Individual landowners were allowed to retain three chia of medium-grade land. Anthony Y. C. Koo, *The Role of Land Reform in Economic Development: A Case Study of Taiwan* (New York: Frederick A. Praeger, 1968), p. 38.

12. Ho, *Economic Development in Taiwan*, p. 166.

13. T. Martin Yang, *Socio-Economic Results of Land Reform in Taiwan* (Honolulu: East-West Center, 1970).

14. T. H. Lee and T. H. Shen, "Agriculture as a Base for Socio-Economic Development," in *Agriculture's Place in the Strategy of Development*, ed. T. H. Shen (Taipei: Joint Commission on Rural Reconstruction, 1974), p. 300.

15. Deposits of the credit divisions of farmers' associations increased from about NT$100 million to NT$2,700 million by the end of 1965. Loans increased commensurately. Wen-Fu Hsu, "The Role of Agricultural Organizations in Agricultural Development" (paper read at conference on Economic Development of Taiwan, June 19–28, 1967, Taipei; processed). Also during this period, credit became available to farmers from the JCRR, government-owned banks, and government agencies and monopolies. Between 1949 and 1960 the proportion of farm loans provided through the organized money market rose from 17 percent to 57 percent. Ho, *Economic Development in Taiwan*, pp. 179–80.

16. Ho estimated that 44.9 percent of the growth of agricultural output during 1951–60 can be attributed to changes in total factor productivity: 10.3 percent to increases in crop area and 34.7 percent to increases in working capital. Ho, *Economic Development in Taiwan*, pp. 147–85.

17. Ibid., p. 178.

18. Yujiro Hayami and Vernon W. Ruttan, *Agricultural Development in International Perspective* (Baltimore: Johns Hopkins University Press, 1971), passim.

19. You-tsao Wang, "Agricultural Development," in Chang, *Economic Development of Taiwan*, p. 176.

20. W. H. Lai, "Trend of Agricultural Employment in Post-War Taiwan" (paper read at Conference on Manpower in Taiwan, 1972, Taipei; processed).

21. The estimation difficulties here are well known, and we do not place much confidence in these numbers.

22. Ho, *Economic Development in Taiwan*, p. 158. Ho derived his figures from S. F. Liu, "Disguised Unemployment in Taiwan Agriculture" (Ph.D. dissertation, University of Illinois, 1966), and Paul K. C. Liu, "Economic Development and Population in Taiwan since 1895: An Overview," in *Essays on the Population of Taiwan* (Taipei: Academia Sinica, Graduate Institute of Economics, 1973).

28. The Future of the Gap Between Rich and Poor

Herman Kahn

In this chapter, Herman Kahn takes the gap question full circle by making two arguments. First, he believes that the gap between rich and poor nations is a positive development that will serve as the "basic 'engine' of growth" in the poor countries, eventually propelling them toward unprecedented levels of growth and thereby eventually narrowing the gap. Second, Kahn argues that a large group of middle income countries, constituting 47 percent of the world's population, have already made great strides and are beginning to close the gap. For the poorest nations, the gap will widen in the immediate future, but thereafter the gap effect also will propel these nations into development and eventually eliminate the wide gaps present today. Kahn goes beyond this prediction to argue that foreign aid programs which seek to reduce the gap are only likely to delay economic development among the poor countries by reducing the force of gap-induced development. In this respect, then, Kahn agrees with the world-system analysts who see foreign aid as slowing growth, but stands their argument on its head by asserting, in effect, that forces within the world system will actually stimulate growth in the poor nations.

Unlike others who discuss the popular concept of the "widening gap" between the rich and the poor, we focus on the positive aspects of the gap. The increasing disparity between average incomes in the richest and poorest nations is usually seen as an unalloyed evil to be overcome as rapidly as possible through enlightened policies by the advanced nations and international organizations. If this occurred because the poor were getting poorer, we would agree, but when it occurs at all, it is almost always because the rich are getting richer. This is not necessarily a bad thing for the poor, at least if they compare themselves with their own past or their own present rather than with a mythical theoretical gap.

In contrast, we view this gap as a basic "engine" of growth. It generates or supports most of the basic processes by which the poor

---

Reprinted with permission from *World Economic Development: 1979 and Beyond*, by Herman Kahn, pp. 60–65. Boulder, CO: Westview Press, 1979.

are becoming rich, or at least less poor. The great abundance of resources of the developed world—capital, management, technology, and large markets in which to sell—makes possible the incredibly rapid progress of most of the developing countries. Many of these poorer countries are also developing relatively autonomous capabilities at an increasing rate.

Current attitudes toward the gap illustrate the world view of many modern liberals. The dramatic increase in the disparity of per capita income between the wealthiest and poorest nations would have been a cause for self-congratulation by the fortunate wealthy nations at an earlier time in history—whether Roman, Greek, Chinese, or Indian. Indeed, when the colonial powers expanded their dominion, their affluence was largely accepted by all parties as a sign of their inherent superiority. Today, however, it is more a source of guilt than of pride for descendants of those same high morale colonialists. Yet such guilt is even less justified today than a hundred years ago.

It is still not widely understood that in light of eventual modernization colonial rule was likely to produce more advantages than disadvantages. Moreover, in much (but not all) of the Third World, the European expansion was more just and humane than most previous conquests by expanding cultures. Without condoning the evils of colonialism, one can nonetheless say that conquest is not an international crime invented by the European peoples. The poverty that exists in the Third World was not caused by European colonization, nor can the current problems of the poor nations be solved by fostering a sense of guilt in the rich nations. The affluent minority of humanity has a genuine responsibility to aid the poor, but largesse dispensed because of guilt is likely to produce counterproductive and self-righteous expectations and attitudes in developing countries.

The modern liberal view holds that an international system that perpetuates inequalities among nations is morally unacceptable. This attitude is indelibly Western in origin and is most prevalent among citizens of what we call the Atlantic Protestant culture area.* As an enlightened modern American, the author has some sympathy with this view but does not expect that a relatively egalitarian world can be achieved in the near future either through violence or through an outpouring of generosity by the advanced countries.

It is one thing to wish the world were a better place, and quite another to make it happen in the very near future. World leaders who proclaim that closing the gap between the rich and poor countries is the most urgent task of our times should ask themselves how this can be done. This alluring goal simply cannot be approached, much less attained, in the next hundred years. The gap might close for the most

---

*Scandinavia, Holland, United Kingdom, United States, Canada, Australia, and New Zealand.

Table 28.1
Population Distribution Among Country Groups

	Population (in billions)		Population (in billions)	Income (Per Capita)
Poor Countries	1.25 billion (29% of world)	Very Poor	1/4	$ 130
		Coping Poor	1.0	300
Middle Income Countries	2.0 billion (47% of world)	Communist Asia	1.0	500
		Transitional	1/2	500
		Mostly Developed	1/2	1,500
Affluent Countries	1.0 billion (24% of world)	Affluent Communist	1/3	4,000
		Affluent Market-Oriented (includes oil-rich)	2/3	8,000

Note: All sums are in "1978 dollars" (i.e., 2/3 of a 1972 dollar or 4/9 of a 1958 dollar). The percentages of 29, 47, and 24 given above are excessively precise but are reasonable estimates; the picture given is not misleading. However, one should note that there are many poor people living in middle income, and even some affluent countries--and some middle income rich people live in poor countries.

rapidly developing countries, but from a practical standpoint, the arithmetic gap will almost surely widen for most of humanity. To anyone who assays the problem with a modicum of seriousness, this conclusion is virtually inescapable.

Actually, the world is doing a lot better than most people realize. Table 28.1 shows the current state of the world, with the countries of the world divided into three broad groups. Two of these groups, communist Asia and the middle income countries, are about as rich as or richer than almost any society before the Industrial Revolution. Therefore, by historical standards, we have to think of them as affluent. Nevertheless, by the standards of today, or at least by the standards of the rich countries today, they do not appear to be wealthy at all but rather to be low income. If a country is rich by the standards of the poor and poor by the standards of the rich one is almost driven to the terminology middle income. We have, therefore, chosen this term. We think of the countries in communist Asia as being on the border between the poor and middle income countries, but normally we will include them in the middle income category. In any case, one can argue that almost half the world's population now lives in countries that have progressed enormously in acquiring wealth and have done so almost completely since World War II.

The progress since World War II has been most heartening. If we had written this book in 1950 we would have been forced to concede that there was no serious evidence that affluence was spreading from the West to other nations with the possible exceptions of Japan and the Soviet Union. Even in those two countries, the standards of living were in fact low (about equal to the average of the middle income countries today). Furthermore, in 1950 there was a genuine question about Japan's ability to recover from World War II. The conventional prognosis was that Japan would become a huge Asian slum. As far as we can discover, nobody predicted anything close to what actually happened. Today, on the basis of the enormous progress during what we later call *La Deuxième Belle Epoque* (1948 to 1973), we must conclude that economic development is simply not a unique product of the West. Indeed, we will argue in later chapters [see Chapter 8 of this volume.—Ed.] that what we call the neo-Confucian cultures of Asia are actually better at economic development than the traditional Western cultures.

The middle income countries generally, and the neo-Confucian countries in particular, are in many cases closing the gap with the rich countries, but this is usually ignored in most discussions. When people talk about "the gap" they are usually now talking about the gap between the 25 percent of the world that is rich and the 30 percent that is poor. This gap could only be closed in the near future by a massive reduction in the affluence of the developed countries and perhaps of the middle income countries as well. Over the next few decades capital investment would have to be shifted to the poorest of the poor countries. The bulk of capital and consumer goods (except for bare necessities, produced in the developed countries) would have to be exported from the developed to the developing nations. If some of our conjectures are correct, something like this may happen to some degree as a result of "natural" forces. However, no political system is sufficiently totalitarian to deliberately and intensively implement such a program on a worldwide scale nor would any sensible people wish to do so.

If such a program could be put into effect, we doubt if it would lead, even in a generation, to the attainment of Western housing standards and educational levels in, say, Bangladesh, as measured by the drastically depressed standards that the West would then have. In short, the most commonly expressed economic goal—"closing the gap"—is absurd as a realistic world goal for the rest of the twentieth century. Moreover, the decrease or elimination of absolute poverty is clearly a higher priority task than the reduction of relative poverty. Maintaining, or even increasing the gap, may be the best way to accomplish this. As President Kennedy once said, "A rising tide floats all ships."

We do not expect anything comparable to the current large gaps to be the final outcome of the present world system, even given the presently widening gaps. To the contrary, we expect the gap in per capita income to be greatly lessened in a historically short period of time—100 or 200 years. This will occur so rapidly precisely because of the wide and still growing gap. The greater the difference in relative income between the rich and the poor countries, the greater the ability of the poor countries to "take off" and the greater their potential growth rate. Rather than being a measurement of the basic problem, the widening gap is in reality a force for transferring the benefits of economic development to the poor. Once economic development starts, the gap facilitates it. As a result, many countries above the lowest levels have been experiencing very rapid growth; for them, the relative gap has declined.

The most that realistically could be achieved in the next decade or two would be to reduce the *rate* at which the gap is *widening*—hardly an inspiring goal. Should we actually set out to achieve it, the most likely result would be to delay the time when the poor nations would become economically fully developed—and even more important, to delay a dramatic decrease in absolute poverty that now seems likely to occur during the next fifty years.

29. Inequality in a Global Perspective: Directions for Further Research

Mitchell A. Seligson

That there is a vast gap between the world's rich and its poor is beyond dispute. The causes and dynamics of the gap, however, are the subject of considerable debate, as the reader of this book will now know. Fortunately, debate over the gap between rich and poor differs considerably from the pattern normally encountered in the social sciences, debates which all too often do not lead to the development of a cumulative body of knowledge. Indeed, it can be said that research in this area represents one of the best illustrations of a cumulative social science continually deepening its understanding of a complex problem. In this concluding chapter I will suggest some directions for future research so that continued rapid progress can be made in our understanding of the problem.

Evolution of Research on the Gaps

Once it became clear that the post-World War II hopes for rapid, universal development in the Third World were not going to be fulfilled, social scientists set their minds to determining why that was the case. It was obvious, then as now, that unless development in the Third World was to surge ahead, the gap between these economies and those of the increasingly prosperous developed countries would inevitably widen. The serious implications of this development for world peace are too great to be ignored.

Early thinking focused on the cultural distinctiveness of the Third World. The observation that these cultures were indeed different from those found in the First World of industrial, capitalist development was enough to convince a generation of social scientists to view cultural barriers as the principal explanation for underdevelopment. Many of these explanations were extraordinarily intriguing, showed creative schol-

This is an original contribution to this volume.

arship, and, moreover, seemed to make a good deal of sense. As research proceeded, however, disenchantment with this perspective began to set in. The more that was known about the Third World the less that cultural factors seemed to be able to explain its underdevelopment. Many researchers found the explanation ethnocentric at best and insulting at worst. Studies also revealed many instances of a single "underdeveloped culture" producing vastly different developmental outcomes; wide variation was observed within supposedly monolithic cultures. In addition, people proved highly capable of tailoring their cultures to conform to more "modern" ways of doing things. Cultures proved to be far more malleable and responsive than had been originally believed. Finally, despite putative cultural limitations, some Third World nations made rapid strides in economic growth; some middle income countries, for example, have been able to achieve higher growth rates in recent years than many industrialized countries. Although not all researchers have abandoned the cultural perspective, as Kahn's discussion (Chapter 8) on the developmental role of the "Confucian ethic" clearly shows, most social scientists have come to accept the critique summarized in Chapter 9 by Portes and Chapter 12 by the Valenzuelas.

With the waning of interest in cultural explanations, other theories emerged. Increasingly, thinking about development has become "globalized." The very nature of the gap problem probably forced such thinking to emerge. After all, in order to study the gap one must first specify the frame of reference in some sort of comparative perspective. Studies can focus on the absolute or relative gap, but these terms have no meaning unless they are situated within a comparative framework; poor people are poor only with respect to rich people.

In this book extensive consideration has been given to the "inverted U curve" of development. In global terms, according to Kuznets and other proponents of this thesis, developing nations are likely to experience a widening internal gap before they see the gap narrow in the later phases of industrialization. Dependency and world-system thinkers agree that the gaps are widening, but do not believe that they will ultimately narrow as industrialization matures because both the widening internal and the widening external gaps between rich and poor are seen as a function of the world capitalist economic system.

Considerable data has been brought to bear on the various theories seeking to explain these dual gaps. It is in the analysis and interpretation of this data that we see the clearest example of cumulative social science in the making. Part Three of this book presents some of the best examples of rigorous testing of theory with data. Some of those examples provide strong support for dependency/world-system explanations, while others refute those explanations just as strongly. While it is too early to predict a definitive resolution of the debate and it is even too early to say which side seems to have the edge, it is possible to look ahead and suggest some directions for future research. A pessimistic interpretation of the present state of the debate is that both sides are locked into their own respective positions and future research will be stalemated. The vital importance of the problem, not only to the world's poor, but to those responsible for helping to secure peace, requires that such a stalemate be avoided. It is therefore appropriate at this juncture to assess where research has taken us and where it ought to go. The contributions in this volume trace the intellectual history of the debate over the gaps; the remainder of this chapter is devoted to outlining the directions in which fruitful further research might proceed.

The International Gap

In GNP per capita terms, a small group of oil exporting nations already enjoy incomes higher than the average income found among industrial market economies. In 1981, Saudi Arabia had a GNP per capita of $12,600; Kuwait; $20,900; and the United Arab Emirates, $24,660; while the mean income of the industrial market economies was $11,120. None of the industrialized countries came even close to exceeding the income of Kuwait and the United Arab Emirates; Switzerland had $17,430, the highest GNP per capita of the industrial countries. The United States, not long ago the world's GNP per capita leader, was far behind at $12,820. Oil-rich Libya was moving up rapidly, with its per capita GNP reaching $8,450, only slightly behind that of the United Kingdom ($9,110).[1]

The rapid growth of the oil economies, however, is certainly the exception to the rule. As was pointed out in Chapter 1 of this volume, the absolute and relative gap between nearly all the developing countries of the world, on the one hand, and the industrialized countries, on the other, is increasing. While South Korea, Taiwan, and Malaysia, for example, are rapidly growing, they have incomes that are only a fraction of those found in the industrialized countries. In GNP per capita terms, it seems clear, there is a near-universal widening gap between rich and poor.

This conclusion, however, is based upon a single indicator, namely GNP per capita. The use of a single indicator of any social phenomenon has long fallen into disrepute in the social sciences. Why then base conclusions about such an important subject entirely upon GNP per capita data? The response to this query from those who use it in their research as a sole indicator of income is that it is by far the most widely accepted indicator. This is true enough, but as suggested by P. T. Bauer in Chapter 23 and confirmed by recent research by the World Bank, the indicator may be misleading. The principal problem emerges not because of the unreliability of data collected on each nation, but because of validity problems associated with converting local currency values into dollars, the standard currency normally employed by those who compare such data.

In order to convert the multitude of currencies used around the world into a single standard, it has long been common practice to use the exchange rate of the foreign currency in U.S. dollars. The exchange rate appeared for a long time to be the only reasonable way to compare the value of different currencies. In fact, however, it is now known that such comparisons introduce considerable distortion in the data. The exchange rate comparisons do not accurately measure differences in the relative domestic purchasing power of currencies. The net result is that the exchange-rate GNP measures greatly exaggerate the gap between rich and poor countries. This exaggeration occurs because international exchange rates are linked to the value of goods and services that are exchanged in world trade. For a developing country in which most of the production does not enter the world trade market, the exchange-rate GNP figures will be an underestimate of true income.

In order to correct for this bias, the United Nations has undertaken the International Comparisons Project which has provided some revealing findings.[2] Using purchasing power rather than exchange rates, one finds that the gap narrows considerably. For example, a country like Sri Lanka exhibits a gap nearly four times as large when the traditional measure is used as when the new, purchasing power index is computed. Countries such as Colombia and Mexico also reveal considerable differences, although these differences are not as great as in the case of Sri Lanka.

It would seem appropriate to suggest that future research on the international gap employ the purchasing power index rather than the exchange rate–based comparison in order to obtain a truer picture of income comparisons. However, one should not leap to the conclusion that the new measure will prove the gap to be illusory altogether. Hence, despite the dramatic narrowing of the international gap in the case of Sri Lanka, as noted above, even using the purchasing power index that country's income per capita is only 9.3 percent of that of the United States. Kenya, in which the GNP per capita is seen almost as doubling with the new index, still confronts income levels that are only 6.6 percent of those of the United States. The revised measure, therefore, does not eliminate the gap between rich and poor. It does, however, provide what appears to be a more appropriate standard of comparison. What remains to be studied is the dynamics of the gap using the purchasing power measure. Specifically, since only limited work has thus far been completed on the new measure, and since only a subset of nations have been included in the calculations, it is not yet possible to determine if the new measure will reveal that the gap is narrowing or widening. The mere fact that the gap narrows through the use of the new index does not necessarily imply that there is an overall trend toward a narrowing of the international gap.

Another way of looking at the gap question is to shift the focus away from per capita income measures and to look at human needs and human development instead. Using this criterion, one obtains a rather different perspective on the international gap question. According to studies conducted by the World Bank (1980: 32–45), major strides have been made in the reduction of absolute poverty since the close of World War II. These studies have found that the proportion of people around the world living in absolute poverty has declined. In addition, there has been a worldwide increase in literacy levels such that over the past 30 years literacy in developing countries has increased from 30 percent to over 50 percent of the population. Even more dramatic improvements have been experienced in the area of health. Infant mortality rates have dropped considerably and life expectancy has been extended. For example, citizens of low-income countries in 1950 had a life expectancy of only 35.2 years, whereas by 1981 that had risen to 58 years (World Bank, 1980: 34; 1983: 192). The World Bank (1980: 35) states that "the gaps in education and health have narrowed—by 15 percentage points in adult literacy and five years in life expectancy" between the industrial countries and the middle-income countries.

Research on the international gap more consciously directed at these indicators of basic human needs may provide a clearer picture of the impact of the gap than that presented by income figures alone. But before one leaps to the conclusion that the human needs approach can demonstrate that the gap is narrowing, some additional context needs to be added to the discussion. While it is true that the *proportion* of people who are experiencing improved education, health and life expectancy has increased, the absolute number of poor people in the world has increased dramatically because of high birth rates in the developing world. Hence, the World Bank (1980: 35) estimates that despite the increases in the levels of literacy, the number of illiterate people has grown by some 100 million since 1950. Moreover, there is increasing evidence that the quality of education in the developing world lags far behind that found in the industrialized countries. The quality gap is especially acute in secondary and higher education where technical advances are so very rapid and the cost of obtaining modern training equipment ever more expensive. It is increasingly difficult for developing countries to adequately train their young people for the skills they need to compete in the high technology world of today.

The education gap has two particularly pernicious implications. First, the increasing frustration that the brightest youngsters face in developing countries as a result of antiquated equipment and poorly prepared teachers results in an increasing tendency for them to migrate to the industrialized nations. Hence, the problem of the "brain-drain" is a growing one, one which promises to continue to adversely affect the ability of poor nations to develop as they steadily lose that sector of their population with the greatest intellectual potential. Second, the high technology nature of contemporary society seems to be creating a higher and more impenetrable barrier between rich and poor countries. The efficiency of modern manufacturing techniques along with the requirement of exceptional precision in manufacturing makes it more and more difficult for developing nations to compete with the industrialized nations. The price advantage that developing nations have as a result of their considerably lower labor costs remains an advantage only for those items that require relatively low technical inputs. Hence, the proliferation of in-bond industries in the Far East and Latin America, where consumer goods are assembled for re-export, only highlights the gap in technology since nearly all of the machinery and a good deal of the managerial skill used in those factories are imported from the industrialized nations. Even without tariff barriers, the Third World faces a growing gap in technology which is serving to reinforce the income gap.

In sum, the use of improved income measures and basic needs data provide important avenues of research for those who wish to study the international income gap. A look at some of these data gives reason for optimism that conditions in poor countries are improving. At the same time, however, there is little reason to believe that the international income gap is narrowing. In fact, it would appear that each passing day finds the world inhabited by a larger number of people who live in absolute poverty, even though the proportion of the world's population in absolute poverty may be declining. This gap, then, seems to remain the single most serious problem confronting the family of nations and one which cries out for the attention of policymakers.

The Internal Gap

However problematical the reliability, validity and availability of data on the international gap, they present an even more formidable barrier to the study of the internal gap. The empirical testing of dependency/world-system explanations for the internal gap has produced widely varying results. Any reader of the major social science journals today would be rightly confused by the varied findings reported in the ever more frequently appearing articles on this subject. In reviewing this growing body of research, Chapter 20 by Muller points out a number of the weaknesses of those articles and goes a long way toward correcting many of them. Beyond the problems reported by Muller, however, it appears that there are at least four chronic problems that beset macro-level empirical tests of internal gap theories and which may ultimately lead down a blind alley of inconclusive findings even after the "best" methodology has been applied.

The first difficulty plaguing these macroanalytic investigations concerns sample skewing. Inequality data are difficult to obtain because many nations do not collect them (or at least do not publicly acknowledge that they do), a problem noted in several of the articles included in this volume. In spite of the availability problem, researchers have proceeded with the data that are available, following the time-honored tradition in the social sciences of making do with what one finds rather than postponing research indefinitely. While such a procedure is often justifiable in many research situations, one wonders if it is justifiable in this one. The principal reason for expressing this cautionary note is that it is probably not the case that the countries reporting income distribution data are a random sample of all nations. Rather, one suspects that there are at least two factors that tend to skew the sample. First, the poorest, least developed nations often do not have the resources (financial and technical) to conduct such studies, and indeed there may not even arise the need for such data to be collected in some of these nations. Second, nations in which the income distributions are very badly skewed are probably reluctant to authorize the collection of such data, and even if the data are collected, governments may not make them publicly available. Hence, the data we do have may reflect a sample that has fewer cases of the poorest nations and fewer cases of highly unequal distribution than one might expect if the sample were random. While it is impossible to prove the second assertion, since one cannot know the extent of inequality until the data are actually collected, even a superficial glance at the list of nations included in the various studies will reveal the large gaps among the world's poorest nations.

The second major problem with macroanalytical investigations is a direct outgrowth of the first. I call this problem the "Mauritania effect," that is, the dramatic differences in results that are produced from the inclusion or exclusion of as few as one or two countries. In one investigation, for example, the inclusion of Mauritania, with a population of only 1.5 million, had a major impact on the results of a key regression equation. The findings, therefore, tend not to be robust when minor variations in sample design occur; one's confidence in the results, therefore, is shaken. An unusually frank comment by a proponent of macroanalytic investigations of this type is contained in Chapter 19 by Weede and Tiefenbach in this volume. They note: "it seems impossible to predict with any confidence what would happen if inequality data on all or about twice as many countries were to become available."

The third problem concerns the general lack of cross-time data. However limited the sample of countries may be for the present period, even less reliable information exists on developing countries for the pre-World War II period. This is a particularly serious problem since both dependency/world-system analysis as well as the traditional developmental approach propose longitudinal hypotheses, whereas data limitations generally impose cross-sectional designs. While such cross-sectional designs can sometimes be a useful surrogate for longitudinal studies, the problem of skewed samples reduces the value of these studies.

One serious manifestation of the lack of longitudinal data emerges in studies that include Latin American cases. As a region, Latin America is more developed than most Third World nations and not surprisingly has somewhat more income distribution data available than other Third

World regions. It is also the case that Latin American nations have been found to exhibit comparatively high levels of both dependency and income inequality. One might leap to the conclusion, as some have, that this proves that inequality is a function of dependency. However, there is another equally appealing thesis, one which suggests that inequality in Latin America is part of a corporatist bureaucratic/authoritarian political culture considered to be characteristic of the region (O'Donnell, 1973; Malloy, 1977; Collier, 1979). One does not know, therefore, if Latin America's comparatively high level of inequality is a function of its intermediate level of development (as Kuznets would suggest), or its dependency (as the dependency/world-system proponents would suggest), or its political culture. To determine which of these hypotheses is correct would require longitudinal data to explore the dynamics of dependency, development and inequality.

A final difficulty with the macroanalytical research is that there is no meeting of the minds as to suitable standards of verifiability. Specifically, there is a wide gulf separating many dependency/world-system theorists on the one hand, and those researchers who seek to test their hypotheses with quantitative data on the other. Cardoso and Faletto (1979), whose book on dependency theory is among the most influential and highly respected works on Latin American dependency (see Pakenham, 1982: 131–132), argue that empirical tests of dependency theory have largely missed the target. Cardoso (1977: 23, n. 12) explains that this is so because the tests have been "ahistorical." In addition, although not rejecting empirical verification as useful, he questions the validity of many of these studies, even those sustaining the dependency approach. Finally, in the preface to the new English edition of their book, Cardoso and Faletto argue that "statistical information and demonstrations are useful and necessary. But the crucial questions for demonstration are of a different nature" (Cardoso and Faletto, 1979: xiii). The thrust of the demonstrations proposed are ones heavily grounded in historical detail and therefore highlight all the more the problem of the lack of longitudinal income distribution data.

In the coming years, it is likely that many more macroanalytical empirical investigations will be published and will continue to add to our understanding. However, it is difficult to imagine how the four major problems enumerated above will be overcome entirely. Given the difficulties apparently inherent (to a greater or lesser degree) in the macroanalytical studies conducted to date, more attention needs to be paid to methodologies that will examine from a microanalytic perspective the question of the origin of domestic inequality. In an insightful critique of the existing empirical research, Ray and Webster (1978: 412) argue that the dependency thesis has "black boxed" the process by which dependency functions, while Smith's (Chapter 14) critique of world-system thinking holds that the approach "neglects the internal dynamics of the periphery." In concluding an extensive review of the dependency/

world-system literature, Palma (1981: 413) argues for micro-studies of "specific situations in concrete terms." And the study by Bornschier, Chase-Dunn, and Rubinson (Chapter 17) concludes by arguing for microsociological studies that would "clarify the specific mechanisms by which these processes operate."

Problems of data availability need not cause the abandonment of future studies of the internal gap. Rather, a series of microanalytical studies would seem like a promising alternative. Such investigations would focus on that "black box" of dependency/world-system analysis, so that eventually it would be possible to trace the ways in which inequality is stimulated in developing countries. The emphasis needs to be placed on drawing the explicit links, if they exist, between income distribution and dependency. Indeed, it can be argued that even if the data problems were not as serious as they in fact are, and if macroanalytical empirical research were to demonstrate unequivocally the existence of a connection between dependency and internal inequality, one would still need to understand how one affects the other, something that cannot be known from the macro-studies.

Some research has already been published that opens the door to this type of analysis. Studies of transnational corporations in Colombia (Chudnovsky, 1974) and Brazil (Evans, 1979; Newfarmer, 1980) reveal much about the internal dynamics of dependency. An even more recent micro-study, however, has demonstrated that imperialist penetration in one African state, Yorubaland, at the end of the nineteenth century, produced a "vibrant and creative" reaction on the part of Yoruba traders in response to new opportunities in the international market (Laitin, 1982: 702).

These microanalytical studies, helpful though they are in beginning to penetrate the "black box," reflect weaknesses that would need to be overcome by those seeking to test the various explanations of income inequality proposed in this volume. First, these detailed case studies, while providing a wealth of rich, descriptive material, betray all of the limitations of generalizability inherent in the case study method. It is to be hoped, of course, that the accumulation of these various cases ultimately will lead to a synthesis; but given the widely divergent methods, time periods, and data bases employed in these studies, it is unclear at this juncture if such optimism is warranted. What is clear is that if a cumulative social science is to continue to emerge in this field, future research will need to be not only microanalytic, but self-consciously comparative as well. Only by applying the comparative method at the outset of a study of the internal causes of inequality will the data generated allow immediate comparisons and subsequent theory testing.

A second weakness of the microanalytic studies conducted to date is that they tend not to test dependency/world-system theory against its competing paradigm. Jackman's chapter (18) makes this point by stating that studies conducted thus far "are deficient as tests of the *relative* merits of the two approaches." What is called for is a design evaluating the contending paradigms simultaneously.

In sum, an appropriate study ought to be (1) microanalytic, (2) comparative, and (3) capable of testing the relative merits of competing paradigms. That certainly is a tall order for any researcher, but one way to achieve this goal and still plan a project of manageable proportions is to focus on key institutions through which dependency mechanisms are thought to operate. In an effort to accomplish this task, one recent study analyzed exchange rate policies as the "linch-pin" that helps "uncover the mechanisms through which these various [dependency] effects occur" (Moon, 1982: 716). A major advance of this study over previous work is the explicit linking of dependency effects to particular policies of Third World governments. Hence, the analysis goes far beyond most dependency literature, which typically makes frequent reference to the so-called internal colonialist *comprador* elite without revealing precisely how such elites affect income distribution. Studies such as Moon's, which examine the impact of other such crucial "linch-pins" through which dependency is thought to operate, are to be encouraged.

Two efforts, therefore, need to be made if one is to hope for the advancement of the debate beyond its present state. First, historians need to assist those working in this field to develop measures of income distribution for prior epochs. Creative use of historical records (e.g., tax roles, property registers, census data, etc.) might permit the reconstruction of such information. This, in turn, would provide the longitudinal data that are so sadly lacking at this time. Second, once the historical data have been gathered, social scientists need to direct their attention to the various linch-pins of dependency and study them in a comparative context. Perhaps with these two efforts underway, significant advances are possible in a relatively short period of time.

Conclusions

The research presented in this volume was not written in a vacuum. Investigators study problems such as the gap between rich and poor because they are concerned; and the great majority of them hope that their findings ultimately will be translated into public policy. Even though definitive findings are still far from our grasp, as has been made clear by the debate presented in this volume, many world leaders have already sought to implement policies to correct the problem.

The many proponents of the New International Economic Order (known as NIEO) freely refer to the dependency/world-system literature as supporting their claims that the gap between rich and poor nations is the fault of world capitalism. They demand that the inequalities be redressed, usually through a massive increase in foreign aid and an even larger increase in the prices paid for basic commodities exported by the Third World nations. Opponents of NIEO, often referring to studies that refute the dependency/world-system thesis, encourage leaders of Third World countries to become more responsible in their economic management and to concentrate their efforts on developing their economies from within. They also suggest that internal inequalities are the result of domestic political decisions rather than a consequence of forces of the international system.

As the gaps between rich and poor grow wider throughout the world, the debate grows more heated. Discussions in international forums today are characterized by increasing intolerance. More distressing, perhaps, is that the academic debate has also taken on a shrillness that only serves to dilute its credibility. It is hoped that this collection of studies along with the suggestions made in this concluding chapter will help, in some small way, to moderate tempers and guide thinking and research toward more productive answers to this important question.

Notes

1. The data are from the World Bank (1983).
2. See Kravis et al. (1975) and Kravis et al. (1982).

References

Cardoso, Fernando Henrique. 1977. "The Consumption of Dependency Theory in the United States." *Latin American Research Review* 12 (3): 7–24.

_____ and Enzo Faletto. 1979. *Dependency and Development in Latin America.* Berkeley: University of California Press.

Chudnovsky, D. 1974. *Empresas multinacionales y ganancias monopolicias en una economía latinoamericana.* Buenos Aires: Siglo XXI Editores.

Collier, David (ed.). 1979. *The New Authoritarianism in Latin America.* Princeton: Princeton University Press.

Evans, Peter. 1979. *Dependent Development: The Alliance of Multinational, State and Local Capital in Brazil.* Princeton: Princeton University Press.

Jackman, Robert W. 1982. "Dependency on Foreign Investment and Economic Growth in the Third World." *World Politics* 34 (January): 175–197.

Kravis, Irving et al. 1975. *A System of International Comparisons of Gross Product and Purchasing Power.* Baltimore: Johns Hopkins University Press.

_____. 1982. *World Product and Income: International Comparisons of Real GDP.* Baltimore: Johns Hopkins University Press.

Laitin, David D. 1982. "Capitalism and Hegemony: Yorubaland and the International Economy." *International Organization* 36 (Autumn): 687–714.

Malloy, James M. (ed.). 1977. *Authoritarianism and Corporatism in Latin America.* Pittsburgh: University of Pittsburgh Press.

Moon, Bruce E. 1982. "Exchange Rate System, Policy Distortions, and the Maintenance of Trade Dependence." *International Organization* 36 (Autumn): 715–740.

Newfarmer, Richard. 1980. *Transnational Conglomerates and the Economics of Dependent Development: A Case Study of the International Electrical Oligopoly and Brazil's Electrical Industry.* Greenwich, Conn.: JAI Press.

O'Donnell, Guillermo. 1973. *Modernization and Bureaucratic Authoritarianism: Studies in South American Politics*. Berkeley: Institute of International Studies of the University of California, Politics of Modernization Series No. 9.

Packenham, Robert A. 1982. "Plus ça change . . . : The English Edition of Cardoso and Faletto's *Dependencia y Desarrollo en América Latina*." *Latin American Research Review* 17 (1): 131–151.

Palma, Gabriel. 1981. "Dependency: A Formal Theory of Underdevelopment or a Methodology for the Analysis of Concrete Situations." In Paul Streetin and Richard Jolly (eds.), *Recent Issues in World Development*. New York: Pergammon.

Ray, James Lee and Thomas Webster. 1978. "Dependency and Economic Growth in Latin America." *International Studies Quarterly* 22 (September): 409–434.

Weede, Erich and Horst Teifenbach. 1981. "Some Recent Explanations of Income Inequality." *International Studies Quarterly* 25 (June): 255–282.

World Bank. 1980. *World Development Report 1980*. New York: Oxford University Press.

World Bank. 1982. *World Development Report 1983*. New York: Oxford University Press.

Index

Other Titles of Interest from Westview Press

Issues in Third World Development, edited by Kenneth C. Nobe and Rajan K. Smith

† *Women in Third World Development*, Sue Ellen M. Charlton

Undermining Rural Development with Cheap Credit, edited by Dale W Adams, Douglas H. Graham, and J. D. Von Pischke

Comparative Development Perspectives, edited by Gustav Ranis, Robert L. West, and Cynthia Taft Morris

International Money and Capitalist Crisis: The Anatomy of Global Disintegration, E. A. Brett

Bibliography on Economic Cooperation Among Developing Countries, 1981–1982: With Annotations, The Research Centre for Cooperation with Developing Countries

† *Culture, Ideology, and World Order*, edited by R.B.J. Walker

Unfinished Agenda: The Dynamics of Modernization in the Developing Nations, Manning Nash

International Dimensions of Land Reform, edited by John D. Montgomery

† *International Political Economy Yearbook*, edited by W. Ladd Hollist and F. LaMond Tullis

† *Theories of Development and Underdevelopment*, Ronald H. Chilcote

† Available in hardcover and paperback.

About the Book and Editor

The Gap Between Rich and Poor:
Contending Perspectives on the Political Economy of Development
edited by Mitchell A. Seligson

Increasing concern has been expressed by Third World leaders and international organizations alike over the growing gap between rich and poor nations. Between 1950 and 1980 alone, the per capita income gap between low-income and industrialized countries grew from $3,677 to $9,648. In addition, within the developing nations themselves, an ever-widening gap separates the rich from the poor.

Other evidence suggests that middle-income countries may be gaining on the rich countries. Some research shows that the gap in education and health is narrowing rather rapidly, and studies of domestic inequality have revealed that growth with equity has occurred in a number of developing nations that have committed themselves to such a policy.

This volume presents the evidence for both sides of the debate. It begins by stating the conventional wisdom—that international and internal gaps are widening—and goes on to examine the major explanations offered, which focus on culture, urban bias, dependency, and world-system analysis. The book then presents empirical studies on the existence and causes of the gap, as well as key case studies that challenge the conventional wisdom.

Unique in its objectivity, this text does not seek to serve either side of the debate, but instead draws upon the best research in the field to highlight major issues and to present studies that have subjected the differing perspectives to rigorous empirical analysis. It will prove especially useful in courses on Third World development, political economy, comparative politics, development economics, the sociology of development, and related topics.

Mitchell A. Seligson is associate professor of political science at the University of Arizona, currently working under an International Relations Fellowship from the Rockefeller Foundation. He is the author of *Peasants of Costa Rica and the Development of Agrarian Capitalism* (1980), coeditor of *Political Participation in Latin America, Volumes I and II* (1978, 1979, with John A. Booth, Holmes, and Meir), and co-author of *Maquiladoras and Migration* (1982, with Williams).